CHILDREN, RIGHTS, AN

CHILDREN, RIGHTS, AND THE LAW

Edited by

Philip Alston
Stephen Parker
John Seymour

CLARENDON PRESS · OXFORD

Oxford University Press, Walton Street, OX2 6DP

Oxford New York
Athens Auckland Bangkok Bombay
Calcutta Cape Town Dar es Salaam Delhi
Florence Hong Kong Istanbul Karachi
Kuala Lumpur Madras Madrid Melbourne
Mexico City Nairobi Paris Singapore
Tapei Tokyo Toronto
and associated companies in
Berlin Ibadan

Oxford is a trade mark of Oxford University Press

Published in the United States
by Oxford University Press Inc., New York

First published 1992
Reprinted (with corrections) 1993, 1995

This is a special issue of the International
Journal of Law and the Family

British Library Cataloguing in Publication Data
Data available

Library of Congress Cataloging in Publication Data
Children, rights, and the law / edited by Philip Alston,
Stephen Parker, John Seymour.
Revised papers from a workshop organized by the Centre for
International and Public Law at Australian National University, July
1991.
Includes bibliographical references and index.
1. Children—Legal status, laws, etc.   2. Children (International
law)   I. Alston, Philip.   II. Parker, Stephen, LL.B.   III. Seymour, John (John A.)
K639.Z9C45   1992   341.4'81—dc20   92-7687
ISBN 0-19-825776-7

Printed and bound in Great Britain by
Biddles Ltd, Guildford and King's Lynn

PREFACE

THE papers and comments in this volume are drawn from contributions to a Workshop on 'Children, Rights and the Law' organized by the Centre for International and Public Law at the Australian National University in July 1991. The purpose of the Workshop was to use the United Nations Convention on the Rights of the Child as a vehicle for exploring some theoretical and practical problems with children's rights. The word 'vehicle' might suggest that the Convention was used merely as a way of going somewhere else. To an extent that is how things turned out. The Convention played a larger part in some contributions than in others. At the same time, all participants recognized that the Convention has intrinsic merit and that, now it exists on paper, attempts should be made to harness its progressive potential.

The papers contained here have all been revised in the light of intensive discussion over the four days of the Workshop. Most of the important editorial decisions were taken at the early stage of settling upon who should be invited to participate in the Workshop and what they should be invited to write about. If there are faults concerning balance and topic selection then the responsibility is borne by the editors collectively rather than the authors individually.

We owe various debts of gratitude. Glen Brennan and Emilija Beswick undertook most of the administrative burden of organizing the Workshop.The Faculty of Law at the ANU, through its Centre for International and Public Law, provided essential material assistance. John Eekelaar and Robert Dingwall, as editors of the *International Journal of Law and the Family*, helped to steer the contents through the production process. The staff of Oxford University Press and especially Richard Hart were, as usual, tolerant of individual acts of editorial delinquency.

PHILIP ALSTON
STEPHEN PARKER
JOHN SEYMOUR

Australian National University
January 1992

INTRODUCTION

Philip Alston* and Stephen Parker**

THE relationship between international human rights norms and their counterparts at the domestic level is an important but often neglected one. In many instances, the international norms are little more than a composite of formulations developed in a handful of states in which innovative approaches to rights have been adopted. In such cases, the development of an international jurisprudence of rights will be greatly facilitated if account is taken of the philosophical assumptions that operated at the national level and of the approach which the courts and other bodies have adopted in applying the norms in question. While the approach ultimately adopted at the international level might bear little resemblance to those adopted in different national contexts, the latter are nevertheless an important starting point. It would make little sense, for example, for international bodies to ignore entirely the relevant United States jurisprudence when dealing with concepts such as 'equal protection' and 'due process', the origins of which are so clearly to be found in American law.

In the case of children's rights, however, the relationship between national and international approaches is rather different, primarily because international law has recently moved significantly ahead of domestic law in this domain. The adoption of the Convention on the Rights of the Child by the United Nations General Assembly on 20 November 1989 signalled the international community's acceptance of a statement of children's rights which, in many respects, is considerably in advance of anything currently formulated in rights terms at the national level. The temptation, therefore, is to assume that reference to domestic analogies is less important and will yield fewer insights than in the case of other human rights. Such an assumption would, however, be entirely misplaced. The reality is that most of the more contentious aspects of the Convention have long been discussed in national level debates, even if not specifically in terms of rights discourse. Moreover, the inevitably superficial nature of the diplomatic negotiations that took place at the international level in order to produce a compromise document such as

* Centre for International and Public Law, The Australian National University, GPO Box 4, Canberra, ACT 2601, Australia.
** Faculty of Law, The Australian National University, GPO Box 4, Canberra, ACT 2601, Australia.

the Convention are not at all conducive to a detailed or nuanced understanding of many of the key issues that arise. Those issues include, for example, the philosophical underpinnings of the concept of children's rights, the practical difficulties in giving substance to concepts such as 'the best interests of the child', the problems that arise in seeking to balance competing and conflicting rights, and the most appropriate mix of responsibilities to be accorded respectively to the child, the family, the community, and the government.

In addition to the innate unsuitability of diplomatic negotiations as a setting in which to explore such issues effectively, the process followed in the drafting of the Convention on the Rights of the Child was, in some respects, especially unsatisfactory. As is frequently the case in the international human rights domain, the original initiative was motivated by a degree of political self-interest that was to be exceeded only by that which characterized the response of some of the governments which were opposed to the initiative. While this is not the place to provide a detailed analysis of the politics of the drafting history of the Convention, it is nevertheless appropriate to note that the original draft on the basis of which the Commission on Human Rights decided to elaborate a Convention was little more than a revamped version of the 1959 Declaration on the Rights of the Child with some singularly undemanding reporting provisions added on. No attempt was made to be comprehensive, political rights were virtually absent, issues of abuse and exploitation were glossed over, and many of the formulations were of questionable appropriateness in a document purporting to state binding obligations. Partly for these reasons, the original proposal, put forward by Poland in 1978, was initially assumed by most Western governments to be little more than a propaganda ploy.

Only when it became clear that the draft, as amended to give it a little more substance, would almost certainly gather enough political momentum to succeed, did other governments begin to formulate positive proposals rather than confining themselves to rearguard blocking manœuvres. The drafting process lasted for over a decade and a regularly changing cast of characters represented most of the governments that were actively involved in the process. There was thus never any sustained opportunity to debate the philosophy underlying the approach being adopted or to consider the overall framework or scope of the Convention. In the end, it was the non-governmental organizations which made the greatest effort to achieve a balanced, coherent and comprehensive approach. But their need to work through, or around, governmental delegations significantly constrained their influence.

None of this is designed to impugn the quality of the Convention that finally emerged. It does, however, serve to underline the importance of taking account of the lessons and insights that can be provided from national level experience in putting the Convention into practice. In terms of international endeavours to promote children's rights, the significance of the essays that follow is a function of two factors. The first is the importance of the Convention itself. In the space of a little more than two years it has (as at 1 January 1992) been ratified by 107 states and signed by another 35 states. No other treaty, particularly in the human rights field, has been ratified by so many states in such an extraordinarily short period of time. The Convention has thus generated an unprecedented degree of formal commitment on the part of governments and the task confronting children's rights advocates will be to ensure that this commitment is matched by action. The second factor is that reference to international legal standards alone can shed only a rather dim light upon the questions of interpretation, emphasis, and application that will arise in the process of seeking to implement the Convention. It is essential therefore that efforts to develop a deeper appreciation of the normative content of the Convention be assisted in part by reference to national experience.

The early contributions in the volume emphasize philosophical problems connected with the very idea of children having rights. More specifically, they dwell on questions of moral foundation. It is easy enough to assert that children have rights. It is also a relatively straightforward procedure to pass legislation or enter into conventions declaring these rights in positive form. If, however, assertions or legislation are to be persuasive and remain coherent in the face of opposition, then a sound set of justificatory principles seems essential. The editors were particularly interested in bringing together a range of moral arguments concerning the status of children as right-holders.

The essays by Campbell, O'Neill, Freeman, and Eekelaar show something of the diversity of views on these matters. O'Neill argues that we can go further to secure the ethical basis of children's positive rights if we try to base them on the idea of moral obligations owed *to* children. Campbell, Freeman, and Eekelaar suggest that the moral rights *of* children are ethically more fundamental. It is from those rights that obligations should be derived. Having said that, there are complex differences and similarities between the four papers which cannot be adequately dealt with in a brief introduction.

One debate which has surfaced in scholarly argument over rights for many years concerns the function that rights have. Are they to enable the right-holder to enforce (or waive) the exercise of her or his will? Or are they to protect the interests of the right-holder? The debate between will and interests theories has been regarded as of crucial importance in arguments over the rights of children. If the will theory prevails then it is not clear that very young children can be said to have any rights. This is because (it is said) they lack the necessary decision-making competence. If the interests theory prevails, then children, no less than other sentient beings, have interests which it may be appropriate to protect in the form of rights.

Although this volume is not another test match in the competition between will and interests theories, there are certainly echoes of the duel. Campbell's stout defence of an interests theory is followed by O'Neill's argument based on obligation. O'Neill's method of justifying ethical principles by reference to agency and rationality seems to share the assumption of will theorists that a certain level of competence is required before a person can be a right-holder.

Freeman and Eekelaar occupy a position somewhere between the opposing camps. Freeman is content to base his argument on rights, rather than obligations, and finds the interests theory to be more coherent and to have greater explanatory power. Having said that, the moral justification for rights is to be found in equality and autonomy. But how can infants exercise the practical autonomy to bring them in line with the justification? Freeman responds with a form of substituted judgment whereby others make decisions under strict conditions. The question to be asked is what sort of action or conduct would we wish, as children, to be shielded against on the assumption that we would want to mature to a rationally autonomous adulthood and be capable of deciding on our own system of ends as free and rational beings? We have, then, an apparent interests theory guided by certain strong assumptions rooted, at least in part, in rational autonomy.

Eekelaar, too, frames his argument in terms of interests and uses a variation of substituted judgment. He emphasizes the role of 'claims' in rights. A system of rights which does not respect at least some claims emanating from the putative right-holders is really no system of rights at all. Where a child lacks the practical capacity to make a claim then it can be made for her or him, but only on the basis of what the child would plausibly have claimed had she or he been capable.

The will/interests tension is matched by a number of other tensions which find expression within the volume. One of these has intriguing parallels with the sameness/difference debate in feminist theory. Are children to be regarded as substantively similar to adults? Or is there something intrinsically different about children? One's position on this may affect the way one defines and protects interests (if one is an interests theorist), or the way one frames adult obligations (if one's theory is rooted in duty), or the way that adults decide *for* children (if one approves of substituted judgment).

Again, a clear contrast can be found between Campbell and O'Neill. Whilst Campbell urges us to recognize the distinctiveness of childhood and to keep clear in our minds the difference between children's interests as *children*, as *juveniles*, and as *future adults*, O'Neill seems to see childhood as simply a stage of dependence on the way, one hopes, to rational autonomy. The main remedy for children, says O'Neill, is to grow up.

Another source of tension, perhaps related to the two mentioned earlier, is that between welfare and rights. Arguably, the success or failure of the Convention could hang on how this tension is practically resolved. The Convention itself advances a best interests criterion—the alternative label for the welfare test—and some might see this as a recipe for more of the old way of looking at things.

In different ways, most of the papers in the volume see some potential conflict between adult decisions motivated by a view of what is in the child's welfare and adult decisions motivated by a desire to respect children's rights. At a distance, at least, is the spectre of paternalism and what we are to feel about it.

To Eekelaar, the gap between welfare and rights is a fundamental one. The core element of a right is the notion of a claim (actual or hypothetical) and this leads him to the conclusion that a so-called right to have welfare done to one is not a right in any meaningful sense. Welfarism, to Eekelaar, is what the children's rights movement is trying to escape from. Others, whilst supportive in general of the establishment of positive rights for children, are not as dismissive of welfarism on moral grounds. Safeguarding welfare seems to be involved in O'Neill's attention to adult duties. Olsen's explicitly feminist critique of the Convention sees some value in a stipulated meaning of paternalism. If paternalism is based on connectedness and intersubjectivity then it is a good and not an evil.

What emerges, perhaps, is that 'welfare', like rights, needs to be carefully defined before it can be approved or disapproved. Parker, for example, attempts to test a consequentialist theory of children's rights which has the avowed goal of maximizing welfare. In line with some recent consequentialist theorizing, he sees value in positive rights as institutional means of reaching certain outcomes. The fact that a discretion-based welfare regime seems to have failed children in many respects does not mean that a *rights*-based welfare regime will suffer the same fate.

The summary so far may give the impression that the papers are heavily theoretical or abstract. Whilst the editors certainly intended that the volume would fill a gap in the literature by emphasizing the importance and complexity of theory-construction, they hope that there is a sufficient balance between theory and practical application; assuming, that is, one can adequately separate them in the first place. The 'case-study' contributions by Naffine, Seymour, Coady and Coady, Parker, and Maclean deal with a variety of difficult areas: juvenile justice, teenagers determined to leave home, definitional problems concerning child abuse, financial support after parental separation, and medical experimentation.

Naffine's paper, in particular, dwells on the gap between 'theory', in the sense of what is supposed to happen, and reality. The assumed dichotomy between 'welfare' and 'justice' approaches to juvenile crime can dissolve if, in practical terms, children are treated little differently under either system. Drawing on empirical research she argues that legislative measures to draw children into the legal process rather than leave them as passive recipients of welfare procedures, seems to have met with little success.

Seymour argues cautiously that a Hohfeld-style rights analysis can take us some distance in showing the issues at stake when a young person and her parents are in conflict.

Coady and Coady warn us against slipping too easily into assumptions that terms have settled meanings. They take child abuse as an example of how definitional flexibility can lead us into profound issues concerning the relationship between the state, the family, and the individual child. Where social consensus runs out over what amounts to child abuse, then questions arise about the proper role of the state in interfering. This leads to a lively rejoinder from Cass about the public/private distinction, a matter taken up also by Olsen.

Parker refers to some emerging empirical research on the damaging effects that parental separation can have on the life-chances of children. The research, he argues, is sufficiently alarming to warrant the framing of a right to child support, informed by a particular welfare goal.

Maclean notes that medical experimentation with children undoubtedly takes place. Given that the patient's consent is regarded as a central prerequisite to the carrying out of experiments, she analyses possible justifications for experimenting on children who lack the competence to give their consent. She concludes that, unless we are prepared to impose on children a level of altruism that we do not impose on those with legal capacity, there is no test which would easily permit the use of children in non-therapeutic experimentation.

The editors are confident that the collection of papers and comments presented here raises some of the important matters that must be considered in the theory and practice of children's rights. Any venture of this nature will have shortcomings, of course. Eekelaar stresses that children should be asked what they want and that their answers should be listened to. A great deal of empirical work needs to be done in finding out what children in different cultures actually want. Yet no children were present, or formally represented, at the Workshop from which this volume springs, nor are their voices heard directly in these pages. It should be said that any criticism along these lines could also be directed at the United Nations Commission on Human Rights. No children participated in the drafting of the Convention.

A degree of ethnocentricity also stands out. All the participants were from affluent western countries (by which is meant affluent western countries where there is an appalling amount of child poverty, maltreatment, and failure to thrive).[1] Furthermore, much of the moral and political philosophy expressed here, with its style of analysis, its categories of rationality, agency, and so on could not be said to be representative of all world-views, even in the West.

Despite these reservations, the volume is offered as a contribution to what must inevitably be a rich and varied debate about the meaning, justification, and practical implementation of children's rights. If the Convention on the Rights of the Child is to improve the lot of children around the world, that debate cannot be side-stepped.

[1] See Cornia (ed.), *Child Poverty in Industrialized Countries: Trends and Policy Options* (forthcoming 1992, UNICEF International Child Development Centre, Florence).

CONTENTS

THE RIGHTS OF THE MINOR: AS PERSON, AS CHILD, AS JUVENILE, AS FUTURE ADULT

TOM D. CAMPBELL*

ABSTRACT

Have children any (perhaps distinctive) rights? The exclusive stress on self-sufficiency and autonomy which typifies the 'will' or 'power' theory of rights, the theory that is used to question the legitimacy and usefulness of attributing rights to children, is inadequate as an expression of the moral significance of persons, particularly children. The equal moral worth of all human persons, including children, is often best protected by ensuring that they have properly protected positive rights justified in terms of their fundamental interests. The 'interest' theory of rights, upon which this view is based, requires us to identify which interests are to be protected and furthered by rights. In the case of children (that is, in law, 'minors') it is helpful to distinguish between their interests as persons (which they have in common with all other persons), as children (which they have as immature and dependent persons), as juveniles (which they develop as they approach maturity) and as future adults (which relate to their future interests as adults). This analysis enables us to refine the principle that 'the best interests' of the child should determine how they are treated by parents, states and others, and may lead us to give rather more emphasis to the rights of the child rather than those of the future adult.

Despite official recognition of children's rights in such documents as the United Nations Convention on the Rights of the Child, the questions of whether children may properly be said to have rights, and if so, whether there are rights which are peculiar to children, remain matters of philosophical controversy. On some assumptions, there is doubt not only concerning the content and distinctiveness of children's rights, but also as to whether rights are the sort of thing that may properly be ascribed to children. In this paper I seek to defend the concept of children's rights, both in relation to the attribution of rights to children and with respect to the substantive distinctiveness of at least some categories of children's rights. In carrying out this task I classify the interests of minors in a way which facilitates the interpretation and concretization of specific children's legal rights, dividing the rights of the

* Faculty of Law, Australian National University, GPO Box 4, Canberra, ACT 2601 Australia.

minor into those rights which relate to his or her interests as a person, as a child, as a juvenile and as a future adult.

Given some proffered analyses of the nature of rights and of what it is to be a bearer of a right, and given certain assumptions about childhood, it seems mistaken to ascribe rights to children, or at least to children of all ages (MacCormick, 1976). Thus, if rights are defined (as they are on the 'will theory' of rights) as normative powers to determine the obligations of others by the exercise of the will of the right holder, and if it is assumed, as it must be, that children do not have the relevant volitional capacities to claim rights, then children cannot properly be said to have any rights whatsoever. In this case, the distinctive thing about children's rights is that there are none. On the other hand, if rights are defined (as they are on the 'interest theory' of rights) as interests which are protected by laws (or other normative rules or standards) then, assuming, as we must, that children have interests, it follows that they may have rights. Such a theory, however, requires us to go on to ask which interests generate rights, and to enquire whether any of these interests are distinctive to children.

I regard a solution to such fundamental controversies as a prerequisite to the determination of the particular rights children have or ought to have. I also regard the question of whether or not children have rights as an important one, the answer to which reveals a great deal about our evaluative outlook. However, for some theorists, the appropriateness or otherwise of ascribing rights to children is an evaluatively arbitrary semantic matter, the answer to which follows from the conceptual apparatus we choose to adopt. In the end, all that counts is that we make the apparatus explicit and clear, and use it consistently. At the other extreme, the decision about whether or not to adopt, defend and refine the language of children's rights may be regarded as a question of fundamental moral and ontological commitment of considerable consequence in the battle to defend the intrinsic importance of children and articulate what it is about children that gives them such value. I incline towards the latter view but, for the purposes of this paper, I simply assume that, somewhere in between the pure conventionalism of the first approach and the metaphysical moralism of the second, there is middle ground, in which we may debate – both as a matter of policy tactics and as an attempt to arrive at a defensible moral map of human values – the philosophical question of whether children have (distinctive) rights, or, as I prefer it to be put, whether or not children ought to have (distinctive) rights (Campbell & Heginbotham, 1991:63–81).

It may, of course, be argued that children are better off without rights. Thus it is sometimes said to be advantageous to children if we concentrate on formulating and implementing our duties towards them and decline to go along with the contention that this commits us to the view that children have correlative rights. Onora O'Neill, for instance, contends that children's needs are not well served by focusing on their alleged moral rights (O'Neill, 1992). On the other hand, it may be a symptom of the vulnerability and lowly social position of children that their status as rights-bearers and the distinctive substance of their rights should be in doubt. Moreover, it is arguably a serious defect in a theory of rights that it cannot readily make room for the reality and distinctiveness of children's rights. The rights of the child serve as falsifiers for those theories of rights which commit us to proscribing the language of children's rights. It may be that there is something very wrong with a theory which makes it impossible to say, for instance, that, in the fullest and most literal sense of the expression, a child has the same right to life as an adult, or, again, that a child does not have distinctive rights, such as the right to receive primary education.

Further, if tackling the issue of children's rights brings into the open what is wrong with such theories, then service may be done to other groups who tend to be excluded from the privileged circle of rights-bearers through, for instance, their failure to exhibit the capacities of normal adults. Arguments against children's rights may reveal confused and descriptively inadequate conceptual positions, and evince a moral viewpoint which is threatening to many social groups, and, indeed represent a dangerously limited appreciation of what it is to be valued as a person of any type. Those theoretical systems which in effect downgrade the status and significance of children by denying them rights, may also manifest a misvaluation of humankind as a whole. To put the matter starkly, the exclusive stress on self-sufficiency and autonomy which is standardly deployed to call into question the attribution of rights to children, is a woefully partial expression of why people count and why we matter to each other.[1]

In passing, it may be salutary to remind ourselves, at this point, that the role of children's rights in philosophical debate has, more often than not, been as a testing ground for theories of right whose main significance is held to lie outwith the world of the child. Philosophers of children's rights have usually been grinding axes for use in more adult battles. It seems significant that children's rights have been analysed not primarily for their own sake, but as part of adult-centred concerns. This in itself may be a manifestation of 'adultism' (if I am permitted to use this barbarism for that form of ageism which discriminates against children).

Partly for these unashamedly partisan reasons this paper seeks to provide a philosophical framework for the analysis and development of children's rights. Section I contrasts the power and the interest theories of rights and considers their application to children. Section II locates children's rights within the terminology of positive and moral rights by developing the idea of intrinsic rights (of which children have a full share) as distinct from instrumental and remedial rights (few of which may be sensibly ascribed to children). Section III counters Onora O'Neill's critique of children's rights, and fastens on her account of dependency and its implications. Section IV sets out a scheme for classifying types of interests that generate the rights of minors from four distinct perspectives: as person, as child, as juvenile and as future adult. It is argued that this scheme of interests clarifies the interpretation and application of minors or children's rights. I conclude by using the proposed classification of minors' rights to contend that those minors who are children often suffer discrimination through an over-emphasis on their position as future adults and an underemphasis on their status both as persons and as children.

I

I have already noted that the dispute between power and interest theories of rights is a central theoretical locus for the conceptual questions surrounding the idea of the rights of the child. On the power theory, a right is a normative capacity that the bearer may choose to use for the furtherance of his or her own interests or projects, a sanctioned exercise of legitimate control over others (Hart, 1982). Such theories may be limited and formal, or they may be fuller and more substantive in their imports. In its limited forms, the power theory is that the formal analysis of the structure of rights must be carried out in terms of the mechanisms available for invoking, waiving and enforcing rights, all of which are said to depend on the exercise of will by the right-bearer. Thus, a right may give a normative control over others which may be used at the discretion of the right-holder to activate those obligations the performance of which she judges to be advantageous to herself or her projects. It follows that only those capable of claiming, demanding or waiving a right can be the bearers of rights. Hence, for instance, small children, being in no position to exercise this sort of control over the obligations of others, have no rights.

The embarrassment for the power theorists of denying rights to children may seem to be avoided by allowing that a proxy, such as a parent, may exercise, on behalf of a child, the discretionary powers which constitute the rights in question. However, on the power theory, this must be less than a full possession of a right since the bearer's will, the exercise of which is definitive for the existence of the right, is not involved. Indeed, it would appear, on the assumptions of the theory, that the proxy is the right-holder. After all, it is she who possesses the power which is said to constitute the right (Campbell, 1983:ch 5). In other words, children's rights exercised by proxies are certainly less than full rights as defined by the power theory. Moreover, at least for some theorists, the process of choosing to exercise one's rights is part of what gives importance to rights, for it is the exercise of choice in matters of importance to the individual that enhances the dignity and exhibits the autonomy of the right-holder.[2] On this view, while the natural capacity to make choices of this sort comes to minors in the course of their normal development, it is only in so far as the individual minor has come to possess these capacities, and hence to resemble an adult, that he or she can have rights. For young children there can be no such choices, and hence, no genuine rights.

In the fuller version of the power theory, rights are related substantively to capacities for choice and rational action in that, at least as far as fundamental rights are concerned, all rights relate to the exercise of practical rationality and self-determination, in that rights have the function of protecting and furthering these capacities.[3] In its purest form, the fuller version of the power theory is that all rights are materially based in the presupposition of the value preeminence of the distinctively rational elements of human nature. It is because human beings have the power of reasoned self-determination that they can have rights, these rights being for the protection of the exercise of these capacities or related to the prerequisites of rational action, such as life itself. In this way, the whole rights viewpoint is a working out of some ideal of Kantian rationalism as the distinctive value-basis of human existence.

Clearly, on the fuller version of the power theory, minors can have rights only to the extent that they have acquired adult-like capacities for reasoned decision-making and willed conduct under the control of rational moral agency. To some people this is an outrageous denial of the value significance of young children which exposes the intellectual and moral limitations of the power theory. Children are no less precious on account of the immaturity of their characteristically adult capacities.

In this regard, the more attractive theory of rights is that which relates rights to the normative defence and furtherance of interests (Campbell, 1983:92–102). According to this – the interest – theory of rights, children have rights if their interests are the basis for having rules which require others to behave in certain ways with respect to these interests. It is enough that there are ways of identifying these interests and arranging and enforcing duties which meet the requirements that they set. There is no presupposition that these interests are expressions of rational capacities, although some of them may be. Nor is there any assumption that the performance of the correlative interest-serving duties must be triggered or set aside by the choice of the right-bearer, although this may often be the preferred way to protect the interests concerned. Rights where the exercise of will by the right-holder is a formal requirement or possibility – which I call option rights – are simply one type of right and do not represent the core of the idea of rights.

At this point the battle-lines are clearly drawn and fiercely contested. Power theorists say that interest theorists miss the distinctiveness of rights, and simply reduce rights to assertions of duty.[4] Interest theorists retort that the duties which go with correlative rights may be distinguished from other duties by the fact that they are grounded in the interests they serve. There are duties which do not derive from interests, such as the duty to worship God, and rights which have no correlative duties, like pure liberty rights which amount to no more than the absence of a duty on the part of a right-holder to refrain from doing that which she is said to have a right to perform; examples would be the right to compete or, in certain circumstances, the right to defend oneself. The interest theory cannot therefore be said to equate rights with duties.

Taking the offensive, interest theorists claim to be able to explain a wider range of rights than the power theorists who have to resort to subtle reconstructions of those specific rights where there is no evident link to capacities of choice. Thus, the right not to be tortured has to be interpreted by a full power theorist as being grounded in something like the fact that torture interferes with the processes of rational decision-making. The interest theorist may retort that it also hurts. Similarly, the interest theorist can persuasively argue that there is nothing particularly indirect about the ascription of rights to mentally handicapped adults and small children, whereas the power theorist, as we have seen, has difficulty with these classes of persons (Campbell, 1985).

Power theorists are on stronger ground in pointing out that the interest theory seems far too broad in that only some interests can plausibly be said to give rise to rights, especially as the theory appears to provide no way of identifying the distinctive features of rights-creating interests. Moreover, the interest theory permits us to indulge in the apparently dubious practice of justifying the coercion of individuals by an appeal to their rights on the basis that paternalistic interventions can protect the vital interests of those who are thereby constrained. Do we really want to speak of the right to be forcibly fed, or the right to be punished? With some plausibility, a power theorist may argue that rights have the important and distinctive function of protecting individuals against unwanted and illegitimate interventions in the right holders' lives (Dworkin, 1977:184–205).

In the stalemate that such well-rehearsed disputes often reach it is tempting to adopt the conventionalist view that the choice between theories of rights is a relatively arbitrary matter to be determined by the tactics of the particular political battle that is being fought, a question of rhetorical strategy rather than substantive disagreement. Everyone believes that children's interests must be protected, it is said, and disagreement arises only over the most effective way of ensuring that this happens. However, even without raising the question of whether it can ever be good long-term tactics to proceed on the basis of apparently advantageous but conceptually muddled views, it is doubtful in this case whether an adequate appreciation of the moral and value status of children can be attained without a satisfactory theory of rights in general and of children's rights in particular. Whether we like it or not, the language of rights is the language in which political priorities are settled and the position of minors must be related to this framework. Thus, for instance, as I shall seek to show, the likely consequence of adopting a power theory of rights is to promote the unfortunate tendency to see the rights of children essentially as relating to their position as near or future adults and their normal progression to that condition. I argue that at the very least this is a partial view of childhood, and is perhaps one which is rooted in the systematic prejudice which normal adults, along with other groups, have in favour of their own variant of the human condition.

On the other hand, if we do adopt an interest theory of rights and seek to apply it to children's rights, then we have to face the challenge of how to identify the interests of children which give rise to a claim for rights. This challenge is taken up in the final section of the paper. However, it needs to be stressed at the outset that adopting an interest theory of (children's) rights in no way commits one to accepting the familiar legal 'best interest' test for determining the legal rights of children. An interest theory of rights, as we shall see, may, rather, lead us towards taking more seriously what children are interested in, or concerned about, rather than the sort of paternalism associated with the 'best interest' rule.

II

To make further progress in the analysis of children's rights it is necessary to introduce the important distinction between moral and positive rights. Few doubt that minors may and should have some positive rights, that is rights (or interests) defined and protected by the actual rules which have legitimacy within their society. Doubt and debate arises over the idea of the *moral* rights of minors, particularly over their possession of those fundamental moral rights to which overriding or near-overriding force is given within most moral theories, and particularly within deontological ones. Moral rights of this sort are not to be confused with those rights which are constituted by the non-legal social rules of a society, the existence and functioning of which are manifested, not in law, but through informal social pressure from family, peers, social and economic superiors and public opinion concerning what is to be expected or 'done' in personal relationships within the society where these attitudes prevail. This sort of so-called 'moral' right is better referred to as a societal right since it is grounded in rules which can be demonstrated to possess societal facticity. Such rights are therefore properly to be seen as a form of positive right, albeit that the rules and sanctions are social rather than legal. Genuine moral rights, if there are any such things, are prior to and may be used to criticize positive rights, whether these are societal or legal.

It may, of course, be doubted whether there are such things as non-societal or non-positivist, 'real' moral rights, for such rights appear to require the existence of moral rules which are independent of any real social recognition, in other words a 'moral law' with an ontology comparable to the traditional idea of natural law and natural rights. This is a highly contentious philosophical thesis which cannot be dealt with adequately here.

However, the controversial natural law versus positivism issue can be partially by-passed by thinking of moral rights in terms of certain kinds of reasons which can be given for affirming that persons ought to have certain positive rights in actual societies, reasons which centre on the identification of interests which are important in and for themselves. This we may consider to be a 'moral-rights style' approach which does not commit us to a questionable ontology of values. On this basis, it is possible to argue that children ought to have positive rights but that these rights are not founded on moral rights or on moral rights style rationales. Thus we might propose giving certain positive rights or powers to children in order to increase the organizational efficiency in schools, or some other utilitarian goal not usually associated with the language of rights. Even relatively absolute positive rights, such as the right to life, may be justified in terms of aggregate happiness, since upholding such rights is a comfort to all living persons who are aware of them and enjoy the sense of security this gives them. This is not the sort of objective which accords readily with the type of moral justification characteristic of theories of moral rights, which centre, not on the general welfare, but on the violated interests of those whose lives have been illegitimately terminated. In contrast to such utilitarian considerations, rights justifications, as they feature in the domain of moral rights talk, characteristically focus on the interests or capacities of the individual right-holder rather than some broader view of social interests.

The reverse possibility may seem less plausible. Why should we deny minors positive rights but grant that they have the very same moral worth as is used to justify giving positive rights to adults? Such a position is, however, far from incoherent. For instance, if we adopt a version of the limited power theory of rights according to which rights are confined to those with the capacity to claim and waive them, and tie this to a justificatory theory which says that such rights are valuable instruments for the protection of interests, then we may well contend that positive rights are good for adults, who know how to use them to protect their interests, but bad for children, who cannot use them to advantage themselves. For paternalistic reasons we may assert the moral rights of children but argue that there are reasons why these should not be enshrined in positive rights.

This would mean saying that children have moral rights but ought not to have positive rights, in which case the analysis of moral rights cannot be given in the terms of a power theory since children do not always have the requisite capacities to claim and hence to possess rights. In other words, affirming the moral rights of children while denying them positive rights involves allowing that the power theory applies to positive rights but not to moral ones. This may be regarded as an awkward concession for power theorists to make.

My own view is that it is best to keep the language of moral rights, if we use it at all, for the assertion of justificatory values which serve as the basis for articulating and instantiating positive rights. Roughly, moral rights may be regarded as those interests which are thought to be of such significance to the life of the human individual that they ought to be given priority in the organization of societal existence wherever possible. This importance is doubtless capable of variations in degree, such that it makes sense to think of some interests giving rise to rights which may only rarely and with special reason be overridden, or other, less significant, interests giving rise to rights of lesser weight which present lesser barriers to countervailing considerations. But all positive rights have the role of protecting, to some extent, the right-holders from purely utilitarian disposals and moral rights may be seen as expressing the grounds for having such positive rights, such as the intrinsic importance of the equal protection of certain fundamental human interests.

However, it cannot simply be assumed that such interests are always best served by giving the person powers which might enable her to protect her own interests. Thus person A may be given positive normative power over certain resources for the purpose of using them for the welfare of person B. Such powers are properly regarded as rights, albeit rights which are normally bounded by accompanying duties concerning how they are to be used. Yet these rights are clearly derivative in the evaluative mode in that they are rights whose existence is justified by their instrumentality in the furtherance of the rights or interests of others. To say that, in such circumstances, A has a right, but B has not, is to confuse the means and the end of the moral relationship, or at least to reverse the flow of justificatory reasoning. The better formulation of such relationships is to assert that A has a duty to B who has the correlative right from which that duty derives, and that, in order to fulfil that duty, A has certain conditional rights to the necessary means to carry out her duties. Such secondary rights are not basic in the hierarchy of societal norms, although they may have an organizational significance of some importance. Certainly the question of whether minors should have such instrumental rights does not seem to lie at the core of the argument about children's rights. The assumption that it does may explain some of the reluctance to attribute rights to children.

Developing these points requires us to draw further distinctions between positive rights, in particular we need to distinguish between *intrinsic rights* (or rights in themselves), and extrinsic or *instrumental rights*.

This distinction is not to be confused with that between absolute and relative (or prima-facie) rights, ie the rights which may never be overridden (absolute rights) and those which have force only if there is no countervailing legitimate consideration (prima-facie rights). In reality, what we are dealing with here is a continuum between the extreme cases stated above. All rights have to be located somewhere on the continuum of exclusionary force, according to their normative capacity to ward off otherwise relevant moral considerations or they would be no rights at all. The purpose of rights is to offer some sort of advance protection against such open-ended decision making. However, whilst all rights have some exclusionary force, the degree of exclusivity given by a right is one of its variables which requires determination (Raz, 1984a).

Exclusionary force has to do with the normative function of rights. In contrast, to classify rights as intrinsic rights is to take a view about their justification. More specifically, to say that a right is an intrinsic right is to say that its justification does not depend on its role in securing some other goal, such as some more basic rights. Ultimately, all rights theories identify certain rights as basic in the sense that they directly identify the interests that the rights protect or further. These are the rights they identify as what I have called intrinsic rights or rights in themselves. Such rights which provide the rationales for complex institutional structures and are, at the same time, logically prior in the process of legal reasoning. At base, issues about children's rights home in on whether children have intrinsic rights, rather than whether they have instrumental rights.

Intrinsic rights need not, however, be absolute, or at the absolute end of the continuum of exclusionary force. Some important interests are not so important as to justify such a status. Moreover some instrumental rights may require a degree of absolutism because of their vulnerability to political pressures and the high significance of the interests that they instrumentally protect. For such reasons, it may sometimes be difficult to tell whether particular rights are intrinsic or instrumental. Thus the right to freedom of expression may be viewed as giving force to the importance of self-expression for its own sake, or it may be viewed as a valuable means for protecting the interests of individuals who use their freedom of expression to draw attention to their grievances. The right to freedom of expression is crucially ambiguous in this way, and such ambiguities need to be resolved before we can go on to raise the question of what degree of exclusionary force should be given to it. Similarly, parental rights, which the UN Convention says must be balanced against the interests of the child, may be interpreted either as intrinsic rights directed toward the protection of the interests of the parent or as instrumental rights ascribed to parents in order to further the interests of their children.

Now, it is possible that all positive rights are or should be instrumental ones, or, more particularly, that children should not have positive rights since their interests are protected by giving instrumental positive rights to others. Thus child-related rights would include the right of child-carers to have access to resources to feed and clothe their charges. This may have some plausibility with regard to the provision of material means of support but not all child-related rights are of this sort. Many interests of children can be protected by laying obligations on others to treat children in certain ways that do not require special access to resources or exemptions from normal normative limitations on the acquisition of resources in order to carry out these obligations. However, it may well be the case that, in relation to the interests of children, there are disproportionate numbers of instrumental rights, simply because young children require care which presupposes the availability of scarce resources. It is a mistake to infer from this, however, that children cannot have rights at all. Indeed the existence of the instrumental rights of others to facilitate the protection and furtherance of children's interests can be viewed as an affirmation that children have their full share of intrinsic rights, and these may be regarded as the rights which are of greatest theoretical and, in the end, practical significance, since other rights derive from them.

Instrumental rights may themselves be divided into two categories. There are those instrumental rights which are instrumental in securing intrinsic rights (call them implementation rights), and those instrumental rights which are instrumental in securing a remedy for the violation of rights, intrinsic or otherwise (call them remedial rights). So far we have considered instrumental rights which are for the purposes of implementation, and found them to be derivative within the scheme of moral justification. However, it is arguable that positive rights are empty if there is no remedy for their neglect. This point may be elevated into the dogma that the remedy is the right. Moreover, in the case of remedial rights, it is often the case that such rights are not ascribed to children because they lack the capacity to invoke or secure remedies for the violations of interests of which they may not even be aware. Again, this absence of children's remedial rights may lead us to the false conclusion that children do not have rights at all, whereas in fact, the remedial rights given to others for the purpose of rectifying violations of children's interests, is founded in the existence of the intrinsic rights which mark the interests which have been violated. Further, while lawyers may not be interested in rights the violation of which permits no remedy, legal philosophers may be even more interested in arguing that all positive rights – whether intrinsic or implementational – should be, where possible, protected by the attachment of remedial rights.

These analytical points clear the way for the claim that, in the most basic sense of rights, intrinsic rights – or rights in themselves – minors, or children, may properly be said to have rights. If we wish to speak in terms of moral rights, we may say children have moral rights because they have that independent intrinsic value which places them on a par with other human beings in terms of their worth and justifies the imposition of duties on others. The fact that they are, at least in the early stages of development, lacking in instrumental rights, both of an implementatory and remedial sort, is a relatively superficial point of theory, although in practice it may render the intrinsic rights of children vulnerable to the vicissitudes of a political and social world in which they have little real power. Indeed, the political challenge of children's rights is, in part, to see to it that this is not what always happens.

III

Before going on to deal in more detail with the distinctive characteristics of children's intrinsic rights, I will consider a recent powerful attempt to cast doubt upon the validity and utility of the rights approach to child policy and the ethics of child care, an attempt which illustrates the strong influence of the power theory of rights in this area. In her article 'Children's Rights and Children's Lives', Onora O'Neill contends that 'when we take rights as fundamental in looking at ethical issues in children's lives we . . . get an indirect, partial and blurred picture' (O'Neill, 1992:24) comparable to viewing the sky only as it is reflected in the façade of a tall building across the street. Professor O'Neill notes that having rights gives rise to legitimate claims and that these claims need not be made by the right-holders since 'it is possible to have institutions which monitor rights'. Further, she acknowledges that children do and ought to have some positive rights. However, she denies that such positive rights are based on what she calls 'fundamental' (moral, natural, human) rights, although, she is prepared to agree that children do indeed have such rights. In other words, whilst children ought to have positive rights, these positive rights are not well grounded in moral rights that they do have.

In her article Professor O'Neill adopts a 'constructive' method, 'which seeks to justify ethical principles by reference to an account of agency and rationality, without relying on claims about desires or preferences' (O'Neill, 1992:40). We may note that this approach echoes the assumptions of the power theory of rights. However, she applies the notions of agency and rationality to the elucidation of obligations rather than rights. This has, for her, the advantage that the Kantian test of universalizability can be readily applied 'by identifying and rejecting any principles of action which cannot guide the action of all members of a plurality of approximately equal rational beings', that is beings who are capable of determining whether the maxims of their actions may be universalized and thus properly followed by everyone in a similar situation (Hare, 1962:7–50). Rights are then derivable as the correlative of the obligations constructed through the process of universalizability. At least, this derivation of rights can be done in the case of 'perfect obligations', namely those obligations where the occasion and force of the obligation are not at the discretion of the obligated agent. This is not, however, the case with 'imperfect obligations', that is obligations which do not specify to whom and in precisely what circumstances the obligations are due. As it turns out, obligations relating to children are characteristically imperfect obligations. Agents' obligations concerning children are typically directed to unspecified children in unspecific circumstances; duties to children are not directed to all children or even to those with whom the obligation holder has a specific relationship. Indeed these obligations are distinctive in that they are not readily capable of being institutionalized as positive rights at all.

In adopting the ancient terminology of perfect and imperfect obligations, Professor O'Neill is not seeking to underplay the moral importance of imperfect obligations. Her emphasis is, rather, that imperfect obligations are not supererogatory, and hence something the performance of which is to be expected only of 'frightfully nice' agents. On the contrary, imperfect obligations have high moral force. These imperfect obligations relate to children's special vulnerability to 'unkindness, lack of involvement, cheerfulness or good feeling' which affects not so much their safety as the quality of their lives. In other words, meeting children's needs requires adult behaviour in relation to these needs which is unenforceable in positive rights because the precise occasions for the performance of these duties cannot be identified. Such consideration cannot be given to all the children that an agent comes across, and yet it cannot be confined to those children for whom the obligation holder has a positive duty of care. Thus it is simply not possible to identify children who might have the rights correlative to such constructed obligations.

It would, perhaps, be unhelpful simply to retort that we may think in terms of imperfect rights equally as well as of imperfect obligations, thus undercutting the priority of obligations over rights in this context. It does seem appropriate to argue, however, that Professor O'Neill makes too much out of an aspect of adult duties to children which is best illustrated by the desirability of making an effort to pay some attention to the children of strangers in whose company you happen to be spending some time. Indeed she considers that the aspect of morality to which she is drawing attention applies to 'all duties to help and to develop others' capacities' (O'Neill, 1992:35). However, it does seem that there is a measure of unwarranted generalization from this undoubted facet of adult–children and other similar relationships to such a grand thesis about children's rights in general. In fact, this apparently central argument, which is based on the existence of obligations which are imperfect but not thereby SUPEREROGATORY, is relatively superficial in comparison with the implications of her basic position on rights, the view that all rights theories of moral justification are inferior to all obligation theories of justification. This position is grounded on the assumption that rights are conceptually related to the protection of spheres of independence, an allegedly incoherent notion, together with the direct claim that paternalism and rights do not go together.

I shall spend only a brief time on Professor O'Neill's general critique of rights since an attack on all rights theories of moral justification is not in itself an attack on specifically children's rights. I only remark that the priority of obligations which she asserts seems to follow from her stress on agency as the constitutive source of all morality, a position she adopts on the grounds that only agents have the necessary cognitive and conative capacities to have obligations. However, it is worth noting, quite aside from the arbitrariness of the starting point that these obligations do not arise from thin air, but are in fact routinely if not always related to the agent's perception of the independent importance of certain states of affairs, notably the welfare of sentient beings, only some of whom will be agents in the relevant sense. It may take an agent to work out how to universalize and hence construct obligations but this does not mean that these obligations must be grounded in agency as the sole source of value.

More troublesome for the situation of children, is the basis of another claim made by Professor O'Neill to the effect that rights concern the independence of individuals and thus cannot take in situations of dependence, such as are fundamental to the lives of children. This difficulty is related to a more basic point about rights, namely that they are alleged to be for the protection of private spaces within which individuals may do as they please.

In fact, this is a particular liberal model of rights which depends heavily on the full version of the power theory according to which the point of rights is to enable individualistic choices to flourish. However, if rights are seen as interests to be protected, there is no need to regard these interests as entirely discrete and private. Indeed many human interests are for the fulfilment of wishes, desires and needs for human relationships of interdependence. It is helpful to think at this point of interests in terms of the idea of a person being interested in something, which may or may not be a future state of that individual (Campbell & McKay, 1978). If a person is interested in her close friends then it may be said to be in her interests that these friends should flourish and, depending on the nature of her interest, that they should flourish in their relationships as friends. Given this interest it is not difficult to think of the duties which could be established to further the conditions in which such friendships may develop and be sustained, such as the duty to permit such persons to meet, and the duty to refrain from telling hurtful lies about one friend to the other. The interests which are guarded by rights are not necessarily individualized in terms of pure self-interest which excludes a concern for other people.

Similarly flawed is the assumption that rights are incompatible with paternalism. Given the type of interest theory sketched above, it can readily be appreciated that some things that people are interested in cannot always be achieved simply by letting them follow their own immediate beliefs about what will contribute to the achievement of their interests or objectives. In such circumstances it may be right to restrain or require activity simply because this will better promote that which the individual is interested in. Thus there may be paternalistic interventions which are justified by reference to the rights of those constrained. To deny this possibility is to adopt a crude form of the full power theory of rights according to which it must always be a violation of rights to restrict individual choice. However, any plausible power theory must allow that not all exercises of choice are to be enshrined in rights, and once we acknowledge the limitations of the full power theory, it is easy to see that important interests for which it is reasonable to accord the individual a protective right may be served by compulsory interventions which are properly regarded as paternalistic.

To resist this conclusion Professor O'Neill would have to fall back on the limited version of the power theory according to which it is a necessary condition of having a right that the right-bearer can choose whether and when to exercise it. She does in fact emphasize that the historical role of the rhetoric of rights has been to stir oppressed people to make claims on their own behalf (O'Neill, 1992:37) which may explain her readiness to accept that rights are indeed incompatible with paternalistic interventions. She notes that children cannot be similarly demanding whereas oppressed groups, with whom she particularly associates the idea of rights, characteristically resist paternalism. But, she thinks, to speak of rights for children, can only be an indirect way of reminding people of their duties towards them. It is better, she argues, to go straight to the idea of obligation without invoking the notions of demanding and claiming rights which obscure the appropriate response to the welfare and lives of children. However, this point does not stand if rights can be conceptually detached from the features which at best characterize only option rights. If the language of rights is seen rather as a priority language which identifies those interests from which our obligations flow, then it is to rights that we should in the first instance look, since they direct our vision towards the persons and the interests which are at stake, obligations being simply the imperative and instrumental reflection of these value assertions. While we cannot expect children to secure for themselves the recognition of their rights, it remains the recognition of rights that is required if their interests are to be given the attention they deserve.

This leaves us to deal with the view that to approach children's lives in terms of rights is 'incomplete' because it cannot capture the significance of imperfect obligations. This is a very much weaker thesis than the contention that we should put to one side the idea of children's moral rights. It may be that in many situations involving close personal relationships, particularly where there are emotional and material dependencies involved, there are to be found, or constructed, many imperfect obligations. This is a position which may well have some force since there is much in desirable human relationships that cannot be caught within the rubric of rules and hence protected by rights. Moreover, it is also possible that once the obligations in question are further articulated it will become apparent that it is possible to spell out the conditions of their applicability, and hence turn the imperfect into the perfect. But, granted all this, it takes us nowhere near the conclusion that it is in general unhelpful to children to construe their normative relationships in terms of rights.

Disposing of Professor O'Neill's critique of children's rights still leaves us with no clear answers to our next question, namely the distinctive nature of children's rights. On this matter, she may have provided us with a lead in her point that children live in situations of dependence and interdependence not individual autonomy. It may be a weakness of the interest theory of rights, a version of which I have relied upon for my response to Professor O'Neill's article, that it leaves us with a very open ended basis for determining which interests are to serve as the ground of rights. In the end this may be a matter of straight substantive moral choice, to which philosophers can contribute only clarification. However, while it is not clear that we can look to an analytical theory of rights at this level of generality to answer such questions, we can at least use it as a starting point for the exploration of the substantive issues of the rights that children should have. Indeed, in rejecting the power theory we have already broadened the base for rights justifications from the narrow confine of those interests which may be characterized as promoting choice and autonomy to take in interests in general, but this simply opens up the field for an infinitely wide range of additional and alternative views. In the next section I seek to make some progress in charting how we might go about identifying the distinctive rights of children by identifying the different sorts of interests involved.

IV

If we raise the question of why children matter, we will often be told that they are the 'future generation', or that they are 'our future', as if the significance of the child could be captured in the image of the adult-to-be who will one day have an important role to play in society. In the shadow of this future, children's lives are governed and moulded often to an extent which involves real suffering and deprivation during the years of childhood. This may be defended in terms of children's rights for it can be argue that we owe it to children to fit them for their future. But the disciplines we enforce in childhood may also be attacked as a violation of children's rights, on the grounds that society is using children as the raw material of its future and depriving them of the happiness and freedom of a real childhood. Or, in a more moderate vein, it may be contended that the interests of the present child are being downgraded for the sake, not of society's future, but of the future of that person. This is less offensive, but may, nevertheless, be construed as a subjugation of the rights of a child to the rights of an adult, albeit, in this situation, the child is father of the man. To sort out this tangle it is helpful to provide a classification of the interests at stake which relate to minors' or children's rights, so that we may clarify the prioritizing choices that have to be made between the different clusters of interests involved.[5]

It is an elementary if sometimes neglected point that children are people. In this context the implication of this apparently uncontroversial supposition is that, if human rights are truly universal then it seems that they should apply to children as well as adults. Indeed, in the debates leading up to the formulation of the Convention on the Rights of the Child, the argument was put that children are covered by the Universal Declaration of Human Rights so that there is no need for a separate Convention for children's rights. And yet, it scarcely makes sense to apply some of the rights in the Universal Declaration to small children. Has a child the right to marry and found a family? The right to work? The right to democratic participation? The child has a present interest in none of these things. These interests and the rights they generate apply to mature individuals, not to people at all stages of their development and, in some cases, their decline. There are rights which everyone has at some stage in a normal life cycle but not at all stages of their existence. One of the stages often so excluded is childhood. However, there are clearly some human rights which are so thoroughly universal that they apply to children: the right to life, is the most obvious, but we can readily name others, such as the right to health care and the right not to be tortured. We may think of these as the rights which children have as persons. Looking at the Convention on the Rights of the Child, we might identify some rights of the minor as a person, for instance, Art 2 the right not to be discriminated against, Art 7 the right to a name and a nationality, Art 24 the right to health care, perhaps Art 26 the right to rest and leisure.

Regrettably, the assumed obviousness of the premise that all children are persons is disputed by those whose analysis of personhood centre on the capacity for rational choice, the very idea which lies behind the full version of the power theory of rights. Yet, these capacities come into play only in the case of mature persons who have attained and retain certain capacities which are characteristic of human beings in their developed state. Such capacities may then serve as the basis for ascribing certain rights to some but not to all human beings. Very young children may thus be excluded from these rights by their lack of the relevant capacities, as may others who, for one reason or another have either not developed them or, having developed, have lost them. If, as the full power theory tends towards asserting, these are all the rights that there are, then children can have these rights only as they develop the capacities which will characterize them as adults. Now, much talk of the rights of children is to the effect that older children ought to be ascribed rights in so far and to the extent that they approximate to mature capacities. Hence arguments for the lowering for the age of consent in various contexts, the right to vote, to marry and to work at a younger age, and the objection to arbitrary age limits, such as sixteen or eighteen at which developing individuals attain the rights of adulthood. It seems discriminatory to deny to 'children' that is persons under a certain age (eg 'minors' in law) rights which they would have if they were over that age and in possession of the capacities they already possess. Indeed it can be argued that 'children' should be required to meet only the level of attainment of the lowest capacities of adults who are accorded rights, whereas in fact, higher standards of rational capacity are required of them than of 'grown ups' when they are assessed for their ability to exercise the normal legal powers of adults, such as consent to medical treatment.[6]

We could regard the movement for children's rights as being, in this way, a movement towards giving adult rights to children. This would certainly fit with the power theory. However, such developments are usually, better construed as redrawing the boundaries between childhood and adulthood, than as extending adult rights to minors. In this case we are not dealing with the rights of children at all, but with the rights of adults who are erroneously being treated as children. This could apply to several articles of the UN Convention, such as Art 13 the right to freedom of expression, Art 14 the right to freedom of thought, conscience and religion, and Art 17 the right to access to information and material in the State's possession.

This line of argument can be taken so far as an attempt to abolish the intermediate stage of adolescence, as a period in which young adults are mistakenly treated as less capable than older adults when in fact they have basically the same capacities and the same interests. Certainly it is hard to see any rationale in terms of capacities and interests in the extensive and variable limitations placed on the freedoms and powers of adolescents. As Martha Minow points out, it seems clear that these variable restrictions have little to do with adolescent capacities and much to do with the desires of older people to deal with such problems as road safety, industrial training, crime and the control of reproduction (Minow, 1986).

Nevertheless, it seems misguided to deny altogether the significance for the growing human individual of the transitional period from paradigmatic childhood to full-blown adulthood. In this phase of development there are elements of both the earlier and the later stages, which means that there are distinctive interests which emerge and claim attention at this period. Further the emerging capacities for different sorts of adult acitvity vary with the sphere in question so that there is no one threshold of adulthood for every aspect of life in society. There are grounds, therefore, for recognizing a 'juvenile' stage of human life which may properly be brought within the scope of the concept of minors' rights. The characteristic aspect of this stage is a largely adult physical development and significant capacities for autonomous choice and conduct guided by the juvenile's own perceptions of the social world and her own scheme of values and beliefs. As a juvenile the child has considerable autonomy interests and many of the rights of the child may be seen as recognizing this fact. Indeed, unless we adopt a highly restrictive analysis of what it is to be capable of autonomy, it is a feature of all but the very earliest stages of human development. The capacity for autonomy involves the ability to select what it is we wish to do and to have, in the light of some information as to the alternatives and their consequences. On this analysis, the autonomy interests of the child stretch right back into the heart of early childhood. Lack of physical independence at these early stages is erroneously confused with lack of the capacity for choice autonomy which is an everyday feature of a child's life even in conditions of extreme dependency. Here we might draw attention to Art 26 'the right to a standard of living adequate for physical, mental, spiritual, moral and social development' as embodying a reference to the stages of autonomy and not simply to preparation for future adult life.

There are, however, distinctively children's interests and subsequent rights which do relate to the rational capacities of adults, namely the rights we ascribe to children in the light of their future as adults. These rights may be regarded as instrumental in so far as their rationale is to serve the interests of the future adult rather than the present child. For instance, aspects of Art 26 (see above), certainly the substance of Art 28 'the right to an education', and Art 29 'the right to develop one's own talents and prepare for a responsible life'. On normal assumptions of personal identity, according to which an adult is regarded as being 'the same person' as the child who has developed into the adult in question, these rights may be seen as being in the interets of the child as a person, but they are sufficiently distinctive to warrant separate categorization. The rights of the child as future person may be identified by considering which rights would not apply if we were to know that the child in question will never become an adult. Clearly this would not affect the child's right to life, but it might affect her right to a certain type of education, for instance. Since the interests in question are for the development of the child they may be called 'development rights'

(Eekelaar, 1986:172). They are properly viewed as the rights of the child only on two suppositions. The first supposition is that the child and the adult are the same person. This may seem uncontroversial but is contested within modern debates about personal identity (Parfitt, 1984). The second supposition is that it is really the interests of the future adult rather than society in general that is the basis for the development training in question. There is a less than subtle distinction between education for the child's future interests and education for the needs of the state.

It is these rights of the child as future adult which tend to be identified as the distinctive rights of children. This is, however, a manifestation of the dominance of power theories of rights which tend to interpret the significance of children either in terms of their emerging adult-like capacities, or because of their position as rational choosers of the future. Yet, there is something seriously incomplete in thinking of children as if their prime significance is the fact that they will one day be adult, or 'real' people. This approach neglects the significance of the experiences of children in their present situations, their present happiness and their current concerns. These genuinely child interests represent at least an alternative core of what it is to be a child, yet the current interests of the child are often subordinated to the training needs of the future person. If we can distance ourselves from the dominant liberal ideology of the assumed superiority of the rational individual we open up the possibility of a more direct look at the needs and concerns of children as such. Some of these, no doubt, can be subsumed under the rights of persons, for all people are something other than the rational persons that some of them may be at certain stages in their lives. The power theory does less than justice to the total existence of adults as well as turning us away from an appreciation of the essences of childhood. Illustrating this from the UN Convention we can identify certain articles as embodying the idea of the rights of the minor as child. Consider in this regard, Art 7 the right to know and to be cared for by one's parents, Art 11 the right not to be illicitly transferred abroad, and particularly Art 19, which refers to a State's duty to protect the child from abuse, neglect, negligence and physical or mental violence. Unfortunately there is no more positive statement of the worth of the minor as child to be found in the Convention. Perhaps this is justified on the grounds that genuine childhood is a relatively short part of a normal human life, although this may underestimate the significance of psychological as distinct from astronomical time.

One device which is sometimes used to validate the alleged superiority of the adult point of view of the interests of the dependent child is the variant of the notion of substituted judgement which says that we, as adults, should choose for the child as she would have had us choose when looking back on her childhood from the position of the grown adult that she has become. This retrospective judgement concerns what sort of parental or societal choices the adult is glad or sad about having been made with respect to her childhood (Eekelaar, 1986:170–1). This device is methodologically dubious in so far as the adult that retrospects is the adult who is produced by a particular sort of education. Apart from that point, however, the whole approach is very much an adult-centred one since it is taken at the point where childhood is over and adulthood is present. It is easy from this sort of hindsight position to welcome sacrifices that were made in the happiness of the child because of the advantages that are now involved. People are inevitably more concerned with their futures than with their pasts. Of course we are glad that we suffered deprivations if these are now redounding to our benefit, for the sacrifices are over and the benefits are to be enjoyed. Moreover, we, as adults, readily forget the miseries of childhood and discount them as childish and unimportant. The method of retrospective substituted judgement does not play fair and equally with the interests of the child as they are manifest in the experiences of childhood.

It is perhaps in the area of infancy or real childhood that most work requires to be done on the issue of determining what rights children ought to have. It is here that Professor O'Neill's points about the dependence of children on a network of relationships has its strongest applications although many of her points relate more to development interests in general. It is certainly tempting to classify the interests of early childhood, in the time of dependence and before the period of adolescence, as genuine childhood and so as the locus of distinctively children's rights. Such an iconoclastic approach would exclude developmental interests and juvenile interests as belonging to different categories, categories which are threatening toward real children's interests and genuine children's rights. This could help to emphasize the point that children matter for their here and now and not only for their, or our, futures. However, we may choose to label these interests the interests of the minor as child, (or perhaps of the child as dependant), if only because there is an advantage in identifying not simply a stage of development but a continuing aspect of life which has relevance to adolescence, and sometimes beyond that. Maybe we should attribute more moral and political weight to 'childishness' as an aspect of all stages of normal human life.

The rights of the child which relate to what I have called 'real' childhood ('infancy' seems too restricted a term) arise in part from its interest in care, security and protection from harm. This is the period in which the difficulty of individuating the child's interests from those of the caring and protecting adults makes it sometimes problematic to formulate rights in ways which have meaningful applications to real messy family situations. ('Messy' in the sense that it is difficult to individuate the separate interests of the individual members of the family). Hence the superficiality of political commitments to abolishing, for instance, child poverty without confronting the issue of abolishing adult poverty. It is in relation to this aspect of children's interests that the challenge to the alleged incurable individualism of rights cannot be evaded. Real childhood occurs when the child is dependent, and must be seen and treated in her connections with other children and significant adults. This does not mean we should, at this stage, abandon talk of children's rights and concentrate on adult obligations alone. Indeed, the analytical messiness of the situation simply recurs when we try to specify the obligations in a practical way. Interests do not have to be empirically and physically distinct entities to be important, and children may be better served by directing our attention to their present interests as dependents even though these are enmeshed in the tangle of others' lives than they are by denying them the recognition that is bestowed by the use of the priority language of rights.

On the other hand, there is more to real childhood than dependence. The right to play, for its own sake, or for the pleasure it brings, could be thought of as arising from the interests of children. Here we may make progress through further analysis of the concept of interests, which I believe ought to be ultimately related in some way or another to what human beings are interested *in* as opposed to what they as juveniles or adults will care about and experience. Such an approach requires extensive empirical study designed to minimize the adult tendency to see children as little adults.

Whatever labels are used, the classification of minors' rights according to the minor's status as person, as child, as juvenile and as future adult, may help in the interpretation of that favourite principle of child law 'the best interests of the child' (which features in Art 3 of the Convention). The classification draws attention to the range of (possibly conflicting) interests that should be taken into account by the law. At the very least this approach reveals the ambiguity of such rights as Art 8, the right to preserve one's identity; or Art 30 the right to enjoy one's own culture or Art 32 the right not to be exploited economically, each of which are capable of different interpretations or applications according to the nature of the sort of interests that they are thought to protect.

Similarly, when proxy decisions are made on behalf of children, the classification of interests may direct proxies to think not only of the interests of the child as future adult but of what the child is currently and appropriately interested in as well as her unchanging interests as a human being, or, if appropriate, the particular interests of the juvenile, as distinct from the future adult.

Beyond that, the suggested classification of the interests of the minor may serve to promote clarity in the determination of the value bases of minors' rights in general. It should certainly help to protect the interest theory of rights against the charge that it fails to identify a sufficiently distinct and discrete sphere of moral discourse. In so doing it may weaken that legitimator of adult elitism – the power theory of rights – and hereby help to remove at least one conceptual obstacle to the practical recognition of the equal worth of minors and adults, old or young, competent or non-competent, an idea which is, I believe, well expressed through the language of children's rights.

NOTES

[1] This theme is developed in relation to persons with mental illnesses in Campbell & Heginbotham (1991:63–81).

[2] This often repeated argument is forcefully stated in the much referred to piece, Feinberg (1970).

[3] Within a much larger project, this is argued in Gerwirth (1977).

[4] As in Simmonds (1985). Note the response in Campbell (1985).

[5] For another such scheme, see Eekelaar (1986:161).

[6] As, for instance, the majority decision in *Gillick* v *West Norfolk Area Health Authority* [1985] 3 WLR 830.

CHILDREN'S RIGHTS AND CHILDREN'S LIVES

ONORA O'NEILL*

A friend who lived in New York could not see the sky from her windows. To discover the day's weather she had to peer at a glass-fronted building opposite, which offered a blurred reflection of part of the sky above her own building. I shall argue that when we take rights as fundamental in looking at ethical issues in children's lives we also get an indirect, partial and blurred picture. If no more direct, clearer and fuller account can be had, we will have to rely on any oblique and partial light which a theory of children's fundamental rights provides. If a clearer, more direct and more complete view of ethical aspects of children's lives is available, we would have good reason to prefer it.

We may begin with a reminder of the appeal and importance of thinking in terms of children's rights. Children easily become victims. If they had rights, redress would be possible. Rather than being powerless in the face of neglect, abuse, molestation and mere ignorance they (like other oppressed groups) would have legitimate and (in principle) enforceable claims against others. Although they (unlike many other oppressed groups) cannot claim their rights for themselves, this is no reason for denying them rights. Rather it is reason for setting up institutions that can monitor those who have children in their charge and intervene to enforce rights. The Aristotelian thought that justice is a relation between equals, so inappropriate in dealings with children, is to be rejected. The lives of children are no private matter, but a public concern which can be met by fostering children's rights.

Many aspects of this view seem to be plausible. I shall not query the thought that children's lives are a public concern or the aim of securing *positive* (legal, institutional, customary) rights for children. I shall, however, query whether children's positive rights are best grounded by appeals to fundamental (moral, natural, human) rights. This conclusion does not threaten children's positive rights, which may have other grounds; nor does it deny that children have fundamental rights. Rather I shall claim that children's fundamental rights are best grounded by

* This article first appeared in *Ethics*, vol 98 (April, 1988), 445–63 and is reprinted with the permission of the University of Chicago Press. In that context the author thanked the readers for *Ethics*, Hillel Steiner, Bob Goodin, Sara Ruddick, Richard Lindley, and especially Sheldon Leader, for helpful and discerning comments.

embedding them in a wider account of fundamental obligations, which can also be used to justify positive rights and obligations. We can perhaps go *further* to secure the ethical basis of children's positive rights if we do *not* try to base them on claims about fundamental rights.

Theories of fundamental rights are most frequently queried from one or another consequentialist perspective. In those perspectives rights cannot be fundamental; if they were they would sometimes obstruct goals of maximizing benefit or of minimizing harm. Since the whole point of appeals to fundamental rights is to 'trump' appeals to other considerations (eg, welfare, convenience, happiness), there is no denying that insistence on respect for fundamental rights is only contingently and at times not closely connected to good results. All of this is well known.

The arguments against theories of fundamental rights offered here neither depend on nor support any form of consequentialism. The perspective from which I shall argue, like that chosen by some writers on rights, is *constructivist*.[1] It differs from those approaches because it offers (in the first instance) an account of the construction not of rights but of obligations. I shall develop a view of obligations that is (broadly) Kantian, indeed more strictly so than numerous accounts of rights that are labelled Kantian. This account of obligations offers, I believe, a fruitful alternative to theories of fundamental rights in all contexts. In the last section of the paper I hope to show that there are particularly strong reasons for adopting it in our thinking about children.

The strategy of arguments will be simple. I shall first argue that theories that take rights as fundamental and those that take obligations as fundamental are not equivalent. The scope of the two sorts of theory differs and does so in ways that matter particularly for children. Then I shall argue that a constructivist account of obligations has *theoretical* advantages which constructivist accounts of rights lack, although rights-based approaches sometimes have *political* advantages which obligation-based approaches do not. Finally, I shall argue that in the specific case of children, taking rights as fundamental has political costs rather than advantages. I conclude that taking rights as fundamental in ethical deliberation about children has neither theoretical nor political advantages and suggest how we could obtain a more direct, perspicuous and complete view of ethical aspects of children's lives by taking obligations as fundamental.

SCOPE: THE PROBLEM OF IMPERFECT OBLIGATIONS

When we have an obligation, we are required to do or omit some type of action. Sometimes we are required to do or omit this type of action for *all* others. Sometimes we are required to do or omit it for *specified* others. Sometimes we are required to do or omit the action for *unspecified* others, but not for *all* others. Obligations of the first two sorts may be thought of as having corresponding rights. Obligations of the third sort cannot plausibly be thought of as having corresponding rights.

It may help to fix ideas if we have in mind examples of obligations of each sort; however, these examples are no more than provisional illustrations. If a fully developed theory of obligations suggests that any of these illustrations is spurious, the illustration can be replaced by an example of a genuine obligation.

First, we are obliged to refrain from abuse and molestation of children, whether or not they are specifically in our charge. This obligation is owed by all agents to *all* children: the right holders – all children – are specified. *Universal* obligations may be said to be *perfect* or complete obligations: they specify completely or perfectly not merely who is bound by the obligation but to whom the obligation is owed.[2] Universal obligations may also be *fundamental*, in the sense that they are not derived from any more basic ethical claim or relationship and do not depend on specific social or political arrangements or on prior acts of commitment. If a universal perfect obligation is fundamental, then the rights that correspond to it are also fundamental rights.

Second, those who have undertaken to care for specific children will have obligations to them, and those specific children will have a right to care of an appropriate standard. Here too the obligation specifies completely or perfectly from whom performance is due and to whom performance is owed, and the obligation is a *perfect* obligation. However, it is not a universal obligation but one owed by specified agents to specified children, whose counterpart rights are special rights. Special rights depend on special relationships. Hence special obligations and rights are not fundamental: rather they are positive obligations and rights whose specific content depends on the specific social and political arrangements and the roles and commitments agents undertake. For example, the specific acts required to fulfil the obligations that teachers or parents may have to children in their charge depend on the specific definitions of these roles in a given society. Such roles and practices and their component obligations and rights are open to ethical criticism and justification in terms of fundamental obligations and rights (Hart, 1955).

Third, we may have a fundamental obligation to be kind and considerate in dealing with children – to care for them – and to put ourselves out in ways that differ from those in which we must put ourselves out for adults. This obligation may bind all agents, but is not one that we owe either to all children (such an 'obligation' could not be discharged) or merely to antecedently specified children. What it will take to discharge this fundamental obligation will differ with circumstances; these circumstances will in part be constituted by social and institutional arrangements that connect specific children to specific others. Fundamental obligations that are not universal (owed to all others) are, when considered in abstraction from social and institutional context, *incomplete* or *imperfect*. This is not just a matter of the indeterminacy of the act or omission enjoined by the principle of obligation, but more fundamentally of the fact that, so long as the recipients of the obligation are neither all others nor specified others, there are no right-holders, and nobody can either claim or waive performance of any right. If there are any fundamental obligations that are imperfect in this sense, then there are some fundamental obligations to which no fundamental rights correspond.[3]

Once imperfect obligations are institutionalized, certain positive special obligations are established to which certain positive rights correspond. For example, one aspect of institutionalizing a fundamental obligation to care for children in particular social circumstances might be to assign social workers a positive obligation to monitor specific children at risk. The children so at risk would then acquire a corresponding positive right to be monitored by those social workers. However, the rights so institutionalized will not exhaust the content of a fundamental imperfect obligation. The obligations of roles such as parent or teacher or social worker are commonly taken to require more than meeting those rights which are institutionalized with the role.[4]

Although imperfect fundamental obligations lack corresponding rights, their fulfilment was not traditionally thought optional: the very term 'imperfect obligation' tells us that. What is left optional by a fundamental imperfect obligation is selection not merely of a specific way of enacting the obligation but of those for whom the obligation is to be performed. Those who do only what the children they interact with have a (universal or special) right to will do less than they ought. They will fulfil their perfect but not their imperfect obligations. In particular parents or teachers who meet only their perfect obligations would fail as parents or teachers. They would not merely fail to be saintly or heroic parents or teachers, that is, omit supererogatory action. They would fail in much that we take to be straightforwardly obligatory for parents and teachers.

Provided the distinction drawn here between perfect and imperfect obligations is retained, various other distinctions are easily accommodated. Because perfect obligations require action for all or for specified others, they have correlative definite, assigned rights, which can be claimed or waived and are in principle enforceable – even in a state of nature. Imperfect fundamental obligations, whose performance is not owed to all or to specified others, do not entail assigned rights and so are not claimable or waiveable by right-holders or enforceable in abstraction from an institutionalized context which allocates recipients to agents. Imperfect obligations can be enforced only when they are institutionalized in ways that specify *for whom* the obligation is to be performed, so defining who holds the counterpart institutional rights and can claim or waive them.

Contemporary ethical writing that is rights based has difficulty in capturing these distinctions. If rights are taken as the starting point of ethical debate, imperfect obligation will drop out of the picture because they lack corresponding rights. The omission would be unworrying if advocates of rights also provided a broader ethical theory which could ground imperfect obligations. Unfortunately, a broader approach to the grounding of obligations is impossible with certain approaches to fundamental rights and repudiated within others. Those who argue that there is an open-ended 'right to liberty', so that any act which violates no other's rights is permissible, clearly leave no room for any obligations other than perfect obligations to respect others' rights. What they leave room for is in fact nothing more than the pursuit of individual prefer-ence, even if it is given a dignified gloss by being classified as an 'exercise of the right to liberty' or as 'pursuit of a conception of the good'.

Those who repudiate an open-ended 'right to liberty' and so could allow for imperfect obligations also surprisingly often deny that the space so provided is governed by any obligations.[5] Modern 'deontologi-cal liberals' take pride in being agnostic about the good for man and argue that insofar as action is not required by respect for others' rights, it is legitimately devoted to pursuit of our varied subjective conceptions of the good, that is, to action that reflects individual preferences. Liberal theorists who allow space for imperfect obligations but then allocate that space to the pursuit of personal preferences do not offer *any* account of imperfect obligations. It is no wonder that some of them characterize action that might traditionally have been thought a matter of (imper-fect) obligation in jocularly trivializing terms, for example, as 'frightfully nice', a matter of 'decency' or of being 'morally splendid' (Thomson, 1986:13–18,58,64).[6] Sometimes such action is seen as a matter of individual preference or style; sometimes it is promoted as superer600-gatory and so (once again) not obligatory. Recent rights-based thinking, whether libertarian or nonlibertarian, obscures the differences between mere expressions of individual style or preference, ordinary acts of kind-ness and consideration which may (in a given context) be matters of imperfect obligation, and truly saintly or heroic action. Without an account of imperfect obligations all of these may seem no more than ways in which we have a right to act, since others' rights are no constraint.[7]

This narrowing of ethical vision makes it hard for rights-based approaches to take full account of ways in which children's lives are particularly vulnerable to unkindness, to lack of involvement, cheerful-ness or good feeling. Their lack may be invisible from the perspective of rights. This may not seem significant if we think only of children in danger but is vital if our concern is the quality of the lives children lead. Cold, distant or fanatical parents and teachers, even if they violate no rights, deny children 'the genial play of life': they can wither children's lives. (Gosse, 1984)[8] Children can hardly learn to share or to show 'the unbought grace of life' if we are concerned only with their enforceable claims against others.

If imperfect obligations could be set aside, theories of obligations and of rights would have the same scope. They would offer two equivalent descriptions of a single set of ethical relationships. When we speak of (perfect) obligations we adopt the perspective of the *agent* and consider what must be done if there is to be no moral failure; when we speak of rights we adopt the perspective of the *recipient* (of perfect obligations) and consider what must be received or accorded if there is to be no moral failure. We would be dealing with two perspectives rather than with distinct accounts of ethical relationships, and the only reason to prefer either idiom would be that the audience for a particular discussion was either in a position to act (so that discussion of its obligations was relevant) or in a position to be affected by others' actions (so that discussion of its rights would be relevant). Many audiences would be in a position both to act and to be affected; for them both perspectives would be important. However, if we think imperfect obligations important, we cannot see a choice between obligation-based and rights-based theories as mere choice of perspective, since the scope of a theory of fundamental rights is narrower. Nor, as we shall see, is a preference for rights-based perspectives vindicated by more theoretical considerations.

THE CONSTRUCTION OF RIGHTS

It is an appealing feature of theories of rights and of obligations that both allow a constructivist account of ethical justification. Foundationalist attempts to provide an objective grounding for ethics have not borne fruit, and the subjective account of the good to which utilitarian consequentialists appeal is widely criticized because it assimilates the good and the desired. Proponents of constructivist theories of rights and of obligations have hopes of avoiding both difficulties. They seek to construct accounts of ethical requirements from minimal claims about human rationality and the human condition;[9] they eschew stronger but controversial views of the metaphysical foundations of ethics.

Constructions that lack foundations cannot be arbitrary accretions. They must be put together on principles which allow the place of each element of the construction to be determined by the position of other elements. We have a ready analogy in space architecture. Space satellites do not have 'foundations' or identifiable 'higher' or 'lower' parts, but their parts must interlock: the construction is not arbitrary. Constructivist accounts of ethical requirements also propose no single foundation, yet do not appeal to a mere plurality of moral intuitions without order. As with other constructions, the parts are to be put together with an eye to coherence and functioning of the structure. The art is to use minimal and plausible assumptions about human rationality and agency to construct an account of ethical requirements that is rich and strong enough to guide action and reflection.

Constructions of rights generally aim to determine the largest set of rights that can be held by each of a plurality of (approximately) equal, distinct rational beings. The appeal of this idea is enormous: it proposes that we construct a rationalist account of ethical requirements which presupposes only that we are separate beings whose interaction is mediated neither by natural instinct nor by supernatural programming, but by processes of practical reasoning. If such beings are to act at all, each must have some 'sphere' of action. If they are without deep inequalities (no natural masters or slaves) it is plausible to think that the spheres should be equal. If the equal spheres are to define rights, these rights and the obligations that are their correlates must be mutually compatible. Of the many possible ways of constructing equal spheres of co-possible proposed rights the one which yields maximal spheres is preferred as affording the best possibility and protection for agency. (Submaximal spheres, it may be thought, would in practice leave some with extra territory, and so undercut the equality of rights.) Such constructions identify ethical requirements with the possession of 'the greatest liberty compatible with like liberty for all'. Each is to be accorded an equal and maximal 'sphere of action', whose boundaries others may not cross, within which it is up to the right-holder alone to determine what shall be done.

Constructions of rights of this type depend heavily on the spatial, indeed territorial, metaphors in which they are standardly presented. If we interpret them as claims that each person has a right to determine what happens within a certain spatial and temporal region we obtain a fully coherent model for the construction. Each right-holder has a space, whose boundaries are definite, and no part of one right-holder's space is included within the space of any other right-holder. The co-possibility requirement is then readily met since obligations reduce to the requirement to keep out of others' spaces. The spaces of right-holders are then made as large as they can be compatibly with the requirement that they be of equal size.

If the spaces of different right holders exhausted the available territory, there could be no imperfect obligations. This might be the case if each right-holder had an open-ended right to liberty, so that anything done by a right-holder within his or her own territory would be permissible but not obligatory and anything done in another's territory would be forbidden. Such an open-ended right to liberty has seemed plausible to some libertarian writers; but we do not have to imagine that the equal, maximal spaces tessellate the available territory. If they do not, there can be spaces which are part of no right-holder's domain. Action in these spaces neither violates rights nor is protected by others' lack of rights to use the same space. Without such interstitial spaces – an ethical no man's land – all obligations must be perect obligations to observe one's own territorial limits, the mirror image of rights that others not infringe those territorial limits or restrict what may be done within them. Interstitial spaces can *allow* for action which is a permissible use of common space. Constructions of rights offer no account of imperfect obligations but need not rule them out.

Despite its coherence, a spatial interpretation of maximal liberties does not fit well with other aspects of theories of rights. One difficulty is metaphysical. A spatial interpretation of rights fits most happily with a physicalist account of act individuation,[10] but theories of rights are more at home with conceptions of human freedom that may be hard to fit into a physicalist picture. It is hard even to see the point of according rights to agents whose freedom of action goes no deeper than uncoerced determination by natural causes. This is a difficult and complex matter, and I shall set it aside to focus on a more immediate difficulty with the project of constructing rights by working out what it would be for all to have maximal, equal liberties.

As long as the spatial metaphors on which constructions of rights depend are taken literally, we have no difficulty in interpreting what is meant by 'sphere', 'territory' or 'space', 'boundary', 'maximal liberty' or 'infraction' of others' rights. However, there are problems (quite apart from those alluded to in the last paragraph) with taking the metaphors literally if the point of constructing an account of fundamental rights is to show how we should co-ordinate uses of a world that we share rather than to partition the world into exclusive domains.

When the literal interpretation is dropped, the territorial metaphors lose sense and precision.[11] When rights (and obligations) are individuated in terms of act descriptions rather than spatial regions we can still tell whether sets of proposed rights are equal and co-possible, but we lose our grip on claims that one right is larger than another, or that some set of rights is maximal. Is, for example, an older child's right to freedom of association *larger* than his or her freedom of conscience? Is either *larger* than the child's right to adequate parental care and supervision? Might we give a different answer in the case of a younger child? By what metric are we to determine the 'size' of a right or of the 'territory' that is constrained by the counterpart obligations the right imposes? Which way of accommodating proposed rights to one another – of guaranteeing their co-possibility – affords the greatest liberty? Can we show that there is a unique accommodation which permits us to identify maximal co-possible equal rights? If we cannot, how can a constructivist approach determine what rights there are?

There is no unique way of accommodating different rights. There are indefinitely many ways of describing possible actions, hence indefinitely many ways of picking out sets of co-possible, equal rights. Without a

metric for rights we could count a set of rights *maximal* only if it dominated all other sets of rights. Since we can always adjust the boundaries
between any two proposed rights, we will find no set of rights that
dominates all others. The principle of construction to which we gesture
in speaking of 'the greatest possible liberty compatible with like liberty
for all' turns out to be radically indeterminate because there are multiple
nondominated sets of co-possible rights. (We can, of course, identify sets
of co-possible, equal rights as *submaximal*, when they are dominated by
another such set: but this is not enough for identifying a unique maximal
set of such rights.)

This problem does not depend on a particular interpretation of
liberty. A negative interpretation of liberty yields a libertarian construction of rights as liberty *rights* not to be interfered with. Libertarian
accounts of rights may seem peculiarly inappropriate to children, since
only children whom we think of (oxymoronically) as 'mature minors'
have much use for liberty rights. Even if we were prepared to settle for a
libertarian account of rights, we could not identify *a maximal* set of liberty
rights. Any pair of proposed equal liberty rights – for example, the rights
of assembly and of liberty of access to public places – can be variously
accommodated, yielding alternative sets of co-possible rights neither of
which dominates the other. Hence we cannot identify any set of proposed liberty rights as maximal.

Positive interpretations of liberty apparently allow for constructions of
rights more widely relevant to children. They construe rights as entitlements to whatever goods or services, as well as forbearances, may be
needed to nurture and sustain the possibility of agency. Unfortunately,
once again we cannot tell which accommodation of various proposed
welfare (or welfare and liberty) rights would be maximal. Is a child's
right to, say, material well-being greater than his or her right to stay
with its family of origin? Of the many ways in which these two rights
could be adjusted, which would afford maximal (positive) liberty?
Without a spatial metric it is not evident how to determine which of
different co-possible sets of equal *liberty* or *welfare* rights is maximal.
Whichever view is taken of human liberty, the notion of maximal liberty,
and so of the most extensive set of co-possible equal rights, is
indeterminate.

A tempting fallback position might be to look for some set of equal co-
possible rights which is avowedly not maximal but rather thought to be
basic. Perhaps a 'core' set of rights that would be included within any
nondominated set of rights can be constructed. However, the requirements for individuating rights outside a physicalist framework show that
no such core set of rights can be determined. Any candidates for inclusion in such a core set can be mutually adjusted to form a further,
distinct set of equal co-possible rights that neither dominates nor is
dominated by the original set.

The scheme of constructing a theory of rights by determining which of the indefinitely numerous co-possible sets of equal proposed rights is either maximal or basic turns out to be indeterminate in ways that flaw the entire project of construction. It is essential to the scheme that human rights are identified by their co-membership in a unique set of rights that are not just equal and co-possible but either *greater* than or *basic* to any other equal and co-possible set. Either way, no right can be identified unless all are identified. Rights that are identified by co-membership of a maximal or basic set of rights can no more stand alone than the poles of a wigwam: their very identification depends on their role in the construction, and if the principles of construction are inadequate the construction 'materials' cannot be picked out.

CONSTRUCTIONS OF OBLIGATIONS

An analogous project for constructing obligations faces fewer difficulties because it does not depend on maximizing nor therefore on there being a plausible metric for obligations. If a plurality of distinct rational beings is to have the same obligations, we can begin constructing the content of those obligations by identifying and rejecting any principles of action that *cannot* guide the action of all members of a plurality of approximately equal rational beings. If there are any such principles, their rejection will be obligatory for rational beings with equal obligations. (Such approaches are versions of Kantian universalizing.) Even if we cannot identify a complete set of principles of obligation, we may be able to identify some members of the set. The advantage of this principle of construction is that it allows obligations to be identified *successively* rather than requiring the identification of all obligations in order to identify any.

An example of the construction of principles of obligation might be the following: we find that a principle of deceit *cannot* guide all communication among a plurality of rational beings, since its adoption is incompatible with maintaining conditions of trust, so with the possibility of communication that deceit itself requires. A principle of untrammelled deception cannot be part of *any* set of universal principles of obligation. We may conclude that nondeceit (at least) is an obligatory fundamental principle of action among any plurality of rational beings who communicate, even if we cannot work out all the other obligations of rational beings. The content of individual obligations constructed by this method can be determined even if we cannot identify a full or maximal or basic set of principles of obligation.

Universalizing methods of constructing obligations are not without problems. They are inadequate unless linked with a theory of action which indicates which level and type of principle of action is to be tested by the method.[12] If principles were judged nonuniversalizable (and their

rejection obligatory) merely because they mention spatiotemporal par-
ticulars, the construction of obligations by universalizing procedures
would produce unsatisfactory results. If the identification of principles of
action is too closely linked to agents' self-consciousness, other unsatisfactory results arise.[13] A constructivist account of obligations will be able to
deliver what it promises only if it resolves these difficulties. Even if the
difficulties are resolved, it may deliver a less complete account of perfect
obligations than constructivist accounts of rights promise. For the
method of construction does not guarantee that all obligations can be
identified: equally it does not postpone the identification of any obligations until all have been identified. A construction made from the agent's
perspective (rather than from the perspective of recipience) may deliver
more, although it promises less, since it does not aim at an 'all or
nothing' construction of ethical requirements.[14]

There are other advantages in applying a constructivist approach to
obligations rather than to rights. In particular, a constructivist account
of obligations not merely allows for imperfect obligations but can also be
extended in a quite natural way to ground some imperfect obligations
that are particularly important for lives that are dependent and vulnerable, including children's lives.

Imperfect obligations are traditionally thought to comprise matters
such as help, care or consideration, and the development of talents, to
whose specific enactment others have no right, but which agents are
obliged to provide for some others in some form. These can be
incorporated within a universalizing construction by a simple extension
of the basic construction. The basis of the universalizing construction is
rejection of action which reflects principles that cannot be universally
acted on by a plurality of distinct rational beings: they are also *vulnerable*
and *needy* beings in the sense that their rationality and their mutual
independence – the very basis of their agency – is incomplete, mutually
vulnerable and socially produced. Our agency is vulnerable to one
another in multiple ways, and particularly vulnerable at certain stages of
our lives. Unless children receive both physical care and adequate
socialization, they will not survive; if they merely survive they may not
become competent agents: without education and instruction appropriate to their society they will lack capacities to act that are needed to
function in the specific contexts available to them. A plurality of distinct
rational beings who are also needy cannot therefore universally act on
principles of mutual indifference. If they did, agency would fail or
diminish for some, who then could adopt no principles of action, so
undermining the very possibility of action on principles that can be
universally shared. Rational and needy beings cannot universally act on
principles of refusing all help to one another or of doing nothing to
strengthen and develop abilities to act. However, it is impossible to help
all others in all ways or to develop all talents or even some talents in all

others. Hence obligations to help and to develop others' capacities must be imperfect obligations; they do not mandate specific acts of helpfulness to specified others or any specific contribution to developing talents in specified others. The construction of imperfect obligations commits rational and needy beings only to avoiding *principled* refusal to help and *principled* neglect to develop human potentialities. The specific acts required by these commitments will vary in different lives. Those who live or work with children are likely to find that they must take an active part both in their care and in their education if inaction is not to amount to principled refusal of those commitments.[15]

Fundamental imperfect obligations cannot be identified with any counterpart set of fundamental rights. Unless and until they are institutionalized, these obligations have no allocated right-holders. When we consider them in the abstract, nothing can be said from the perspective of recipience; no right-holders are specified; there is nobody to claim or waive performance. However, if a constructive argument shows that universal indifference to helping others and universal neglect to develop human capacities for action are matters of (imperfect) obligation we will have reason to act to try to further these obligations. In particular we will have reason to construct and support institutions that realize and foster the discharge of these obligations.[16] For example, where we can foresee the incidence of need in broad outline (as we can for children) and the incidence of opportunity to meet or deny needs (as we can for those who in a given society are charged with the care of children) we may find strong reasons to establish a legal and social framework that secures certain positive obligations and so positive rights to care and education of a certain standard for children. The argument behind such a grounding of children's statutory and customary rights will appeal to a combination of perfect and imperfect obligations, and use these to work out how the actual practices of a caring for and educating children of a particular society at a given time should be developed or modified. An argument for the same legal and social changes which appealed directly to children's fundamental rights would have the more daunting task of demonstrating in abstraction from particular institutions and practices that each child has a fundamental right to specific forms of care and education.

POLITICS: THE RHETORIC OF CHILDREN'S RIGHTS

None of these arguments shows that it is always pointless to talk about children's fundamental rights. Whatever we say about fundamental perfect obligations can, after all, be stated just as accurately in terms of the counterpart fundamental rights. However, since children depend so much on others who perform their imperfect obligations, a shift to the idiom of rights in discussions of children risks excluding and neglecting

things that matter for children. Yet we all know that the idiom of rights
has become a common and respected way of approaching ethical issues
to do with children. The success of this idiom, we have seen, cannot be
attributed either to its being the only or obvious nonconsequentialist
approach to fundamental principles that matter for the treatment of
children, or to its pre-eminent theoretical coherence. What then
accounts for its present prominence? Why does so much current discussion of fundamental ethical issues focus on children's rights and not on
obligations to children?

I believe that a large part of the answer to this question is historical
and that a short consideration of that history suggests good reasons for
caution in using the rhetoric of rights to think about ethical issues on
children's lives.

The rhetoric of rights was separated from its parent theories of natural
law and human obligations in the eighteenth century. The discourse of
rights is an entirely legitimate descendant of older discussions of obligation and justice, of virtue and happiness, which have been ubiquitous
both in popular and in philosophical discussion in ethics since antiquity.
Rights can readily be derived from a theory of obligations merely by
considering perfect obligations from the perspective of recipience.
However, the legitimacy of the discourse of rights becomes problematic
when it aspires to become the sole or fundamental ethical category.

The shift to the perspective of recipience may sometimes have a
liberating force. On the surface it may seem strange that a shift away
from the perspective of agency to that of recipience could liberate or
energize. Since rights will be unmet, indeed violated, unless those who
hold the counterpart obligations do what they ought, it may seem puz-
zling that an idiom which addresses recipients rather than agents should
be at all important. However, the rhetoric of rights had powerful uses in
its original context of confrontation with absolute monarchies and other
undemocratic and oppressive institutions. By adopting the perspective
of the recipient of others' obligations, it insists that the recipient is no
mere loyal *subject* who petitions for some boon or favour but, rather, a
claimant who demands what is owed and is wronged if a rightful claim is
denied. Of course, claims, like petitions, may go unheeded by the powerful; but unlike petitioners claimants construe such rejection as injustice.
The rhetoric of rights disputes established powers and their categories
and seeks to empower the powerless; it is the rhetoric of those who lack
power but do not accept the status quo. Those who claim their rights
deny that the powers that be may define who they are, what they may
do, or what they are entitled to. Although the rights of the powerless can
only be met, as they can be thwarted, by the action of the powerful, the
powerless in claiming their rights assert limits to others' power (which
they may fail to establish). The charters and declarations of the human
rights movement from the grand eighteenth-century documents to the

UN Universal Declaration of Human Rights, as well as the activities of contemporary movements for civil rights, women's rights, and minority rights, constantly appeal over the heads of the powers that be, urging those who are powerless to claim their rights and so to take the first step away from dependence.

If the powerless gain recognition for the rights they claim, those on whom the counterpart obligations fall must acknowledge and fulfil them. Sometimes these obligations will be fulfilled with little urging from those whose rights are acknowledged; sometimes enormous 'pressure from below' is needed before there is change. The political point of the rhetoric of rights is therefore evident: rhetoric has to be one of the main weapons of those who lack power. This also explains the easy and frequent misuse of that rhetoric to claim spurious rights even when no corresponding obligations can be justified. Many of the rights promulgated in international documents, including the International Declaration of the Rights of the Child, are perhaps not spurious, but they are patently no more than 'manifesto' rights, (Feinberg, 1980)[17] that cannot be claimed unless or until practices and institutions are established that determine against whom claims on behalf of a particular child may be lodged. Mere insistence that certain ideals or goals are rights cannot make them into rights; but a proleptic rhetoric of rights may be politically useful in working to set up institutions that secure positive rights that constitute (one possible) realization of fundamental imperfect obligations.

We have already seen that a constructivist account of fundamental rights faces *theoretical* difficulties in dealing with ethical issues to do with children. A rights-based approach suffers not only from the *general* difficulty that its construction is indeterminate, but from the specific problem that it cannot ground the imperfect obligations whose fulfilment is so important in children's lives. Such theoretical difficulties might, however, not lead to political failure. The perspective of rights may be ideologically and politically important in spite of its theoretical difficulties because its rhetoric empowers the powerless. Can appeals to children's fundamental rights be politically significant, in the way that other appeals to rights have been? Do they or can they help empower children or their advocates to wring recognition and fulfilment of obligations from the powerful?

Appeals to children's rights might have political and rhetorical importance if children's dependence on others is like that of oppressed social groups whom the rhetoric of rights has served well. However, the analogy between children's dependence and that of oppressed groups is suspect. When colonial peoples, or the working classes or religious and racial minorities or women have demanded their rights, they have sought recognition and respect for capacities for rational and independent life and action that are demonstrably there and thwarted

by the denial of rights. No doubt oppression takes its toll, and those who
have been treated as dependent all their adult lives often lack confidence
and are more subservient and less autonomous than they may become:
but the potential for empowerment is there, and activity and agitation to
claim rights that are denied may itself build confidence and autonomy.
But the dependence of children is very different from the dependence of
oppressed social groups on those who exercise power over them.

Younger children are completely and unavoidably dependent on those
who have power over their lives. Theirs is not a dependence which has
been artificially produced (although it can be artificially prolonged); nor
can it be ended merely by social or political changes, nor are others
reciprocally dependent on children. The dependence of oppressed social
groups, on the other hand, is often limited, artificially produced, reduc-
ible and frequently matched by the reciprocal dependence of the privileged on the oppressed, who provide servants, workers and soldiers. It is
not surprising that oppressors often try to suggest that they stand in a
paternal relation to those whom they oppress: in that way they suggest
that the latter's dependence is natural and irremediable and their own
exercise of power a burden which they bear with benevolent fortitude.
The vocabulary and trappings of paternalism are often misused to mask
the unacceptable faces of power. It is not mere metaphor, but highly
political rhetoric, when oppressors describe what they do as
paternalistic.

Child-rearing and educational practices are often harsh and ill-
judged. Yet they are fundamentally different from other exercises of
power in that (with few exceptions) parents and educators seek to reduce
(some or all of) children's incapacities and dependence. Even when they
are reluctant to lose their power over children, they do not want specifically childish dependence to continue indefinitely. This is not because
parents or educators are always high minded but because children's
dependence is a burden for those on whom they depend. When power
over children is systematically used to perpetuate forms of dependence
or subservience which are not peculiar to childhood, we criticize not just
those child-rearing and educational practices but also whatever wider
social relations keep those who have left childhood in positions of economic and social dependence. The rhetoric of rights may have relevance
and resonance for the *adults* of such societies, who find themselves still
dependent and powerless even when they lose the peculiar dependence
of childhood. Yet an appeal to rights will have little chance of empowering those who are still children: if they are too young they will be wholly
unable to respond to the appeal; if they are old enough to respond they
will probably find themselves well on the way to majority and to the
ending of the forms of disability and dependence that are peculiar to
children.

The crucial difference between (early) childhood dependence and the dependence of oppressed social groups is that childhood is a stage of life, from which children normally emerge and are helped and urged to emerge by those who have most power over them. Those with power over children's lives usually have some interest in ending childish dependence. Oppressors usually have an interest in maintaining the oppression of social groups. Children have both less need and less capacity to exert 'pressure from below', and less potential for using the rhetoric of rights as a political instrument. Those who urge respect for children's rights must address not children but those whose action may affect children; they have reason to prefer the rhetoric of obligations to that of rights, both because its scope is wider and because it addresses the relevant audience more directly.

Since the ranks of childhood are continuously depleted by entry into adult life, no 'children's movement' on the model of the women's movement or of civil rights movements can be envisaged. However, 'mature minors' can find themselves in a position partly analogous to that of oppressed social groups.[18] Their minority may sometimes be prolonged unnecessarily by civil disabilities and modes of life that damage their social development and postpone competence. Mature and maturing minors who are restricted and damaged by civil liabilities and infantilizing social practices can use the rhetoric of rights to help secure greater recognition and independence. This rhetoric may galvanize and empower those who find themselves with many mature capacities but still with the burdens of minority; it may even hasten the maturing of capacities. Vicarious action to secure rights may be valuable for other minors, whose maturing has been delayed or undermined by infantilizing (even if well-meant) treatment. For the majority of children, however, the rhetoric of rights is merely one indirect way of reminding others of some of their obligations.

If we care about children's lives, we will have a number of good reasons not to base our arguments on appeals to children's fundamental rights. Some of these reasons are the theoretical difficulties of theories of fundamental rights. To look at rights is to look at what is ethically required indirectly by looking at what should be received. Constructivist accounts of what should be received are radically indeterminate, hence blurred. All rights-based approaches are incomplete in that they tell us nothing about what should be done when nobody has a right to its being done: they are silent about imperfect obligations. The view we get from the perspective of rights is not merely indirect, but blurred and incomplete.

Other reasons against involving children's fundamental rights are political. The rhetoric of rights is mainly useful to agents who are largely powerless but able to exert at least rhetorical pressure from below. Children are more fundamentally but less permanently powerless; their main remedy is to grow up. Because this remedy cannot be achieved rapidly they are peculiarly vulnerable and must rely more than other powerless groups on social practices and institutions that secure the performance of others' obligations. The great disanalogies between children's dependence and that of members of oppressed social groups suggest that the rhetoric of rights can rarely empower children.

These conclusions will be uncongenial to some of those who have hoped to add the momentum of the human rights movement to activism on behalf of children. I think that hope is illusory because it exaggerates the analogies between children's dependence and the dependence of oppressed social groups. Nor do I think we should be surprised that rights-based approaches have not proved congenial or illuminating ways of handling the full range of fundamental ethical issues that face those who live with children. Theories of rights were born and developed in large part in repudiation of paternalistic models of just political and social relations. Their proponents have repudiated the justice of familial analogies which liken kings to fathers, see colonial powers as mother countries, women and underedeveloped peoples as childlike, and just social relations as patriarchal. However, it is no mere analogy when we speak of mothers and fathers as parents, and children are not just metaphorically childlike. There are good reasons to think that paternalism may be much of what is ethically required in dealing with children, even if it is inadequate in dealings with mature and maturing minors. Nothing is lost in debates about the allocation of obligations to children between families and public institutions if we do not suppose that fundamental rights are the basis of those obligations. However, a fuller account of fundamental obligations to children and of their appropriate institutionalization in families and in public institutions is a further story. The task of this paper has been to show why that story needs telling.

NOTES

[1] The term 'constructivist' is particularly associated with Rawls' project of giving an account of justice whose justification is neither foundationalist nor subjective nor merely stipulative. Here I use the term without close examination to cover approaches which seek to justify ethical principles by reference to an account of agency and rationality, without relying on claims about desires or preferences. Compare Rawls (1971); Rawls (1980:515–72); as well as Dworkin (1977:150–83), esp 160 ff; Gewirth (1982); Shue (1980).

[2] They are not and cannot be completely specific about the act or forbearance that is owed: no act description can be fully determinate. Some accounts of the distinction between perfect and imperfect obligations suggest that the difference is only or mainly that the latter leave more 'latitude' to act in various ways. Although it is plausible that imperfect obligations leave *more* latitude, I shall rest nothing on this difference since it does not provide a clear demarcation between perfect and imperfect obligations. *Any* principle of obligation must leave action underdetermined: deliberation and adjudication are indispensable in the application of principles of perfect as well as of imperfect obligation.

[3] Although fundamental perfect obligations, like fundamental imperfect obligations, often need institutional embodiment (cf Shue, 1980) this does not obliterate the difference between them. It is only in the case of perfect obligations that right-holders are identifiable prior to institutionalization.

[4] There are various reasons for thinking that the content of fundamental obligations cannot be completely institutionalized. First, the positive obligations of institutions are specified not only by the positive rights they create or confer, but by their mandates, goals and purposes as well. (We understand well enough that institutions like individuals can fail in their obligations without violating any rights, that there can be positive as well as fundamental imperfect obligations). Second, and more specifically, the obligations of institutions charged with securing public good, or averting public harms, cannot be exhaustively decomposed into obligations to respect individual rights. Third, certain obligations may be premised on the discretion of the obligation bearer to allocate the performance of the obligation: those who see charitable giving as obligatory commonly think that there are no corresponding rights since the allocation of such giving is at the discretion of the one who gives. I am indebted to Sheldon Leader for clarification of these points.

[5] Dworkin (1977:266–78) specifically denies that there is an open-ended 'right to liberty', yet he also insists that liberalism is agnostic about the good for man; see Dworkin (1978:113–43).

[6] Similar turns of phrase are used by many other writers.

[7] Compare further arguments to some of these conclusions in Raz (1984:182–200), esp 185–6.

[8] For variations on the theme of withering parenting, see Mayor (1973); Keane (1982). Recent philosophical writing on ethical issues affecting children often stresses the danger of relying too much on *positive* rights, which typically come into play in adversarial contexts and so are destructive of intimacy and family life. See, eg O'Neill & Ruddick (1979), esp pt 2; Blustein (1982); Shrag (1980); Schoeman (1980). The objections raised in this article to rights-based approaches to children's issues are not objections to children's *positive* rights. On the contrary, one of the aims of the approach is to ground positive rights adequately (while accepting that there is much to be said against overemphasizing adversarial contexts in thinking about children's lives). However, we are ill-placed to object to an overemphasis on *positive* rights unless and until we can offer an account of *fundamental* obligations to children. Given the dearth of obligation-based approaches, and in particular the lack of accounts of the grounds of fundamental imperfect obligations, in recent philosophical discussions of children's issues, I believe that the literary illustrations are revealing and not redundant. Some recent discussions of 'rights to do wrong' are, I believe, also a sign of the failure of modern liberal political theory to show what, apart from appeals to fundamental perfect obligations and their corollary rights, could ground judgements of wrongdoing. This is not an unavoidable situation: we have only to look back to the structure of the Kantian enterprise, or to the tradition of civic humanism (cf Skinner, 1984) to see that a serious account of imperfect obligations is compatible with taking perfect obligations, and so rights, seriously.

[9] There are other ways of making rights the fundamental ethical category. Theories of natural rights typically rely on a theological framework; some optimists simply posit that rights are fundamental. I take it, but will not here argue the point, that only a constructivist approach could offer good reasons for thinking rights fundamental. Constructivist approaches to rights have been used both by libertarian writers and by those who seek to establish welfare as well as 'liberty' rights; see the works referred to in n 2 above.

[10] The spatial metaphorics are closely associated with classical writing on rights – eg in Hobbes and Locke. For the combination of libertarian constructivism with a physicalist theory of action, see Steiner (1974–75:33–50).

[11] For discussions of the limitations and difficulties of spatial interpretations of rights, see Taylor (1985): esp 218 ff; O'Neill (1979–80); Dworkin (1977:270 ff).

[12] This topic has been closely debated in discussions of Kant's concept of a maxim. For recent treatments, see Bittner (1975:485–9); Höffe (1977:354–84); O'Neill (1985).

[13] This large topic embraces questions about the ideological context of ethical reasoning. The literature both on ethics and on ideology is immense, but the literature linking the two outside relativist frameworks is so far rather unsatisfactory. I have made preliminary attempts to forge some links in O'Neill (1985a);(1986);(1988).

[14] These points are compressed here. I have worked through them in more detail in O'Neill (1986:ch 6–8).

[15] The background to these points lies in Kant's treatment of the 'contradiction in the will' version of the Formula of Universal Law. I have offered an interpretation of the argument that connects it to considerations of human need and vulnerability in O'Neill (1986 ch 7–8); O'Neill (1985a); O'Neill (1985b).

[16] It is a point of controversy whether imperfect obligations should ever be legally enforced. I shall take no stand on the matter. All that is claimed here is that in institutionalizing such obligations we make them *enforceable*; the modes of enforcement may use social or psychological

sanctions rather than legal ones. It may be the case that certain sorts of sanction that are available ought not to be used to enforce certain types of obligation. If it is the case (it seems plausible, but I have not argued the point here) that the act descriptions in principles of imperfect obligation are less determinate than those in principles of perfect obligation, legal enforcement of imperfect obligations may have to be indirect – that is to say, it may work only by way of constituting certain institutions on whom specific interpretations of principles of imperfect obligation are laid as positive obligations.

[17] Although manifesto rights cannot be claimed or enforced as they stand, they propose principles to be institutionalized. For example, the United Nations Declaration of the Rights of the Child includes the rights 'to grow and develop in health' (principle 4), 'to an atmosphere of affection and of moral and material security' (principle 6), and to 'an education which will promote his general culture and enable him on a basis of equal opportunity to develop his abilities and his sense of moral and social responsibility' (principle 7). None of these 'rights' is well formed as an enforceable claim, but they can be seen as ideals that should inform the construction of institutions that secure enforceable claims.

[18] See O'Neill & Ruddick (1979:pt 3), for discussions of the situation and predicaments of 'mature minors'.

THEORY, RIGHTS AND CHILDREN: A COMMENT ON O'NEILL AND CAMPBELL

C. A. J. COADY*

We should bring to a discussion of children's rights some sense of the constraints that need to govern an adequate theory of the topic.[1] There are at least seven plausible candidates for such constraints.

(1) Positive rights (either of law or social convention) need a justificatory underpinning of a broadly moral kind. Here it is natural, but not self-evidently compelling, to speak of moral rights. O'Neill (1992) has urged that it is better to underpin positive rights with moral obligations and that this is especially required when discussing children's rights. Real-politik theories of rights which discuss this justificatory level are inappropriate to the discussion of children's positive rights since children themselves have so little purchase upon political power.

(2) A philosophical account of rights must give due weight to the idea that, as Ronald Dworkin has picturesquely put it, rights function as 'trumps' against the project of doing good. Even a utilitarian account must explain, or explain away, the 'appearance' that rights restrict, on behalf of individuals or groups, the benefit maximizing operations of others on behalf of the collective good. In this connection, certain liberal theorists are given to speaking of the requirements of rational autonomy and the need for moral space to pursue different conceptions of the good. Campbell (1992) thinks that this idea smacks too much of rationalism, indeed Kantian rationalism, and discriminates against the moral value of children's lives – partly because children do not yet have this rational autonomy and partly because there is more to everyone's life than rationality. I will have more to say of this later; for now I want merely to stress that Campbell's own concern for rights as protections of fundamental human interest should meet this constraint, as he thinks it can. It needs to be noted here that rights also function as 'trumps' against the project of doing good to yourself. I may exercise a right and thereby (even knowingly) do myself a harm. So a person may corrupt himself by exercising the right to read or view pornography.

(3) Related to (2), is the fact that rights should always be such as to allow that it might be wrong to exercise a right. I may be acting within my rights by not intervening in a fight in order to protect the weaker

* Philosophy Department, University of Melbourne, Parkville, Victoria, 3052 Australia.

party, but it may be wrong of me, all things considered, not to intervene.

(4) The account of children's rights should be both realistic and unsentimental about the facts of childhood and adulthood. Children can be inspiring and delightful, as can adults, but they can be tiresome and irritating, as can adults; they can be loving and altruistic, as can adults, but they can also be cruel and selfish, as can adults; they can be intelligent and perceptive, as can adults, but they can also be stupid and dull, as can adults. Indeed, there are so many similarities and continuities between childhood and adulthood that it is hard, without lapsing into sentimental romanticism, to say what is so different about the two phases other than the way social structures treat them. (Hence the attraction of the view of children as 'little adults' about which Campbell is perhaps too scornful). Yet there are important natural differences between childhood and adulthood to which I shall later turn – central to them is the notion of maturity.

(5) The perspective of rights seems to be, as O'Neill (1992) insists, predominantly one of recipience rather than agency and this fact is related to the naturalness of talk about waiving, not insisting upon, transferring, and indeed even forfeiting rights. We may not want to receive various things to which we are entitled, we may yield the benefit to others, and certain events may deprive us of our entitlements to receipt or possession of a good. This perspective may have to shift somewhat in dealing with certain rights but any theory needs to give some account of how natural it is to think in this way.

(6) Rights talk should allow that it may be *good* to satisfy certain desires or even interests but that we have no right to claim satisfaction of those interests. So it may be good for an ill patient to have a heart transplant, but if there is only one donor organ available and five people who need the transplant then that patient may not have a right to the transplant. Perhaps none of them strictly have a right to it, or perhaps only the one who satisfies certain criteria does.

(7) The possibility must be seriously entertained that there is no single analysis of rights that will do justice to all the nuances and functions of rights-talk. The concept may be essentially polymorphous and we may have to say that the power/will analysis captures one important conceptual area in which rights are spoken of and the interest analysis another, perhaps other analyses other areas, and leave it at that with a few lofty remarks about family resemblance. Or, we may confront this same phenomenon with a strategy of regimentation by sticking to our favourite theory and treating divergences from it as secondary, derivative, or corrupt. Of course, it may be that there is just one definition that will cover all the important uses of the term 'rights', but we should, at least, be alive to the possibility that it isn't so.

To turn now to the papers by Campbell (1992) and O'Neill (1992). They are divided on the basic questions of whether obligations or rights are more ethically fundamental, of whether it is philosophically useful or even appropriate to speak of moral rights for children, and of whether it is politically sensible to campaign for the welfare of children on a platform of rights. O'Neill thinks that obligations are a more basic moral category than rights where Campbell seems to think rights more basic in some sense, and O'Neill decides against rights on the two questions to do with children whereas Campbell supports them. I think I disagree with both of them on the first point and sympathize with Campbell on the second and third. The first question raises too many issues of too great a complexity to discuss here but, in brief, my view is that the notion of virtuous character is more fundamental than either obligation or rights, though this is not something I will develop further. On the other matters, I want to begin by questioning a basic move of O'Neill's which Campbell concedes. This is the crucial inference from the existence of imperfect obligations to the non-existence of corresponding rights. What O'Neill says about this is that there is a general convertibility of obligations and rights except for those obligations called imperfect and that the failure of convertibility for these is both part of the reason for obligations being more fundamental than rights and for the dubious value of rights discourse as a way of improving the lot of children. Imperfect obligations are those which require us to do or omit some type of action for unspecified others but not for all others (O'Neill, 1992). She gives the example of the fundamental or basic obligation to be kind and considerate in dealing with children, and later, obligations to promote the development of people's talents, to offer cheerfulness and 'the genial play of life' (or at least not to be cold and cheerless so that 'the genial play of life' is denied to children). Of these, she insists that there are and can be no rights holders corresponding to the imperfect obligation since these obligations are not owed (or allocated) to any specific persons. 'When we consider them in the abstract, nothing can be said from the perspective of recipience; no rights holders are specified; there is nobody to claim or waive performance' (O'Neill, 1992).

Insofar as these claims constitute an appeal to pre-theoretical intuitions, then I must say that I am unpersuaded. O'Neill means her imperfect obligations to be more than supererogatory urgings and indeed to have quite demanding import and, if so, I am unclear that we cannot convert them to corresponding rights. Why not say that children have a right not to be denied 'the genial play of life', that they have a right to a cheerful environment, a right to consideration and kindness? It may be replied that we cannot say so because imperfect obligations leave it open to context and circumstance when and how and to whom the agent owes his or her obligation. To this, however, we may surely reply that once these details are available there will be particular children who have a right to the relevant actions. Moreover, in advance ('in the abstract'), it is clear to what reference class such rights will attach – namely, the class

of children. Nor is it true that there is nobody to waive or claim performance. No particular person is specified in the statement of obligation but
this does not mean that particular children in need of kindness or urgent
help cannot claim or even waive performance. Furthermore, their claims
may well act as 'trumps' against broadly utilitarian schemes of social
improvement – this is part of the power of the Dickensian defence of
children (in *Oliver Twist* and elsewhere) against the cold-hearted
'philosophical' social reformers of his time.

For these reasons, I find O'Neill's claims re imperfect obligations 'not
proven', but I have far too little confidence in pre-theoretic intuitions
about rights to say that these considerations decisively show her to be
wrong.

What then of the great battle Campbell describes between power and
interest theories of rights? (See Paton, 1972, for discussion of the opposition and MacCormick (1982), for a defence of something along the lines
of an interest theory.) Here, I think that Campbell's concern to vindicate
the interest theory over the power theory leads him to fasten onto what
may be merely accidental features or psychological associations of the
theory or of the predilections of some of the theorists associated with it.
So he insists that 'the full power theory tends towards asserting'
(Campbell, 1992) that the only rights there are, are those which involve
the agent's exercise of rational choice and this rules out very young
children as bearers of rights. Earlier (Campbell, 1992) the theory is said
to be 'clearly' committed to this. I can see what he means and I have
little sympathy myself with analyses of personhood in terms of such
strong rationality criteria as would rule out small children (as well as
lots of adults too). Nonetheless, there is surely room for a power theory
which gives an important role to rights as protections for autonomous,
reasoned decision-making as well as recognizing the need to protect
other vital human interests. Such a theory might well emphasize the
centrality of the capacity for reasoned decision-making and rational
moral agency as a determinant or partial determinant of the kinds of
being who shall be rights holders, without insisting that rights so
ascribed can only protect the activity of rational decision making.
Moreover, since we are talking of a kind (or, I would be happy to say, a
species) of being, this emphasis could include small children, damaged
adults etc, as members of that kind, whilst excluding trees and most (if
not all) animals. Such a moderate 'full' power theory might not satisfy
Campbell but it is, I think, more defensible than the version he attacks.

Moreover, the 'thin' power theory remains untouched by such criticisms. If we take the version of it Campbell gives, (and which he
attributes to Hart (Campbell, 1992)) a right 'is a normative capacity
that the bearer may choose to use for the furtherance of his or her own
interests or projects, a sanctioned exercise of legitimate control over
others', and this cannot be accused of an obsessive concern with ration-

ality. Nonetheless, it does have the right depending upon the possibility of the bearer actually choosing to use the 'normative capacity' and this will not apply to small children. Thin theorists may reply that a proxy can exercise the power on the child's behalf but Campbell objects that this entails that the child is less than a full possessor of the right, which would seem, on the assumptions of the theory, to be possessed by the representative or proxy. As an objection to the thin theory this seems to me unnecessarily hostile. The example of very young children certainly shows the formulation of the theory to be inadequate, but it is easily adjusted to meet the counter-example. We merely change 'bearer' to 'bearer or her representative'. Some such amendment is, in any case, needed to cover cases where a palpable right holder is temporarily incapacitated but needs to claim a right and can do so through the agency of another. [Incidentally, Campbell is wrong, I think, to hold that, on the original definition, the proxy will be the right-holder since although she does the choosing she is not choosing to further her own interests and projects. What is true is that, on the original definition, there is no clear right-holder]. The amended definition is then closer to the interest theory but Campbell may still object that it makes the rights of the small child more secondary than they really are. This is a serious objection but I am not sure what force should be accorded to it. The small child's rights to life, to nourishment, to a kind environment, to education, are still full blown 'normative capacities' leading to empowerments, it is just that others will usually have to act on its behalf.

At this point, I suspect that what is really important about the battle lines is less definitional than justificational. It is not so much a question of what is a right but of what facts justify the ascription of this or that right. (Of course, the questions are related). We may adopt a modified 'power theory' along the lines I have suggested and then argue about what general facts justify the ascription of such normative capacities and hence what specific facts justify the attribution of this or that right. In any case, on the matter of 'moral rights' Campbell is prepared to move some distance in the direction I am suggesting since in Section II he defends what he calls a 'moral rights style' approach which he hopes by-passes the ontological problems of the status of moral rights by concentrating upon underlying justificatory reasons for the granting of positive rights. Whether or not this strategy does avoid the ontological commitments that worry Campbell will not concern me here. What is clear is that Campbell is seeking to satisfy what amount to constraints 1 and 2 by this strategy. His commitment, in the case of intrinsic rights, is to justifications in terms of the 'interests or capacities of the individual right-holder rather than some broader view of social interests' such as might rather appeal to utilitarian theorists.

What we might then see the appeal to individual interests as doing is serving as a demystification of moral rights. Or, if this is too inflam-

matory a phrase, as a way of resisting an appeal to moral rights which
takes them as *sui generis* or in need of no further explication. The question
then becomes what are we to make of this justificatory appeal to
interests?

There are several clarificatory points to be made about interests. The
first is that whether interests are identical with or supportive of rights
they cannot be identified with mere desires or preferences. However we
finally analyse it, an interest must be a deeper notion than a want or a
desire or a preference. This is partly a matter of conceptual analysis and
partly a requirement of the sort of normative theory that rights talk
embodies and Campbell supports. As far as conceptual analysis, it is
perfectly acceptable, and sometimes true, to say that someone wants
something which it is not in their interests to have. And, as this sort of
locution suggests, our preferences and desires are things we are more
likely to be authoritative about than our interests (though, of course, we
are not infallible about any of those things). Again, although we can talk
about real desires and real preferences as contrasted with actual ones,
the move is usually one to be suspicious of especially when someone else
is telling us what our real desires and preferences are. In the case of
interests, the talk of real interests gets more purchase and is less easy to
dismiss by counterassertion. If I am thinking of applying for a new job
and a friend tells me that this is not in my real interests (though I have
expressed an interest in it) then her comment opens up a discussion
about the way the prospect fits into the values, interests, concerns and
needs that I will admit to having. The verb form 'being interested in'
and related expressions can obscure the distance that lies between
desires and interests. As for the requirements of normative theory, a
theory of moral rights (or a moral rights style theory) should be wary of
connecting interests too closely to desires, preferences or the like because
these are much better adapted to a utilitarian style approach which
commits itself merely to maximizing desire or preference satisfactions
wherever they occur and has no particular concern for their value as
such nor for the fact that they belong to this or that individual.
Moreover, basing our approach to rights on mere preferences and
desires will readily lead to violations of constraint 6 since there may be
certain things that I want and it would be good for me to have but to
which I have no right. There is also the risk of running foul of constraint
3 since I may very well have a right and act on it, without violating the
rights of others, even where this goes against my own interests or
declared preferences, or the interests, desires etc of the others. Any
version of the interest theory needs to be sensitive to such considerations.

It is particularly important to distinguish interests from desires and
preferences when operating at the level of the basic moral justification of
positive rights, because here, as Campbell stresses, we are usually concerned with fundamental interests (Campbell, 1992). All this is far too

sketchy, but it reaches to important theoretical and practical questions. The theoretical issues concern how we should demarcate those interests which are relevant to the analysis and justification of rights from those which are not. Campbell shows his awareness of this problem at several points but does not do a great deal to solve it beyond the reference to fundamental interests. My own suggestion is that the search should focus upon the concept of need, which has its own obscurities, but which has the advantage of having an even stronger normative overtone than interests and *a fortiori* than desires or preferences. It also connects more directly to the idea of human nature and its demands, an idea which has claims to be of central ethical significance. Here again, a properly developed theory would have to negotiate the requirement of the constraints, especially, 2, 3, and 6. (In this connection see the interesting paper by Wiggins (1985).)

The practical significance of characterizing interests more carefully emerges in the final sections of both Campbell's and O'Neill's papers where they discuss the more 'applied' issues raised by the debate about children's rights. Campbell is anxious to stress, amongst other things, the importance of paying attention to the interests which children have as children rather than as potential adults. He is very concerned to avoid the imposition of adult concerns and perspectives upon what is distinctive (and distinctively valuable) in the life of children. O'Neill, by contrast, tends to think of childhood as essentially incomplete and dependent; its miseries and disabilities as something to be cured by growing up. She actually says that, compared to other disadvantaged groups, children 'are more fundamentally but less permanently powerless; their main remedy is to grow up.' (O'Neill, 1992).

To take O'Neill's position first. The passage quoted sounds more heartless than her overall position really is; indeed, it makes childhood sound something like flu. The paper does show a tendency to disregard the degree to which children sometimes suffer severe setbacks to their development and disturbing frustrations of their current needs which cannot be remedied by moving into adulthood, if only because the setbacks and frustrations cause not only present unhappiness but determine for the worse what sort of adulthood they are going to grow into. One of the most important facts about childhood, particularly early childhood, is the degree to which the child's experiences and the treatment he or she receives is so profoundly formative of the child's future as adolescent and adult. Whatever Freud's faults as a theorist, this is one lesson that we have rightly learned from him and earlier thinkers such as Rousseau and Froebel. Because O'Neill is insufficiently sensitive to this dimension of childhood, she finds it too easy to dismiss the significance of talking of rights which protect the needs children have to a normal development of their potentialities. This represents a lack of realism about children which offends against constraint 4. The immaturity of children is not just a matter of their being powerless, but of their being in a process of development for which adults must take a degree of responsibility because often adults know more about what children need for a sane and healthy life and what can cause possibly irreparable damage.

On this matter, Campbell, it seems to me, has a clearer vision but he errs in the opposite direction, partly because he treats the notion of the child's interests in a way that sometimes assimilates them too closely to its mere desires and preferences. Except for the very young, children can think for themselves, develop ideas, friendships and concerns, but they are necessarily lacking in the knowledge which experience of the world and of people can, in time, provide. Consequently, Campbell's insistence upon 'giving more weight to what children are actually interested in as opposed to what they as juveniles or adults will care about and experience' (Campbell, 1992) needs to be very carefully unpacked if it is not to canonize severely uninformed desires in the sanctified language of rights. Elsewhere, he qualifies the point by talking of what 'the children are currently and *appropriately* interested in' (my emphasis) (Campbell, 1992) and the qualification is important, but it weakens the force of his general critique of those who view the child's interests from the point of view of the adult. If 'the point of view of the adult' means an informed view of what human beings need to live well, it can hardly be irrelevant to what interests of the child are inappropriate. Of course, we should attend carefully to the details of a child's life, aptitudes, desires and expressions of interest in order to be more attuned to what its needs are. It would nonetheless be unrealistic sentimentality to ignore the twin facts that the child's perspective and understanding of the world it must grow in are necessarily partial and limited (though increasingly less so with time), and that the child's desires, preferences and indeed many of its interests are the result not of some autonomous natural process called childhood, but of the shaping and formation by other human beings, many of them adult, and some of them, significantly, parents. There are no doubt dangers in the method recommended by Eekelaar (Eekelaar, 1992) and rejected by Campbell, of making retrospective substituted judgements on what a child's interests really are, but I suspect that this is sometimes a fair way of discovering what interests are 'appropriate'. The parent who was sexually abused by her father and has suffered in adult life from the effects of the experience, will judge that her own daughter's real interests are in avoiding the same involvement, even if the child is presently interested in that sort of relationship with her father.

More generally, I doubt that there is very much that is really distinctively different in kind about the lives of children and adults except what is related to immaturity of physical and psychological powers. The former is overcome in the later phases of childhood and so is a good deal of the latter. What young children need, as the Convention on the Rights of the Child makes plain, is roughly what adults need only perhaps more of it. They need rather more in the way of food, affection, protection from exploitation and so on. They need to play, but so do adults (though the forms of play will sometimes differ); they need education, but so of course do adults. Here incidentally, I should express a specific point of difference from Campbell. He imagines (Campbell, 1992) what we would say of the rights that apply to a child whom we know is never going to grow up. A dramatic case would be a child with AIDS or leukemia. He holds that we should think differently of such a child's rights to a certain kind of education though not her right to life. But I think that we should treat this child's educational needs much the same as any others (always allowing for any difficulties of a physical, emotional or intellectual kind caused by the illness). Education of any sort is never merely an instrumental good and the child's present interest in learning largely remains whatever its future prospects. To return, however, to the distinctiveness of childhood. Campbell mentions (Campbell, 1992) the Convention's articles 7, 11, and 19 as positive assertions of the value of the minor as a child where he seems to be saying that these articles do acknowledge rights which reflect 'the essence of childhood'. But in fact the rights in question are all rights that adults either have or should have as well. The difference is that they will apply somewhat differently to children because of a difference in their circumstances rather than their 'essences'. I sense here a certain unrealism about children which may violate constraint 4.

NOTES

[1] I am indebted to Dr. Robert K. Fullinwider, of the Institute for Philosophy and Public Policy in the University of Maryland, and Visiting Scholar in the Philosophy Department of the University of Melbourne, for helpful comments on the constraints that should govern a theory of rights.

TAKING CHILDREN'S RIGHTS MORE SERIOUSLY

MICHAEL D. A. FREEMAN*

ABSTRACT

This article argues that the conditions experienced by many children make it important that their rights should be taken seriously. Rights are important if children are to be treated with equality and as autonomous beings. This means believing that anyone's autonomy is as significant as anyone else's. This article examines arguments supporting this position and applies it to the UN convention.

INTRODUCTION

We have begun to take children's rights more seriously – at least on one level.

The international community has framed its much-lauded Convention on the Rights of the Child (United Nations, 1989). It has convened a World Summit on the subject (UNICEF, 1991). Legislators and judges, in the Western industrialized world at least, have become conscious of the need to recognize the individuality and autonomy of older children. Institutions, including Ombudsmen, have been established in a few countries, Norway, New Zealand, Costa Rica and Israel (Flekkoy, 1991).

England has its *Gillick*[1] decision and has recently implemented new children's legislation, which is not only more child-centered, but the clearest recognition yet of the decision-making capacities of children.[2] But, despite Government protestations to the contrary,[3] the law of the United Kingdom still falls far short of the ideals of the United Nations Convention.[4] Although the British Prime Minister of the 1980s could state: '. . . children come first because children are our most sacred trust',[5] she presided over a steep rise in child poverty and deprivation (Bradshaw, 1990). The same Government, which proudly vaunts its commitment to children by pointing to the Children Act 1989, could also boast (though it would prefer the evidence was discretely veiled) that the number of children living in families with incomes around the supplementary bene-

* Professor Michael Freeman, University College London, Faculty of Laws, Bentham House, Endsleigh Gardens, London WC1H 0EG.

fit standard (that is subsistence level) increased between 1979 and 1985 by 49 per cent.[6] The number of homeless households has doubled since 1981.[7] There has been a dramatic increase in the number of young people who are homeless and living rough on the streets of large cities.[8] Though there has been a decline in infant mortality, rates have declined more slowly than in some other comparable countries, and are still high in comparison with, for example, France, Italy and Sweden (National Children's Home, 1989). And 'causes of death which can be regarded as "preventable" . . . cause infant deaths in Social Class V at about three times the rate for Social Class 1' (OPCS, 1988). These examples could be multiplied. But, whatever the state of deprivation of children in relatively prosperous Britain, it is nothing as compared with much of the rest of the world, with children the legitimate objects of extermination squads in Brazil and Guatemala, dying of starvation in much of Africa and of radiation in parts of the former Soviet Union and living in shanties, refugee camps and as prostitutes for Western tourists in many countries of the third world (UNICEF, 1991).

It would be idle to pretend that the answer to all this lies in theory or, indeed, that deliberations at academic conferences will have any immediate impact on the lives of children. But we can and must believe that the state of childhood will be improved if we are prepared to take children's rights more seriously, to transcend the rhetoric of international documents and domestic legislation and tease out the moral argument for the recognition of children's rights (Worsfold, 1974; MacCormick, 1982; Lucy, 1990). It was Oliver Wendell Holmes, the jurist and judge, who commented that the world to-day was governed more by Kant than Bonaparte (Holmes, 1897). Rights, of course, are never given but are fought for.[9] In searching out the moral grounds for the recognition of children's rights we must believe that this fight will be strengthened and that, ultimately, the condition of childhood will be ameliorated. And this it may achieve if it can transcend the impoverishment of political discourse with the inconsistencies and hypocrisies all too commonly found therein.

THE IMPORTANCE OF RIGHTS

Ubi ius, ibi remedium. Where rights exist redress is possible. This is lawyers' discourse and its roots go deep into legal culture. Lawyers have not articulated the reason why this correlativity should be so important. Perhaps to them it has been obvious. Philosophers and jurists have, however, sought out the justification. Rights are 'valuable commodities' (Wasserstrom, 1964).

It is useful to reflect upon what a society without rights would look like. Such a society would be morally impoverished. It might well be a benevolent society in which people were treated well, but they would have no cause for complaint if standards were to fall. A world with claim-rights is, as Joel Feinberg has put it, 'one in which all persons . . . are dignified objects of respect'. And he adds: 'No amount of love and compassion, or obedience to higher authority, or *noblesse oblige*, can substitute for those values' (Feinberg, 1966). What is clearly delineated here is the close association between rights and dignity (a concept itself to which all too little attention has been given) (but *cf* Sedler, 1986), and rights and respect, an association which, of course, is at the root of Ronald Dworkin's thinking about rights.[10] In today's world there is little need to construct or imagine what a society without rights would look like: we only need to take a look at countries like Romania or Albania to see the reality: indeed, a peep into Romanian orphanages or homes for the mentally handicapped in Albania tells us much about the plight of children produced in such morally impoverished environments.[11]

Children easily become victims.[12] That much is clearly recognized in the United Nations Convention.[13] They have not been accorded either dignity or respect. They have been reified,[14] treated as objects of intervention rather than as legal subjects, labelled as a 'problem population' (Spitzer, 1975), reduced to being seen as property.[15] They complete a family rather as the standard consumer durables furnish a household (Kellmer-Pringle, 1980). Because children have lacked the moral coinage of rights, it has been easy to brush their interests aside in the sweep of consequentialist thinking. Where the goal is the maximization of welfare, children do not seem to have counted or to have carried much weight. Consequentialist thought is capable of justifying rights but only as rules of thumb for maximizing welfare. But the interests upheld by rights are not just desires to seek pleasures and avoid pains, as utilitarians claim, or rank individualism, self-indulgence or egoism, as Burke, Bentham and Marx in various ways argued (Waldron, 1987). Rather, these interests are our plans and projects, our concerns and our states of mind without which our lives would be bereft of much of their meaning. The recognition and protection of these interests is that which makes human life more human. In this sense civilization is dependent in part upon a culture which acknowledges the integrity and personality of each individual. That is why *apartheid* and racial segregation are wrong, why the marital rape immunity could not be defended (Freeman, 1985) and why the sexual abuse of children (Freeman, 1989; La Fontaine, 1990), which reduced them to objects, disciplinary practices like 'pin-down', rationalized as control measures (Levy & Kahan, 1991), and corporal punishment, legitimate only in the case of children (Newell, 1990; Freeman, 1988b) are grave infringements of the interests of the human beings targeted by the practices in question.

BUT ARE RIGHTS IMPORTANT FOR CHILDREN?

Those who accept the moral importance of rights as 'trumps'[16] are often still inclined to deny the necessity of thinking in terms of rights when it comes to children. The arguments put tend to take one or more of three forms.

First, there is the argument that the importance of rights and rights-language themselves can be exaggerated. That there are other morally significant values, love, friendship, compassion, altruism, and that these raise relationships to a higher plain than one based on the observance of duty cannot be gainsaid (Kleinig, 1976). This argument may be thought particularly apposite to children's rights, particularly in the context of family relationships. Perhaps in an ideal moral world this is true. Rights may be used to resolve conflicts of interests and in an ideal world there would be harmony and these would not exist. But it is not an ideal world – certainly not for children. Children are particularly vulnerable and need rights to protect their integrity and dignity. 'Solitary, poor, nasty, brutish and short' (Hobbes, 1651) may not be a description of a state of nature (rather a construction or 'thought experiment' on Hobbes' part (Hampton, 1991)) but it may come close to describing what a world without rights would look like for many children. Of course, it may be said that where children have rights this creates conflict. They complain about their treatment; they make legitimate claims; they challenge authority. Were they not able to do so life would be easier, quieter for adults (parents, teachers, social workers, police etc). But there would still be conflict: it would simmer below the surface, occasionally boiling over. Think of our treatment of prisoners, who are endowed with few rights and the riots which periodically erupt (Woolf, 1991). It is difficult to see how this would make the world a better place. When Kleinig asserts that 'a morality which has as its motivation merely the giving of what is due . . . is seriously defective'[17] he is only partly correct. Such a morality both allows for the observance of minimally decent standards and the opportunity to express and reciprocate the other morally significant values to which he refers.

The second argument is in one sense related to the first. It assumes that adults already relate to children in terms of love, care and altruism, so that the case for children's rights becomes otiose. This idealizes adult–child relations: it emphasizes that adults (and parents in particular) have the best interests of children at heart. There is a tendency for those who postulate such an argument to adopt a *laisser-faire* attitude towards the family. Thus, the only right for children which Goldstein, Freud and Solnit (1979) acknowledge in *Before the Best Interests of the Child* is the child's right to autonomous parents. A policy of minimum coercive intervention by the state accords, they maintain, with their 'firm belief as citizens in individual freedom and human dignity' (Goldstein, Freud &

Solnit, 1979:12). But it hardly needs to be asked *whose* freedom and *what* dignity this is thought to uphold. It is difficult to see how the creation of a private space in this way can be said to protect the humanity of the child. There is a strand in the recent English Children Act of 1989 which reflects very much the same philosophy.[18]

The third argument equally rests on a myth. It sees childhood as a golden age, as the best years of our life. Childhood is synonymous with innocence. It is the time when, spared the rigours of adult life, we enjoy freedom, experience play and joy. The argument runs: just as we avoid the responsibilities and adversities of adult life in childhood, so there should be no necessity to think in terms of rights, a concept which we must assume is reserved for adults. Whether or not the premise underlying this were correct or not, it would represent an ideal state of affairs, and one which ill-reflects the lives of many of today's children and adolescents. But for many this mythic 'walled garden of 'Happy, Safe, Protected, Innocent Childhood' (Holt, 1975)is just plain wrong, with poverty, disease, exploitation and abuse rife across the globe.

The case put forward by those who wish to deflate the importance of rights for children does not, accordingly, withstand critical scrutiny.

Rights are important because those who lack rights are like slaves, means to the ends of others, and never sovereigns in their own right.[19] Those who may claim[20] rights, or for whom rights may be claimed, have a necessary pre-condition to the constitution of humanity, of integrity, of individuality, of personality. It is surely significant that when we wish to deny rights to those who have attained chronological adulthood, such as blacks in South Africa or the Southern States of the USA or the mentally retarded, we label them children ('boys'). To be a 'child' one does not have to be young. Foucault's aphorism that 'madness is childhood' (Foucault, 1967) rings very true. Childhood is, of course, a social construction, a man-made phenomenon: it has not always 'existed', as Ariès (1962), Illich (1973) and others (James & Prout, 1990) have reminded us.[21] Those in authority determine who is a child.

BUT SHOULD WE BE LOOKING TO OBLIGATIONS RATHER THAN RIGHTS?

A more oblique attack on children's rights or rather on the appropriate way morally to justify them, is put by Onora O'Neill in 'Children's Rights and Children's Lives' (1992). She does not question the view that children's lives are a public concern, rather than a private matter. Nor does she query the aim of securing positive rights for children. What she does question is whether children's positive rights are best grounded by appeals to fundamental rights. She claims that 'children's fundamental rights are best grounded by embedding them in a wider account of fundamental obligations, which can also be used to justify positive rights and obligations' (O'Neill, 1992:24–5). It is her contention that 'we can perhaps go *further* to secure the ethical basis of children's positive rights if we do *not* try to base them on claims about fundamental rights' (O'Neill, 1992:25).

Her argument is closely reasoned and no summary can do it justice. The strategy of her argument, as she put it, is:

. . . that theories that take rights as fundamental and those that take obligations as fundamental are not equivalent. The scope of the two sorts of theory differs and does so in ways that matter particularly for children . . . (T)hat a constructivist account of obligations has *theoretical* advantages which constructivist accounts of rights lack, though rights-based approaches sometimes have *political* advantages which obligation-based approaches do not . . . (T)hat in the specific case of children, taking rights as fundamental has political costs rather than advantages (O'Neill, 1992:25).

She concludes 'that taking rights as fundamental in ethical deliberation about children has neither theoretical nor political advantages', and a more 'perspicuous and complete view' of ethical aspects of children's lives 'can be obtained by taking obligations as fundamental' (O'Neill, 1992:25).

My differences with O'Neill are several. She cannot envisage a children's movement: I can. Indeed, there are prototypes or at least germs of children's movements already in existence. There have been school strikes and attempts at school unionization (Hoyles, 1979). There is in Britain the National Association of Young People In Care and similar organizations elsewhere. There are any number of adult writers who propagate children's rights. There are children's legal and other advisory centres and children's ombudsmen. To say that these are movements on behalf of children rather than children's movements is only a partial answer for the other rights movements were equally preceded by prototypes and led by enlightened members of the oppressing 'class'. Think of John Stuart Mill or the National Association for the Advancement of Coloured People. A children's movement could emerge.

Secondly, she thinks the dependency of children is 'very different' (O'Neill, 1992:38) from the dependency of other oppressed groups. 'Appeals to children's rights', she argues, 'might have political and rhetorical importance if children's dependence on others is like that of oppressed social groups whom the rhetoric of rights has served well' (O'Neill, 1992:37). There are, she believes, four ways in which children's dependence is different from the dependence of other oppressed groups. It is not artificially produced, though she concedes it can be artificially prolonged. It cannot be ended merely by social or political changes. Others are not reciprocally dependent on children whereas slave-owners, for example, need their slaves. The 'oppressors' usually want children's dependency to end. I do not deny that children's dependency is different from that of other groups, but I do not think it is quite as different as O'Neill would have us believe. To some extent it is artificially produced. The lessons of history tell us this: our own experiences and intuitions enable us to realize that many adolescents have the capacity to be less dependent than many adults. For example, if competence rather than age were the test, we could safely give the vote to many fourteen-year-olds and have little compunction about disenfranchizing large sections of the adult population (Lindley, 1986:125–33). Some (clearly not all) of it can be ended by political, if not by social change. They may not be changes of which we approve (and I certainly would not approve) for example, encouraging children to be gainfully employed. But they are changes which would decrease dependency. The reciprocal dependency argument can also be over-played: think of the parent who needs to be loved and shown affection by his or her child. Some child abuse can apparently be explained in this way: children who cannot, or more usually are not old enough to, show affection being battered by inadequate parents.[22] Certainly, some older children perceive a parent's dependency in this way. It is not unknown for children, in the divorce setting, to think that a particular parent cannot survive their loss, with the result that their decision, if asked, as to where to live may be influenced by what they see as a parent's welfare rather than their own.[23]

A third difference I have with O'Neill follows on from the second. She perceives children as a special case. Whilst she concedes that the fact that children cannot claim rights is no reason for denying them rights, the claiming/waiving dilemma seems to be the root of her thinking. She does not discuss what she believes the theoretical underpinning of rights to be, but the references to claiming and waiving suggest she is wedded to the will theory.[24] A series of inconclusive test matches may, as Neill MacCormick (1982) put it wittily, have been played out between the will and interest theories of rights,[25] but he, I think, showed convincingly that, in the case of children's rights at least, the interest theory was more coherent and had greater explanatory power.[26] Children have interests to protect before they develop wills to assert, and others can complain on behalf of younger children when those interests are trampled upon. Questions of 'by whom' and 'how' have not been satisfactorily answered. Howard Cohen's suggestion of the 'child agent', who would 'supply information in terms which the child could understand, to make the consequences of the various courses of action a child might make clear to the child, and do what is necessary to see that the right in question is actually exercised' (Cohen, 1980:60) is appealing, if ultimately, flawed.

It cannot be right, as O'Neill states, that the child's 'main remedy is to grow up' (1992:39). First this underestimates the capacities and maturity of many children. Both in moral and cognitive development, many children reach adult levels between twelve and fourteen, though the ability to reason improves quite obviously through adolescence.[27] We expect adolescents to be criminally responsible at the age of fourteen (indeed, we are prepared to impose criminal responsibility on them at ten), but we are less willing to accept the correlativity of responsibility and rights. Secondly, what O'Neill ignores is the impact on adult life that parenting and socialization leave. A child deprived of the sort of rights envisaged in the UN Convention will grow up very differently from one accorded them.

It is then O'Neill's contention that if we care about children's lives, there are good reasons not to base our arguments on rights. These arguments are both theoretical and political. Instead she argues we should look to improve children's lives by identifying what obligations parents, teachers and indeed the wider community have towards children. 'A construction made from the agent's perspective may deliver more, though it promises less, since it does not aim at an "all or nothing" construction of ethical requirements' (O'Neill, 1992:34). But a construction of rights need not aim at absolutism either. There are very few (if any) absolute rights and these must by definition belong to children too. If there is an absolute right not to be tortured (Gewirth, 1982), the torturing of children for whatever reason is beyond deliberation. O'Neill's concern with 'accommodation' problems seems to assume that those who construct rights are looking for 'unique' solutions. The spatial metaphor she employs is helpful to a point but is ultimately flawed because it is taken too literally and is used to explain too much. She says that when a literal interpretation is dropped, territorial metaphors lose 'sense and precision' (O'Neill, 1992:31), that we lose our grip on claims that one right is larger than another or that some set of rights is maximal. For example, she questions how a rights-based theory can determine whether an older child's right to freedom of association is larger than his or her freedom of conscience and whether either of these rights is larger than the right to adequate parental care and supervision. There are no right or necessarily even best answers to these questions. Much will depend on the age of the child: older children have greater need for association rights than small children and younger children require closer parental care than more mature children do. But, at least so far as older children are concerned, which right is greater should depend upon which they, that is the recipients, perceive to be of greatest significance to them, unless, as will be argued later, the exercise of a right is destructive or irreparably debilitating. It is not a question of what 'significant others' such as parents, and teachers would accord them.[28] How this is constructed is considered in a later section of this article.

THE LIMITS OF RIGHTS

Having emphasized the importance of rights, three points must be briefly addressed.

First, crucial though it is to see children's rights recognized, we must be careful not to mistake the words for the deeds. This is particularly significant now that we have begun to take children's rights seriously. The passing of laws, the implementation of conventions, is only a beginning: it is a signal that must be taken up by governments, institutions and individuals. For some years English children's legislation had a provision, in fact now diluted,[29] that local authorities, in reaching any decision about children in their care, had to give 'first consideration' to children's welfare and 'due consideration' to the wishes and feelings of the child (Child Care Act 1980 s 18). In practice, this was honoured more in the breach than in the observance, justifying the comment, often made, that it was mere tokenism (Gardner, 1987). But, it is worse than this, because it is easy to take the words for the act and assume that with the enactment of rights-bestowing provisions the conditions of children's lives has changed. The importance of legislation as a symbol (Edelman, 1977) cannot be underestimated, but the true recognition of children's rights requires implementation in practice. Indeed, unimplemented, partially implemented or badly implemented laws may actually do children more harm than good.

Secondly, the passing of laws can have less than desirable side effects and unintended consequences. Rights can all too easily backfire. Reform movements intended to enhance children's rights and the concomitant development of professional structures to implement such reforms can generate their own sets of problems, and these may undermine children's rights or otherwise deleteriously affect the quality of children's lives. It is not uncommon for the reforms of one era to become the problems of the next. Many examples could be given: the invention of the IQ test (in 1907 a benevolent measure by which an objective test was substituted for the injustice of the subjective method then used for placing children in institutions – now associated with the stigma of labelling); the juvenile court system (lauded as a way of 'saving' children and then conceptualized in terms of children's rights but today widely associated with the diminution of basic rights) are just two. Looked at in this way, can we be sure that an injection of more rights for children into the juvenile justice system would not lead to an increase in more informal 'justice without trial' (Skolnick, 1966), or that more rights for children in the divorce process would not become a method of social control of mothers and in the process harm also children, as, indeed, may be happening in regimes which are developing to control pregnant women? This is not to advocate caution in furthering children's rights, but care in so doing, and to recommend adequate surveillance of the institutional practices of those to whom the task of operationalizing children's rights is entrusted.

Thirdly, rights without services are meaningless, and services without resources cannot be provided. 'No law', wrote Monrad Paulsen (1974) in relation to mandatory child abuse legislation in the United States, 'can be better than resources permit'. Many think the good intentions of the 1989 Children Act in England will founder because of inadequate resources: local authorities are already re-defining statutory definitions of 'in need' to take account of what they see as realities (Barber, 1990). There is, in other words, little point creating an improved legal framework or instituting greater rights for children, unless in addition resource allocation is addressed, and redressed.[30] Children are not interested in symbolic politics. Ultimately, the question of rights for children resolves into questions of distributive justice. If we are not prepared to accept this, we may as well give up the fight to see children's rights improved.

WHY SHOULD WE TAKE CHILDREN'S RIGHTS MORE SERIOUSLY?

We must now seek out the moral justification for taking children's rights seriously.

Our point of departure is to ask why we believe it is morally important that adults should be regarded as rights-holders with all that this entails (Sumner, 1987). When this is answered, we can turn our attention to children and investigate whether any of the supposed reasons for discriminating against children stand up to rational scrutiny.

Why, therefore, should we take rights seriously? As the language used indicates, we cannot today investigate this question without taking note of the writings of Ronald Dworkin (1977, 1978). He has not addressed children's rights and much of his relevant writing has tackled specifically rights against the state (or constitutional rights). Some, but far from all, children's rights come into this category. Nevertheless, the insights offered can be generalized.

It is Dworkin's thesis that if persons have moral rights to something, they are to be accorded these rights even if a utilitarian calculation shows that utility would be maximized by denying it to them. He invokes Rawls (1972) to illuminate the moral foundations of the rights thesis. Rawls proposes a methodology of reflective equilibrium whereby we try to fashion formulations of moral principles to the cut of moral judgement until we no longer feel inclined to change our judgements to fit the theory or our theory to fit the judgements. The ideal is a perfect fit. Rawls' mechanism for this reflective equilibrium is the social contract model: it conceives of persons in the 'original position', behind a 'veil of ignorance' and thus ignorant of their identity, interests and entitlements, choosing the structure of the society in which they will live.[31] Dworkin believes that these individuals 'have a responsibility to fit the particular judgments on which they act into a coherent program of action' (Dworkin, 1978:160). Thus interpreted, Dworkin believes the contractual mechanism can be dropped. It is nothing more than a moral metaphor. Instead, he believes that we can, and should, focus on the idea that all other principles derive from the principle of equal concern and respect for each person.

For Dworkin anyone who proposes to 'take rights seriously' must accept the ideas of human dignity and political equality. He argues in favour of a fundamental right to equal concern and respect, and against any general right to liberty. The advantage of his so doing, as John Mackie acknowledged in an important article (1984), is that the right to equal concern and respect is a final and not merely 'a prima-facie right', in the sense that one person's possession or enjoyment of it does not conflict with another's. Dworkin puts this forward as a 'postulate of political morality' (1978:272) a fundamental political right: governments must treat citizens with equal concern and respect.

But why do we have the rights we have? (Bedau, 1984). Is this by itself sufficient to explain a right-based moral theory? The question is still left open as to where rights come from. Why do we 'have' the rights we do? I am not talking here of legal rights. The answer to why we have these can be answered within the legal framework itself (the statute says . . .) or historically by depicting the struggles (for the vote, trade union rights etc) that were ultimately successful.

What 'is' there then when there 'are' rights? As Jan Narveson put it there 'must be certain features or properties of those who "have" them such that we have *good reason to acknowledge* the obligation to refrain from interfering with, or possibly sometimes to help other bearers to do the things they are said to have the right to do, or have those things they are said to have a right to have' (Narveson, 1985:164).

Rights then are dependent on reasoned argument, which is not always forthcoming. Thus, Nozick merely asserts peremptorily that 'individuals have rights' (Nozick, 1974:ix). Justifying principles can, and have, been sought. One common answer links rights with interests. This takes us part of the way, but not far enough. Feinberg is right to suppose that the 'sort of beings who can have rights are precisely those who have (or can have) interests' (1966).[33] But to argue from this is unacceptable. There is much that is in my interests but to which I can in no way make a justifiable claim. This is rather different from O'Neill's objection to finding rights where there are imperfect and non-institutionalized obligations only.[34] But it enters a caveat at least against the indiscriminate use of the 'manifesto' sense in which rights are sometimes used.[35]

Another argument often put forward is purely formal. It is that all persons ought to be treated alike unless there is a good reason for treating them differently. Dworkin, for one, accepts this. He envisages the right to treatment as an equal (Dworkin, 1977:226–9)[36] as a morally fundamental idea. It is that which requires that each person be accorded the same degree of concern and respect as every other person. Though attractive, as already indicated, this reasoning alone is not without its difficulties. A problem lies in deciding what constitutes a 'good reason' for treating people differently. Gender and colour are now almost universally accepted to be indefensible distinctions but age is not so regarded by policy-makers (Eekelaar & Pearl, 1989) or philosophers. Nor, on one level, should it. We cannot but accept that children, particularly young children, have needs (Kellmer-Pringle, 1980) that cannot be met by recognizing that they have rights on a par with adults.[37] That much will become clear later in this article. But, looked at generally, the principle appears more egalitarian than it is. Its potentiality for undermining egalitarianism cannot be overlooked.

An appealing argument has been advanced by William Frankena (1962). He argues that humans are 'capable of enjoying a good life in the sense in which other animals are not . . . . It is the fact that all men are similarly capable of enjoying a good life in this sense that justifies the prima-facie requirement that they be treated as equals'. Superficially, this is an attractive argument. But it question begs. Are all persons, even all adults, capable of enjoying a good life? All children are capable of so doing, even if their capacities during childhood are limited. But there are dangers in using an argument like this: it can easily lead to the deprivation of rights on the grounds that it is meaningless to the person in question – the decision to allow the sterilization of mentally handicapped women has been so justified in England and elsewhere (Freeman, 1988a). It can also be argued that, without more, it fails to show how factual similarity can be said to ground the obligation which Frankena claims. Nor is it entirely clear how factual similarity should lead to egalitarian treatment, for it would be possible to argue that two persons were similar, whilst supporting unequal treatment on the grounds that the value of one person's happiness is greater than that of other persons.

Space precludes the consideration of other arguments, but they are all in some way defective. Dworkin himself attempts to identify the existence of a moral right against the State when, for 'some' reason, the State would 'do wrong' to treat a person in a certain way, 'even though it would be in the general interest to do so' (Dworkin, 1977:139). It is, however, clear that what is 'wrong' for the State to do is what the State has an obligation not to do. Dworkin, in other words is defining rights in terms of duties. But, why is it 'wrong' for the state to act in a particular way? It is because the individual has a 'right' on which state action of a particular sort would illegitimately trample. This suggests the argument is inherently circular (MacCormick, 1983).

Thus, Dworkin's arguments take us so far – but not far enough.

Equality by itself cannot explain what Dworkin is trying to explain: namely, that rights as such 'trump' countervailing utilitarian considerations. Something more is needed. I suggest that this additional concept is autonomy.

A plausible theory of rights needs to take account not just of equality but also of the normative value of autonomy (Feinberg, 1986; Frankfurt, 1981; Haworth, 1986; Lindley, 1986; Dworkin, 1988; Young, 1986), the idea that persons as such have a set of capacities that enables them to make independent decisions regarding appropriate life choices (Mill, 1859). The deep structure of the rights thesis is equality and autonomy (Richards, 1981). Kant (1785) expressed this by asserting that persons are equal and autonomous in the kingdom of ends (Mulholland, 1990). It is the normative value of equality and autonomy which lie at the root of the Rawlsian contractarian conception. To see people as both equal and autonomous is to repudiate the moral claim of those who would allow utilitarian calculations of the greatest happiness of the greatest number to prevail over the range of significant life choices which the rights thesis both facilitates and enhances.

Utilitarianism, by contrast, demands that the pattern of individual life choices be overridden if others are thus made better off. The result of this is that life choices become in effect the judgement of one person, the sympathetic onlooker whose pleasure is maximized only when the utilitarian principle is upheld. But such an assimilation contradicts the central theses of equality and autonomy – the fundamental tenet of ethics that people are equal and have the capacity to live as separate and independent beings. To treat persons as utilitarianism requires is to focus almost obsessively on aggregated pleasure as the only ethically significant goal and to ignore the critical fact that persons experience pleasure and that pleasure has human and moral significance only in the context of a life a person chooses to lead.

It is the rights thesis that protects the integrity of the person in leading his or her life. One of Dworkin's insights was to link Rawlsian contractarian theory to the language of rights. One of his failings was to fail to appreciate that both notions at the root of Kantian moral theory (equality and autonomy) were equally morally significant. When we take both equality and autonomy seriously, we are back to the contractarian thinking to be found in Kant and in the contemporary constructivism of Rawls. Equality is, I believe, best expressed as an original position of equal beings: autonomy as the putative choice of those beings under a 'veil of ignorance'.

To believe in autonomy is to believe that anyone's autonomy is as morally significant as anyone else's.[38] Nor does autonomy depend on the stage of life that a person has reached. Only human beings are 'persons'. A legal system may attribute 'personhood' to an inanimate entity, a corporation, an idol, a god or even to animals but these do not become 'persons' in the sense used here. What is it, then, about human beings that makes them 'persons'? Recent writers are in general agreement. For Haworth (1986) it is 'critical competence', for Lindley (1986) it is a capacity for reasoning. These tests are not unlike that constructed by Lord Scarman in the *Gillick* case. Lord Scarman offered no guidelines as to when a child reached '*Gillick*-competence' and, in terms of age, legal commentators since have assumed this was reached during adolescence.[39] It is, however, clear once criteria for personhood are examined that many children acquire critical competence considerably earlier.

A good account of the criteria is in Lindley (1986:122):

Certainly consciousness is a requirement. More specifically a person is a creature which has beliefs and desires, and acts on its desires in the light of its beliefs. However, this is insufficient for personhood. What is required in addition is the capacity to evaluate and structure one's beliefs and desires, and to act on the basis of these evaluations.

He also approves Frankfurt's account of freedom of will and the concept of a person (Frankfurt, 1981). According to Frankfurt, to be a person, a creature must have 'second-order volitions', that is desires about which desires she wants to become her will. As Lindley phrases it, 'people have wills, insofar as they do not necessarily act on their strongest inclinations, but have the general ability to act on the results of their deliberation' (1986:122–3). He argues that a crucial requirement is possession of the concept of 'a self' (1986:123): someone has to be able to think of himself 'as a being with a future and a past, a subject of experience, a possessor of beliefs and desires' (1986:160). Of course, it is not clear exactly when children acquire these concepts, and there may be gender and class differences, but at seven it would not be uncommon and at ten it may be thought that most children have become persons in the sense depicted here. In England their education attainments are now 'examined' at seven and they are criminally responsible at ten.

To respect a child's autonomy is to treat that child as a person and as a rights-holder. It is clear that we can do so to a much greater extent than we have assumed hitherto. But it is also clear that the exercising of autonomy by a child can have a deleterious impact on that child's life-chances. It is true that adults make mistakes too (and also make mistakes when interfering with a child's autonomy). Having rights, means being allowed to take risks and make choices. There is a reluctance to interfere with an adult's project. This reluctance is tempered when the project pursuer is a child by the sense that choice now may harm choice later. As Lomasky (1987:160) puts it: 'what counts as damage . . . is determined by what will likely further or diminish its eventual success in living as a project pursuer'.

This is to recognize that children are different. Many of them have lesser abilities and capacities. They are more vulnerable. They need protection. Without welfare rights being recognized, they will not be in a position to exercise autonomy. Of course, all of this is true, but it is not as true as we have come to believe. Children are different, but they are not all that different. There is a 'developmental trajectory' (Kleinig, 1989) through which we all pass. Age is often a suspect classification. If we are to apply a double standard, we must justify it. Double standards are not necessarily unjustifiable: things which appear to be alike may, on further reflection, not be as alike as they looked at first appearance. The onus lies on those who wish to discriminate. Hitherto, it has to be said that they have not discharged this burden very convincingly. How many of the structures, institutions and practices established to 'protect' children actually do so? Think of the juvenile court, the care system, observation and assessment centres, reporting systems where abuse has been identified, 'child protection' registers for children 'at risk', and ask whether the 'official' version of the truth withstands critical examination. But ask also whether, and to what extent, we are prepared to encourage children to participate in decisions regarding their life choices. It is much easier to assume abilities and capacities are absent than to take cognizance of children's choices.

If we are to make progress we have to recognize the moral integrity of children (Miller, 1987). We have to treat them as persons entitled to equal concern and respect and entitled to have both their present autonomy recognized and their capacity for future autonomy safeguarded. And this is to recognize that children, particularly younger children, need nurture, care and protection. Children must not, as Hafen (1977) put it, be 'abandoned' to their rights.

THE LIMITS OF AUTONOMY

In looking for a children's rights programme we must thus recognize the integrity of the child and his or her decision-making capacities but at the same time note the dangers of complete liberation. Too often writers on children's rights have dichotomized: there is either salvation or liberation (Margolin, 1978), either nurturance or self-determination (Rogers & Wrightsman, 1978) – in Richard Farson's pithy phrase, the one protects children, the other their rights (1978).

To take children's rights more seriously requires us to take more seriously than we have done hitherto protection of children and recognition of their autonomy, both actual and potential. The view presented is premised on the need to respect individual autonomy and to treat persons as equals. Actual autonomy is important but it is as much the capacity for autonomy that is at the root of this thinking. Here, once again, the constructivism of Rawls' theory of justice may be prayed in aid. It is the normative value of equality and autonomy which forms the substructure of the Rawlsian conception of the social contract. The principles of justice which Rawls believes we would choose in the 'original position' are equal liberty and opportunity, and an arrangement of social and economic inequalities so that they are both to the greatest benefit of the least advantaged, and attached to offices and positions open to all under conditions of fair equality and opportunity. (See also Rawls, 1982).

These principles confine paternalism (the philosophy at the root of protection) without totally eliminating it. Those who participate in a hypothetical social contract would know that some human beings are less capable than others. They would know about variations in intelligence and strength, and they would know of the very limited capacities of small children and the rather fuller, if incomplete, capacities of adolescents. They would employ the insights of cognitive psychology (Melton, 1987). They would also bear in mind how the actions of those with limited capacities might thwart their autonomy at a future time when their capacities were no longer as limited.

These considerations would lead to an acceptance of interventions in children's lives to protect them against irrational actions. But what is to be regarded as 'irrational' must be strictly confined. The subjective values of the would-be protector cannot be allowed to intrude. What is 'irrational' must be defined in terms of a neutral theory capable of accommodating pluralistic visions of the 'good' (Rawls, 1987). Nor should we see an action as irrational unless it is manifestly so in the sense tha it would undermine future life choices, impair interests in an irreversible way. Furthermore, we must tolerate mistakes, for, as Dworkin rightly observes, 'someone may have the right to do something that is wrong for him to do' (Dworkin, 1978: 188–9). We cannot treat persons as equals without also respecting their capacity to take risks and make mistakes. We would not be taking rights seriously if we only respected autonomy when we considered the agent was doing the right thing. But we also would be failing to recognize a child's integrity if we allowed him to choose an action, such as using heroin or choosing not to attend school, which could seriously and systematically impair the attainment of full personality and development subsequently. The test of 'irrationality' must also be confined so that it justifies intervention only to the extent necessary to obviate the immediate harm, or to develop the capacities of rational choice by which the individual may have a reasonable chance of avoiding such harms.

The question we should ask ourselves is: what sort of action or conduct would we wish, as children, to be shielded against on the assumption that we would want to mature to a rationally autonomous adulthood and be capable of deciding on our own system of ends as free and rational beings? We would, I believe, choose principles that would enable children to mature to independent adulthood. One definition of irrationality would be such as to preclude action and conduct which would frustrate such a goal. Within the constraints of such a definition we would defend a version of paternalism: not paternalism in its classical sense for, so conceived, there would be no children's rights at all. Furthermore, it must be stressed that this version of paternalism is a two-edged sword in that, since the goal is rational independence, those who exercise constraints must do so in such a way as to enable children to develop their capacities.

All paternalistic restrictions require moral justification. In many cases it is not difficult to adduce sufficient and convincing reasoned argument. Thus, it is not difficult to present the case for protecting children against actions which may lead to their death or to serious physical injury or mental disability. Nineteenth century legislation which made it illegal for children to go down coal mines or up chimneys or into factories can thus readily be defended (though it may not have been passed to protect children). So can laws designed to protect children from sexual abuse and exploitation. There are clear dangers in the suggestions of writers of the 1970s like Holt (1975) and Farson (1978) that a child's right to self-determination includes a right to a sexual relationship with whomsoever he or she pleases. The 'discovery' of sexual abuse since has all but put an end to these demands (Miller, 1984; Nelson, 1987). On the other hand, 'ages of consent' as such are meaningless: the crucial factor is the presence or absence of exploitation, so that age *difference* may be of greater significance than the age of the child. A system of compulsory education, and concomitantly restrictions on employment, can also be defended, contrary to the argument of some liberationists (Duane, 1972), though the perimeters, content and goals of 'education' would be very different from those conventionally stipulated.

What should legitimize all these interferences with autonomy is, what Gerald Dworkin (1972) has called, 'future-oriented' consent. The question is: can the restrictions be justified in terms that the child would eventually come to appreciate? Looking back, would the child appreciate and accept the reason for the restriction imposed upon him or her, given what he or she now knows as a rationally autonomous and mature adult? It may readily be conceded that this is not an easy test to apply. It involves something akin to what Parfit (1984) has called 'ideal deliberation'. (See also Brandt, 1979). As he puts it: 'What each of us has most reason to do is what would best achieve, not what he *actually* wants, but what he *would* want, at the time of acting, if he had undergone a process of "ideal deliberation" – if he knew the relevant facts, was thinking clearly, and was free from distorting influences'. But what are 'relevant facts'? And how are hypothetical preferences to be considered? Can distortion of values be eliminated? The problems are real, but the effort to disentangle them remains worthwhile.

The dichotomy drawn is thus to some extent a false divide.

Dichotomies and other classifications should not divert us away from the fact that true protection of children does protect their rights. It is not a question of whether child-savers or liberationists are right, for they are both correct in emphasizing part of what needs to be recognized, and both wrong in failing to address the claims of the other side.

To take children's rights more seriously requires us to take seriously nurturance and self-determination. It demands of us that we adopt policies, practices, structures and laws which both protect children and their rights. Hence the *via media* of 'liberal paternalism' (Freeman, 1983).

THE CONVENTION

It would be wrong to conclude without asking how the world's statement of principles matches up to the model and reasoning embodied in the 1989 UN Convention here set out. Certainly, it recognizes a large number of rights. Most are expressed in terms of rights (for example, freedom of expression, thought, association, social security, education), though some are conceptualized as duties upon states (for example, the provision dealing with sexual abuse). Nothing of moment hinges upon the distinction: it is certainly not a reflection of any philosophical considerations. The rights enumerated concentrate heavily on protection and on the granting to children by adults of what they think children need. But, significantly, Article 12 requires states to 'assure to the child who is capable of forming his or her own views the right to express those views freely, in all matters affecting the child, the view of the child being given due weight in accordance with the age and maturity of the child'. Whether the Convention would have looked the same had its framers consulted children on its contents is a matter upon which we can only speculate.

On the other hand, an article such as Article 29 is of great significance. The education of the child is to be directed *inter alia* towards the development of the child's personality, the development of respect for human rights, the preparation of the child for responsible life and to inculcate tolerance. As a provision which emphasizes choice and which sees education in broad terms, it is a recognition of children's rights in its widest sense. The law of England certainly falls far short of these ideals (Newell, 1991) and recent practice undermines them further.[40] So does the law of the USA (Bitensky, 1990).

The Convention is a beginning, but only a beginning. Those who wish to see the status and lives of children improved must continue the search for the moral foundation of children's rights. Without such thinking there would not have been a Convention: without further critical insight there will be no further recognition of the importance to children's lives of according them rights.

NOTES

[1] *Gillick* v *West Norfolk and Wisbech Area Health Authority*, [1986] AC 112. But see now *Re R* [1991] 4 All ER 177.

[2] Children Act 1989. See, in particular, ss 1 (3)(a); 4 (3) (b); 6 (7) (b); 10 (8); 20 (11); 22 (4) (a), (5); 26 (3); 34 (2), (4); 38 (6); 43 (8); 44 (7); 64 (2) (a).

[3] Notably, those of the Minister for Health, Virginia Bottomley. See for example, her statement, reported in *Community Care*, 850, 4 (7 February 1991).

[4] For a detailed exposition of the shortcomings see Newell (1991). A similar exposé of US laws and practices is Cohen & Davidson (1990).

[5] She said this at the George Thomas Society Inaugural Lecture on 17 February 1990.

[6] 28.6 *per cent* of all children were living around this standard. This figure is derived from official Department of Social Security statistics.

[7] This figure is extrapolated from National Children's Home statistics, in particular annual 'Factfiles' entitled 'Children in Danger'. See also Bradshaw (1990:40–2).

[8] It has been estimated that over 150,000 experience homelessness every year as a result of leaving home or care and being unable to find or afford accommodation. See Gosling & Diarists (1989). Changes in social security rules that removed entitlement for sixteen and seventeen-year-olds and reduced it for other young people have aggravated this situation. See Craig & Glendinning (1990).

[9] See the view of Cohen, 1980 that 'rights' are a 'militant' concept. Bentham by contrast, called it 'terrorist language', thus making it very clear where he stood.

[10] But, of course, not only Dworkin. See also Benn (1988).

[11] This is not intended to take issue with the thesis presented by Glendon (1991) on the dangers of an exaggerated rights discourse, where rights rhetoric becomes almost a 'dialect'. Nor is it the place to examine the communitarian thesis of Taylor, MacIntyre, Sandel and others, save to say that I am far from convinced that individual rights and community values are incompatible.

[12] Or an 'endangered species' as one writer Max (1990) has recently put it. On 'blaming the victim', see Ryan (1976).

[13] See, in particular, Articles 6, 9, 11, 16, 19, 20, 22, 23, 24, 27, 32, 33, 34, 35, 36, 37, 38, 39 and 40.

[14] Reification involves 'treating a notational device as though it were a substantive term . . . a construct as though it were observational' (*per* Kaplan, 1964:61). 'The "name" and the meanings assigned to it become the thing to which we react. The thing is symbolized by the name; the name takes on an existence of its own' (*per* Pfuhl, 1980:28).

[15] There are many illuustrations of this. One graphic recent case study is Groner (1991) an account of the *Morgan* v *Foretich* custody/access dispute.

[16] The term derives from Dworkin (1978a) where an account of rights as 'trumps' against a background of utility considerations is developed.

[17] Kleinig (1976:14). A revised version is Kleinig (1982:ch 15).

[18] In particular the presumption of non-intervention in s 1 (5).

[19] This is similar to Isaiah Berlin's 'positive liberty': 'I wish to be an instrument of my own, not other men's acts of will. I wish to be a subject, not an object . . . deciding, not being decided for, self-directed and not acted upon by external nature or by other men as if I were a thing, or an animal, or a slave incapable of playing a human role, that is, of conceiving goals and policies of my own and realizing them' Berlin (1969:131).

[20] They do not have to be able to exercise them at this point of time.

[21] But this should be looked at critically, if not sceptically, in the light of Pollock (1983).

[22] In saying this (for which there is some evidence) I should not be taken to be endorsing the psycho-pathological model of child abuse (Freeman, 1983:117–20).

[23] Therefore the view that perhaps they should have the right not to be asked to express any preference. And see *M* v *M* [1977] 7 Fam Law 17.

[24] See the discussion in White (1984:107–108).

[25] See the discussion in Simmonds (1986).

[26] But cf Tuck (1979:ch 1); Lucy (1990:217). Lucy describes the debate as 'rationally irresolvable'.

[27] It is difficult to generalize since class and gender may be crucial variables, but the evidence on moral and cognitive development suggests that many reach adult levels between twelve and fourteen.

[28] It is the case that in practice it will be adults who will impose the limits implied here and discussed in detail below. But the test of intervention is grounded in the objective standard of values of the individual parent, teacher or other adult authority.

[29] See Children Act 1989 s 22(3) where the obligation is to 'safeguard and promote' the child's welfare, rather than to give, as before, 'first consideration' to it. 'First consideration' was interpreted by Lord Brandon in M v H [1988] 3 WLR 485 as being no different from giving 'first and paramount' consideration as then required by the Guardianship of Minors Act 1971, s 1.

[30] See Wikler's view (1979:377–92) that ultimately questions of rights resolve into questions of distributive justice.

[31] Rawls has not stood still and his articulation of the 'original position' argument has developed. The parties in the hypothetical deliberations of the original position are now identified as giving priority to the Kantian interest in the development and exercise of their moral powers of rational autonomy and fair dealing. Expressed thus the value of Rawlsian constructivism to my arguments is enhanced.

[33] Reasoning like this was employed in Re B [1987] A.C. 199, on which see Freeman (1988a).

[34] O'Neill seems to take it for granted that if there are rights they must be 'perfect' ones. 'Imperfect' rights clearly have less value than 'perfect' ones, but conceptually they make no less sense than 'imperfect' obligations.

[35] Where there is said to be a right wherever there is a need. This is logically fallacious and could provide a recipe for anarchy.

[36] Here the distinction is drawn between 'equal treatment' and 'treatment as an equal', the latter being 'normatively less fundamental' (per Western 1990:102).

[37] The ambiguity of 'need' is depicted well by Woodhead (1990:60). His thesis, that we must disentangle the scientific from the evaluative, the natural from the cultural, contains important insights which repay study.

[38] Mill (1859).

[39] See now Re R [1991] 4 All ER 177. Also useful is Re C, The Times, 1 October 1991.

[40] See the editorial in the Times Educational Supplement, 'Keeping The Issues out of Geography', 18 January 1991, 19 (Issue no. 3890).

AUTONOMY AND THE APPROPRIATE PROJECTS OF CHILDREN: A COMMENT ON FREEMAN

CATHERINE LOWY*

In urging us to take children's rights more seriously, Professor Freeman adopts the Dworkinian theory of rights, but he wants to go beyond Dworkin's foundation for such a theory in equality of dignity and respect for persons and adds a principle of autonomy. This leaves him with the problem that is the occasion for my comments. Michael Freeman does not just argue that some rights relate to the right-bearer's nature as an autonomous being, but rather that rights as such are grounded in what he called the 'deep-structure' of the value of autonomy. The question which arises then, is whether such a theory of rights can meet the challenge of accommodating the rights of children. The status of children as autonomous beings, is to say the least, severely contested, as Neil MacCormick (1976) incisively points out:

Children are not always or even usually the best judges of what is good for them, so much so that even the rights which are most important to their long-term well-being, such as the right to discipline or to a safe environment, they regularly perceive as being the reverse of rights or advantages. It does not follow that adults act well if they permit their children to waive those rights, or if they enforce them only at their children's insistence.

The way in which Freeman deals with this challenge to his theory of rights, which is after all a theory of rights for children, is to argue that what is important about autonomy in the case of children is not so much actual autonomy as the *capacity for autonomy*, presumably to be exercised at some later part of the life-span. (This suggests that the underpinning of the general rights theory here endorsed involves not so much equality and autonomy as equality and the capacity for autonomy.) It is here that Michael Freeman tells us when it is justified to protect that capacity for autonomy at the expense of children's present irrational acts or decisions. An irrational action is to be construed as one which would undermine future life-choices and 'impact interests in an irreversible way'. This seems to be too strong. I hope as the mother of small children, but not just in that capacity of course, that the myriad actions from which they must

* Department of Legal Studies, La Trobe University, Melbourne, Victoria 3083 Australia.

be, and I hope, are protected, are not viewed in the light of their future welfare so far in advance that an action which results in a treatable fall or burn is not one from which I rush to protect them, or even one from which they have a right to be protected. (This is despite the validity of the Millian point raised by Freeman that the occasional mistake is a good way of avoiding later such irrational acts.)

Again, and in a slightly different vein, the paradigmatic cases for justified intervention on this account, for older children than the ones I have just had in mind, are 'using heroin' and 'refusing to attend school'. Here the reasoning is that the consequences are such as to impact on later lives of the objects of the intervention in such a way that they would seriously impair rationality, undermining future life-choices.

One way of construing what is suggested here, is that the autonomy of children is to be restricted in the light of the expectation that the object of the intervention would at some future time 'consent' to the intervention. Or to put it in terms of the kind of theory which is being hinted at rather than developed here, when the encumbrance of the irrationality that comes of the status of childhood has been removed, the object of the autonomy limiting intervention will be grateful for, or approve of, the intervention. To take an uncontroversial example, lack of skin cancer in late middle-age will make our children grateful to us for insisting that they wear hats on sunny summer days. This position is more plausibly put as a requirement, not so much of consent, but of hypothetical consent, since we can have no evidence other than that of a hypothetical kind, for events which are to take place far in the future with respect to the desires, interests, proclivities and so on of human beings. (Even in this case, which I have called uncontroversial, it is not at all difficult to imagine a change in the scientific orthodoxy closer to the earlier prevailing view of the importance to health of exposure to the sun early in life, which would of course drastically influence the likelihood of future consent or gratitude.)

Despite the appeal of this kind of theory for justified paternalistic intervention, Freeman is too sanguine about justifying paternalistic interference with children in this way. There is a set of problems for such accounts which arises particularly sharply in the application to children. The puzzle as to who it is who does the consenting in the future is particularly acute. On the kind of theory of personal identity advanced by a philosopher such as Derek Parfit (Parfit, 1984), the later source of consent or gratitude for the current intervention will just not be the same person at all. We do not need to accept such philosophical revisions of the common-sense notion of personal identity, to see the problem of the identification of the earlier with the later self over the period of change which precisely constitutes the maturation process: Such theories are open to the charge that the hypothesis of future approval of present paternalistic intervention is self-fulfilling. This objection is most telling when applied to children and the educative process; the values instilled via the interventions are the very values which become the reason for the future approval.

Is there another approach to children's rights which is able to take into account autonomy as centrally as Freeman wants to do, but which is able to accommodate our reluctance to let children, especially young children, have their way on all and every occasion and which is not reliant on mere *capacity* for autonomy to generate autonomy-respecting rights? It is just such an approach that I want to sketch.

Even very young children, beyond the stage of infancy, are capable of projects in the sense in which I want to use that word.[1] A project at least involves a structure of related expectations determined by a set of positive interests; an interest in, for example freedom from pain is not enough. Projects have many features by which they may be distinguished one from the other. For instance, they may or may not be long-term goal directed, conscious or complex. They may or may not be part of a distinguishable life-plan. The most important feature of projects in the context of our concerns here is that they may or may not be appropriate to a person's current circumstances. It is possible for quite young children to have projects the most important positive fetaure of which is their appropriateness. Respecting the autonomy of children involves respecting their projects when these are appropriate and this is what centrally connects children's current autonomy, as opposed to their mere capacity for autonomy, with children's rights. I would want to argue for a general right to pursue such appropriate projects for children from which particular rights might be, but need not be, derived in a usefully generalizable way.

The right to pursue current projects is acknowledged both by Freeman, when stating his views in a less abstract mode and by the International Convention which is the subject of this Volume. For instance, Freeman talks of the importance of the right of freedom of association for older children. One might add a less formal right of choice of favourite companions for younger children as part of their general right to pursue appropriate projects, projects which, *pace* Freeman, may have no substantial consequences for their future mature autonomous decision making. Articles 13, 14, 15 and 16 of the Convention may be read as mere, and faint echoes of the adult rights to freedom of speech, association and privacy. They may, on the other hand, be read as rights accruing to the appropriate projects of children.

The appropriateness of such projects has little to do with rationality. Children might have passionate attachments and aspirations which are irrational, but which though inappropriate for a mature person may be entirely appropriate for a child, and the pursuit of which, if threatened, we may be able to protect by reference to one or more of the Articles I have just cited.

It is a mistake to construe deviations from adult standards of rationality as harm in every case and to seek to protect our children from such deviations as though they constituted harm. Equally, it is a mistake to construe the role of autonomy in the lives of children as a matter of capacity only. This becomes clear if we think of the way in which we consider it important to respect the autonomy of children suffering from terminal diseases. They, like other children, have appropriate projects which are protected by autonomy-respecting rights. Their relationship to the present and the future, and the balance between them, should make clear to us that relationship and that balance in the case of other children as well. Children are notoriously incapable of taking a long-term view, or forgoing present satisfaction for future gains. While we may well be aware of this fact, we need to be careful of robbing them of their present in the very process of attempting to provide an autonomy-respecting theoretical underpinning for their rights.

NOTE

[1] My use is different from the extensive and systematic use of the notion of projects by Lomasky (1987). My own first use of the notion appears in *Bioethics* (1988).

CHILDREN IN THE CHILDREN'S COURT: CAN THERE BE RIGHTS WITHOUT A REMEDY?

NGAIRE NAFFINE*

ABSTRACT

The United Nations Convention on the Rights of the Child demands that children appearing before courts of law be treated well. They should receive a fair hearing; they should be allowed to speak freely; they should be presumed innocent until proven guilty; they should not be compelled to give testimony; and they should be treated with dignity. Their best interests should be the court's primary concern. This paper considers whether Australian children are the recipients of this sort of treatment in the criminal courts of law.

It concludes that in at least two Australian capital cities, Adelaide and Sydney, children receive quite a different style of justice. Typically, they waive their right to contest and generally remain passive spectators throughout the proceedings against them. Recent legislative endeavours to draw children into the legal process seem to have met with little success.

INTRODUCTION

'In all actions concerning children . . . the best interests of the child shall be a primary consideration.' This instruction is contained within Article 3(1) of the Convention on the Rights of the Child which specifically embraces the actions of courts of law. The location of this Article within a document designed to secure and to strengthen children's rights would lead one to believe that the goal of securing the child's best interests in court is fully sympathetic with the goal of strengthening their legal rights. Indeed we may go further than this in our reading of Article 3(1). Because it designates 'all actions concerning children', all of the rights identified within the Convention must have as their primary goal the achievement of the child's best interests. To strengthen children's rights, it would seem, is first and foremost to have their best interests at heart.

In this paper, we examine the application of Article 3(1) of the Con-

* Ngaire Naffine, Lecturer in Law, The University of Adelaide, GPO Box 498, Adelaide, South Australia 5001 Australia. The author wishes to thank Joy Wundersitz and Fay Gale who participated in the Adelaide research. The empirical work was supported by a grant from the Australian Research Council awarded to Fay Gale. The author wishes also to thank Stephen Parker and Michael Hogan for their thoughtful comments on the manuscript and their suggestions for its improvement.

vention to the Australian system of juvenile justice. The particular focus of enquiry will be the children's court operating in its criminal jurisdiction. Two related questions will be posed. Has the recent move towards a language and philosophy of formal rights secured the best interests of children brought before the children's criminal court, as the Convention might lead us to expect? And at a broader philosophical level, is the idea of the child's best interests compatible with the idea of children's rights in the light of the Australian experience?

Two other Articles of the Convention are relevant to this enquiry. Article 12 of the Convention requires States parties to allow children to express their views freely, particularly in the context of judicial proceedings. Article 40 invokes 'the right of every child . . . accused of . . . having infringed the penal law to be treated in a manner consistent with the promotion of the child's sense of dignity and worth'. To this end, it demands that accused children 'be presumed innocent until proven guilty' and that they receive 'a fair hearing according to law, in the presence of legal or other appropriate assistance'. Such children should 'not be compelled to give testimony or to confess guilt'. In the course of this enquiry, we will also consider whether Australian children are accorded these protections in the criminal courts.

A BRIEF HISTORY OF CHILDREN'S JUSTICE

In the criminal sphere of children's justice, the notion of the child's best interests may be thought to sit oddly within a larger plan to strengthen children's rights. Indeed, for those who are familiar with the history of children's justice, any endeavour to equate children's 'best interests' with children's 'rights' may well be regarded as inappropriate. The idea of 'the child's best interests' as an overriding goal for criminal justice has come to be associated with the removal of rights for children, rather than with their augmentation. To appreciate why this is so, we need to foray, briefly, into the history of Australian criminal justice for children.

THE COMMITMENT TO WELFARE

Until the end of the seventies, the 'welfare' approach to young offenders prevailed in all Australian jurisdictions. This was a style of justice which employed the terminology of the caring professions. The needs and vulnerability of children provided its central focus. Its main proposition was that criminal children need treatment, not punishment, and that the burden on the court was to find the suitable cure rather than the appropriate and proportionate penalty. Its stated primary concern was with the best interests of the child: with their identification and achievement.

In many respects, the welfare model was sustained largely at the level of rhetoric, as Seymour (1988) makes clear. For much of the time, the style of criminal justice offered to Australian children was not markedly different from that offered in the adult sphere. Though the scale of penalties was reduced, and an effort was made to separate criminal children from their adult counterparts, children's and adult courts of law looked much the same. Physically the courts were similar and procedurally there were few concessions for children. Perhaps a more convincing distinction between justice for children and justice for adults was the greater power to intervene and control on the part of the children's court. While conventional sentences were more restrictive in the children's sphere (children's courts functioned as courts of summary jurisdiction and so were more limited in the range of penalties), the children's magistrate had jurisdiction to deal with the unruly (as well as the criminal) child, who could be institutionalized, for her own good, until she attained the age of majority (Bailey-Harris & Naffine, 1988).

JUSTICE ENDORSED

From about the mid 1970s, ideas about criminal justice for Australian children underwent a gradual transformation. Disenchantment with the dominant 'welfare' view of young offenders as essentially needy individuals requiring the state's benign intervention was strengthened by a new commitment to formal due process of law for children and to the imposition of greater controls on the powers of the State in relation to young offenders. The shift from 'welfare' to 'justice' for children gained momentum in certain jurisdictions and then spread to others (Freiberg, Fox & Hogan, 1988; Seymour, 1988).

The repudiation of the welfare model was a salient theme in the 1977 Report of the Royal Commission into the South Australian system of juvenile justice (Mohr Report, 1977). As a consequence, new reforming laws designed to bring children's justice more in line with the adult model were enacted only a few years later. There followed a number of enquiries and reports on the treatment of young offenders in other Australian states in which the sentiment expressed uniformly was that greater formality and legality would benefit children brought before the courts.[1] Consistently, the style of justice scrutinized, criticized and found wanting was that characterized by informality and discretion.[2]

THE CRITIQUE OF WELFARE

Those who rejected the welfare model employed a complex set of arguments to advance their cause. Paradoxically, the welfare model was considered both too soft and too harsh in its treatment of children. It was considered too soft in the sense that it regarded children as inherently weak and vulnerable. In the welfare view, young offenders were not responsible for their criminal actions and indeed criminal behaviour was interpreted as a cry for help. As offending children could not be held accountable for their behaviour, it was up to the state to decide what was in their best interests (Morris & Giller, 1987; Pratt, 1989).

The effect of the welfare approach was to sever the crime from the punishment, so that neither the gravity nor the triviality of the criminal behaviour necessarily determined the extent of the punishment thought appropriate. The welfare model thus was perceived also to be too soft in the sense that children were not always punished to the degree that the crime was thought to demand. And when the punishment did not fit the crime, the community was frustrated in its demand for a fitting retribution (Bayer, 1981; Clarke, 1985; Debele, 1987).

For related reasons, the welfare model was perceived also to be too harsh. In the name of helping the child, it accorded to the State considerable powers to intervene and to control the behaviour of children. Because the seriousness of the crime did not set the limits to state intervention, as in the adult jurisdiction, children could also be treated with severity. Particularly in the case of children deemed to be uncontrollable, rather than criminal, the State was able to exercise complete authority (Andrews & Cohn, 1974). For her own best interests, the unruly child could be institutionalized until the age of majority for a range of trivial and non-criminal behaviours such as disobeying her parents and mixing with 'the wrong sort'. Intrinsic to the welfare model of juvenile justice was therefore a high degree of discretion which was, at times, associated with a highly punitive approach: what might be regarded in the adult sphere as an abuse of due process (Bailey-Harris & Naffine, 1988).

In the 1970s, there was an interesting convergence of thinking by the critics of children's justice from the Left and from the Right. Both were discontented with the welfare model, but for different reasons. The convergence took the form of a common solution to the problem of how to deal with young offenders. Those from the Right considered the model too soft in that it treated children as irresponsible and helpless. Better, they thought, that children were seen as possessed of a high degree of autonomy, that they be thought responsible for their actions and so punished appropriately for their offending. The state had been too lenient in its sentencing and it was time that it took a firmer line with anti-social children and held them accountable for their offending.[3]

Critics from the Left expressed concerns about the arbitrariness of children's justice and the potential for exceptionally harsh punishment when a child was thought to be out of control. Children, they thought, would fare better in a system which was bound by conventional notions of the Rule of Law. Thus the shared solution to children's justice adopted by reformers from the Left and from the Right was a more formal, adversarial model in which children were to be treated much the same as adults. Both intellectual schools sought a greater degree of certainty, consistency and proportionality in the State's response to criminal children. Both advocated a more rigorous application of the law and less reliance on welfare notions of remedial treatment. The consensus was that children should be viewed as rational and responsible individuals invested with the full array of legal rights (Morris et al, 1980; Morris & Giller, 1987).

Set against this debate, article 3(1) of the United Nations Convention, with its focus on the child's best interests, might well be viewed as inherently controversial. To both sets of critics of children's justice, the rhetoric of welfare, and in particular the notion of the child's best interests, has produced unwelcome results. To those from the Right, the idea of the child's best interests has been used to justify lenient sentences. To those from the Left, this idea has excused the exercise of wide discretions and a consequent abuse of state power in the children's jurisdiction.

To both critics, the invocation of children's rights has been seen positively to require the rejection of the welfare idea of the child's 'best interests' and the associated notion that it is the State (which may be variously lenient or severe), not the child, which decides what those interests should be. Or put another way, in the criminal sphere of children's justice, the concept of the child's best interests has been contaminated by its association with the welfare model and its perceived abuses of children's and citizen's rights (depending on the viewpoint).

EVALUATING THE FLIGHT FROM WELFARE

In response to these debates, there have been concerted legislative efforts to modify criminal justice for Australian children, nearly always in a manner which is sympathetic to the notion of a more formal rights-based justice for children (Freiberg, Fox & Hogan, 1988; Seymour, 1988; National Workshop, 1990). With the recent ratification of the United Nations Convention on the Rights of the Child, it is timely to evaluate these changes. In what follows, the intention is to take a closer look at some of the current theories and practices of children's criminal justice and, in the light of these findings, to consider the wisdom of the attack on welfare and the notion of the child's best interests.

SOME CURRENT THEORIES: THE PURSUIT OF CHILDREN'S JUSTICE IN AUSTRALIA

The effort of Australian reformers to draw children into the criminal process – to ensure their effective participation and to secure their rights – has taken a number of specific forms though the 'justice' rhetoric has displayed a remarkable consistency. In South Australia, for example, the Report of the Royal Commission (Mohr Report, 1977) which formed the basis of the laws now governing young offenders (The Children's Protection and Young Offenders Act 1979) relied heavily on ideas of formal due process for children.

To Commissioner Mohr, who conducted the South Australian investigation, there should be 'no erosion of the fundamental rights of accused persons nor indeed of convicted persons under the guise of "helping the child".' Justice Mohr took it to be 'fundamental' that 'no child shall be found guilty of a crime by means which would not, and do not apply, in the adult world'. He was convinced that the best way to help children was to accord to them all the rights of the adult accused (Mohr, 1977:7). In support of his argument for a formal system of justice for children based on strong rights, Mohr drew support from the American Supreme Court decision of *In Re Gault*.[4] There he found favour with the notion that '[d]ue process of law is the primary and indispensable foundation of individual freedom. It is the basic and essential term in the social compact which defines the rights of the individual and delimits the power which the State can exercise.' As a consequence, Mohr insisted that a clear distinction be drawn between court hearings for needy and neglected children and those charged with criminal offending. When found guilty, criminal children would be subject to determinate sentences. In addition, he advocated the removal of the vague charge of 'in need of care', which provided the basis of 'uncontrollable' children being arrested and brought before the courts. (All three recommendations were to become law.) Only criminal children, Mohr believed, should be tried by the courts and, for their own benefit, their cases should be heard in a manner which reflected their status as criminal defendants. In other words, criminal cases involving children should be seen for what they were – adversarial proceedings – and so children should be accorded the full array of adult rights.

A similar emphasis on legal rights for children was to be found in the reports on children's justice produced in other Australian states and similar reforms have ensued. As Seymour observes in his critical history of Australian juvenile justice, in Western Australia, Queensland, Victoria, and New South Wales, one can observe a shared disenchantment with a welfare style of justice and a new faith placed in formal justice. Consistently, there have been 'demands for reforms which emphasise the distinctive nature of criminal proceedings [as well as] moves to diminish the tendency to see young offenders as being indistinguishable from children in need of care' (Seymour, 1988:166). Consistently it is being said that children will fare better if it is recognized that criminal proceedings for children are precisely that.

Law reform is a complex process. It tends to be characterized by compromise and negotiation between theorists, researchers, bureaucrats and politicians.[5] What finally appears on the statute books may therefore bear only an indirect relation to the models of justice imagined in their

pure form. This is certainly true of the various Australian endeavours to
secure rights for children in the courts via legislation. The processes
which led to the current New South Wales legislation, for example, are
Byzantine in their complexity (Hogan, 1990; Luke, 1990).

It is possible, nevertheless, to discern in the new laws several affirma-
tions of the justice approach. Thus the new laws have tended to ensure
the separation of welfare and criminal matters and to delineate more
clearly the procedural protections for the young accused. The current
New South Wales legislation, proclaimed in 1988, thus impels a court to
'have regard to the following principles:

(a) that children have rights and freedoms before the law equal to those
enjoyed by adults and, in particular, a right to be heard, and a right to participate, in the processes that lead to decisions that affect them;
(b) that children who commit offences bear responsibility for their actions but,
because of their state of dependency and immaturity, require guidance and
assistance . . .
(e) that the penalty imposed on a child for an offence should be no greater than
that imposed on an adult who commits an offence of the same kind. (Children
(Criminal Proceedings) Act, 1987).

The Victorian legislation is even more forceful about the need to
protect the formal legal rights of children. According to s 18 of the
Children and Young Persons Act, 1989:

(1) As far as practicable the Court must in any proceedings –
(a) take steps to ensure that the proceeding is comprehensible to – (i) the
child . . . ; and
(b) seek to satisfy itself that the child understands the nature and implications
of the proceeding and of any order made in the proceeding; and
(c) allow (i) the child . . . to participate fully in the proceeding; and
(d) consider any wishes expressed by the child . . . .

Here we can observe a new concern for children's comprehension and
involvement in the legal process. Also prominent is the idea that children's courts should pay the same attention to due process as their adult
counterparts. We are witnessing a new desire to remove the euphemistic
language of welfare and to stress what is thought to be the true adversarial nature of children's court hearings. Only recently, the Senior
Magistrate of the New South Wales Children's Court set his imprimatur
to this approach to the children's court: as a place where children are
accused of crimes, where their criminal responsibility is determined and
where they are sentenced accordingly (Blackmore, 1990).

The advocates of the new justice model are returning, in effect, to a
more classical idea of liberal justice, one which emphasizes the agency
and volition (and therefore the criminal responsibility) of young persons
charged with crimes. As free, rational actors, rather than as children
primarily in need of the state's assistance and intervention, it is

appropriate that young defendants should now be brought into the legal process, encouraged to play an active role in their hearing and also to be made more accountable for their offending. Prominent, once again, are notions of criminal agency and criminal responsibility with the associated notion of proportionate punishment (Bortner, 1982:3).

CURRENT PRACTICES: ENTRENCHING BUREAUCRATIC PROCEDURAL JUSTICE

With the endorsement of a rights-based justice for children, one might anticipate a number of changes to the operation of the children's court. Perhaps one would expect to find more children taking up the traditional legal rights we associate with adult justice. We might be looking for greater precision, care and formality in the court process. We might expect more active participation of children who are now willing to 'express [their] view freely' in the manner identified in Article 12 of the Convention. We might anticipate a greater emphasis on the presumption of innocence (in accordance with Article 40 of the Convention) and so expect more challenges to the statements of police and perhaps a greater proportion of children insisting on their right to contest their guilt.

In what follows, the intention is to make some modest observations about some past and present practices of children's justice in South Australia and New South Wales, rather than conduct a systematic evaluation of Australian children's courts before and after the new justice laws. Some of these observations are based on interviews conducted with lawyers in South Australia and Sydney, New South Wales (Naffine & Wundersitz, 1991b). Others are drawn from a study of guilty pleas in the South Australian children's court, the details of which have already been documented (Naffine, Wundersitz & Gale, 1990; Wundersitz, Naffine & Gale, 1991). Still others are based on extensive observations of the Adelaide and Sydney Children's Court (Naffine & Wundersitz, 1991b; Naffine, 1990b; Blackmore, 1990; Naffine & Wundersitz, 1991a). These disparate data will nevertheless help us to assess whether the reformers' expectations are being met.[6]

Though in many ways commonplace, the following observations on the children's court have tended not to inform the thinking of those who are most influential in securing legislative change. Another purpose here is therefore to consider why the ideas of many of the reformers have not been informed by a detailed knowledge of the practical workings of the system. Why is there such a gap between practice and theory?[7]

PLEADING GUILTY

The most important right of children charged with a crime is to insist on their innocence. Justice Mohr (1977), the architect of the South Australian laws, seemed to regard the trial as the centre-piece of criminal justice. He emphasized the need to remove the obscuring language of welfare, to recognize the adversarial nature of proceedings in the children's court and to strengthen children's rights within them. This is why, in response to his recommendations, social welfare cases were removed from the criminal jurisdiction, why the criminal court was identified more clearly as an institution bound by due process of law and why determinate sentencing was introduced.

In view of the priority now accorded children's formal legal rights, one might expect to see significant numbers of young South Australian defendants pleading not guilty. Indeed, the rate at which children elect to go to trial could well be regarded as a basic indicator of the success of adversarial, rights-based justice. The available evidence reveals, however, that few children are willing to challenge the prosecution.

South Australia has a three-tiered system of juvenile justice. There is a Screening Panel (introduced by Mohr) which decides whether a case should go before what is known as a Children's Aid Panel for warning and counselling or to the more formal Children's Court which is empowered, *inter alia*, to fine and to detain. In order to qualify for an appearance before an Aid Panel, the less harsh alternative, the child must admit guilt (Nichols, 1981). Of those children offered the alternative of the Aid Panel rather than Court (and this group is usually about 60 per cent of alleged offenders), it is usual for about 98 per cent to admit the allegation. So for example, in the financial year 1985–1986, a representative year, 5,468 children were given the option of a Panel Hearing and chose to admit the charge. This figure represented 97.8 per cent of children offered the opportunity of a Panel Hearing. In other words, when given the chance to appear before the less punitive Aid Panel, only 2.2 per cent of children refused to admit the charge (Naffine, Wundersitz & Gale, 1990:198). Though the rate at which children profess their innocence is lower at the level of the Children's Court, it is still high. For the 1988–1989 financial year, for example, only 4.6 per cent of Court matters were completed by way of a trial. While it is true that a few of these non-contested matters can be accounted for by the withdrawal of the prosecution case, it appears that the vast majority are the result of either an initial or late plea of guilty. Such statistics indicate that adversarial justice is clearly the exception rather than the norm in the Children's Court.

It has recently been estimated that of the total population of children who enter the South Australian juvenile justice system charged with an offence, some 95 per cent admit the allegation. A further 3 per cent of cases are resolved through the police withdrawing their case and then 2 per cent of children formally sustain a plea of not guilty (Naffine, Wundersitz & Gale, 1990; Wundersitz, Naffine & Gale, 1991).

When Mohr commenced his enquiry, Aid Panels were already in place and the Children's Court was essentially as it is today: a summary court of justice operating much like an adult summary court, but with greater informality than its adult counterpart and with a reduced scale of penalties. Then there was a host of reasons why children would prefer to plead guilty. Those reasons remain and help to explain the current findings.[8]

Usually children regard themselves as outclassed by the prosecution which has access to far greater resources and can usually rely on the evidence of expert and amenable witnesses (that is, the investigating police officers) (Naffine & Wundersitz, 1991b). The guilty plea is (often rightly) perceived to be the quicker route to justice and is therefore also generally regarded as less painful than a trial. In South Australia, the provision of an Aid Panel which carries the benefit for the child of avoiding a Court hearing but which requires, in the first instance, an admission of guilt provides a specific incentive not to contest (Nichols, 1981).

In many ways, children are also tacitly encouraged to waive their right to a trial. The message they receive consistently from the police and even from many lawyers is that their basic instincts are right. There is little point in bucking the system (as their lawyer is likely to indicate, the prosecution is indeed better placed to win) and the normal and sensible course of action is to plead guilty (which, anyway, as the lawyer will also intimate, is not likely to lead to a severe sentence in view of the reduced scale of penalties) (Naffine & Wundersitz, 1991b).

Mohr was committed to the notion of formal adversarial hearings for children and yet he did not address these basic problems of children's justice. In fact he did not even refer to the rate of guilty pleas which he should have known to be high. Instead he spoke with optimism about the benefits of the trial and failed to refer to the many inherent pressures in the system to plead guilty.

The high rate of guilty pleas is not a phenomenon peculiar to South Australia.[9] Though it is difficult to obtain statistics in most other jurisdictions, figures are issued for New South Wales. These indicate that here too the vast majority of children tender a plea of guilty (Naffine, Wundersitz & Gale, 1990:200) In other words, from the available statistical evidence it is clear that, typically, children's hearings proceed by way of a guilty plea which entails a waiver of the most fundamental legal right: the child's right to rely on the presumption of innocence and contest the case – that right which forms the focus of Article 40 of the Convention.

LAWYERS IN THE CHILDREN'S COURT

Quantitative data help to discern overall patterns in the processing of young offenders but may fail to give a vivid sense of its day-to-day operation, in all its detail. The perceptions of those who work in the Children's Court provide a qualitative means of evaluating its processes and so flesh out the bones of the statistics. Lawyers practising in the Children's Court, for example, are in an ideal position to describe and interpret the nature of proceedings.

In South Australia, legal representation for children is in the main publicly funded. In the central Children's Court in Adelaide there are two permanent full-time salaried public lawyers. In the other metropolitan courts, children have access to public lawyers who also deal with adult matters. Interviews conducted with the majority of lawyers who spend a significant part of their time representing children were remarkably uniform in their revelations about South Australian children's justice (Naffine & Wundersitz, 1991b).

With so many children pleading guilty to the charges laid against them, there is little real legal work to be done in the children's court. Though lawyers do regard themselves as the 'voice' of the child in the court-room, they concede also that their only real task is to construct a plea in mitigation of sentence. Generally, they are not in the business of challenging the prosecution and 'shooting holes in the police case' (Naffine & Wundersitz, 1991b:17). This is not to say that lawyers do not confer a benefit on the young defendant. In their own reckoning, they may well help to improve the child's legal position in informal ways prior to the hearing by negotiating charges with the police. As a result of these exchanges, charges may be reduced or dropped. But by the time the case gets to court and formal justice resumes, the main task of the lawyer is simply to present the child – who has pleaded guilty – to the magistrate in a sympathetic light for the purposes of sentencing.

The popular idea of the lawyer as the hired gun of her client is openly disputed by children's lawyers. In what they colloquially refer to as the 'kiddies' court', sentences are perceived to be lenient (in view of the summary scale of penalties) and so there is not the same pressure to engage in legal conflict. Rather than 'go for broke', an approach which might only antagonize the magistrate in the lawyers' view, the aim of the children's representative is to obtain what is commonly referred to as a 'realistic' outcome by way of penalty.

This 'ideology of triviality', to borrow Doreen McBarnet's phrase, is one which has been observed to pervade the practice of law in English magistrates' courts (McBarnet, 1981a). Because adult summary courts deal with minor offences and can only mete out minor penalties, it is difficult for jurists to develop a great deal of interest in summary justice, according to McBarnet. While this attitude may be thought undesirable in the adult sphere of justice, it is even more objectionable in the children's court where defendants can acquire a record for the most serious of offences. And yet what McBarnet observes of the adult summary court may be said of the Children's Court. As we will see below, 'the relative triviality of the penalties . . . provides the crucial legitimations in law for the lack of due process in summary justice' (McBarnet, 1981a:206).

It is generally assumed by advocates of the 'justice' approach, that children's legal rights and in particular their active participation in court will be strengthened if they have recourse to a lawyer. However, there is a sense in which the opposite is true. The presence of a lawyer in court may sometimes help to dilute (rather than augment) the adversarial nature of proceedings. Though lawyers recognize that they supply the child's 'voice' in court, they do not necessarily regard this as a voice of challenge. Indeed, on the contrary, often they regard themselves as a sort of court-room facilitator. Because they are familiar with the language, forms and conventions of the court-room, lawyers help to oil the proceedings so that cases can flow smoothly. As one South Australian lawyer put it: 'It's easier for the magistrate to operate through the lawyer and to get the salient information from the lawyer than to drag it out of the child in court.' Moreover, with the un-represented defendant, the court cannot assume, as it usually does, that the child is apprised of her legal position.

In the central Sydney children's court, legal representation is supplied by some forty private lawyers who place their names on a rotating roster. This brings them to court about once a month. Interviews conducted by the author with eleven of these lawyers indicate similarities between the two jurisdictions.

The summary nature of justice in the Children's Court seems to generate a feeling among certain Sydney lawyers that children's matters are less testing than adult work. Again, the suggestion is of an 'ideology of triviality'. Not only are the sentencing risks perceived to be less severe (because of the reduced penalties), but there is also a sense in which the legal work is thought to be less taxing. As one Sydney lawyer put it:

Naturally kid's courts matters aren't as serious as other matters. I think [representing children] is very good grounding [for a new lawyer]. You're not playing for terribly high stakes . . . [also] the complexity of matters . . . is not as serious.

Because the work is varied and the penalties are thought to be low, Adelaide lawyers also indicated that the Children's Court was a good training ground for people newly entering the profession. They recognized that the children's jurisdiction gave them an opportunity to deal with very serious criminal matters (everything short of murder) but for smaller stakes. Or as a Sydney lawyer described his monthly visit to the Children's Court, in a more flippant mood: 'I enjoy it. It gets you out of the office'.

This is not to say that the Sydney lawyers did not view their work as important. Indeed many seemed to regard their participation in the duty lawyer scheme as their particular contribution to the social good. Several lawyers expressed grave concerns about the parlous social and economic plight of young offenders. Their monthly visit to the children's court was therefore a way of helping and comforting youths in difficulty as well as satisfying the child's basic right to legal representation.

And yet it was also recognized that as the guilty plea was the norm, the lawyer's court-room role was limited. While several Sydney lawyers admitted that they could improve the legal position of their client before court, by negotiating charges with the police prosecutor (though one lawyer suggested that a minority of children's lawyers engaged in this practice), by the time the matter reached the court-room it appeared that their major task was to plead for clemency rather than to enter into debate about points of law and procedure. The lawyer could endeavour to convince the magistrate not to record a conviction. He could then try to persuade the magistrate of the value of a lenient sentence.

COURT OBSERVATIONS

Extensive observations of the Adelaide Children's Court (some 200 appearances: Naffine & Wundersitz 1991b) and of the central Sydney Children's Court confirm that there is minimal confrontation and conflict between the two formal adversaries.[10] Nor is there a tendency on the part of lawyers to insist on their client's formal rights, in the manner anticipated by the justice reformers. Indeed there is little in the way of formal legal advocacy in the children's court.

In Adelaide, a typical case unfolds like this. At the request of the magistrate, the defence lawyer indicates whether the child intends to plead guilty to the charge, which as we know he usually does. The magistrate then reads the charge to the defendant and the young person pleads guilty as indicated. The guilty plea is taken as full proof of the crime alleged and so the police prosecution proceeds to describe to the court what are termed the police 'facts' (Naffine & Wundersitz, 1991b). The police 'facts' are aptly named as they become the official version of the incident for the purposes of the hearing. Both sides use this term to refer to the police version of events from this point on in the case. Rarely are the 'facts' probed in any way, which is perhaps not surprising given that any differences between the prosecution and defence have probably been ironed out, in an informal manner, well before the hearing. When the prosecution completes his rendition of the 'facts', the defence lawyer formally admits them and proceeds to plead in mitigation of sentence.

Rarely do children speak in court. Rarely are the police challenged. Typical of proceedings is speed, routine and an appearance of efficiency. Cases are often dealt with in a matter of minutes. As more than one lawyer has described the process, it is not unlike a 'sausage machine': child in; child out (Naffine & Wundersitz, 1991b).

Children's hearings in Sydney are even more streamlined. The charges are not read aloud, merely handed to the magistrate. The defendant is not required to plead. The lawyer does it for him, so that on occasions the child's plea has been entered before he even reaches the court-room. The police 'facts' are also tendered rather than read aloud, so much of the case proceeds without the need for the verbal exchange of information. The lawyer then orally delivers a plea in mitigation.

Though often brief, the plea for leniency may do a number of things. It may indicate the child's good record at school or her endeavours to find employment or the difficulties he is facing at home. We may learn of the illness of a parent or of a chronic history of child abuse. Usually the stories are affecting. Each one is designed either to illustrate the disadvantages under which the defendant has laboured (mercy should be shown) or to reveal that the child has promise and will perform well in the future, if not hamstrung by a severe sentence. In essence, there is little legal work here. Rather, the plea in mitigation is a plea for clemency. Again, rarely do children speak in court. Rarely are the police challenged. Their view of the incident remains intact and few questions are raised about the procedures they adopted in acquiring their evidence. Characteristic of proceedings is an appearance of speed, routine and efficiency. Often cases are completed in a matter of minutes. A typical hearing proceeds in the following manner:

At 2:17 the child's lawyer pleads guilty on behalf of his client to a charge entailing the consumption of drugs. No charge has been read out in court, though all parties (excepting the defendant) have in front of them the relevant documents. The Police Prosecutor hands what he refers to as 'the facts' to the Magistrate which the Magistrate reads to himself. The lawyer gives a brief plea in mitigation. The magistrate asks whether there is any difficulty with employment. The defendant's work supervisor who is sitting in the public gallery vouches for the defendant (in this respect an exceptional event). The magistrate sentences the child (in this instance, it is only a caution). The defendant is never addressed and never speaks. The hearing is completed at 2:31. Or to cite another case on another day with another magistrate: At 12:20, the Magistrate asks whether he is to be taking a plea and the lawyer indicates a plea of guilty. (No charges have been read to the defendant, though it is assumed he has been shown a copy.) The Police Prosecutor says: 'I tender the facts' which are read in silence by the Magistrate. (No police 'facts' have been read out.) The lawyer gives a plea in mitigation and the Magistrate then finalizes the case at 12:23 by dismissing the charge (there will be no penalty for the child). The defendant does not speak, nor is he spoken to. Three minutes have passed.

The overwhelming impression one gains of children's criminal proceedings in both States is that of administrative efficiency. This is not to say that children are not treated with dignity, nor that some magistrates do not make a conscious endeavour at times to extract words from the defendant, even if it is only a show of remorse at the point of sentencing. The compassion and humanity of magistrates, lawyers and police is often manifest. Repeatedly, there are shows of kindness to the young defendant. But still the compelling feeling is that there is a need for haste and that there is little time to spell out the details of the matter for the benefit of defendants nor seek to involve them in their own legal matter.

Essentially the children's hearing appears to be the preserve of experts. It is for lawyers – who provide the 'voice' of their clients and whose very presence implies that the child's rights have been protected – and it is for police who present the 'facts'. Generally it is unintelligible to the lay person, often for the simple reason that too little information is presented orally in court. In the Sydney Court, the atmosphere can be eerie as the case proceeds mainly through a silent reading of charges and 'facts'. With experts running the matter, it is possible to proceed with the aid of a sort of legal short-hand, without lengthy explanations to the defendant about the nature of the proceedings. For example, 'facts' can be 'tendered' without further comment or explanation. If the child is represented by a lawyer, as she usually is, there is little need to use plain English in court. Hearings can therefore be conducted in a manner which is rapid and routine and without contest or challenge. The norm is for defendants to remain entirely silent.

THE REALITY GAP

It is plain that many of the endeavours of the rights-reformers of children's justice have not been realized. Much of the evidence in fact suggests that the new laws have made little difference in court. Children's hearings still proceed much as they have always done: as modified, summary courts of justice.[11] Passivity rather than participation, characterizes the young defendant. Typical, rather than exceptional, is the waiver of rights, rather than their invocation. For many defendants, their court-room experience is fleeting and, very likely, incomprehensible.

In defence of the reformers it may be said that recent legislative statements to the effect that children should take an active role in their proceedings may be regarded more as exhortation than expectation.[12] It is well known that children are particularly difficult to draw out: that they are shy and often inarticulate. Parliamentary efforts to involve children in legal proceedings therefore may simply be regarded as educational: they may encourage judges, police and lawyers to listen to children and to take them more seriously. Articles 12 and 40 of the Convention, however, require more than this from our legislators. They demand a concerted endeavour to invest the young defendant with volition. Also, the continuing vigour with which reformers endorse the justice approach makes it fair to ask, how and why good intentions have gone wrong? Much of the problem, it will be suggested, has to do with what may be termed a reality gap endemic to much legal thinking.

The idea of the reality gap may be stated simply. Lawyers as theorists (and this includes those who engage in law reform) tend to think of the law in terms of the decisions of judges rather than the acts of the legislature (Cotterrell, 1986). Moreover, they think of law in terms of the judicial decision-making of the superior courts of justice.[13] At this elevated judicial level, cases are conducted with a high degree of formality, slowly and with a vigilant eye to the procedural and evidentiary rights of the accused. Considerable time is spent in both the preparation and the presentation of the case. The trial itself is regarded as the linchpin of the adversary process where all the benefits of the Rule of Law are to be witnessed. Here the public may behold all the protections made available for the accused: the presumption of innocence, the right to silence, the elimination of extraneous evidence which is prejudicial to the accused, the careful testing of the Crown case (Packer, 1964; McBarnet, 1981). It is an impressive array of rights.

But the reality of most criminal procedure is the magistrates' court where the vast majority of the work is done. Most adult defendants appear before the courts of summary jurisdiction, not the superior courts of law. In the lower courts, justice is characterized by speed, informality and the routine plea of guilty. Typical of most cases is the defendant's waiver of most legal rights. In the summary court, cases tend to be emptied of their legal content. The prosecution case may comprise only the briefest resume of the alleged incident followed by a guilty plea and then a short plea in mitigation of sentence from the defence counsel (Naffine, 1990a).

For most of this century, even the most serious young offenders have received the summary style of justice, not the formality of the superior courts. And yet this commonplace fact has done little to inform or modify the thinking of the reformers. When the critics of 'welfare' from both the Left and the Right advocated the shift to the 'justice' model, they continued to speak in terms of superior court justice, with its formality and its careful invocation of rights. They did not look at what was actually happening in the children's courts and what was likely to continue.

The theory of children's justice is derived from adult superior court justice – with its emphasis on informing the defendant, encouraging participation, invoking legal rights, ensuring that what children have is at least as hedged in by due process as adult justice. But children are receiving the reality of adult summary justice, which is a very rough sort of justice. It is streamlined, fast, technical and has little of the dignity and formality of the higher courts. The defendant is expected to remain silent and indeed is expected to plead guilty.

The children's hearing is conducted in the jargon of professionals and makes few concessions to the lay person. It possesses few of the features anticipated by either the critics from the Left or from the Right who advocated a more formal, rights-based model of children's justice. The panacea of the 'justice' model was intended to bring to children all of the presumed benefits of formal due process of law. But the style of law which was to be accentuated in the children's court was that of the adult summary courts, with all its shortcomings. It was not the justice of the superior courts, from which the justice model drew its inspiration. In short, the reality gap means that children have been offered reforms which derive their philosophical justification from the theory (though not necessarily the practice) of the adversarial adult trial. This is the touchstone of reforming rhetoric. But what they are in fact receiving is summary justice according to the adult model, with some minor adjustments. This is a form of justice which is regarded as highly defective by anyone familiar with its operation.

SUSTAINING THE REALITY GAP

Few of the present findings on the practices of the children's court as a summary court of justice would come as a surprise to empirical criminologists. There is already a common understanding among a growing number of students of the summary courts that there is little due process and volition here. It is well known that adult defendants plead guilty 'to get it over with', because the process is the punishment (Feeley, 1979). Indeed the adult criminal court has been likened to a degradation ceremony in which the defendant has no real role to play (Carlen, 1976; Bankowski and Mungham, 1976; Blumberg, 1976). And yet law reformers continue to draw inspiration not from the empirical literature, which shows how criminal justice actually functions, but from the legal ideal of the Rule of Law and adult adversary justice of the superior courts.[14]

There is a host of reasons why the thinking of law reformers about the law often has so little to do with what is actually happening in the courts for most of the time: why it is that law reformers tend not to equip themselves with a basic working knowledge of what the courts do before they seek to change them (Seymour, 1988). One is the intellectual gulf between legal theory and social research to be found in most of our law schools. The tendency of law schools not to examine the law in its context has been the subject of adverse comment by the Pearce Report (Pearce, Campbell & Harding, 1987).

The expository tradition in legal education is also responsible for the tendency of lawyers not to consider the law in action (Sugarman, 1986). In this style of pedagogy, still dominant in many law schools, the law is interpreted as an accumulation of rational principles rather than as a social practice. The empirical study of law is regarded as more fitting to the social sciences (Naffine, 1990b). Accordingly, the more practical subjects which pay attention to the operation of the law – such as women-and-the-law courses – are given marginal status in law schools and carry little prestige (Graycar & Morgan, 1990). The tendency of legal educators to focus on the judgements of superior, appellate courts and to ignore the operation of the lower courts (where most of the work is done) further limits the intellectual focus of the student of law.[15]

Still another reason for the reality gap is that those who engage in the reform of the law are often members of the judiciary whose most recent experience of justice has been acquired from the Bench of higher courts. Lawyers who become judges are unlikely to have acquired a close acquaintance with lower court justice. Furthermore, the pool of lawyers from which judges are drawn are not those which tend to specialize in law for the poor and law in the lower courts. Judges are usually former barristers who practised in the most prestigious areas of the law, dealing with corporations and the world of commerce. It may also be said that the very nature of formal legal reasoning makes for a divorce from reality and encourages lawyers not to look critically at their own ideas. In this intellectual style, legal analysis is thought to be a technical exercise in a quite particular style of logic which excludes matters of policy, politics and moral values (Cain, 1976; Peller, 1985; Mason, 1987). An enquiry into the 'social facts' surrounding any particular legal decision is therefore extraneous to the judicial function (Zines, 1986:360).

CONCLUDING THOUGHTS

In at least two Australian capital cities, children appear to receive neither the intended advantages of formal justice nor the questioned benefits of the welfare model. Indeed there appears to be little philosophical coherence to the practice of children's justice (Luke, 1990; Hogan, 1990). We may conclude that Article 3(1) of the United Nations Convention is at best imperfectly observed in these places. In other words, the recent move towards a language and philosophy of formal rights for children has tended not to secure their 'best interests'.

To arrive at this conclusion, this study has employed some quite specific indicators of justice: the extent to which children plead guilty, the attitude of children's lawyers to their court-room role and the willingness of children to participate in the court process. Clearly there are other measures one might employ. One might consider, for example, the impact of the new laws on trends in sentencing or on the consistency of

children's justice across the two jurisdictions considered. Indeed there
are suggestions that on these indicators the new laws may be proving
beneficial to children.[16] And yet the measures of children's justice selected in this study – in particular, pleas and participation – embrace rights
which have been emphasized by the Convention and which may therefore be regarded as fundamental.

Articles 12 and 40 give priority to the right of children to express their
views freely as well as to experience the full benefits of the presumption
of innocence. In the light of these demands of the Convention, children
in the Adelaide and Sydney courts fare poorly. This enquiry has
revealed that it is the exception rather than the norm for a child to
express herself in court, let alone to invoke her right to insist on her
innocence.

These findings prompt us to consider what might be done to improve
the situation of the young person in court. Should the practice of children's courts be brought more in line with the ideas of the reformers –
should it be brought closer to the justice model as the reformers conceive
it? – or would it be better to abandon notions of formal justice for
children? Or perhaps we should look for some other approach to the
young offender, perhaps one which revives the less fashionable notions of
welfare?

Our discovery that children's justice is theorized in a certain way, but
practised in quite another, does not mean that all would be solved if the
theory advanced (that of formal justice) were translated into practice.
Though it is more considered and measured in its steps, formal or higher
court justice does not necessarily cater for children – which is precisely
why summary courts were developed for them. Higher court justice is
conducted in an even more remote and technical language than the
summary courts of law, a style which does little to promote comprehension. It is ritualistic, formal and designed to promote awe for the institutions of the law.

Perhaps the central problem of superior-court justice is its conception
of the person. The human model it draws upon is that of the self-
sufficient classic liberal individual, able to sustain informed choices and
act in her own interests. The emphasis is upon rights derived from
volition; it is based on a will theory of rights (MacCormick, 1982:154).
Children, however, are even less able to assert themselves than adults.
As O'Neill (1992) has remarked, children 'cannot claim their rights for
themselves' which is why 'The Aristotelian thought that justice is a
relation between equals [is] inappropriate in dealings with children'.
And, as we have seen, even most adults elect to have criminal proceedings dealt with quickly through the guilty plea. If few adults feel able to
demand their basic rights, why should children?

With the justice model, we seem to be confined to two unhappy
options: the streamlined justice of the summary courts and the awesome

formality of higher court justice. Both styles of justice presuppose a defendant who is capable of looking after himself, of invoking his own rights through an act of positive will. Though we have seen that the legalism of the summary court is characterized more by the abandonment than by the invocation of children's rights, the tacit assumption remains that once a lawyer is present (and mostly they are), the child has made an informed decision and that the lawyer is always acting on the child's instructions. The fiction is that the child who pleads guilty has engaged in a positive act of volition and that their lawyer is merely an agent. In truth, children are passive and are swept along in a tide of events generally not of their own making. Similarly, children appear unsuited to the rigours of higher court justice – which presupposes a confident, rational and informed defendant, capable of invoking her rights. Neither style of justice would appear to be in the child's best interests.

By contrast, the virtue of the welfare model was its recognition of the vulnerability of children and the variabilty and the specificity of their needs. In some ways, it offered a more convincing view of children. It recognized that children do not always act with volition; that often it is better that the court itself endeavour to preserve their interests. In a sense it was based on what MacCormick (1982:154) calls an interest theory of rights: it assumed that children's interests should be protected, whether children demanded them or not. The weakness of the welfare approach was its tendency, in what it deemed to be the child's best interests, to ignore the wishes of the child and to intervene to a degree which was not warranted by the offending behaviour.

In view of the besetting problems of conventional justice for children, documented above, it may be timely to reconsider the strengths of the welfare approach and to endeavour to eliminate its deficiencies. To this end, it may be possible to conceive of a children's court which specifically caters for children – which is designed to secure their best interests, and to ensure real comprehension and participation at a level which makes sense to children – but whose powers to intervene and help are conditional and confined. This would be a court which is charged to act in the interests of children but which is also obliged to respect children's rights.

Put another way, children's courts would come closer to meeting the demands of the United Nations Convention were there a shift of responsibility for the implementation of children's legal rights – from children to the courts themselves. O'Neill (1992) makes the point well: 'rights will be unmet, indeed violated, unless those who hold the counterpart obligations do what they ought'. Or as another legal philosopher sees it, children should be able to possess rights, in particular the right to have their interests protected, which do not depend on their ability to invoke them. Otherwise children will have few rights and few interests (MacCormick, 1982).

With this in mind, we might conceive of a type of children's court which is required positively to proceed in a manner which is beneficial to children and which children can understand and so have their say – because they know what is going on. This court could be prevented, by law, from proceeding against a child unless it was positively demonstrated that children's rights had been respected. It could be required, for example, to point to evidence that the child had received an adequate explanation of all of the ingredients of the charge, the relevant defences, the nature of the proceedings that would be followed in the court in the prosecution of that charge (which would enable the child to intervene and speak up in court where necessary) as well as the ramifications of a criminal conviction (which may make children think harder about pleading guilty). At the hearing, the child could be led through the proceedings and encouraged to participate at all stages.

In short, the best interests of the child might be served, in a manner sympathetic to the goals of the Convention, were it encumbent upon the court, not the child, to secure those interests. It may be possible then to reconcile the idea of the child's best interests and the idea of strong formal, legal rights for children. There remains a very real risk of paternalism: if it is up to the court to decide what is good for children, there is the potential for the court to be highly intrusive, for the child's own good. (Already, we have seen the abuse of discretion associated with the uncontrollability charge.) But it should be possible to hamstring the court so that it is obliged to do the right thing by the child because it is held accountable for its actions.

Perhaps what is impeding progress in this direction is the likely cost of such a style of justice. Certainly, it would be slower, less routine and so less efficient (from the point of view of the administration of the courts). No longer could the court assume the routine guilty plea. Instead it would be put through its paces and be obliged positively to engage the child. This would take time, money and effort. Another problem would seem to be the limited nature of the legal imagination. For analysts of children's justice, the welfare model remains under a cloud. It is still associated with discretionary paternalism and an abuse of power. And so we appear to be left with either the routine legalism of summary justice or the ritualized formality of the higher courts.

But why limit ourselves to the past or present forms of children's justice? For it is possible to conceive of a different type of children's court, one which wrests at least some of the control of the proceedings from the legal experts and hands it to the child; one in which proceedings are comprehensible, where children's choices are therefore informed, and where the court carries an enforceable obligation to ensure that the interests of children are paramount.

NOTES

[1] See for example the Edwards Report (1982) which considered the treatment of young offenders in Western Australia, the Carney Report (1984) which considered the Victorian legislation as well as the several reports conducted in anticipation of the current New South Wales legislation (Luke, 1990; Hogan, 1990).

[2] This is a debate which was also conducted in Britain and the United States and indeed much of the Australian rhetoric was drawn from overseas (see, for example, the ideas contained in Parsloe (1978); Morris et al (1980) and Morris & Giller (1987). It is therefore appropriate to cite the international literature when explaining the critique of welfare. Seymour (1988) has been particularly critical of this derivation of theory. He maintains that Australia adopted ideas, particularly from America, which had an unsuitable provenance in that there were important differences between juvenile justice in the two countries.

[3] The reasoning employed in the Mohr Report (1977), to be discussed below, provides a good illustration of this convergence. In effect, Commissioner Mohr drew on both sets of criticisms of welfare, maintaining that children should be given the benefits of a certain and predictable court and then should be held responsible for their offending.

[4] 387 US 1, 1967.

[5] I am grateful to Michael Hogan for his advice about the nature of the law-reform process, particularly in New South Wales.

[6] All research conducted in Sydney was undertaken by the author for the purposes of a national study of juvenile justice. This is a collaborative project with F. Gale and J. Wundersitz which was funded by the Australian Research Council.

[7] Again it should be noted that the law reform process is complex. While theorists and researchers may well be aware of the realities of the court-room, others who are perhaps more influential in the process (politicians and judges for example), may be less attuned to these facts.

[8] Mohr's failure to refer to the available statistics on guilty pleas is symptomatic of the divorce between lawyers and the socially scientific study of law. That is, Mohr relies on formal notions of the Rule of Law and yet does not consider its practical operation. This 'reality gap' in legal thinking will be analyzed below.

[9] Nor is it peculiar to the Children's court. The large majority of adult defendants also elect to plead guilty (Naffine, 1990a).

[10] Observations were conducted by the author: above n 6.

[11] The tenacity of the magistrates' court model in the juvenile sphere of justice has been noted recently by Seymour (1990). He has anticipated that, notwithstanding the recent efforts to introduce more formal justice for children, 'in the majority of cases . . . it will be business as usual'.

[12] Again I thank Michael Hogan for this thoughtful comment about the different purposes of legislation.

[13] See for example the focus on superior court justice in Sallmann (1985).

[14] Again the reasoning of Justice Mohr in the Mohr Report (1977) provides a clear demonstration of this tendency. He invokes the forms of higher court justice to illustrate what is ideal in criminal procedure. And yet his brief is to evaluate and improve the Children's Court which is committed to a summary style of justice.

[15] Law students not only spend most of their time studying the judgments of higher courts which deal with only a small minority of cases but they also concentrate only on those cases which are thought important to the evolution of some legal doctrine. Indeed magistrates courts, where most of the work is done, are not courts of record so what happens therein cannot be studied in the form of written judgments. If the law student is to study the lower courts, she must rely on direct observation – which tends not to be regarded as the appropriate work of a law school or of a lawyer but is rather the (intellectually less taxing?) work of social scientists. From the point of view of lawyers, magistrates courts do not deal with interesting or hard law, even though, as McBarnet (1981) has pointed out, were these cases thought to possess sufficient prestige and were they sufficiently remunerative, they would receive far more attention and would suddenly become more interesting. There is nothing inherently less legal about the ingredients of a less serious crime tried in the lower court. It is just that it is perceived to be less interesting.

[16] This was a view offered to the author by one of the architects of the New South Wales legislation.

AN 'UNCONTROLLABLE' CHILD: A CASE STUDY IN CHILDREN'S AND PARENTS' RIGHTS

JOHN SEYMOUR*

ABSTRACT

Using a case-study of an 'uncontrollable' child as its starting-point, this paper examines the usefulness of rights language in illuminating disputes between parents and teenage children. Hohfeld's distinction between rights and privileges is employed in order to explore the meaning of a teenager's assertion that she has a right to independence and the meaning of the parents' answering claim to a right to control her. The obligations of parents and society towards rebellious teenagers are also discussed. It is argued that, if these teenagers do possess a right to be free of control, the effective exercise of this right depends on society's acceptance of a duty to provide the necessary supporting services. Further, the focus on obligations leads to a consideration of different conceptions of parenthood. The prevailing model reflects the view that such rights as parents possess in respect of their children derive from their obligations. An attempt is made to analyse these derivative rights: it is proposed that a distinction can be made between parental powers and parental authorities. Such an analysis, however, is not the whole story. Simply because of their status, parents also possess what are described in this paper as recognized interests. The paper concludes by considering how the concepts of powers, authorities and recognized interests assist in our understanding of the issues posed by the case-study.

INTRODUCTION

Case Study

Mary, aged fifteen, has been in conflict with her parents for some time. Her mother is very possessive and her father has high expectations of his children. Although both parents are conscious of the need to give Mary increased freedom (in such matters, for example, as choice of friends and clothes), in practice they have not proved to be very flexible. A social worker's report described them as 'firmly disciplinarian, autocratic and rigid'. They constantly criticized Mary's behaviour and she was unwilling to negotiate or compromise.

* Reader in Law, Faculty of Law, The Australian National University, GPO Box 4, Canberra, ACT 2601 Australia. The author wishes to thank Tom Campbell, John Eekelaar and Stephen Parker for their comments on earlier drafts of this paper.

Mary decided to leave home and moved into a refuge. Her behaviour there was unsatisfactory and she was asked to leave. She stayed in two further refuges; she was described as 'manipulative' and resisted social workers' efforts to find her a job. She left each of the refuges voluntarily because she found their regimes too restrictive. By this stage she had acquired a poor record with youth refuges and was unwelcome at most. She was next reported as being found by members of the police drug squad in a flat occupied by three men who were charged with burglary, possession of stolen property and possession of prohibited drugs. Mary's parents were angry and distressed and tried to persuade her to return home. She refused on the ground that they would be too strict with her.

In the view of her social worker, Mary 'is determined to become independent and seems headstrong in pursuit of this goal. She resists assistance from her family, welfare and other support agencies.' The worker's reports suggest that Mary is immature and confused.

Discussion

The purpose of this paper is to examine some of the issues raised by a case of this kind. In particular, I shall consider whether our understanding of the dispute between Mary and her parents is assisted by an analysis which employs the language of rights. This question is posed because in such a dispute both parties are likely to invoke rights supportive of their positions. The parents will claim a 'right' to control her and she will claim a 'right' to live where she pleases.

To assist in determining what Mary and her parents mean by their statements, it is helpful to refer to Hohfeld's analysis of legal relationships (Hohfeld, 1923). He identified a series of 'jural correlatives'. For our purposes it will be necessary to consider only his distinction between rights and duties, on the one hand, and privileges and no-rights on the other. For Hohfeld, the identifying feature of a right, in the strictest sense, was that it embodied a claim which inevitably imposed a duty on another person. The example he gave was of X's right that Y should stay off X's land. An invariable correlative is that Y has a 'duty' to observe X's claim. A 'privilege' Hohfeld defined as a liberty or freedom from the right or claim of another. If X has a privilege, he is not constrained by any rights or claims of Y. X owes no obligation to Y and hence has the opposite of a duty. Y has what Hohfeld called a 'no-right' because he is unable to make demands of X. To continue the earlier example, X has a privilege of entering on to his own land and Y has a no-right to prevent him from doing so.

This analysis clarifies what Mary and her parents are saying. In Hohfeld's terms, Mary may be claiming a 'privilege', not a 'right'. Her use of the word 'right' is a way of emphasizing a belief that she should not be constrained. She is asserting that no one may stop her leaving home. Her parents would deny this. Their position is that they believe they may invoke the law in order to re-establish control over Mary. They are claiming that they have 'rights' which the law will enforce. Hohfeld's model is, however, not entirely appropriate here, since we are not dealing with a reciprocal relationship in which the parents' rights are matched by correlative duties imposed on Mary. This aspect will be considered later in the paper.

Before further examining the different positions adopted by Mary and her parents, it is necessary to make a preliminary point about the way in which the word 'rights' is used in this paper. Although the distinction between legal rights and moral rights may sometimes become blurred, every effort has been made to confine the discussion to the former (in the sense of interests recognized by the law).

MARY'S RIGHTS

To what extent does rights language assist in illuminating the nature of Mary's conflict with her parents? If it is accepted for a moment that she is claiming a right, rather than a privilege (a distinction to which I shall return), it is apparent that she is asserting a right to her autonomy. Yet when her position is described in this way, it can be argued that she is not demanding a right which flows from the status of childhood. Mary is not saying that she is entitled to special consideration because she is a child; rather she is seeking to escape from what she sees as the shackles of childhood and to be treated as an adult. Both O'Neill and Campbell (in papers published in this volume) draw attention to the significance of this fact. The former notes that libertarian accounts of rights are inappropriate to children and sees the concept of the 'mature minor' as an oxymoron (O'Neill, 1992). Similarly, Campbell observes that the movement towards giving adult rights to children might be better seen as redrawing the boundaries between childhood and adulthood. So construed, the movement has nothing to do with the rights of children (Campbell, 1992).

This analysis can, however, be taken a little further. Society has set certain age limits and it is presumed that children below these ages lack full capacity.[1] Mary's claim can be seen as an assertion that the presumption should be rebutted in her case and that she possesses the capacity to make her own decision as to where to live. There is some judicial support for her view; for example, in *Gillick*'s case[2] a majority of the House of Lords accepted that in certain circumstances a girl under sixteen may obtain contraceptive advice without parental consent, provided she has sufficient understanding and maturity to appreciate what is involved. Quite how broad a theory may be built on the foundation of this ruling is not clear. One interpretation is that it has opened the way for case-by-case decisions in a range of situations whenever children are old enough to argue that they have the capacity to make informed assessments.

If this view is accepted, it might be seen as establishing a new right for older children, one which could be defined as:

an entitlement, in all disputes, to have their actual capacities determined, rather than being subject to presumptions based on their ages.

A number of comments can be made about this formulation. The point noted earlier is worth repeating: it is odd to describe as a right of childhood a claim not to be treated as a child. This, in its turn, draws attention to a more fundamental question. If the suggested right were adopted, what would be the implications for the concept of childhood? The setting of age limits, arbitrary as these are, does mark off a period in an individual's life when special protection is provided. If the assumptions which underlie the establishment of this period of quarantine – assumptions as to dependence and vulnerability – are rejected and case-by-case decisions made, the result could be a radical revision of society's policies towards its children.

Some, of course, would argue that this would be no bad thing. They would urge that the proclamation of the proposed right would lead to the replacement of a somewhat fuzzy benevolence with a more clear-sighted variety. This, however, would be to beg the question whether the suggested principle would be unacceptable because it would undermine the concept of childhood. This, in turn, prompts a further question. If the principle were adopted, would it have this effect?

Such an outcome would be most unlikely, because of the legal system's long-standing attachment to paternalistic child welfare policies. In practice, a ruling in a case involving a dispute about a child's capacity to make an independent decision will rarely be made solely on the basis of the child's maturity and comprehension. Rather, the tendency will be to assess this capacity by reference to what is thought to be in the child's best interests. If the decision is felt to be contrary to those interests, the most likely result will be a conclusion that the child lacks the capacity to make it. Thus the law's recognition of the special position of children will continue and the suggested right will be read down and will not mean what it says.

My argument, therefore, is that the postulated right would either involve the abandonment of the concept of childhood or it would be interpreted in such a way as to preserve that concept. If society believes that its children are special and deserve protection and guidance, it must accept that disputes in which they are involved will be handled by persons operating within a particular frame of reference. The alternative is to accept that children who display a certain level of maturity should be treated in the same way as adults. We cannot have it both ways.

This analysis is consistent with the idea of childhood embodied in the United Nations Convention on the Rights of the Child. The Preamble notes that earlier Declarations and Covenants had agreed on the need for special care, assistance and safeguards to be provided for children.

That there is an inevitable tension between the urge to treat the young solicitously and the desire to make case-by-case decisions, is, however, reflected in the fact that Article 5 requires those responsible for children's care to deal with them in a manner consistent with their evolving capacities. Further, Article 12 recognizes the importance of taking into account children's views; these views are to be given 'due weight in accordance with [their] age and maturity'. This, of course, brings us back to the paradox of the mature minor and the likelihood that maturity will be assessed by those operating within a paternalistic frame of reference.

The foregoing discussion has adopted Mary's assertion of a 'right' as its starting point. As was noted earlier, however, an acceptance of Hohfeld's terminology requires a distinction to be drawn between rights and privileges. If Mary is saying no more than that no one may stop her leaving home, she is claiming a privilege rather than a right. This raises questions about the utility of employing such a classification in the context of her dispute with her parents. On one view, her statement has little legal significance. Were she to inform a bystander that she has a 'right' to leave home, the response might be: so what? This reply might seek to give the same value to her claim as would be given to an assertion that she has a 'right' to adopt any hairstyle she chooses.

Yet to disregard both claims on the ground that they are no more than assertions of a freedom to choose, is to overlook an important point. Such claims have certain legal implications. As Hart has observed:

[W]here a man is left free by the law to do or not to do some particular action, the exercise of this liberty will always be protected by the law to some extent, even if there is no strictly correlative obligation upon others not to interfere with it. This is so because at least the cruder forms of interference, such as those involving physical assault or trespass, will be criminal or civil offences or both, and the duties or obligations not to engage in such modes of interference constitute a protective perimeter behind which liberties exist and may be exercised (Hart, 1982:171).

To greet Mary's statements about her freedom to leave home or to choose a hairstyle with a 'so what' response is to ignore the legal significance of Hart's 'protective perimeter'. If she is correct in either or both of her claims, she is not saying something which can be dismissed as none of the law's business. Although there is an important difference between the two claims – one has more far-reaching consequences than the other – both raise genuine questions about legal status. In particular, to agree that no one may interfere with her decision to live where she chooses is to make a significant statement about the types of powers which she may exercise and which may be exercised over her.

Further, Hart's analysis draws attention to a matter raised by Hohfeld's classification. In the latter's terms, the corollary of Mary's view about her freedom to leave home is that her parents have a 'no-right' with regard to her because they are unable to make demands which the law will recognize and enforce. Hart seems to share this view: in his opinion, the invocation of liberties (Hohfeld's 'privileges') does not impose 'strictly correlative' obligations on others. Yet if Mary is correct in asserting that no one may stop her leaving home, this may impose something resembling an obligation on her parents, an obligation not to interfere. In this context, the 'protective perimeter' assumes a significance which the label 'privilege' might obscure. Perhaps she has a fully-fledged right which imposes a correlative duty on her parents? Or is it something less than this? The problem with an attempt to identify a right of this kind is that there is no legal rule which expressly states that she is free to leave home; nor is there one which explicitly indicates that her parents may not prevent her from doing so.

All this, of course, is based on the assumption that, whatever terminology is used, Mary is correct in her assertion that no one may stop her leaving home. It is not the purpose of this paper to undertake a detailed examination of criminal, tort and child welfare law in order to determine whether controls may be imposed on her. One or two comments will, however, be offered in order to throw further light on the nature of the claims made by Mary and her parents.

If Mary's position regarding her parents is that they may not take direct action to control her, she is probably correct. Were they to seek physically to restrain her, they might be liable (both in tort and criminal law) for assault. Similarly, if they tried bodily to remove her from the flat in which she is living, liability for kidnapping or false imprisonment might arise.[3] On this basis, it seems clear that the parents do not possess a right over her which they may assert themselves.

Do they have a right which others may enforce on ther behalf? A possible source of such a claim is to be found in child welfare laws relating to 'uncontrollable' children. Such laws exist in England and some Australian jurisdictions.[4] On examination, however, it is apparent that these laws do not exist to give effect to whatever rights a parent might possess with respect to a teenage child. Rather, their primary purpose is to provide procedures for dealing with children thought to be at risk because of their unruly behaviour. Their focus is on the extent to which this behaviour indicates that the child is in need of care.[5] The secondary purpose – now less explicitly acknowledged – is to establish mechanisms by which the state can control troublesome juveniles and so protect itself from the threat which they pose. Thus the fact that Mary's parents may request the police or welfare authorities to invoke these laws does not mean that they have personal rights which the law will enforce. Uncontrollability laws fulfil broad social functions; they do not provide parents with a remedy which is the equivalent of an injunction.

Mention should also be made of an Australian procedure which expressly seeks to respond to situations such as that which has arisen in Mary's family. In New South Wales, one of the grounds on which a child may be considered to be in need of care is 'substantial and presently irretrievable breakdown in the relationship between the child and one or more of the child's parents'.[6] Similarly, in Victoria, Children's Court proceedings may be taken by a parent or child on the ground that there is 'a substantial and presently irreconcilable difference' between them.[7]

Would the application of procedures of this kind confer on Mary a right to leave home? Is this a right in the full sense, in that it is matched by a correlative duty on welfare officials to facilitate her departure? The answer to these questions is unclear. The effect of the provisions outlined is to bring a juvenile in Mary's situation into the child welfare system. The primary purpose of this is to determine whether she should be made the subject of state intervention and also to decide if some form of court-sanctioned care or supervision should be imposed. If this is the outcome, one result will be the curtailing or extinguishing of many of the powers of Mary's parents over her. Yet this is not the same thing as saying that the procedure has the effect of validating her assertion that she has a right to leave home. What will have occurred is that the state will have endeavoured to replace one set of controls with another. Alternatively, of course, a court dealing with Mary's case under these procedures might conclude that nothing can or should be done to interfere with the choice which she has made. In this case it might be said that the outcome is the equivalent of a declaration that Mary is entitled to be free of control. On this analysis, she will have been justified in claiming a special type of privilege, one which the law will affirmatively recognize.

Thus scrutiny of the use, by Mary and her parents, of rights language identifies a number of important issues arising from their dispute. In particular, examination of the significance of her claim that no one may stop her leaving home throws light on the nature of childhood, the emergence of autonomy and possible legal responses to the demands made by the parties to the conflict. The analysis, however, takes us only a certain distance. Focusing on Mary's assertion of a right to leave home must not be allowed to divert us from the consideration of a related question: should Mary be supported in her assertion of her autonomy? Posing the question this way identifies the need to move from debate about the meaning of rights to an examination of the obligations which society might owe to a young person in her situation.

A QUESTION OF OBLIGATIONS?

To re-cast the problem in this way is to adopt O'Neill's view that:

rights-based approaches have not proved congenial or illuminating ways of handling the full range of fundamental ethical issues that face those who live with children (O'Neill, 1992:40).

It should be noted that this comment not only advocates a change in perspective, but also (in its reference to ethical issues) embodies a broader approach than has previously been adopted in this paper. Earlier, it was pointed out that, when dealing with children's and parents' rights, I have endeavoured to confine myself to a discussion of legal rights. In shifting the focus to obligations, I – like O'Neill – raise both legal and moral issues, though my ultimate purpose is to deal with those obligations to children which the law imposes on parents.

Central to O'Neill's argument is the proposition that, if we want to assist and protect children, we should concentrate not on their rights, but on the obligations of others towards them.

'Those who urge respect for children's rights must address not children but those whose action may affect children; they have reason to prefer the rhetoric of obligations to that of rights' (O'Neill, 1992:39).

She is not alone in drawing attention to the importance of obligations. Freeman has stated that 'much talk about rights is really talk about obligations' (Freeman, 1983:38) and Raz has noted that to describe a person as having a right is to say that an aspect of his or her well-being is a ground for holding another to be under a duty (Raz, 1984a:1). O'Neill's analysis is, however, particularly useful and warrants further examination. In emphasizing certain aspects, I am conscious of the danger of misrepresenting and over-simplifying her approach. Her concern is primarily with young children and with the appropriateness of advocating children's rights while pursuing paternalistic policies towards them. It follows that her arguments are developed in a context quite different from that which is explored here. Nevertheless, the adoption of her analysis illuminates some of the issues discussed in this paper.

The crucial feature of this analysis is its emphasis on the value of paying close attention to obligations when problems involving children arise. Central to this argument is O'Neill's three-fold classification of society's obligations towards children (O'Neill, 1992). Obligations owed by all persons to all children she describes as 'perfect' and 'universal' obligations. They confer rights on all children. Then there are obligations imposed on specific persons with regard to specific children. These are 'perfect' but not 'universal'. They confer rights on specific children against specific persons.

It is the third category which is of special relevance to this paper. This embraces 'imperfect' obligations. The example O'Neill gives is an obligation to be kind and considerate in dealings with children. Such an obligation is not owed to all children because it cannot be discharged. Nor is it owed to specified children:

'[S]o long as the recipients of the obligation are neither all others nor specified others, there are no right holders, and nobody can either claim or waive performance of any right' (O'Neill 1992:27).

This is the important factor: we are here dealing with obligations which do not confer rights. It follows that such obligations will be overlooked if we adopt a theory of rights as our frame of reference.

The relevance of this to Mary's dispute with her parents is that it draws attention to the fact that a crucial question is not whether Mary has a right to leave home, but whether society owes an imperfect obligation to children in her position. Further, as O'Neill points out, it is possible for an imperfect obligation to be institutionalized. Her example is of an identified category of children at risk whom social workers are legally obliged to monitor. In this situation, an inchoate obligation to care for children would be transformed into an obligation which confers a positive right on specific children.[8]

My argument, therefore, is that further understanding of Mary's position is gained by asking questions about the types of obligations which society might owe to someone in her position. Is there an imperfect obligation to support her assertion of her autonomy? At a more practical level, is it possible to envisage such an obligation being recognized by law so that a child in a particular category can seek to enforce its performance?

Let us consider how society's obligations in this context might be formulated. A principle such as the following might be adopted:

Society has an obligation to provide adequate support services to enable any child of sufficient capacity who wishes to do so to live independently of his or her parents.
The adoption of this principle would confer the following right:

Any child of sufficient capacity has the right to determine his or her place of residence.
Such a right would come into existence only in consequence of the express recognition of an obligation.

It is not proposed to discuss the desirability of accepting such an obligation and its correlative right. My point is that thinking in terms of obligations illuminates some important implications of Mary's assertion of her independence. When we seek to define society's obligations in this context, we can appreciate how far-reaching these implications are. In particular, this undertaking prompts the question: should society accept an obligation to provide the necessary social security, housing and health services to support all mature children who wish to leave home?

The proclamation of such an obligation would be unpalatable to many. Some would argue that the result would be to undermine the family and that the State should encourage the preservation of the family unit rather than putting resources into services which would facilitate children's departure from home. This perception of the importance of the family's role is reflected in the Preamble to the United Nations Convention, which accepts that the family provides 'the natural environment for the growth and well-being of all its members'.

For those who hold this view, the only acceptable course might be the recognition of a very narrowly defined obligation with regard to children who leave home. This could, for example, be expressed in terms of society's acceptance of responsibility only for children who are justified in leaving their parents. An illustration is provided by Australia's social security law, which makes provision for payments to homeless children. Such children qualify for an additional sum if they are receiving the Job Search Allowance (the name given to one form of unemployment benefit). Young recipients who are not living at home are entitled to the supplementary payment if they have left home because their parents will not permit them to remain or because of 'domestic violence, incestuous harassment or other exceptional circumstances'.[9] This definition reflects the view that normally the State should underwrite children's bids for independence only if they are homeless through no fault of their own.

A WAIVER OF RIGHTS?

Before considering the views of Mary's parents, it is worth pausing to note that there is another way that she can express her claim. So far, the analysis has been in terms of her assertion of a right to live independently. Yet it is possible to view any rights which she might possess from a quite different perspective. It can properly be said that children have a right to support and protection. To speak of such a right is to employ terminology which conforms exactly to Hohfeld's usage: here the children's rights are matched by the parents' correlative duties to support and not to abuse or neglect them. One way of interpreting the stand taken by Mary is to argue that, although she has a right which imposes a duty on her parents, she wishes to waive that right. She wishes to cast off the protective mantle which the law provides.

As Wellman has pointed out, the possibility of children waiving their rights raises difficult problems (Wellman, 1984). A parent's duty to cosset a child gradually diminishes; for example, the restrictions imposed on the movements of a very young child must in time be lifted. The duty to protect must give way to the duty to assist the child's development towards independence. Yet what Wellman describes as the resulting duty of non-interference can be over-ridden. The example which he gives is of his duty to allow his teenage daughter to go out by herself; this duty can be displaced if she takes a job which requires her to walk home late at night in a dangerous area. In such a situation, a duty to accompany her might revive.[10]

The crucial question is whether, and in what circumstances, the daughter is able to make a decision to reject an offer of protection. As

Wellman notes, the parent/child relationship is different from a contractual relationship. A party to a contract may make a decision to waive rights under that contract, but in the case of a child, any purported waiver can have consequences in the distant future, consequences which the child lacks the maturity and experience to assess. The child may therefore lack the capacity to relieve the parents of their obligations. This is because the parent/child relationship subsists; it cannot be brought to an end in the way that a contractual arrangement can be extinguished.

The relevance of this analysis to the situation of Mary and her parents is clear. Although she has a right to protection, it is not one which she can unilaterally decide to renounce. Her parents' obligation to provide judicious protection remains, regardless of her wishes. The parents may not be over-protective, but nor may they abandon her. The special nature of the parent/child relationship locks both parties into a dispute which cannot be resolved by asking whether Mary may waive her rights against her parents.

THE PARENTS' RIGHTS

Let us now change the focus and consider the significance of the assertion by Mary's parents that they have rights over her. In examining their position, I shall initially revert to a less precise use of the word 'rights'. Later in the paper an attempt will be made to scrutinize the concept of parental rights.

The claim made by Mary's parents raises questions about the legal nature of parenthood[11] and for the purposes of this paper it is helpful to distinguish between two contrasting views. One sees parents as having certain fundamental rights simply because they are parents. The other sees such rights as parents possess as existing only to allow them to fulfil their obligations towards their children. The crucial difference between the two models is that one regards parents as entitled to derive some benefit from parenthood, whereas the other defines parenthood solely by reference to parents' duty to promote their children's welfare. It is worth noting that – not surprisingly – the United Nations Convention does not indicate whether one model is to be preferred rather than the other. Article 18.1 requires parents to make children's best interests their 'basic' concern and so emphasizes parental responsibilities. Article 5, however, sees parents as having some fundamental entitlements. It provides that:

States Parties shall respect the responsibilities, rights and duties of parents . . . to provide, in a manner consistent with the evolving capacities of the child, appropriate direction and guidance in the exercise by the child of the rights recognized in the . . . Convention.

Those familiar with recent developments in family law might object that any notion of fundamental parental rights and consequent benefits is now outmoded. There is some truth in this. Nevertheless, while this notion does reflect nineteenth century attitudes, an examination of these attitudes helps to illuminate the nature of parenthood today and aids our understanding of the dispute between Mary and her parents.

Analyses which incorporate some idea of benefit do not deny that parents have obligations to act in their children's best interests; indeed, they may well see these obligations as the most important characteristic of parenthood. The significant point, however, is that these analyses do not view parenthood as a sphere of responsibility which begins and ends with the performance of obligations. An example of the synthesis of two different concepts is found in Blackstone's *Commentaries*:

The *power* of parents over their children is derived from . . . their duty: this authority being given them, partly to enable the parent more effectually to perform his duty, and partly as a recompense for his care and trouble in the faithful discharge of it (Blackstone, 1791:452).

Blackstone's reference to 'recompense' indicated that he believed that parents should derive some benefits from their children. At the time when he was writing it was accepted, for example, that parents were entitled to the benefit of their children's labour while they lived at home. This right continued to be recognized by the English common law until well unto the twentieth century; the result was that parents could sue those who deprived them of their children's services.[12] Another illustration, noted by Blackstone, was a child's obligation to support parents in their old age. This had been incorporated into the Poor Law of 1601.[13] The current law no longer recognizes a parent's claim to benefits of this kind. In *Gillick* Lord Scarman expressed the view that the 'reward element' to which Blackstone referred had been 'swept away'.[14] This conclusion, however, does not necessarily mean that the notion of benefit can be disregarded in contemporary analysis of the legal nature of parenthood. It is possible that parents may still seek to lay claim to other forms of benefit. One such claim is of a more subtle kind than a demand for services or support. Although difficult to define, its essence lies in proprietorial concern to ensure that children grow up into certain sorts of persons. Implicit in this desire is an expectation that children will be a source of satisfaction to their parents. This, in its turn, involves parents' perceptions of children as extensions of themselves.

It is not easy to discover material which expressly recognized this aspect of parenthood. It was embodied in the attitudes which prevailed in upper-middle and upper-class Victorian England, where it was accepted that parents had an interest in equipping a child to occupy an appropriate station in life. The training and education of children and parents' concern that they should make suitable marriages were all directed to ensuring that the children would maintain the family's prestige and place in society. It was accepted that parents should want to make their children in their own image.

The Victorian *pater familias* did not simply seek to do what was best for the child; through the child he sought to ensure that the family tradition – *his* tradition – was carried on. The proper development of the child was something in which he took a selfish (as well as an altruistic) interest. A clear example of this view was provided by Dickens in his description of Mr Dombey's pleasure at the birth of his son, Paul. The reader is left in no doubt that he was a valued possession whose purpose in life was to ensure the continuance of 'Dombey and Son'. As Mr Dombey put it, Paul had 'to accomplish a destiny' (Dickens, 1846:4). Another illustration was provided by a father of seven, writing in 1836, just before Victoria's accession. One of his sources of satisfaction was that his children had grown up to be 'respected in any polite circle' (Grylls, 1978:51).

Whether the English common law expressly recognized this concept of parenthood is not clear. In the much-criticized judgments in *Agar-Ellis*, there was reference to the father's control 'over the person, education and conduct of his children', while the father was described as having 'the right to the custody and tuition of his children'. Further, the father's rights were characterized as 'sacred' and it was thought that to ignore these rights would be 'to set aside the whole course and order of nature'.[15] Although the matter was not specifically addressed, it is difficult to escape the feeling that the judges were here referring to something more fundamental than the father's powers to advance his children's welfare.[16]

The extent to which decisions like *Agar-Ellis* can be taken as providing a general indication of the nineteenth century law's attitude to parenthood is, however, questionable. Complicating the picture is the fact that in the past much of the analysis of parental rights was an analysis of *paternal* rights. When Victorian judges dealt with family disputes, it was normally the relationships within patriarchal families to which they directed their attention. Although this century has seen an increasing recognition of the position of mothers, the result has not been their acquisition of the rights possessed by nineteenth century fathers. Instead, a different concept of parenthood has emerged. Thus one response to the Victorian case-law is to dismiss it as irrelevant to any enquiry into the current nature of parents' rights. A further difficulty is caused by the fact that, both last century and this, the English courts have assumed that the interests of parents and their children usually coincided. What parents want for their children is often presumed to be what is best for their children; talk of children's welfare can thus mask the possibility that the courts have arrived at outcomes which satisfy parents' demands to control and mould their children. In addition, judicial discussions of the nature of parental authority normally occur in the context of disputes as to whether the state should intervene to override a parent's wishes. Again, in such disputes the assumption that parents know best regularly prevails and the courts therefore decline to interfere. In cases of this kind, there is no need for the courts to enter into any discussion of parents' motives and hence the nature of their rights is not scrutinized.

All this naturally prompts the question whether the model of parenthood under discussion is either hopelessly elusive or no more than an historical curiosity. In my view the model should not be dismissed on these grounds. The main reason for this assertion is that the considerations which have been identified – parental expectations and aspirations – are often the real issues underlying disputes caused by 'uncontrollable' children. The disagreement between Mary and her parents can be seen as the result of the parents seeking to impose their views as to the sort of person they wish her to be. Her behaviour does not conform to their expectations and it is for this reason that they are asserting that their 'rights' have been ignored. Although they might express their claims in terms of a desire to safeguard her welfare, the fact remains that this desire is not the whole story. To focus on this aspect is to miss an important element in their motivation.

Nor can a case such as Mary's be dismissed as an isolated and untypical example. In multi-cultural societies such as England and Australia the phenomenon of parents from ethnic minorities seeking to impose their views on children who wish to adopt the standards of the dominant culture is well recognized. It may well be that these parents must learn that the law will not support them, but the point which needs to be stressed is that the real nature of their demands can be understood only against the background of a concept of parenthood such as I have tried to outline. Further, although perhaps formulated with a different purpose in mind, Article 29 (1) of the United Nations Convention states that children's education should respect their cultural identity. There is an obvious potential for conflict between this principle and a child's assertion of an autonomy incompatible with the parents' culture.

Let us now turn to the contrasting view of parenthood – that which stresses obligations rather than personal benefit and which therefore views parents as vehicles for the advancement of their children's welfare. This view was clearly articulated by the House of Lords in *Gillick*. The proposition at the heart of the majority judgments in this case was expressed by Lord Fraser as follows:

[P]arental rights to control a child do not exist for the benefit of the parent. They exist for the benefit of the child and they are justified only in so far as they enable the parent to perform his duties towards the child, and towards other children in the family.[17]

A similar statement was made by Lord Scarman:

[P]arental rights are derived from parental duty and exist only so long as they are needed for the protection of the person and property of the child.[18]

These principles were far from novel. Indeed, both Lord Fraser and Lord Scarman cited the statement by Blackstone to which reference has already been made.[19] As has been noted, the difference between the *Gillick* principles and Blackstone's formulation lay in the rejection of the additional notion of parental 'recompense'. This change was an understandable result of the increased emphasis which the law had placed on children's welfare as the dominant consideration in cases involving disputes over their upbringing.[20] Yet what appears to be an unexceptional consolidation of the law raises questions about what it means to be a parent. It is one thing to assert that, in case of disagreement, the best interests of the child should be the primary criterion. It is another to draw out this principle's implications with regard to parental rights.

One way to do this is to re-state the difference between the two models of parenthood in somewhat different terms. To conclude that any rights that a parent has over a child may be exercised only to the extent that they benefit that child is to adopt a particular concept of parental rights. In Campbell's terminology, such rights are not *intrinsic*; they are not fundamental entitlements which all parents can invariably assert. Rather, they are *derivative* (since they owe their existence to the logically prior set of obligations which parents have towards their children) and *instrumental* (since they may be exercised only in fulfilment of those obligations) (Campbell, 1992).

If it is accepted that parents no longer possess intrinsic rights in respect of their children (and cannot, therefore, look to them to fulfil their own expectations and needs), the question to be addressed is: what form do their derivative/instrumental rights take and what does this tell us about the status of parenthood?

THE NATURE OF PARENTS' RIGHTS

The first step towards answering this question is to return to the search for a more discriminating terminology. The following analysis points the way to such a terminology, although it does not pretend to provide a comprehensive classification. What are offered are no more than organizing concepts, a frame of reference which may prove useful in examining the current legal role of a parent. The terms chosen are: Powers, Authorities and Recognized Interests. These will be examined in turn.

Powers

Parents' powers enable them to do things to children and to make decisions affecting them. These include the power to select a child's name, to determine a child's school, religion and place of residence, to administer corporal punishment, and to restrict a young child's freedom of movement. Such powers may be included in the reference, in Article 5 of the United Nations Convention, to the 'rights and duties of parents . . . to provide . . . appropriate direction and guidance'.

Authorities

An authority is exercised to enable a child to do what the child would do if he or she had the capacity. Frequently a parent's use of an authority relates to the child's dealings with the outside world; in Campbell's terms, the parent acts as a proxy in this situation (Campbell, 1992). A clear example is the giving of consent to an uncontroversial operation, such as an appendicectomy. The effect of the parent's consent here is to confer on the surgeon immunity from civil and criminal liability (Montgomery, 1988:334).[21] Other examples include giving consent to marriage, taking and defending court actions, appointing a legal representative, agreeing to an apprenticeship and to the issue of a passport.[22]

Recognized interests

This concept is the most difficult of the three to define. It is designed to encapsulate the notion that there is something special about the status of a parent. When matters affecting a child arise, a parent occupies a position different from that occupied by all other members of the community. For example, a parent may pick up and fondle a young child when similar actions performed by another person might result in liability for assault. Another illustration of a parent's special role is that when disagreements arise relating to a child's dealings with the outside world, the parent will normally expect to be consulted. A manifestation of this is found in legislative provisions requiring parents to be present at proceedings in children's and juvenile courts.[23] Similarly, the position occupied by parents is reflected in laws relating to a non-custodial parent's access to children following a divorce.

In short, a parent has a special interest in a child's welfare, an interest to which the law must always pay regard. This interest reflects an expectation that the parent will normally be involved in important decisions affecting the child. This is not to say that a parent's wishes will inevitably, or even usually, determine the outcome in the case of a dispute. All that is being asserted is that in those situations where a parent does not possess a power or authority, the parent will still possess an interest which the law will recognize. Parents' views will usually be taken into account and these views carry special weight. As Lord Fraser observed in *Gillick*,[24] '[I]n the overwhelming majority of cases the best judges of a child's welfare are his or her parents'.

It might be objected that analysis in terms of powers, authorities and recognized interests raises more problems than it solves. Clearly there are difficulties with such a classification. The boundaries of the categories are not fixed. For example, it could be argued that the requirement for parental consent to the issue of a passport allows the exercise of a power (to control the child's movements) rather than an authority to act as a proxy. Nevertheless, it is my view that the above analysis helps us to understand the nature of claims relating to 'parents' rights'. For instance, Mrs Gillick's objection to the provision of contraceptive advice to under-age girls could be described as a dispute over who has the authority to give consent, but might in reality be a dispute over whether the mother had the power to control their behaviour.

Further, when we examine parents' powers and authorities, it will be seen that a distinction must be made. In some areas a case-by-case approach is adopted. *Gillick* provided a clear example: the question posed was whether the children had acquired the necessary capacity. This recognition of gradually developing autonomy, desirable as it might be, is a source of uncertainty. In other areas, however, the limits of the parents' powers and authorities are plain. This is the case when the legislature has intervened to provide clear guidelines. In such matters as the issue of a passport and the taking and defending of court actions, the legislation has created an irrebuttable presumption of juvenile incapacity. With regard to decisions of this kind, therefore, parents may confidently assert that they have unchallenged authority in respect of their children. Another way of putting this is to adapt the much quoted statement by Lord Denning that a parent's right to the custody of a child is a 'dwindling' right.[25] Some powers and authorities 'dwindle' as the child becomes more mature, but others remain unimpaired until specified ages are reached.

There is no discernible pattern: in some matters, case-by-case decisions can be made on the basis of children's capacity and in others the parents' authority is absolute. One can speculate that administrative convenience has demanded greater clarity with regard to certain parental authorities. These relate to children's dealings with the outside world (government and court officials, for example) and it is understandable that these officials should formulate clear rules. It seems that some of a parent's powers are more problematic; it is difficult to imagine legislative provisions defining the limits of a parent's power in such matters as place of residence and choice of religion.

Further, there are some authorities which parents may be unable to exercise. Some decisions are so controversial that it cannot be assumed that a parent, acting as proxy, may be permitted to make them. Examples are the authorisation of the sterilisation of a mentally incompetent child and the switching off of a life-support machine of a brain-damaged neonate.[26] Again, the distinction between powers and authorities is useful; normally powers may be exercised by parents and it is only in case of dispute that a decision by a court is needed. The exercise of certain authorities, in contrast, is beyond parental competence.

Finally, there is another distinction which should be noted. Earlier in this paper, reference was made to Campbell's contrast between intrinsic and derivative/instrumental rights. Examination of my suggested classification of parental rights reveals that, while powers and authorities may properly be described as derivative and instrumental, recognized interests are intrinsic. They have a fundamental quality and so represent a special form of right.

CONCLUSION

The conclusions based on the analysis offered in this paper can be formulated in both general and particular terms. Certain conceptual issues can be identified, but it is also important to try to address basic questions about the likely outcome of the dispute in which Mary and her parents are embroiled. With regard to the theoretical aspects, my examination of this dispute has sought to identify the way in which the use of rights language contributes to our understanding of youthful claims to autonomy and of the law's response to these claims. This paved the way for a discussion of broader questions relating to a child's relationship with his or her parents and the wider community. The nature of this relationship can be illuminated by considering the obligations which parents and community owe to children.

Whether the parent/child relationship should be understood primarily in terms of parental obligations is a question which draws attention to the usefulness of distinguishing between two models of parenthood. One regards it as legitimate for parents to view their children as repositories for their own values and aspirations. The other sees the parental role as beginning and ending with the performance of obligations and hence not conferring benefits which the law will protect. Although it is the latter view which may now prevail, I have argued that the former should not be completely ignored. It would probably still be held by many parents and cannot be dismissed as an anachronism. This point is underlined by the fact that the Court of Appeal in *Gillick* emphasized the importance of preserving parental authority and saw itself as protecting parents against any infringement of their right to control children up to the age of eighteen.[27] It was left to a majority of the House of Lords to formulate the alternative model, based on parental duties.

The implications of this approach have yet to be fully explored. I have suggested that, given the changes which the concept of parenthood is undergoing, it is helpful to speak of parental powers, authorities and recognized interests. Use of this classification reveals important distinctions which are obscured by rights language. One view of parental powers and authorities is that they exist only to the extent that they allow parents to fulfil their obligations. This notion leads to these parental rights being characterized as derivative or instrumental, rather than intrinsic. Their retention is therefore conditional on their exercise being in furtherance of children's welfare. Another implication seems to be that parents cannot claim powers and authorities over their children as a recompense for their performance of their duties. Parents' acceptance of their obligations may not impose matching obligations on the children. Finally, if we turn to the question of the likely outcome of the conflict between Mary and her parents, we can draw out some of the consequences of the foregoing analysis. Given the emphasis which has been placed on the contingent nature of parental powers and authorities, the logical starting point is to seek to identify the obligations which the parents owe to the fifteen-year-old Mary. They must protect and maintain her. The duty of maintenance is particularly important in the context of their dispute with their daughter; they are probably unable to make their performance of this duty conditional on her conformity to their wishes. At least in Australia it seems to be the law that parents' obligations to maintain their children are not extinguished by unfilial behaviour. Perhaps Mary's parents will be required to accept that not only might they be unable to impose their views on her, but they might also be compelled to provide maintenance for her until she attains the age of eighteen.[28]

Beyond the duties to protect and maintain, Mary's parents have an obligation to foster her attainment of what Freeman has called a 'rational independence' (Freeman, 1983:4). From this cluster of obligations, there derive certain powers and authorities; in addition – but quite separate – are recognized interests. In combination, these constitute what the parents would describe as their 'rights' over her. In the context of the dispute in which they are presently involved, they are invoking certain powers and recognized interests.

The appropriateness of parents exercising their diminishing power to determine a child's place of residence must be assessed on a case-by-case basis. With regard to Mary, the question which must be asked is whether this power has been extinguished. Applying the *Gillick* principle, one test to be applied is whether she has acquired sufficient capacity to make an informed decision. The available information suggests that she may not yet have done so.

The situation is, however, complicated, as an objective assessment of her capacity would not in reality be the determining factor, should the dispute result in court proceedings. In practice, any decision would be greatly influenced by a consideraton of what course of action would be most likely to advance Mary's welfare. Further, this approach cannot necessarily be dismissed as misplaced paternalism. Such powers as the parents possess are derived from their obligations towards her. Whatever Mary may think, the obligation to protect her (in this case from herself) cannot be unilaterally brought to an end. Yet we might be forced to conclude that, although the obligation remains, the power required to fulfil it has been lost.

Another, more practical, question can be asked about the claimed power. Even if such a power theoretically exists, is there any means by which the parents or society can seek to exercise it? Perhaps in this case any remaining obligation to provide protection simply cannot be discharged. Resort to coercive intervention might be seen as bolstering the parents' control over Mary, but it cannot enforce obedience to their wishes. This might lead to the conclusion that the parents' obligation to foster her independence has superseded their obligation to provide protection and that the new obligation is one from which no powers are derived. This is not to say that the duty to facilitate the exercise of autonomy will never give rise to concomitant powers. As Hafen has noted, there are dangers in thrusting independence on the young too soon (Hafen, 1976:650). There will be occasions on which parents will be obliged to employ the remnants of their powers of control in an effort to avoid these dangers. In Mary's case, however, this might prove impractical.

Her parents, therefore, may have to accept that their 'rights' over her consist of no more than recognized interests. They can expect to be consulted by those making important decisions affecting her and their views will be given special weight. For example, if their dispute with her were to lead to court action, they would be entitled to be involved and have their opinions considered. To this extent they would occupy a special position, by virtue of their status as parents. It seems that they must come to terms with the fact that at this stage of Mary's development, the law will not acknowledge that they have a recognized interest in seeking to ensure that Mary will grow up into the sort of person they want her to be.

NOTES

[1] Article 1 of the United Nations Convention on the Rights of the Child selects eighteen as the normal age of majority, and this is the general age of majority in Australia, see Gamble (1986:18), and in England and Wales, Family Law Reform Act 1969 (UK), s1.

[2] *Gillick v West Norfolk and Wisbech Area Health Authority* [1986] 1 AC 112.

[3] See *R v D* [1984] 1 AC 778 and *R v Rahman* (1985) 81 Cr App R 349.

[4] See Children Act 1989 (UK), s 31(2)(b)(ii), Children's Protection and Young Offenders Act 1979 (SA), s 12(1)(b) and Children's Services Act 1965 (Qld), s 60.

[5] The fact that the state has an obligation to intervene when a child's environment is unsatisfactory is acknowledged in Article 20 (1) of the Convention.

[6] Children (Care and Protection) Act 1987 (NSW), s 10(1)(c).

[7] Children and Young Persons Act 1989 (Vic), s 71.

[8] The foregoing analysis fits the pattern established in a number of the Articles of the Convention. While several of these recognize broad 'manifesto rights' (Feinberg, 1980:153), their significance is increased by the fact that their proclamation is accompanied by the imposition of imperfect obligations on the relevant state agencies. For example, the recognition, in Article 23 (1), of the right of mentally or physically disabled children to a full and decent life is matched in Article 23 (2) by provisions relating to the obligations of States Parties to extend the necessary assistance to those caring for these children. Similarly, Article 28 not only recognizes children's right to education, but also specifies the matching obligations which States Parties should accept in order to give meaning to this right.

[9] Social Security Act 1991 (Cth), ss 5(1) (definition of 'homeless person'), 559 and 1067-B1.

[10] As Carney pointed out in his oral commentary on this paper, this analysis raises some questions. Is Wellman speaking of a moral duty to accompany her or of a power to insist on doing so?

[11] The following analysis is intended to apply to parents who have the guardianship of their children.

[12] For a discussion of the common law relating to parents' actions for the loss of children's services, see Balkin & Davis (1991:750–3). Actions for loss of children's services have been abolished in the United Kingdom, see s 5 of the Law Reform (Miscellaneous Provisions) Act 1970 and s 2 of the Administration of Justice Act 1982. The current law in Australia is discussed by Balkin & Davis (1991).

[13] See 43 Eliz. c 2 (1601), s 7.

[14] [1986] 1 AC 112, 185.

[15] In re *Agar-Ellis* (1883) 24 ChD 317, 326, 330, 329, 336.

[16] Another example was provided by *Wellesley* v *Duke of Beaufort* (1827) 2 Russ 1; 38 ER 236. There the court was clearly concerned that the children should be educated in a manner befitting their rank and station. Lord Eldon told the cautionary tale of a youth 'the representative of a very old baronet' who had wished to marry the daughter of 'a common bricklayer'. The marriage had been prevented. (At 29, 246).

[17] [1986] 1 AC 112, 170.

[18] Ibid 184.

[19] Ibid 170, 185.

[20] This emphasis is reflected in Article 3 (1) of the United Nations Convention. This states that in all actions concerning children, 'the best interests of the child shall be a primary consideration'.

[21] Although not fully exploring the distinction, Montgomery points to the need to distinguish between the right to consent on behalf of a child and the right to control a child's behaviour. See Montgomery (1988:335).

[22] See Marriage Act 1961 (Cth), ss 13 and 14; Supreme Court Rules 1970 (NSW), Pt 63, Rule 2; Supreme Court Rules 1986 (Vic), Rule 15.02(1); Industrial Training Act 1975 (Vic), s 26; Industrial and Commercial Training Act 1989 (NSW), s 29(1); Passports Act 1938 (Cth), s 7A(2).

[23] See for example, Children's Protection and Young Offenders Act 1979 (SA), s 69(1); Children and Young Persons Act 1989 (Vic), s 18(1)(c) and Children and Young Persons Act 1933 (UK), s 34(1).

[24] [1986] 1 AC 112, 173.

[25] *Hewer* v *Bryant* [1970] 1 QB 357, 369.

[26] See for example, *In re B (A Minor) (Wardship: Sterilisation)* [1988] 1 AC 199; *Re Marion* (1991) FLC 92–193 (sterilisation); *In re J (A Minor) (Wardship: Medical Treatment)* [1991] 2 WLR 140 (switching off life-support).

[27] [1985] 1 All ER 533.

[28] This conclusion is somewhat tentative. Under s 66B(1) of the Family Law Act 1975 (Cth), parents' 'primary duty' to maintain their children appears absolute. Under s 66H(1), the duty can remain after a child attains the age of 18 if financial support for education is necessary. One judge has taken the view that a parent should meet his obligations under this provision only if some parental rights are retained. Watson J was not impressed by the claim for maintenance made by a youth over eighteen who argued that his father's rights over him had been extinguished. He commented: 'An adult son cannot demand a slice of the paternal cake with one breath and spew out filial abnegation with the next' (*Mercer and Mercer* (1976) FLC 90–033, 75, 131). Whether this case can be taken as a general authority for the proposition that parents can demand rights in return for the performance of obligations is doubtful.

'RECONCILING THE IRRECONCILABLE'?: A RIGHTS OR INTERESTS BASED APPROACH TO UNCONTROLLABILITY? A COMMENT ON SEYMOUR

TERRY CARNEY*

Rebellious or independently minded young people, who neither breach the criminal law nor fall within the scope of 'child protection' laws, pose a dilemma for law and social policy alike. It is argued in this paper that analyses of the position which present the issues in terms of rights, privileges and duties are ultimately unhelpful: they may clarify debate, but they do not provide a secure foundation for legal policy.

This paper considers other bases for resolving the critical dilemmas which are posed when 'independently minded' young people claim recognition for personal judgements which they have made about where their destiny lies. It is argued that 'social rights of citizenship', and an analysis based on competing 'interests', provides a better foundation for social policy, because it explicitly recognizes the 'connectedness' of the young person with other members of the community. This is advanced as the basis on which to define the role and the limits of legal involvement in the contest between the young person, their parents, and the State.

1 INTERESTS OR RIGHTS?

Rights analysis can be problematic when relied on to found rather than to express (or translate) claims made on individuals or society itself. Two main theories of rights are advanced in the literature; a 'will/power' theory (the ability of the holder of the right to require another to accept defined obligations)[1] and an 'interests' theory (where rights are the legally protected interests of the right bearer). As Campbell points out, the first theory poses difficulties for young children who lack capacity to form the requisite will (theories positing a mature adult potential seek to overcome this by postulating a hypothetical retrospective 'substitute'

* Terry Carney, Faculty of Law, University of Sydney, 173–175 Philip Street, Sydney NSW 2000 Australia.

expression of will), and the latter both leaves unanswered the question of the basis on which the protected interests are to be divined, and is inclined to be under- and over-inclusive (Campbell, 1992).[2]

Alternative frameworks also have drawbacks. Thus in rejecting rights analyses of children's interests for an obligations theory, O'Neill (1992) makes one particularly dubious contention in characterizing rights solely in terms of recognizing individual 'zones of autonomy'. Like Campbell, this paper rejects this as failing to recognize the 'connected-ness' of human life, and of the prospect that rights are founded in social relations (other than instrumentally to advance the interest of the collec-tive itself). Adapting Harris (1987), this paper therefore turns back to theories of 'social rights of citizenship' as the basis for founding those rights (Marshall, 1973).

2 FROM STAKEHOLDERS TO SOCIAL RIGHTS

Children's law necessarily balances the interests (social claims) of three stakeholders:[3] the independent interests of the child (in a safe, support-ive environment which respects appropriate 'choice' rights), the family (through deference towards its autonomy in childrearing), and the state (with its historic *parens patriae* role of being the parent of last resort and 'protector' of dependent or vulnerable people). Not all of those interests are appropriately recognized by the law, not all will find expression at any one time, and, of those which do find expression, not all will (or need) be expressed as legal 'rights'. When the stakeholders express their claims in the language of rights they may be doing so for rhetorical or political advantage (the assertion of a moral or ethical value), and, in any event, they will argue for positions which reflect differing values and conceptions of 'rights'. Thus Sampford (1986:32–3) argues that rights have at least four forms of expression: negative (or 'choice'), protective (or 'basic'), positive (or 'developmental'), and psychological (the capa-city to exercise developmental rights). Different elements (and forms) of law give priority to different aspects of these rights. Writers who adopt a Hohfeldian 'rights/duties' frame of reference (eg Seymour, 1992) risk falling between two stools: they neither satisfy conservative critics (who would call for the law to grant families or children maximum autonomy of action), nor those commentators who would argue that the law has a major role to play in securing the *social rights* of children (or families). There are two main reasons for this.

First, by seeking to find a 'socially progressive' correlative duty which is owed to the child either by their parents or the State, Hohfeldians implicitly reject a role for law in simply securing a zone of immunity (the purely self-regarding right to be left alone): a right which may be claimed even in the face of evidence that the consequence of honouring it may be less than optimal. Second, by focusing on the tension between the first two of Sampford's rights (negative versus protective) at the expense of the others, such writers overlook the role of law in creating and sustaining environments within which social rights may flourish (developmental or psychological above).

3 WIDER CONCEPTIONS OF RIGHTS?

A more satisfying frame of analysis then, may be to return to the more amorphous concept of 'interests' as a basis for identifying the different elements (and forms) of law which accord priority to the four different types of 'rights' chronicled by Sampford.

One view of the neglect laws for example, is that they aim to secure protective rights (or what Eekelaar calls 'basic interests'). These are said to encompass entitlements to 'general physical, emotional or intellectual care [which is] within the social capabilities of [the] immediate care-giver' (Eekelaar, 1986:170). But there are two manifestations of this: a right to be protected against a negation of access to those entitlements; and the positive securing of that access. Seymour (1992) applies this same distinction to a consideration of the case of the 'unruly' adolescent.

The risk entailed in this analysis is that debate about the function of law may narrow to the choice between two roles: either law protects against risk by removing the child, or it serves to reinforce the educative/protective authority of the child-rearing function of parents. In the case of the adolescent, though, this latter rather endorses an 'ideal' parent/child position, which it is conceded the law may be unable to enforce in the face of the adolescent who votes with their feet (or otherwise thumbs their nose at the theoretical authority of their parent(s)).

What is relegated in such an analysis is a fuller consideration of Sampford's positive rights ('developmental interests'). These can be translated as universal opportunities to access resources to develop talents and thus 'minimize the degree to which they enter adult life affected by avoidable prejudices incurred during childhood' (Eekelaar, 1986:170) – or the 'equality principle' (Dingwall, 1984:106). This is a claim for recognition of a 'social right': one of the welfare rights of citizenship (Marshall, 1973:67). Arguably this lends itself to recognition only through welfare legislation (distributive laws providing cash transfers or services). This then is the basis for grounding general rights to adequate income support and accommodation for young people who are homeless: it rests in a recognition of the claim of young people as people with an entitlement to enjoy a level of social intercourse (citizenship). It is not a narrow, easily trumped right which is grounded in a basic interest (such as avoidance of starvation or privation), nor a right which is a proxy for parental or social rights (in shaping future adults): it is a 'ranking interest'.

4 COMPETING INTERESTS AND PARENTAL CAPACITY

These interests (social and individual claims) compete for attention. Adolescents who neither breach the criminal law nor fall within the ambit of 'child protection' laws, constitute one of the vortexes where the interests are harder to discern and in a frequent state of flux (and disarray). Seymour graphically documents this conflict and indeterminacy (Seymour, 1992). But there is nothing very special about this. Interests and rights, however expressed, are often in conflict. Thus the protective mantle of welfare rights of citizenship clash with rights to self-expression. Any legislation is a compromise; one which may defy logical analysis, reflecting nothing more or less than the prevailing political and community will (whether democratically arrived at or the product of powerful shapers of opinion).

In the field of parent-child relations however, the mix of values frequently raises more profound questions of political and moral philosophy (Mnookin, 1978:5). This is a product of the overlay of the 'family interest'. In the service of political pluralism, or religious freedom or adult autonomy, a family-centred rationale has often been vigorously advocated (Wald, 1976:248). An assumption of parental capacity to manage the upbringing of children is deeply embedded in social, ethical and economic attitudes to the family. The two clear incursions on this principle are risk to the welfare and development of the child and offences by children. In the case of risk, parental rights may at highest be assumed by the State – or be monitored and regulated by it. The principal debates are about the bases of intervention (needs or harms), the forms of state involvement (family conferences or courts), and the nature of the responses (state care or home-based orders). Currently a 'harms model', administered by courts charged with the re-unification of the family where possible, is favoured.

In the case of the offender, the State interest is two-fold: to foster the development of the young person as a law abiding citizen, and to protect the public. A more solicitous attitude has generally been taken towards juvenile offenders, but the principal debates have been about such questions as: the extent to which the needs of the offender might displace the restriction that state intervention not be disproportionate to the gravity of the offence; the degree of recognition of procedural rights of the child; the forum for adjudication (court or administrative body); and the nature of the sanctions. Currently a 'justice' rather than a 'welfare' model prevails.

Apparently common to both cases is the lack of relevance of the *competence* of the parent. In the case of children at risk the 'child-centred' character of the prevailing philosophy (eg the 'welfare and best interests' principle), favours a dispassionate stance to the issue of parental capacity (or 'fault'); deficiencies of parental care which can readily be remedied do not serve to justify intervention at all (because the harm is not ongoing), and the incursion on parental authority otherwise is a *consequence* of the finding of unacceptable levels of risk to the child (whether from neglect or direct actions). So also with offending. The offence by the child similarly serves as the pre-condition for intervention and determines the shape of that response; any loss of parental rights over a child placed in custody is once again the *consequence* not the rationale for intervention.

5 GLOSSES ON PURITY: THE STATUS OFFENCE

The so called status offences (including exposure to moral danger, uncontrollability, and truancy), break from the specificity principle currently prominent in established neglect and offender jurisdictions: intervention is not grounded on specific harm to the child or a specific breach of a predetermined criminal prohibition. This departure from the rule of law is the primary source of opposition from lawyers (Gamble, 1985:101–2), while other disciplines point to a lack of evidence of successful interventions.

Status offences have mixed (and differing) rationales, however: this mixture is the basis for calling it a 'hybrid' category. Thus uncontrollability is arguably more concerned with the public interest (in quelling pre-delinquency and rebellion) than with the rights of the child. Truancy and exposure also have this element (truancy may undermine confidence in public education, and exposure may be a harbinger for a career of immorality or crime), but the major apparent focus is to secure 'basic' or 'developmental' interests (an acceptable environment for social development). Harm to self rather than to others is more prominent. Parental competence is also much more central to such conceptions.

6 PURITY OR PATERNALISM?

Parental capacity, then, has not always been incidental, and may not remain so. Historically speaking, parental capacity was once at centre stage in both settings, and there is evidence of its return to prominence. Thus neglect laws were once redolent with features of parental incompetence, slackness or waywardness.[4] And until quite recently, it was common for young offender legislation to provide for parents to be held accountable for the offences of their children.[5] Moreover, status offences such as 'uncontrollability' have been (and continue to be) recognized either within the offender or the neglect branch (and occasionally as a hybrid). The popularity of the New Zealand 'family conference', as a central mechanism for resolving without reference to a court, all but 2 per cent of neglect and 4 per cent of offences reported to police (CYPFAct, 1989; Hassall & Maxwell, 1991:6–7), suggests a resurgence in such approaches.

If the waywardness of the parent (such as encouragement of a career in juvenile crime) is to serve as the basis for an intervention against the child which cannot be independently grounded in risk to, or actions by, the child, serious moral and practical questions arise. As Wald argues, 'a policy that attempts to increase socialisation at the cost of increasing emotional damage [to children] should be unacceptable' (Wald, 1982:19). The remoteness of the remedy from the real source of concern, the vagueness and imprecision of grounds for intervention, and doubts about whether the child is better off as a consequence of the intervention – are the three principal objections to status offences.

7 CONCLUSION

In the 1981 Report of the Australian Law Reform Commission, these reservations were accepted. However that document went on to argue that the concerns could be allayed by hedging the grounds with restrictions and then incorporating them in the definition of circumstances in which a child is in need of protection. Thus the report agreed in the main with the case against the status offence, but refrained from 'completely abandon[ing] the field' (ALRC, 1982:227). It proposed that the grounds of neglect should include 'behaviour . . . likely to be harmful' where parents or guardians are unable or unwilling to prevent its occurrence, 'incompatibility' between children and their parent(s) or guardian(s), and *persistent* truancy which 'is or is likely to be, *harmful* to the child' (ALRC, 1982:232). The attraction of this was that it highlighted the fact that a species of harm to the child is the justification for state action. Where issue can be taken with that report is its implicit assumption that the law is restricted to one of two roles; either it secures choice rights for the young person or it protects their 'basic interests' (in this case through the inclusion of status offences in the neglect provisions, which protect 'basic interests').

The wider position preferred here rests on Marshall's citizenship theory, which recognizes a social right to full participation in society characterized as being equally important to guarantees of political rights (universal suffrage) and civil rights (equality before the law).[6] Social reciprocity is the nub of this thesis: the citizen and the state owe mutually responsible duties to each other; welfare is not simply a 'good' owed unconditionally to the citizen on pre-ordained terms.

This wider conception of social rights builds on two important elements of a traditional analysis of the welfare state – principally the recognition of the moral duty of the state to protect vulnerable people irrespective of fault; and compliance with the principle of the rule of law (that entitlements should not be at the whim of the state or be subject to arbitrary change). But it adds a state responsibility to foster the positive developmental interest of (young) citizens in participation in the life of the community; a duty which translates into the provision of positive income, housing, employment and training measures to enable young people to participate at a reasonable level.

The conception of rights which appears to be implicit in the ALRC Report and the Seymour paper in the present volume, is narrower. While defensible in its own terms, this approach passes up a role for law in securing access to social rights of citizenship.[7]

NOTES

[1] The more expansive version of this insists also on Kantian rational capacity, see Campbell (1992).

[2] Allowing the interest in survival to justify paternal action of force feeding.

[3] 'Stakeholder' is an omnibus term designed to meet the feminist critiques of the artificiality of 'intervention/non-intervention' analysis, and the arguments that rights analysis misreads the significance of 'social connectedness', indeterminacy, and the pervasive impact of patriarchal power structures in denying legitimacy to the voice of women and children within the family; see further Morgan (1988).

[4] Thus the heads of neglect in the *Neglected and Criminal Children's Act* 1864 (Vic) covered vagrancy, association with immoral people, lack of a settled abode, waywardness and begging: s 13(1)–(5).

[5] Remnants of this remain in some Australian jurisdictions, Seymour (1988).

[6] Marshall (1973); Harris (1987); Cf. Goodin & Le Grande (1987) (arguing that citizenship is too woolly a concept to be of explanatory power).

[7] See further, Carney (1991).

'THERE OUGHT TO BE A LAW AGAINST IT': REFLECTIONS ON CHILD ABUSE, MORALITY AND LAW

MARGARET M. COADY* & C. A. J. COADY**

ABSTRACT

The United Nations Convention on the Rights of the Child, which forms the background to our discussions in this conference, is a sober, moderate plea on behalf of a group that is often powerless, disadvantaged and under-represented in a world dominated by adults. It is certainly not an extremist document, and its faults, we believe, lie rather in the area of conservative (though possibly necessary) compromise with entrenched cultural forces, for example, in the specification that fifteen be the age under which children should not be made to serve in the armed forces. There are also occasional forays into conceptual and ethical waters that are more troubled than the authors of the convention seem to recognize. The repeated, but unscrutinized, references to 'the best interests of the child' as a determining criterion are amongst these, and some of the references to child abuse suffer from a degree of vagueness that could allow for unacceptable interpretations. In what follows, we are less concerned directly with problems internal to the document itself than with problematic ways of thinking about children, child abuse, morality and the law that exist already in our community and others like it. These ways of thinking are significant in the context of our discussions because they will put flesh upon the document's bare bones, giving a living reality to its ringing phrases and interpreting its unclarities. The Convention takes as one of its starting points the fact that there are many children today suffering physical and psychological damage from adults, as well as from more impersonal economic and social structures and natural catastrophes. We have no intention of disputing such palpable and distressing facts. Nonetheless the present furore about child abuse and the legislative changes implemented and sought need cool appraisal lest hysteria and faddism combine with legitimate concern to produce alarming social and political outcomes that may be hard to reverse. In what follows we attempt such an appraisal of elements in the debate about child abuse.

THE PROBLEM OF CONCEPTUAL FLEXIBILISM

Any discussion with moral and philosophical dimensions can benefit

* Margaret Coady, School of Early Childhood Studies, University of Melbourne, Private Bag 10, Kew, Victoria 3101 Australia.
** Tony Coady, Philosophy Department, University of Melbourne, Parkville, Victoria 3052 Australia.

from conceptual or definitional clarification. This should be obvious enough but it is seldom appreciated in public debate just how distorting the lack of such clarity can be. An example from historical debate about the early days of Australia provides an instructive illustration.

The early European settlement of Australia was very largely composed of convicts and their jailers and the vast majority of the women in the early colony of New South Wales were convicts. Recently, partly under the impetus of feminist historians, there has been much debate about the treatment and status of these women. That their treatment was generally bad is pretty plain and a good deal of the mistreatment was sexual. There is a ready acceptance by both modern feminists and earlier clerical moralists that the moral and social status of so many of these women was that of prostitute. This consensus fuels quite different political agendas – writers like Anne Summers have large numbers of the women condemned to a life of prostitution by male power structures whereas the Reverend Samuel Marsden, one of the early colony's most influential puritans, was anxious to uphold a model of female virtue that most of the convict women (and many other women, come to that) would fall short of. On close examination, however, it turns out that the common, agreed premise of the feminist and the preacher is either false or ill-defined. If the term prostitute means one who sells sexual services then the available evidence strongly suggests that the vast majority of the convict women were not prostitutes. To begin with, prostitution was not a transportable offence and the terms 'whore' or 'prostitute' were used either as mere terms of abuse for women who did not come from the respectable classes, or who engaged in any form of promiscuity, or even as denoting those in stable sexual relationships who had not had the benefit of a Church of England marriage. The term 'concubine' was a useful bridging expression for this last group suggesting something very close to whoring. Marsden compiled a list called 'The Female Register' in 1806 which classified the infant colony's adult women into three exclusive categories of 'married', 'widowed' or 'concubine'. Since the only form of marriage Marsden recognized was that performed within the Church of England this consigned not only faithful *de facto* wives but also Jewish and Catholic women married according to the rites of their own communions to the bin of concubinage (Hughes, 1988; Summers, 1975).

The extended usage of terms like 'whore' and 'concubine' can of course be defended by recourse to considerations of neglected resemblances but such extensions can very easily mislead, and surreptitiously promote objectives and agenda which would otherwise be more carefully scrutinized. Many convict women who settled into stable and even permanent relations in New South Wales in the early Nineteenth Century did so under coercive pressures which had economic aspects so that one can find analogies with the selling of sexual services. Nonetheless, the striking disanalogies remain and words like 'prostitute' serve to mark them. We need a label for working (consciously or unconsciously) with extended and wide understandings of crucial moral and political concepts; we propose to call it 'flexibilism'. In the matter of child abuse, we should be particularly wary of flexibilism (Coady, 1986).[1]

As Hacking (1988) and several others have pointed out, the modern concern for child abuse arises from earlier anxieties about child battering, and even earlier ones about cruelty and neglect. A great deal of the concern for children's well-being that is at the heart of campaigns against child abuse, and even a lot of the typical instances of abuse, can be found in Charles Dickens' *Oliver Twist*. Two notable changes have, however, taken place in the years since the publication of Dickens' book. The first is that Dickens is concerned with the damage done to children by institutions and ideologies ('philosophers' as he calls them – it is the Benthamite reformers he means) and also by the criminal classes amongst whom they 'fell'. The typical modern document on child abuse is not a novel but a newspaper feature, a social agency report or a government manifesto and its primary focus is not on the ravages of institutions, pet theories and hardened criminals but of 'ordinary' families. The second change is that, where Dickens only gestures at a sexual aspect of the treatment of children (in the person of the prostitute, Nancy), the most recent emphasis is upon sexual damage. Where Dickens' audience was being sensitized to the harms of starvation, beating and emotional cruelty, inflicted by impersonal functionaries viewing themselves as the embodiments of society's moral concerns, modern audiences are being warned about much more hidden, often subtle harms inflicted by kith and kin. Not that sexual harms are always subtle; there is nothing subtle about rape. Nonetheless, incestual violations often occur in contexts which do not match the common settings for adult rape, nor are all the things referred to as sexual abuse blatantly damaging to the supposed victims. A recent Australian report, commissioned by the Law Reform Commission of Victoria, states that 'sexual abuse refers to a variety of behaviours ranging from exhibitionism to intercourse, from intimate kissing and cuddling to penetration with an object' (Goddard, 1988:66). No doubt there are many cases of exhibitionism and 'intimate' cuddling which are damaging to children, but equally there are many which are not. (The author may have some special sense of 'intimate' and other expressions in mind but this does not emerge in the report.) If there are no further threatening aspects, like the display occurring in a confined space, most healthy ten-year-olds are likely to be no more than amused, intrigued or, at worst, a bit alarmed by a street encounter with a 'flasher'. When talk about child sexual abuse arises in a setting of legislative recommendations such conceptual flexibilism is cause for alarm.

There is a point of connection here with other forms of child abuse. It might be thought that, whatever the ambiguities of sexual or emotional interactions, surely physical violence is always abusive and should be dealt with by the law whether it occurs within the family or outside of it. Article 19 of the Convention on the Rights of the Child is clearly informed by this thought when it insists that States who are parties to the Convention 'should take all appropriate legislative, administrative, social and educational measures to protect the child from all forms of physical or mental violence, injury or abuse, neglect or negligent treatment . . . while in the care of parent(s), legal guardian(s) or any other person who has care of the child.' The concern for the rights of the individual child expressed in this article is legitimate but its expression is simplistic. That this is so is shown both by the fact that violence is arguably not always immoral and that, where it is immoral, it is not always appropriate that it be the concern of the law. The first point is illustrated by the examples of just wars, just revolutions and legitimate police violence and, more relevantly here, by the example of just physical punishment of children by parents. (All these are rejected by some critics or other but their objections, though serious, are hardly decisive.) The second point is important and often overlooked, especially by groups who are, rightly, seeking to publicize the State's apparent indifference to severe violence or neglect inflicted upon women and children in domestic settings. In spite of the seriousness of such concerns, it remains true that we would view with astonishment the idea that the police should be called in to prosecute children, or deal with them in other ways, whenever they fight with each other in the home or give way to anger and hit their parents. This is so even if quite a lot of pain or damage is caused by the assaults. The explanation of this lies partly in the fact that law enforcement is seldom much exercised about momentary, contained assault like a flare-up of shoving or punching in a bar, but, more significantly, it lies in the recognition of the social value of there being spheres of life in which the State intervenes coercively only with some reluctance. The family is such a sphere though by no means the only one. While there are convincing arguments why the State should hesitate to intervene coercively in the family, there is no doubt that appeal to the sanctity and privacy of the family has been used as an excuse for non-intervention by law enforcement officers in cases such as assaults on spouses or children where there is clear justification for intervention. Often the aggressor is arrested only after repeated calls to police from the victim. This hesitancy on the part of the law enforcement officers may be due to a number of factors including the volatility of the emotional situation and difficulties of producing evidence in court, but appeal to the privacy of the family sphere has often been used to justify such inaction (Scutt, 1983).

There is an extensive and important literature criticizing what has been called the 'public/private dichotomy'. Much of this literature stems from those Marxist-inspired analyses which demonstrated the way in which women's work of caring for the young, the ill and the elderly, of cooking and cleaning and so on, contributes to the economy and yet has been overlooked and downgraded because it has been done in the 'privacy' of the home (Zaretsky, 1976). The unequal power relations within the home have gone uncriticized because they are not visible to the public eye (Dalley, 1988; Olsen, 1985; Okin, 1989). More fundamentally, Frances Olsen and others argue that the family is constituted by the laws of the state in that as Olsen puts it 'the state is responsible for the background rules that affect people's domestic behaviours' (Olsen, 1985). There is no doubt that any useful distinction between the private and the public will have to allow for interactions, even 'constitutive' interactions, between what is private and what is public. Nonetheless the wholesale rejection of any contrast between what is public and what is private contains the seeds of confusion and danger. Where 'public' refers to openness to the scrutiny and intrusion of all citizens, then collapsing the distinction means removing protections and guarantees from the lives of individual citizens, whether young or old, male or female, rich or poor. What has been gained from the critics of the public/private dichotomy is a greater understanding of the power relationships within groups such as families and of the necessity for individuals in groups to be able to gain redress for exploitation which occurs within these groups. The Convention goes some way toward providing this redress in that children are given individual rights which could be used against exploitation in families, schools and other communities in which they participate.[2] It is interesting that one of the rights which the Convention wishes to gain for children, and one that has been most vigorously resisted by conservative defenders of the family, is the right to privacy.[3] Those who refuse to give any meaning to the public/private distinction are unwitting allies of those on the other side of the ideological divide who do not wish to recognize this right to privacy.

CHILD ABUSE AND THE LIMITS OF LAW

The complex issue of how and why we should determine limits to the operation of law cannot be fully treated here, but it is remarkable how much ignored it is in the debates about child abuse and other matters affecting the development of the child. This is all the more remarkable given that the liberal tradition has such a strong commitment to the idea that the law should not intrude into certain areas of morality, often labelled 'private' morality. Moreover much conservative theory emphasizes the rights and powers of the family against the State.[4] Yet there are early tendencies in the movement against child abuse and the broader movement to secure children's rights, which raise grave worries about the legal enforcement of morality and 'lifestyle' and about unwarranted state intervention in family life.

It is worth remarking that, in this connection, there are several emphases in the Convention that are at least in tension with each other where they are not straightforwardly at odds. Certain of its more categorical denunciations and demands (such as that against all forms of violence in Article 19,(1)) show no easy harmony with reiterated stress on the importance of the family and of respect for 'the child's ethnic, religious, cultural and linguistic background' (see Article 19,(2)). The question of physical or psychological chastisement of the child comes to mind as one in which the background mentioned may well sanction some forms of physical and/or mental violence.

A principal reason why the issue of lifestyle and the State gets so little attention is the phenomenon of conceptual flexibilism already referred to. The striking paradigms of child abuse are the battered infant or the raped daughter and these are so clearly the sorts of immorality that ought to be the concern of the law (on any theory: liberal, conservative, socialist, feminist) that we hardly notice that the concept has been extended to take in quite different 'immoralities'. We have already cited a wide and amorphous legal definition of sexual abuse. On child abuse generally the matter is no better. Consider the US Child Abuse Convention and Treatment Act which now deems it child abuse for a physician to limit intensive care of a newborn with irreparable life-threatening handicaps (Hacking, 1988). Again, the NSW legislation would have it that a child is abused if it is exposed to behaviour that psychologically harms it (Care and Protection Act 1987, s 3(i)). But it is perfectly possible for all sorts of normal, well-intentioned activities aimed at a child's good to cause psychological harm to some children. One need only reflect on the way some children react to even non-bullying swimming lessons.

These are legal definitions, and particularly worrying because of their direct link to State interventions and penalties, but definitions abroad amongst theorists, commentators and activists can have strong indirect effects upon the operation of the law. Here we find definitions which characterize child abuse as an 'unacceptable' way of bringing up children. Kaufman, for instance, cites workers in Victorian sexual assault centres arguing for mandatory reporting because it would more clearly delineate 'acceptable or unacceptable mores and morals' (Kaufman, 1988:23). Garbarino and Gilliam say that child abuse 'may be described as a form of situationally determined incompetence in the role of caregiver. It stems from the combination of social stress and a relatively low level of skill as a caregiver' (Garbarino & Gilliam, 1980:29). The British Department of Health and Social Security in 1980 issued a circular on child abuse recommending ways of keeping a register on cases of non-accidental injury to children which gave as one criterion for inclusion on the register, 'severe non-organic failure to thrive' (Parton, 1985:113).

Critics have pointed to the way these definitions and criteria are congenial to more interventionist activities by social workers and to the antagonisms this gives rise to. Packman, for instance, found families in Britain referring to social service officers as 'the SS' and social workers as the 'Gestapo' (Parton, 1985:127). What is less often remarked is the fact that the extended definitions necessarily rely upon moral or philosophical conceptions and theories which are either presently insecure or (in W. B. Gallie's happy phrase) 'essentially contestable' (Gallie, 1964:157). They also raise important questions about our understanding of morality and its relation to the exercise of state power through the law. If morality is concerned with what it is to live well then it will inevitably involve more than the rules, prohibitions and codes that it is often identified with. Its province will extend to outlooks, world-views, metaphysical beliefs and theories; its rules will be partially determined by these and by changes consequent upon more demonstrable discoveries and advances in the sciences. Moreover, morality is also a matter of spirit, sensitivity and appropriate emotional response to the needs and concerns of others. This dimension which has been called a 'care focus' is often in danger of being swamped by the stress on morality as abstract, general code. It is a dimension which is specially relevant to the intimate relations involved in the upbringing of children.

This rich understanding of morality is, or should be, an important ingredient in the debate about the limits of law. There is no need to deny that some of the same behaviours are prohibited by both law and morality (eg, murder and theft). Nor need fear of the state's invasion into the realm of morality be based upon generalized scepticism or relativism about moral truth; one needs much less drastic assumptions about morality than that. The three most relevant seem to be:

1 Moral knowledge can be distinguished from moral opinion. It is certainly known that torturing innocent children to death is morally wrong but this item of knowledge contrasts strikingly (at present) with our grasp of the truth (if it is a truth) that abortion is morally wrong or that (nearer to our topic) corporal punishment of children is morally wrong. These latter beliefs are properly matters for debate upon which reasonable people may reasonably continue to disagree. Sometimes the disagreement persists because of present inability to resolve empirical issues – such as what effect mild physical violence has upon children. Sometimes it persists because the disputants have quite different moral ideals or conceptions which are connected with religious outlooks, none of which are outright vicious, and so do not call for state suppression. Sometimes the disagreement rests on divergent metaphysical or theoretical convictions, often having something of the flavour of religious beliefs, which permanently or temporarily defy rational resolution. An instance

of divergence is provided by the influence of Freudian, or other related psychological theories, and outlooks reacting against them. This is particularly significant in the child abuse area where the determination of whether something is either sexual or non-sexual abuse will often turn on claims about normal or healthy development and what prevents it. For example, many believe that a child is abused if it is deprived of schooling but others, such as John Holt, think that schooling is destructive of the child's proper development. (The general effect of Article 28 of the Convention is to ignore the complex issues raised by this controversy and to decide the matter, without argument, against those who think like Holt.) In the sexual area, different attitudes to nakedness provide an example. Some hold that a child develops healthier sexual attitudes if nakedness is normal in the home whereas others believe that this endangers moral development.

2 Unlike law, morality essentially goes beyond an interest in behavioural conformity to a concern for the way in which an agent holds moral views and acts upon them. There are two aspects to this concern. First, reason, intention and motive are, to some degree, at the heart of morally good behaviour. The legal imposition of conformity to norms does not contribute to an understanding of their significance nor to the appropriate spirit of adherence to them. These internal features of morality need to be cultivated by moral education and tend to be undermined by the legal imposition of conformity.[5] Such impositions are tolerable when they are clearly required for community safety as in laws against rape, murder, fraud, etc, but the conflation of law and morality is always to the disadvantage of morality. Second, emphasis on behavioural conformity would seem to be inimical to the encouragement of that care and sympathy which are essential in a child's moral development.

3 Even if the most stringent moral realism in epistemology, semantics and metaphysics were granted, it would remain true that there is more to morality than moral truths. The moral life requires the concrete application of moral norms, values and principles to the messy particularities of life and this means that a moral agent must strive to acquire the difficult skills of practical judgement and prudent discrimination. Our moral problems are peculiarly our own, not in the sense that others cannot make true judgements about their solutions, but in the sense that individuals need to cultivate self-reliance by understanding and dealing with moral issues if they are to take charge of their lives. This involves some risks of harm to self and others and the state is naturally concerned to limit such risks, but if we value moral autonomy we must allow some room for risk. The upbringing of children invokes moral autonomy in two related ways. The adult should be concerned to foster moral self-reliance in the child but is also called upon to exercise the capacity in the fostering process. Indeed, it seems likely that one of the most efficacious

means of encouraging autonomy in the child is the parent's example of its exercise.

The flexibilist talk of 'failure to thrive', 'incompetence as a care-giver', and so on needs to be judged against this background as does the way 'sexual abuse' has been extended to take in behaviour which may or may not be damaging to the child but which conflicts with the social reformer's ideal of sexual behaviour. A good deal of the conduct being incorporated into the category of abuse and being made subject to the law is either contestably immoral (belonging to the realm of 'moral opinion') or where it is plainly immoral, its treatment as illegal will have bad moral effects. This latter point involves considerations (2) and (3) above. Laws whose only point is to promote morality may well have the opposite effect by swamping important internal aspects of moral behaviour covered under (2) and (3). Lying, verbal cruelty, adultery and other forms of disloyalty are immoral but arguably should not be illegal (except in special contexts, such as lying in a trial or in contracts), partly for pragmatic reasons, but partly for the reasons advanced above. Or to take a rather different case, greed is a vice and it has many, varied manifestations. Some of these are the concern of the law, as when greed leads to murder or theft, but the operations of the vice are often less palpable though nonetheless important; the overcoming of these faults is a matter for moral education, self-examination, and social interaction since these agencies employ predominantly moral processes rather than coercion. Preference for these processes certainly has its costs – poor schools or poor parents or poor friends may produce corrupted people: people who are, for instance, materialistic, selfish, idle, hedonistic or uncaring. But when the processes work well, they will produce genuine moral virtue and this is not something that the law can produce.

MUST LEGAL ENFORCEMENT UNDERMINE MORALITY?

The general thrust of this argument may be challenged in several ways. One is to reject the account of morality given and another is to accept its broad outline but to claim that coercion is not as inimical to morality as the argument would have it. There is something to be said for each of these strategies though it is seldom in fact said in the debate about child abuse. The first strategy insists that the internal account of morality presents merely one peculiarly modern (post-Kantian?) view of it. Earlier societies, and even some today, have operated with a much closer fusion of law and morality than that advocated by writers like Mill (1957).[6] We doubt that the conception of morality employed in the argument is as modern as alleged – there is certainly evidence of a similar approach in Aristotle[7] – but, in any case, the fact that it is modern is hardly an objection to it and it is even less of an objection when it is urged by those moderns whose outlook shows that they share its central assumptions and concerns. The most ardent anti-liberals on the left, for instance, are moved by a passionate concern that the oppressed be liberated, empowered, take control of their own lives and so on, yet it is precisely concerns of this general sort that the conception of morality under challenge actually embodies. No doubt, the conception has been subject to ideological employments of a distorting and damaging kind but we should beware of jettisoning the baby along with the bathwater.

The more substantial difficulty is posed by the second strategy. This reminds us that it won't do to be too pious about such notions as freedom, reason and autonomy in connection with morality because, just as the acquisition of any skill involves a good deal of mere training, so the acquisition of the virtues will involve a good deal in the way of humdrum drilling and training of the mind, character and emotions. The objector will urge that this is particularly clear in the case of the moral (and other) education of children. Similarly, it is claimed, the coercive role of the law can provide a form of training or shaping of moral character in the citizen.

Perhaps the best line of reply to the second objection is to acknowledge that it has some force but not nearly enough. To take the case of young children first: corporal punishment in the form of a spontaneous (or relatively spontaneous) response to an offence may very well have the effect of providing a child with an understanding of how behaviour of a certain sort will be perceived and reacted to by others. This in itself may be an important step in moral development, but it is clearly defective as ethical instruction unless at least accompanied by an account of why people are right to perceive and react as they do. In other words, what is required to transform the display of force into a genuine contribution to character-building is precisely an attempt at a reasoned presentation of what is wrong with the sanctioned behaviour.

There is, incidentally, some empirical evidence to show the effectiveness of such reasoning, in the absence of corporal punishments, on surprisingly young children.[8] Perhaps there is a case for certain forms of violent punishment (and certain forms of non-violent coercion) as part of the moral education of children but against it must be set the argument that the child may well take the wrong lessons from the resort to even moderate corporal punishment, lessons such as the confusion of might with right, the undue regard for fear as a motive, and too great a respect for violence as a means of solving conflicts. This counter-argument may not be sufficient to offset all value for corporal punishment as a part of the process of moral education for the child – this issue is clearly controversial – but it highlights the fact that, even with young children, coercion is a second-best and, as such, no more than a supplement to reason and example in moral education. For adults, of course, corporal punishment has virtually disappeared from modern legal systems and is not advocated even by those who see punishment as a form of moral education.[9]

Nonetheless, other coercive and fear-based measures such as the operation of the law and police activities are sometimes seen as morally educative for adults. Whether the state should be in the business of itself giving moral education to adults is pretty dubious. Mill, for instance, thought the State should not even provide moral (or any other) education to children (Mill, 1957:159). Whatever we think of that, it is one thing to want the State to educate adults morally and another again to want this to happen through coercion. If we assign any role to forms of coercion in the case of children, its justification will advert precisely to the ways in which their developmental status differs from that of adults.

LAW AS EDUCATION?

The discussion of this second objection leads naturally to consideration of an argument which is commonly used to support child abuse legislation. When faced with the objection that some proposed law is unenforceable or dangerous to civil liberties or ineffective in preventing harms, its advocates will often resort to the supposed educative value of the change. There are several ambiguities in this defence which need to be clarified before it can be usefully discussed. There is an obvious sense in which law can be, if not educative, at least informative, without any cause for anxiety. This is the sense in which it is informative about what the law is. It is usually an important feature of law that it be openly promulgated and its content and central implications clearly expressed. Second, there is the fact that a sub-set of laws are properly concerned with educational matters – such as those establishing compulsory schooling. Third, there is the claim which, as already mentioned, is defended by Hampton, that the justification for punishment, including State punishment of law-breakers, is to be given in terms of education. Hampton's version of this puts the justification as aimed at the moral education of the offender. We have grave reservations about her position, but, in any case, it should be distinguished (as she herself does distinguish it) from a fourth position which can easily be confused with it (Hampton, 1984:219). This is the thesis that laws, or some laws, should be made with a view to the moral education of the community at large. It is this thesis which is often invoked in the child abuse debate, though sometimes conflated with one or more of the other three. That it is different can be seen from the fact that the rationale for the making of laws need not coincide with the rationale for punishment of law-breakers.

What then of the fourth position and its role in the child abuse debate? One employment of the idea occurs in the Victorian Law Reform Commission's report on Sexual Offences Against Children where the authors say, 'although the law has only a limited effect in preventing criminal behaviour, its symbolic and educative functions are of considerable importance'. They then quote from a previous Commission Report which said, 'A significant role of the criminal law is to define unacceptable conduct. In declaring certain types of sexual behaviour to be criminal, the law plays a crucial part in the development and maintenance of community attitudes and expectations' (Victorian Law Reform Commission, 1988:18). Elsewhere they refer to the law's role in 'declaring', 'asserting' and 'advocating' certain values (1988:72). The Australian survey of workers in Victorian sexual assault centres, cited earlier, showed that those in favour of a form of mandatory reporting gave as one of their chief reasons for supporting it that such a measure would provide for 'the clearer delineation of acceptable or unacceptable mores and morals' (Kaufman, 1988).

Child abuse is not of course the only area in which such sentiments are expressed. Arguments of a similar kind have had currency in debates about sexual harassment, seat-belt legislation and drink-driving laws. Even within what we have been calling the fourth position, however, it is necessary to make further distinctions. There are blatant moral wrongs which people are nonetheless unaware of, and this for different sorts of reasons. Consider the recent Italian rape case where several youths attacked a woman in a Roman street late at night, were caught while the rape was in progress and one of them, on being arrested, exclaimed: 'You mean this sort of thing is a crime!' If the report can be believed he was claiming to be unaware that what he was doing was morally, and not just legally, wrong (he was presumably not trying to distinguish morality from law). It is hard to be certain of the bases for this absurdly false belief about a moral matter – it may be due to a failure of moral understanding or lack of factual information or both. The idea that women, or certain classes of them, deserve or like such treatment still has wider currency than suspected. A case in which factual error (of a nonmoral kind) produces ignorance of blatant moral wrongs occurs in the child abuse context. Very young children can sustain serious physical injury merely from being shaken hard. Here is a case where what might well seem a morally neutral or minor matter is demonstrably seriously wrong but the demonstration requires certain (non-contentious) medical information which people may well lack. Again there was a time when some people did not know the dangerous effects upon their driving skills induced by relatively small amounts of alcohol and hence were unaware of the risks to themselves and others of drinking and driving. Whether the central cases of child abuse are wrongs that the perpetrators are typically unaware of in any of these ways is, however, open to grave doubt. Indeed the available evidence suggests that they usually know quite well that they are doing wrong (Heath, 1985).

On the other hand, there are putative moral wrongs which are more controversial and in respect of which it is implausible to claim that there is some relatively obvious demonstration of their wrong which the promulgation of a law will serve to bring home to an audience. It is here that the exercise of legal enactment as a form of education is most dubious since it is precisely in such cases that moral insight and understanding are most endangered by pressure or coercion. Yet it is in these areas that the law as education argument is very commonly heard. In Sweden, for example, legislation prohibiting corporal punishment is defended in these terms. We suspect that such pressures create a situation in which the sort of consensus required to underpin a pluralist state is most at risk. John Rawls has called our attention to the 'overlapping consensus' on which a liberal democracy, and indeed, a just society, must depend (Rawls, 1987). If areas that are beyond any consensus obtained by reason are enforced by laws determined by group pressures, then the State is likely to be viewed as an instrument of narrowly sectional interests – whether they be those of religious fundamentalists or radical feminists.

The point comes out even more clearly if we consider an interesting variation of the 'law as education' theme. In response to the claim that the sway of law puts too much coercion into the moral life it may be replied that the educative force of the law lies not (or not so much) in its threat of force, but in the subject's perception that the law embodies a communal wisdom about what is morally right. This interpretation of the theme, in our opinion, puts the best face possible upon it.

Whatever scorn we philosophers heap upon it, the argument from authority does rightly have force, in some contexts, and it is at least an argument, an appeal to reason of sorts, rather than a mere threat. Certainly we rely upon the word of experts and authorities, whose views we are in no position to check, for a great deal of our reasonable beliefs. The idea of a moral expert is, for a variety of reasons, more problematic but it certainly has some place in the education of children and we do not, in any case, intend to dispute its legitimacy here. Nor do we mean to dwell overmuch on the factual question of whether people really conform to the law because of a reasoned regard for authoritative opinion or through fear of sanctions, though there is clearly significant room for disagreement here. Our point is rather that the argument requires that there be available the sort of moral expertise which is precisely lacking in the case of much that is described as child abuse. When there is lacking a rational consensus on the empirical or moral data or even rudimentary agreement on the theoretical framework within which such data can be understood, then the assumption that the law embodies a communal wisdom about morality is unwarranted. As Natalie Abrams points out, if you want to develop a broad definition of child abuse then it will be parasitic upon a normative theory of parenting and, far from commanding general consent, such a theory is hardly in existence. She opts for a wide definition of child abuse in terms of violations of a child's dignity but rejects 'the automatic connection frequently made between definitions of abuse and neglect and grounds for coercive state intervention' (Abrams, 1979:162). Hers is no doubt a tenable theoretical strategy, but we doubt that it makes much practical and political sense given the way 'the automatic connection' she describes has become a cultural reflex. It is surely better to operate with a much narrower concept of 'child abuse' so that the reflex can do less damage.

NOTES

[1] One of us has written of the problems facing flexibilist definitions of violence: C. A. J. Coady (1986). A wide or flexibilist approach to violence often underpins the flexibilist view of child abuse. Consider, for instance, Liz Kelly's view that sexual violence is a continuum which includes a father's being 'very controlling' or criticizing a daughter, or engaging in a variety of unwelcome verbal behaviours (Kelly, 1988:121).

[2] Very young children will need to have these rights as individuals exercised for them by others. On many occasions the best person to exercise these rights on the child's behalf will be a parent, though at other times this will not be so. This difficult issue is discussed by other contributors to this volume.

[3] Article 16 of the Convention states *inter alia* 'No child shall be subjected to arbitrary or unlawful interference with his or her privacy, family, home or correspondence, nor to unlawful attacks on his or her honour and reputation'.

[4] Gutmann (1987:28) usefully distinguishes between three types of political theory about the state and education. Two of these – 'the family state' identified with Plato and 'the state of families' identified with Locke – emphasize the special importance of the family for political theory and the state of families 'places educational authority exclusively in the hands of parents'. By contrast 'the state of individuals' (identified with Mill) is less concessive to parental rights but still cautious about the state's replacement of the family as an educative force.

[5] This point has been eloquently argued by classical liberals such as Humboldt, Green and Mill. It has been criticized by Mabbott (1967) and McCloskey (1973).

[6] In recent writings a contrast is often made between *Gemeinschaft* and *Gesellschaft*. O'Hagan (1984), for example, characterizes the distinction in the following way. *Gemeinschaft* refers to a form of social organization which emphasizes communalism and in which law is designed to be an instrument of moral education. *Gesellschaft* on the other hand describes a society of free and equal human beings who contract to live together in peace, a society in which there is a strict separation between law and morality. O'Hagan makes extensive use of Tonnies' descriptions of *Gemeinschaft* and *Gesellschaft*.

[7] See Aristotle, *Nicomachean Ethics* Bk II, Ch 4, where it is argued that merely doing acts that are called virtuous is not enough to make an agent virtuous because the agent must know what he is doing, must choose the acts 'for their own sakes' and must act from 'a firm and unchangeable character' (1105a22–1105b12).

[8] The experimental evidence indicates that techniques such as explanation of the consequences for the victim of a child's injurious behaviour, statements of moral principle and the like produced significantly higher 'reparation scores' than techniques like physical chastisement. In the jargon of psychology, 'reparation' covers reactions aimed at showing sorrow or regret or at comforting the victim. The children involved in the study were aged between $1\frac{1}{2}$ and $2\frac{1}{2}$. See Zahn-Waxler, Radke-Yarrow, King (1979).

[9] For a version of the 'punishment as moral education' thesis, see Hampton (1984).

THE LIMITS OF THE PUBLIC/PRIVATE DICHOTOMY: A COMMENT ON COADY & COADY

BETTINA CASS*

1 INTRODUCTION: THE CONVENTION ON THE RIGHTS OF THE CHILD

The preamble of the Convention on the Rights of the Child extrapolates from the basic principles of earlier United Nations Declarations and reaffirms the fact that children, because of their vulnerability, need special care and protection. It goes on to emphasize the caring and protective responsibility of the family 'as the fundamental group of society and the natural environment for the growth and well-being of all its members and particularly its children'.

But it does not succumb to a romantic, conservative fallacy about the goodwill of all families, declaring that the 'best of the interests of the child' must prevail and that, in the event that parents and guardians fail to provide adequate protection and care as is necessary for the child's well-being, it is the responsibility of States to provide that care (Part I, Article 3). The Convention goes further to stipulate some of the conditions under which direct state intervention to protect the 'best interests of the child' is warranted; namely, in cases involving 'abuse or neglect of the child by parents'. Given that the primary responsibility of States is to ensure that a child not be separated from his or her parents against their will, the exception to this must occur only when 'competent authorities subject to judicial review determine, in accordance with applicable law and procedures' that such an act is necessary for the best interests of the child (Part I, Article 9). The Convention goes on explicitly to stipulate the legal and public policy measures necessary to provide such protection against maltreatment by parents or guardians:

States Parties shall take all appropriate legislative, administrative, social and educational measures to protect the child from all forms of physical or mental violence, injury or abuse, neglect or negligent treatment, maltreatment or exploitation, including sexual abuse, when in the care of parent(s), legal guardian(s) or any other person who has the care of the child (Part I, Article 19 (I)).

* Bettina Cass, Department of Social Work and Social Policy, University of Sydney, Sydney NSW 2006 Australia.

In addition, States are charged with the responsibility to establish appropriate social programs for the prevention of abuse and the treatment of victims.

There are interesting matters of the principle of 'subsidiarity' operating here: a supranational body (the United Nations) is indicating to signatory nation states the various responsibilities of families and State authorities in relation to the protection of the physical and psychological well-being of children; charging families with major responsibility but then indicating that the principle of the 'best interests of the child' must prevail against the interests of parents where practices are doing manifest harm to children as defined by each State's law and procedure. Of course it is the latter point which is contentious: raising the necessity to scrutinize those laws and their implementation in any jurisdiction which stipulate the conditions under which and the manner in which officials may intervene in family relationships to remove or otherwise protect children against the actions or neglect of their parents (or guardians).

In this regard, the history of Australian State and Territory authorities removing Aboriginal children from their parents on the grounds of the 'interests of the moral and physical welfare of the child' is too recent and too terrible (the NSW Aborigines Welfare Board which administered a separate system of welfare for Aboriginal children having been abolished only in 1969), to engender complacency (Chisholm, 1985).

It is clear that the alleged dichotomy between private and public, between the privacy of the family and the public domain of the state and its instrumentalities, is challenged fundamentally when the principle of 'protecting the best interests of the child' is interposed between these two apparent polarities. In Australia it was part of child welfare orthodoxy that whereas Aboriginal children might be the object of state intervention to protect their welfare (ie, to protect them from the identity of Aboriginality), and that the children of the poor and 'unworthy' mothers might require protection from their class heritage, the dominant consideration, in all *other* cases, was the protection of family privacy and autonomy (Wilkinson, 1986).

One of the possible interpretations of the Convention, and no doubt one of the reasons why it has incurred the displeasure of political conservatives, is its fundamental questioning of the family/state dichotomy: it is the role of families to nurture, care for and protect children, and the role of States to provide adequate resources and services (education, health care, childcare, family income) to enable them to do so; it is the role of States to structure their laws in relation to adoption, the protection of children's identity, the protection of family and children's free movement, the rights of children *vis-à-vis* both parents and their joint responsibilities to them. In other words, there is recognition here that family responsibilities and therefore the context of childhood itself, is constituted (at least partially) by state law and practice (which are of course culturally and historically specific). Universally applicable tenets are enumerated with the purpose of strengthening the authority and resolve of governments to bias their laws in favour of the rights of children in families and institutions: not because these units are currently free of or outside of the public domain, but because they are already constituted by it, in ways which may not be conducive to the protection and well-being of children. The implication is that the constitution of family life in signatory States may, in fact, not be conducive to the best interests of children in all circumstances, and that parents are not the best and final arbiters of what constitutes the best interests of their children: an implication which places upon governments the proper role of child protection in the first instance, not merely the last instance. In an extraordinary way, this brings into families of all classes, the respectable working class, the advantaged and the elite along with the poor and the disadvantaged, the possibility of state intervention in respect of children, so as to protect their interests in ways which are prescribed and enforced by governments, legislation and courts: a set of practices to which poor families and subordinate racial groups have long been subject.

What the Convention does is firstly to question the public/private dichotomy; secondly, and even more fundamentally, to disaggregate the rights of children from the rights of 'families', to constitute children as independent actors with rights *vis-à-vis* their parents and *vis-à-vis* the state. In this way, the rights of parents to deal with their children as they define permissible and desirable are constrained and circumscribed. And this disaggregation entails another implicit individualization of interests: the disaggregation of the rights of parents: women's interests from men's interests. No wonder the Convention is contentious, when the very crux of the conservative ideology of family as unified, private and inviolate is exposed.

It is in the writing of feminist lawyers, sociologists and philosophers that the notion of family/state impermeability and family as the site of a unity of interests has been most ably exposed (Land, 1979; Pateman, 1989; Graycar, 1990). The thrust of this literature is *not* to deny the value of a sphere of private and intimate life beyond the monetized relations of the market or the bureaucratic rationality of the modern state, but to note the many ways in which 'private life' is constituted by market and state power. The power relations of intimate life cannot be understood without reference to the relative position of men and women, adults and children in the labour market, or without reference to the laws regulating marriage, divorce, child protection, domestic violence. It is not the 'right to privacy' which might be expected in democratic theory which is questioned in this literature, but the so-called 'right to privacy' which is no more than a protection of patriarchal rights to maintain relations of inequality and dominance under the guise of family inviolability. The challenging of the public/private dichotomy is a challenge to the market processes and legal systems which construct gender and age vulnerabilities, and then fail to provide protection or redress.

2 MARGARET COADY AND C. A. J. COADY 'THERE OUGHT TO BE A LAW AGAINST IT: REFLECTIONS ON CHILD ABUSE, MORALITY AND LAW' — A COMMENT

In this section, I turn to an examination of Coady and Coady's paper, as an interesting example of a contribution to the family/state debate where the boundaries between the two are seen as ideally relatively impermeable, or at least, where the moral preference lies with a shoring up of the boundaries to protect family life from unnecessary interventions.

The paper is proposed as a 'cool appraisal' of child abuse as definition and policy, but it is from the outset steeped in its own ideological stance. A social theorist concerned with the ethics of discourse in social policy writing cannot object to a paper which is deeply infused with ideological values, but she must be wary when the paper purports to be ideologically neutral. The authors are concerned with the autonomy of the family as a sphere into which 'the State should intervene coercively only with the greatest reluctance'. The paper addresses the legal and social policy treatment of child abuse and particularly the official definition of what constitutes 'abuse'. The authors adopt the word 'flexibilism' to denote an officially sanctioned or imposed elasticity of definition, such that a continuum of behaviours and practices is encapsulated within the definition and given similar legal and social policy treatment. Flexibilism is used also to denote the construction of moral and political concepts, in this case 'abuse', where the concept allows for elasticity, ie, an inclusivity rather than an exclusivity of what constitutes abuse.

This concept of flexibilism is then subjected by the authors to an example of definitional elasticity. In taking to task the definition of sexual abuse adopted by a Research Report commissioned by the Victorian Law Reform Commission which defines sexual abuse as referring to 'a variety of behaviours ranging from exhibitionism to intercourse, from intimate kissing and cuddling to penetration with an object', the authors state (without any supporting evidence) that ten-year-olds are likely to be at worst 'a bit alarmed', but not harmed, by a street encounter with a 'flasher'. There is a trivialization of the meanings of abuse to which the authors are party in this example, as alarming for informed discussion as the alleged flexibilism of the report which is under scrutiny. What evidence is there that public exhibitionism causes no harm?

Certainly, it could be argued, and with conviction, that the intimacy

of family and kin relationships in which most child abuse occurs constitutes an additional invasion into the child's right to be protected from
harm in the environment socially constructed as 'safe', and that exhibitionism in this context would therefore probably cause more harm than
'public exhibitionism'. This is an hypothesis which needs exploration –
but the authors do not raise this question.

The nub of the paper's philosophical position lies in its view that not
all forms of violence within families are defined as the business of the law
or the state because of: 'the recognition of the social value of there being
spheres of life in which the State intervenes coercively only with the
greatest reluctance. The family is pre-eminently such a sphere.' The
paper takes the view that the family is a social sphere in which the
boundaries between its practices and that of the state is, and should
remain, relatively impermeable, unless it can be shown that great harm
is being done in a continuous way to certain family members. The
critique to be made of this position includes the following set of
observations.

The family is already legally constituted to enforce the authority of
parents; economically constituted to enforce the power of primary
breadwinners over those who are dependent, or who earn less; politically
constituted to ensure that democratic rights are practised only by adults.
Indeed to speak of *coercive interventions* by the State in the context of child
protection is to engage in a process of flexibilism: if the object of state
intervention is to protect children from harm, then coercion has already
been perpetrated, *not* by the State, but by the adult perpetrator of physical or sexual abuse.

The authors condone fully interventions into family life which are
consistent with the paradigms of 'battered infants' and the 'raped
daughter', which are designated as the sorts of immoralities that ought
to be the concern of the law (in any theory – liberal, conservative,
socialist, feminist). But they are concerned that the concept has been
extended to include quite different 'immoralities' which, as far as the
authors are concerned, are much more problematic, because the
evidence of harm is much less.

As with sexual abuse, where the definition held up to scorn involved
public exhibitionism; the example given to criticize the wider usage of
physical abuse is also one taken from public rather than family life: the
US Child Abuse Prevention and Treatment Act which brings within its
ambit the actions of physicians in relation to limiting the intensive care
of newborn children with life-threatening handicaps. We are dealing
here with examples which do not allow for a full description and analysis
of the types of behaviour (physical violence, sexual abuse, psychological
abuse) which may inflict a variety of harms on children in a variety of
settings. In addition, each example is derived from public or relatively
public settings, while the intent of the paper is to argue that the 'family'

is a privileged sphere, in which legal definitions of child abuse should take special care not to proscribe practices which may cause little or no harm to children, and where family autonomy should be protected.

The authors are particularly concerned about the extension of the definition of abuse to include the incompetence of caregivers, and the ways in which this may legitimize welfare workers' interventions. They imply that the definition of what is immoral necessarily involves a definition of the moral, which they hold should include a 'care focus', particularly in respect of the intimate relations of family life and the upbringing of children. They note that various laws, like the Swedish law against corporal punishment, might undermine the overlapping consensus of liberal democracy. John Rawls is invoked to suggest that the law against corporal punishment is one which might place at risk the consensus required to underpin a pluralist state.

If areas that are beyond any consensus obtained by reason, are enforced by laws determined by pressure groups then the State is likely to be viewed as an instrument of narrowly sectional interests – whether they be those of religious fundamentalists or radical feminists. (Coady & Coady, 1992)

This is the nub of the argument: if there are no laws proscribing corporal punishment of children, are we to believe that the State's condoning of such practices reflects the capture of the State by the narrow sectional interests of some school masters and some parents – to the exclusion of the interests of all children and all parents who do not use or condone the use of corporal punishment? Which sectional interests can we presume to be using the State as its instrument when a set of practices which clearly discriminates against children is defined as part of an 'overlapping consensus'? Overlapping consensuses do not, presumably, need to be traced back to their holders; only those views traceable to distinct social movements which appear to violate liberal or conservative orthodoxies. Indeed, one could use John Rawls' theory of justice to mount a very plausible case against corporal punishment as undermining the conditions of a just society. After all, if the 'veil of ignorance' were applied we might wish to devise a just society as if our own place in it were as young people in schools, where corporal punishment might be regularly used or as young people in households where parents or guardians hold that flogging instils moral behaviour. The exercise of the 'difference principle' invoked by Rawls would then lead to the formulation of laws which discriminate in favour of the need of the least socially and economically advantaged, indeed of the most vulnerable. In this case, I would judge that laws against corporal punishment might easily be seen as upholding the overlapping consensus of a just liberal democracy (Rawls, 1972).

Coady and Coady subject the efficacy of physical coercion of children as a tool in moral education to some, albeit limited, scrutiny. They conclude that 'coercion is a second-best, and, as such, no more than a supplement to reason and example in moral education'. A rigorous use of Rawlsian reasoning would require a thorough-going questioning of the notion 'second-best'. The physical coercion of children, ie the infliction of physical harm, is better viewed as the *antithesis* of reason in moral education, indeed, as the exercise of an 'example' which is directly contrary to reason. If the intention of the reasoning is to instil the conviction that 'might is right', then coercion and reason would be supplementary, indeed complementary. But if adult/child relations are to be premised on the 'overlapping consensuses' of a liberal democracy concerned with justice, then the interests of children to be educated morally without fear of the infliction of violence require strong legal protections.

In their conclusion the authors argue that only a narrow concept of child abuse is warranted, so that the automatic connections made between the definition and the sphere of 'coercive state interventions' is also strictly limited, so as to do least damage. The problem with this conclusion is the authors' view that state intervention is 'coercive', not the behaviours and practices which invoked the actions of the state. Nowhere is the idea of state intervention as 'protective' of children's interests invoked. Indeed, if the analysis of what constitutes child abuse were to *begin* with a disaggregation of family members' interests and focus on the rights and needs of children for a nurturing and safe environment, then the definition could proceed to be as *inclusive* as required to protect the child's physical and emotional well-being, and each addition of a range of damaging behaviours could be made, based on the 'duty of care' which is the essence of adults' responsibility to children.

Finally, a brief word about the authors' critique of the view that laws which intervene in the realm of morality cannot be educative, or at least, that this is no defence of the worth of a law, and no justification for a law's existence. It is not considered problematic in the 'central cases of child abuse' that laws should declare publicly that certain behaviours are considered both morally and legally wrong, and subject to strong sanction. However, it is held that there are more controversial areas in which the wrong being done is less easy to demonstrate and the exercise of legal enactment might endanger 'moral insight and understanding'. Here the example used is the Swedish law against corporal punishment, discussed earlier.

More pertinent would have been an example of what aspects of, say, sexual practices within the family the authors might hold not to be a proper area for legal enactment within the rubric of abuse. It would appear that it is precisely in this area that arguments about 'law as educative' are most persuasive in indicating to a range of formal and informal networks that certain behaviours are damaging to children's welfare, and that there are overlapping consensuses in a liberal democracy which hold that to be the case. Under these conditions, what might otherwise appear to be moral ambiguities are at least resolvable at one level – the level of legal enactment – and a culturally and ethnically diverse society is able to set about the debates required to ensure that people are properly informed, that the formal legal and informal practices and policies required to protect children's welfare are widely understood and properly debated. The penalties and remedies to be arrived at are another matter, but to hesitate to intervene in family practices so as to maintain family autonomy, unless the demonstration of harm to children is one of the 'exemplary' cases, may be to protect the perpetrators to the considerable harm of the victims.

A child-centred focus on the subject of abuse would need to start with very different questions:

What legal formulations and sanctions are required to ensure that children, whose economic and social vulnerability give them few, if any individual resources, are enabled to live and develop within the family and other social institutions without the infliction or fear of infliction of physical and emotional harm?

How can laws serve an educative and preventative purpose in informing the key social actors, and children themselves, about their rights to protection?

How can legal protections, sanctions and other social policy remedies redress the clear power imbalance between children and those adults who hold the 'duty-of-care'?

A moral position based on the 'duty-of-care' would need to begin with a profound scepticism about the dichotomy of the public and the private and go on to disaggregate the interests and rights of family members, in this case, the rights of children *vis-à-vis* their parents, and the rights of children *vis-à-vis* the state.

CHILD SUPPORT: RIGHTS AND CONSEQUENCES

STEPHEN PARKER*

ABSTRACT

This paper is a preliminary attempt to construct a theory of children's rights which could plausibly be adopted by interpreters of the United Nations Convention on the Rights of the Child. It takes child support as a test case and, by way of example only, looks at the recent Child Support Scheme in Australia. The theory put forward in the paper is a consequentialist one with the goal of maximizing welfare. Specifically, it encompasses the welfare value of a community of people who have not been let down by adults in the past ('the good of non-betrayal'). It differs from most recent theorizing about children's rights which proceeds from *a priori* concerns with liberty, autonomy or respect. Whilst similar conclusions on many matters might be reached on either approach, one advantage of a consequentialist theory (it is argued) is that it lends itself readily to a transformative political strategy.

INTRODUCTION

Article 27(4) of the *United Nations Convention on the Rights of the Child* ('the Convention') provides that States Parties shall take 'all appropriate measures' to secure the recovery of maintenance for the child from her or his parents, both within the State Party and from abroad. Article 27(1) requires that States Parties recognize the right of every child to a standard of living adequate for the child's physical, mental, spiritual, moral and social development. Article 26(1) recognizes, in terms, the right of the child to benefit from social security, although paragraph (2) acknowledges that the provision of social security benefits should take into account the resources and the circumstances of the child and persons having responsibility for the maintenance of the child.

* Faculty of Law, The Australian National University, GPO Box 4, Canberra, Australia 2601. I would like to thank Lisa Wright for her research assistance and the Faculty of Law, ANU which paid for it. I am also indebted to Professor Rebecca Bailey-Harris and to the other contributors to this volume for their comments on the original paper from which this is drawn. If those comments have not all been taken on board then that probably represents a victory for stubbornness over prudence.

THE AUSTRALIAN CHILD SUPPORT SCHEME

Australia, which has now ratified the Convention, introduced a Child Support Scheme ('the Scheme') in 1988–9. Leaving aside the maintenance of children whose parents live in different States Parties, the Scheme seems to deal with all the matters covered in the above-mentioned Articles. It is designed to secure the recovery of maintenance from parents; it is designed to improve the standard of living of a class of children; and it is designed to make social security provision subject to a prior obligation owed by parents.

Space does not permit a full description of the Scheme and the events leading to its establishment.[1] Certain points need to be made at this stage, however, so that the later discussion on rights to child support is more easily understood.

The old system of court-ordered child maintenance in Australia came under increasing scrutiny as the public expenditure costs of sole parent families were appreciated. Coupled with growing awareness of the economic consequences of divorce on women and children, this appreciation led to moves to take child support assessment out of the hands of judges and practitioners and put it in the hands of public servants who would administer a formula.

A Child Support Agency was established within the Australian Taxation Office and, since 1st October 1989, the Agency has been applying a resource-sharing formula. It assesses child support levels, collects the money (normally by deduction from the liable parent's wages or salary alongside Pay As You Earn Income Tax) and pays it into a Child Support Trust Account. The money is withdrawn by the Department of Social Security and passed on to the custodian. Whilst doing so, the Department can adjust any sole parent's pension also being paid to the custodian by applying new, more precise, means tests.

Social security saving is the sub-text for all of the Scheme. By taking more money from liable parents and by channelling it through the Department of Social Security, the old priorities are reversed. In the past, in practice, social security was often the primary source of support for sole parents. Now, social security is supposed only to top maintenance up. In effect, the financial relationship between the state, men, women and children after relationship breakdown has been altered.

The basic formula under which child support is calculated was devised by reference to the limited information that existed about the proportion of income devoted to children in families on different income levels. In essence, the absent parent's taxable income is identified, an amount is notionally taken out in respect of his commitments for self-support and new children, and then the balance is subjected to a percentage depending on the number of children for whom child support is being calculated. The product is the child support that he must pay. The self-support allowances are pegged at social security rates and the table of percentages will produce considerably higher amounts of periodic child support than was usually paid under the old regime.

The upshot is that, unless the Scheme is subverted,[2] it will do more good for children than the old system. The extent of that good depends partly on the operation of social security rules and partly upon parental circumstances.

No custodial parent is directly compelled to apply for an assessment of child support. If, however, the custodian is claiming social security then it is a precondition of entitlement that she takes reasonable action to claim maintenance. In practical terms, most sole parents will be claiming pension and, subject to some administrative rules defining when it is not reasonable to take maintenance action, if they want pension they will have to apply for an assessment of child support. It follows that a custodial parent *not* claiming social security need not apply for child support and she can make a private agreement with the other parent (as in the old days).

Opting out can take other forms. In particular, parents can register a 'Child Support Agreement' with the agency and provide for a different figure from that which the formula would produce. They can also provide that a different form of wealth transfer (such as a lump sum or share in the home) be substituted for the formula amount. Again, the control is social security. The rules are complex but their thrust is that opting out is largely curtailed if it leads to more social security being paid. Acting as a kind of backstop, the Family Court has jurisdiction to depart from the formula in special circumstances or to order other wealth transfers in substitution or in addition.

Work incentives for liable parents and custodians were also a consideration in the design of the Scheme. The self-support component and the level of percentages were fixed, in part, so that liable parents do not pay a real rate of marginal tax and other deductions which inhibit work efforts. Custodians can earn up to Average Weekly Earnings before their child support is affected. Very few custodians will earn over this amount (probably less than 10 per cent) and so most custodians can work, all other circumstances permitting, and their earnings will not affect their child support. Their earnings may well reduce any sole parent's pension also being claimed, however, and this again was part of the design.

WHY A THEORY OF CHILDREN'S RIGHTS IS NEEDED

The purpose of this paper is not directly to ask what might be thought the obvious question: does the Scheme comply with the Convention? The provisions of the Convention, when taken on their face, are sufficiently indeterminate that they could be held satisfied by a wide range of systems producing higher or lower amounts of maintenance. In the event of Australia being challenged, any decision-maker would have to (or at least ought to) import a more specific set of requirements into the Convention, a theory if you like, and then test the Scheme against it. There is no obvious way of predicting what that theory would be and so any answer to the obvious question of whether the Scheme complies with the Convention is inevitably: it all depends.

Instead, the paper asks a more limited and preliminary question: What is involved in constructing a theory of children's rights capable of importation into the Convention? I attempt to answer that question by developing my own theory and I do so by reference to the Child Support Scheme. To be clear, I am not predicting that a decision-maker *would* adopt this theory. It is inconceivable that she would go through the argumentative steps of the paper. Nevertheless, some kind of goal-based or programmatic approach is imaginable and the task of the paper is to clear away some obstacles and suggest some directions.

The exercise, then, is a normative analysis with a practical purpose. It puts forward tentatively a theory of children's rights as a contribution to the debate about how to interpret and apply the Convention. It is a first-order exercise on which further work needs to be done. If, however, it is a theory with holes, that is at least one characteristic it shares with other theories of children's rights.

THE MOTIVE BEHIND THE THEORY PRESENTED HERE

It will be seen later that the theory presented in this paper is a consequentialist, or exclusively goal-based, one. It is possible that the component parts could be taken out of their consequentialist housing and placed within a different set of principles. Despite the reservations of some contributors to this volume, I have persevered with the development of a consequentialist theory of children's rights, not simply for the challenge, but also to provide a contrast with what seems to be the emerging dominance of Kantian and other deontological principles in policy debates about children. In particular, it provides a contrast with the contributions by Michael Freeman, Onora ONeill and John Eekelaar in this volume, although it is possibly more congenial to that of Tom Campbell.

THE STRUCTURE OF THE PAPER

I begin by discussing theories of children's rights through looking at the way that rights theories generally may be categorized. This is followed by a discussion of consequentialism and an argument that there is a place for rights within a consequentialist framework. The theory of the paper is then presented and put into operation by reference to the interest of a child in being financially supported after parental separation. The final substantive section of the paper looks specifically at the Australian Child Support Scheme.

The function that the Scheme has in the paper needs to be made explicit. It is there to make the children's rights theory more concrete, to show its potential uses and its weaknesses. Although towards the end of the paper I discuss briefly whether the Scheme does satisfy the theory, even if the answer I give is shown to be misguided that would not of itself make the exercise pointless. My intention is to use the Scheme to help evaluate the theory, not to use the theory to evaluate the Scheme.

It is assumed throughout that the subjects are infant children, so that no question arises about their capacity to make relevant decisions. This is the approach which tests a children's rights theory to its extremes.

THEORIES OF CHILDREN'S RIGHTS

Because the children's rights theory put forward here differs in a fundamental respect from those of other contributors to this volume – namely in its consequentialism – it may help if I situate it within rights theories generally. If nothing else, this should help the reader identify more readily my lapses into error.

It seems that some disagreements in rights debates cannot be rationally resolved. This irreconcilability has become apparent as the participants have paid more attention to the deeper theories, or foundation principles, on which their positions rest. Jeremy Waldron (1984:3) has argued that if two theories of rights rest on opposing commitments, for example one to liberty and the other to substantive equality, then these differences will manifest themselves in discussion about rights.[3]

Assuming, as I do, that Waldron is correct, there is no possibility of a single paper dealing adequately with the whole range of competing positions because it is impossible to debate fully the relative merits of their foundation principles. A large measure of assertion is required in order to proceed. The limited purpose of the discussion immediately below is to lay out some of the alternatives in a way which gives context and shape to the position I am taking.

CATEGORIZING RIGHTS THEORIES

One way of categorizing rights theories is by reference to which one or more of three aspects they focus upon (Martin and Nickel, 1980):
(i)   the normative elements which constitute a right;
(ii)   the function which a right serves; and
(iii)   the justification for saying that a right does or should exist.

The *normative elements* (as in (i) above) which are most commonly put forward are duties, claims, liberties, powers and immunities. The older view that a right has a duty as its exclusive correlative, so that rights and duties are but two sides of the same coin, was shown to be inadequate by the more complex scheme made famous by Hohfeld. His taxonomy of rights as claims, liberties, powers and immunities has been more appealing because its set of correlatives connect more realistically with the differing situations of *non*-rightholders. So, for example, whilst a claim-right gives rise to a duty in another, a power-right does not give rise to one in such a direct sense, except perhaps the duty to acquiesce in the exercise of the power.

For the purposes of the present paper, this does not need to be taken further because child support rights under my adoptive theory will take the form of claim-rights. That is, a child will have a right to the payment of money, or its equivalent, and a specific person or agency will have a duty to pay it. (The question of how an infant child can be said to have a claim is one which is returned to below.) A fully developed theory of children's rights would obviously have to account for more than child support interests. It would need to deal, inter alia, with the child's interests in being nurtured and in having her or his choices considered carefully. It may well be that a fully developed theory will be constituted by a *cluster* of normative elements, of which claims and duties are only two. Although I do not have to consider that here, such a theory seems attractive in principle (Wellman, 1982:14; Sumner, 1987:45).

The *function* that a right serves (as in (ii) above) is usually debated within a dichotomy of will and interest theories. (The labels differ and there are derivatives of each, but this simple presentation suffices here.) The will theory argues that rights confer powers upon people to require that their will or choice should hold sway. It is this function that distinguishes rights from desires, needs, merits and so on. The interest theory, by contrast, holds that the function of a right is to protect or further the rightholder's *interests* (Campbell, 1983:92; Sumner, 1987:45).

A common objection to the will theory, and one which is directly relevant to present concerns, is that it seems incapable of including young children and others who lack the capacity to make choices. This objection is explicitly conceded by will theorists who argue that whilst young children cannot have rights they do nevertheless have moral standing sufficient to give rise to duties in others.[4] The virtue of the interest theory, its advocates claim, is that it can incorporate children directly. Whilst it is said there may be substantial overlap between the two theories when it comes to most adults (because they have an interest in their choices being respected) the two theories diverge over young children.

Rights theories can also be categorized by reference to their justificatory basis, or *foundation principles* (as in (iii) above). Appeals to liberty, autonomy, utility or welfare seem to feature in various forms as justifications or foundations for rights, whether moral or positive.[5]

THE THEORY DESCRIBED

Against that rather swashbuckling account of how competing rights theories might be categorized, this is the theory of children's rights which the paper seeks to construct and defend. It can be described as a restrictive consequentialist interest theory, the goal of which is the maximization of welfare. I will work through its elements by following (i), (ii) and (iii) above and then seek to defend its major features.

A children's rights theory must be able to include, whatever other normative elements it may include, claims which impose a duty upon another. An immediate rejoinder is that young children are in no position to 'make' claims. My presentation of the interests theory acknowledges, however, that rights are *ascribed* to people by human practice. It does not presuppose that there is anything intrinsic to human beings which through the application of reason leads inevitably to a conclusion that they have rights. If the whole theory falls, then this part may go with it. Until then, there is nothing objectionable in ascribing a claim to someone, in saying that they *have* a claim, even if they cannot personally pursue it. This deals with (i) above.

The function of children's rights is to protect the interests of children. I will shortly expand on this when I turn to the kind of interest that child support legislation must protect in order to comply with my theory ('the normal case interest') but this deals, provisionally at least, with (ii) above.

The justificatory basis, as in (iii) above, which requires us to respect children's claims to have certain interests protected as rights is a consequentialist one, the goal of which is the maximization of welfare. It is commonly supposed that consequentialists cannot take rights seriously. Indeed, this is sometimes put forward as the principal objection to the most celebrated form of consequentialism, classical utilitarianism. Because of this, a little time must be spent arguing that a restrictive form of consequentialism does have a place for rights.

CONSEQUENTIALISM

Consequentialism in its broadest conception is the view that the ultimate, foundational criterion of the rightness of actions refers to consequences (Johnson, 1991). A theory is therefore consequentialist only if it appraises actions in terms of the value of their consequences (Sumner, 1987:165). Consequentialists are also committed to the pursuit of some synoptic or global goal. Their moral framework is therefore not merely good-based but *goal*-based also.

Non-consequentialist theories, often described loosely as deontological theories, differ in at least one fundamental respect from consequentialist ones. There are always possible occasions when the right thing to do is not the good thing to do. Thus, one can be under a moral duty to do something, in particular to respect a person's rights, even if to do otherwise on a particular occasion would produce more good.[6] To some non-consequentialists, the principle of producing good or preventing evil, no matter how these terms are defined, is not a moral criterion or standard at all. To others it is simply not the *only* basic or ultimate one (Houlgate, 1988:11).

It is standardly thought that a consequentialist cannot be committed to the idea of moral rights. Ultimately, it is said, he or she must always preserve the option of doing what has the most desirable consequences in terms of the goal. In contrast, a non-consequentialist may say that, regardless of the consequences, one should respect another's moral rights or perform one's own moral duty.

The most common set of consequentialist theories are utilitarian ones. Although there is a confusing range of utilitarian theories, some stand out quite clearly. Classical utilitarianism in the tradition of Jeremy Bentham holds that good is pleasure and evil is pain or misery. The right thing to do is that which maximizes net pleasure. But the goal of utilitarianism need not be expressed in terms of hedonism. One might replace hedonism with the notion of preference satisfaction so that, for example, self sacrifice or altruism can be added to pleasure (Goodin, 1991:243).

Whilst hedonistic and preference utilitarianism might seem to focus on short-sighted concerns from the individual's point of view, *welfare* utilitarianism suppresses short-term interests in favour of protecting people's long-term welfare interests from a non-agent relative point of view. To Goodin:

Welfare interests consist just in that set of generalized resources that will be necessary for people to have before pursuing any of the more particular preferences that they might happen to have. Health, money, shelter, sustenance and such like are all demonstrably welfare interests of this sort, useful resources whatever people's particular projects and plans. (Goodin, 1991:244).

Utilitarianism is generally aligned with liberal political theory, one reason being that the goals which different versions set themselves seem to emphasize individual liberty or some other central liberal value. Liberalism is not a defining feature of consequentialism as such, however. One could, for example, set goals that might be described as feminist or socialist. Certainly, welfare utilitarianism is a common form of consequentialism that can come close to crossing the boundary between liberalism and socialism.

Criticisms of consequentialism are legion and are not rehearsed in detail here.[7] It is common to hear that consequentialism lacks sufficient respect for the difference between persons, or for justice or rights. Doubts are also expressed about the feasibility of formal procedures which appropriately identify, measure and then compare pleasures, preferences, welfare (or whatever).

In the face of these criticisms, modified forms of consequentialism have been put forward. One example is rule utilitarianism under which an act is right if and only if it conforms to the utilitarianly best rules. In other words, rules are placed as intermediate devices so that the agent does not appraise the value of each possible action by direct reference to the goal. Rule utilitarianism has been criticized because, inter alia, it offers no moral ground for complying with the rule when it is clear that breaching it will produce more good. It seems to be a failed attempt to compromise between the intuitive attraction of utilitarianism and the intuitive attraction of respecting rights and enforcing duties because of their intrinsic importance.[8]

A more recent modified form of consequentialism can be called restrictive consequentialism. It is not rule-consequentialism because justification is still sought at the level of acts rather than shifted to the level of rules. It has superficial similarities with rule utilitarianism, however, because it offers a range of arguments for saying that individual acts of calculation should not always be trusted or respected and that other procedures may be needed. The justification for these other procedures is, ultimately, that more good is done this way.

One elaborate argument that more good is done by having procedures in addition to individual acts of calculation is an argument from fallibility. L. W. Sumner's *The Moral Foundation of Rights* is an extended defence of the place of rights within a consequentialist moral theory. The author argues that whilst the direct strategy of evaluating acts by reference to the goal is best for someone 'who is extremely powerful, highly knowledgeable, exceptionally bright, and rigorously impartial' (Sumner, 1987:187), decision-makers in the real world have only limited control over the agenda they are faced with, they have limited information and power, they are idiosyncratic, they have prior commitments and they are subject to pressures. Strategies are required, based on estimates of fallibility, to constrain individual decisions so that the favoured outcome is more likely to be achieved. In the same way that a person who has given up smoking might guard against moments of weakness by asking friends to promise not to offer a cigarette, so too can 'pre-commitments' be instituted in public life.

A different, but complementary, argument for constraints has been put forward by Phillip Pettit in the context of welfare state philosophy (Pettit, 1986). Pettit argues that welfare state philosophy, conventionally concerned only with outcomes, can have a place for rights. An outline of his argument serves the dual function of showing that rights can be respected within a consequentialist framework and also introducing welfare considerations (which are at the heart of the children's rights theory being put forward here).

Pettit argues that a consequentialist cannot take 'fundamental' rights seriously. He is talking about natural rights; that is, rights which (i) do not require social or legal recognition (ii) are universal and (iii) must not be violated if intrinsic wrongness is to be avoided. The consequentialist cannot tolerate fundamental rights because she must always remain free justifiably to infringe them if to do so would maximize probable value; for example by avoiding greater infringements by others of others' rights (Pettit, 1986:72). *Non*-fundamental rights are not, however, always ruled out. It is possible that by instituting non-fundamental rights one can thereby maximize probable value.

At this point, a distinction must be drawn carefully. The consequentialist as a designer of systems (as 'constitution-maker' in Pettit's phrase) always seeks to maximize probable value. At the level of *evaluation*, therefore, she cannot feel bound by rights. At the level of *decision*, however, she may feel that non-fundamental rights lead to the best outcomes. That is, she can bind herself to decide particular questions in accordance with rights, although she reserves the possibility of arguing for change to the system if those decisions no longer produce the goods. The reason for believing that decision-makers can justifiably be bound by rights at the level of decision is because of the essential by-products that rights can have. Where those essential by-products contribute to maximum probable value then a 'constitution' can justifiably enshrine them. Using this argument, Pettit says that a consequentialist can advocate the protection of citizen's claims to welfare in right-form. This is because of the essential by-products of institutional rights. These essential by-products may be described as: the saving of computational time and trouble; the tenure or assurance that rightholders enjoy, the dignity conferred when title to a benefit is a proprietary one; and the avoidance of temptation for claimants to exaggerate their deservingness in the hope that they will maximize their chances in a (non-rights) balancing process.

THE GOOD OF NON-BETRAYAL

The normative children's rights theory presented here works within a restrictive consequentialist framework aimed at welfare outcomes. Considerably more work would need to be done in identifying the component values that make up 'welfare' for the purposes of a fully-fledged children's rights theory. The raw materials of the goal will include, however, things necessary for both individual and collective well-being. It will have a pluralist rather than a monist theory of value.

One item on the inventory – which (at last) takes us nearer to the point of the paper – is the good enjoyed by a community which *justifiably believes that the opportunities in life of all its members have not been impaired by the reasonably avoidable adverse consequences of past adult choices*. This hardly rolls off the tongue and so, for the sake of economy, it can be described as the 'good of non-betrayal'. The description is not entirely apposite because the good is not merely in avoiding the *fact* of non-betrayal but in the individual and collective *knowledge* that betrayal has been avoided. 'Betrayal' is a strong word, and it will be qualified by the later discussion of what impairment is reasonably avoidable, but our growing knowledge of the harm that adults can do to children, intentionally or otherwise, indicates that an arresting term is required. To jump ahead for the purposes of clarity, I will argue that the old child maintenance system did have reasonably avoidable, adverse long-term consequences for children. Early empirical evidence suggests that many children suffer continuing impairment of their life chances as a result of parental separation. The essential by-product of institutionalizing child support rights is the reduction of this impairment. Institutionalizing such rights contributes to the good of non-betrayal.

The foundation principle of the theory does not therefore proclaim nor seek to protect any fundamental right of a child to liberty, autonomy or whatever. Rather, it points to the valuable consequences for us all of promoting children's long-term welfare. By a circuitous route, this has dealt with (ii) above.

My linking together of claims (ie (i)), interests (ie (ii)) and welfare (ie (iii)) is consistent with an argument by Lucy that the interest theory tracks utility/welfare whilst the will theory tracks liberty/autonomy (Lucy, 1990:237). Some writers, such as Eekelaar and Freeman in this volume and MacCormick (1982:ch 8) seem to propose what might be described as a diagonal path. They say that (what sounds like) a non-consequentialist principle justifies the protection of interests. They cut across from a foundation principle like autonomy or liberty to an interest theory of rights rather than a will theory. The diagonal path leaves unanswered the awkward question of how one goes about selecting interests for the special protection that right-hood involves. If it is always up to the individual to assess her or his interests, so that rights are agent-relative, then the individual must be capable of making the choice. That is not open to us if we are dealing with infants. It seems to follow that the promotion of certain interests to the status of right-hood must be based on a process that is not agent-relative; hardly a promising start for a theory based on the autonomy or liberty of agents.

One possibility, advocated in terms by Eekelaar and Freeman (in this volume and elsewhere), is to determine the matter by asking, on the basis of certain assumptions, what the child *would* have chosen had she had the practical autonomy to do so. Stated differently, one engages in substituted judgement by asking what should the child thank you for on reaching the age of autonomy? Although I do not have to decide the matter, because I am only concerned with putting forward a *plausible* theory of children's rights capable of adoption, I suspect this diagonal linking of autonomy and interests confuses the matter unnecessarily.

So far, my approach has been unspecific about distinctions between moral and positive rights. Because the consequentialist rejects the notion of natural (ie 'fundamental') rights, the distinction between moral and positive rights may simply be the extent to which they are institutionalized. Like Campbell (1983:22) I prefer to reserve rights-talk for legal and quasi-legal settings, so that 'moral rights' are better described as *justified demands* for the protection of interests in a law-like manner. Essential to the thesis, however, is the need to keep these reasons for having positive rights always in mind. As we will see, they have a continuing relevance in defining, interpreting and applying positive rights. They do not drop out of the picture once words appear on a statute book or a treaty.

The next task is to show how my theory deals with two related questions:

(i)   What is involved in picking out interests as deserving of promotion to right-hood?; and

(ii) What is involved in protecting them so that they achieve right-hood?

PUTTING A GOAL-BASED INTEREST THEORY INTO OPERATION

To decide how an interest is properly picked out in line with the theory presented here, one must return to the foundation principle. (For obvious reasons, all the examples are drawn from child support circumstances and from here on the baffling strands of the paper may start to come together.) As was foreshadowed, the cluster of welfare values which contribute to the foundation principle for the theory include the good of non-betrayal: that is, the good enjoyed by a community where everyone justifiably believes that their opportunities in life have not been impaired by the reasonably avoidable adverse consequences of past adult choices.

This leads me to frame the child's interest in being supported financially in a manner borrowed from Eekelaar and Maclean (1986), although it operates here in a different context than it does in their thesis. The interest to be protected by the ascription of a right is 'the normal case interest'. Eekelaar and Maclean's proposals for a resource-sharing child support regime include the concept of a 'normative standard' which would operate as an upper limit on maintenance liability. They describe it as:

. . . designed to encompass the principle that, if available resources can prevent it, children should not fall below, or further below than can be avoided, a standard of living enjoyed by most children in their society. The concept goes beyond the ideal of 'belonging' to, or 'participation' in a community which is employed in the poverty literature. The children should not merely be entitled to feel that they are part of the community of intact families, but that they are a *standard case* of that community (Eekelaar & MacLean, 1986:122). (Original emphasis.)

The normal case interest (as I call it) requires an attempt to be made to apply the same amount of resources to the child as would have been applied in an average two-parent family *on these income levels*. The italicized words are important. The normal case interest does not involve comparison with a stereotypical family at large. It requires a comparison with families on similar income levels. As presently stated, the normal case interest therefore works within, and does not challenge, unequal distribution of wealth and advantage between social classes and the sexes. There is no reason in principle, however, why the consequentialist approach should not include redistributive values, from which different formulations of interests could be derived, so that the status quo *is* challenged.

What grounds are there for saying that a foundation principle of welfare justifies protection of the normal case interest in the urgent and peremptory manner characteristic of a right? The makings of an answer can be found in recent research, the early findings of which have begun to paint an alarming picture of the long-term consequences to children of parental separation. Some of the findings about the consequences for men[9] were described by MacLean and Wadsworth (1988).[10] The findings go beyond the immediate or short-term financial and emotional consequences of relationship breakdown, devastating though they may be.[11] They relate to the life chances of children many years after separation. Space does not allow them to be described in any detail and so this account is much abbreviated.

The UK Medical Research Council's *National Survey of Health and Development* is a follow-up study of approximately one-third of all children born in Britain in one week in March 1946. The sample is stratified for social class. The most recent contact with that sample was at the age of thirty-six, when the numbers had been depleted from 5,362 to 3,996. In conjunction with earlier follow-up studies, it is possible to compare the children whose parents had separated with those whose parents had not. We are also now sufficiently advanced in time to begin tracing the consequences into the next generation because people born in 1946 are themselves within the active period of family formation and dissolution. By the age of thirty-six years, the men from 'divorced homes' were proportionately more likely to be unemployed. One paragraph from Maclean and Wadsworth gives an indication of what this meant:

Amongst the population of those unemployed and seeking work parental divorce may present the beginning point in a chain of vulnerability in which poor educational attainment, and in 17 per cent of the men, chronic illness in adult life, had the cumulative effect of making them insecure and irregular workers at the lowest end of the employment spectrum. Since, in comparison with the population of employed men, they were also more likely to be single (32 per cent of this unemployed group as compared with 7 per cent of employed men) or divorced (24.5 per cent of this group as compared with 13 per cent of the employed) rather than married (38 per cent of this group compared with 80 per cent of the employed) they were also likely to be relatively short of the kind of support that marriage can provide. One man described his circumstances as '. . . not feeling as if you were part of society' (Maclean & Wadsworth, 1988:162–3).

As for income, this was still significantly low at thirty-six amongst men who had had childhood experience of parental loss. Low income was connected with relatively low educational attainment, itself positively correlated with parental divorce.[12]

It is not my purpose here to evaluate these findings in methodological terms, assuming I were capable of it, nor to deal with questions of cultural and temporal specificity which they undoubtedly raise. All that can be done is to assert the existence of evidence, which if it continues to sustain conclusions like these, will amount to a powerful resource on which a consequentialist theory based in welfare can draw.

Maclean and Wadsworth in the conclusion to their article speculate on some directions which should be considered in the light of these findings. One passage is particularly relevant:

Clearly private law cannot create resources to help this group; but family law can consider the ways of assessing and enforcing child support, the question of equity between children of the same parent in different households, and even the possibility of compensating children for the consequences of their parents' decisions (Maclean & Wadsworth, 1988:164).

To be clear, I do not claim that the evidence of long term impact of parental separation necessarily entails my particular definition of the affected child's interest (ie the normal case interest). In fact, I claim only that that interest is one, and perhaps the minimum one, which the theory requires to be protected by reference to that evidence. Needless to say, protecting the normal case interest in child support could not, of itself, *eliminate* the impairment of life chances, but the consequentialist is concerned with doing something about it.

A recapitulation of the argument so far may help the reader to rejoin the ship. The children's rights theory put forward here holds that children may be ascribed claims to have certain interests specially protected by institutional rights. It is a consequentialist theory concerned with welfare outcomes. These welfare outcomes await fuller development but they involve, at the least, value being attached to the good of non-betrayal. This is the good enjoyed by a community which justifiably believes that the opportunities in life of all its members have not been impaired by the reasonably avoidable adverse consequences of past adult choices. On the breakdown of a relationship adults make choices, whether they are litigants, legal practitioners or judges. To reduce the reasonably avoidable adverse consequences of these choices for children, the normal case interest should be protected in right-form at the level of decision-making.

Assume, for the purposes of making progress, that the argument is persuasive. How should the normal case interest be protected? A list of formal standards for the promotion of an interest to that of a right is important to the theory. In one way or another, the list is designed to prevent back-sliding. It is designed to reduce the consequentialist temptation to revert to mere goal-rights at the level of decision (Scheffler, 1988:199). Goal-rights are 'tradeable across persons', unlike strict rights. They can be infringed if this reduces the violation of others' rights by others. They tend also to be expressed in imprecise ways. Australia's old child maintenance system involved, at best, goal-rights. Children's interests were thrown into the pot without any precise privileging or weighting and in practice they rarely came out again. Having said that, the promotion standards presented here are expressed in open-ended terms, and further development of them is required.

STANDARDS FOR JUDGING LEGISLATION

Four standards which call for discussion are those of distinctiveness, motive, benefit and enforcement.

Distinctiveness is about the properties that distinguish this interest from the interests of others differently situated. If, for example, a child's interest is not relevantly different from an adult's interest then we might have an interest which is potentially constitutive of *a* right, but it would not properly be called a children's right. Depending upon the subject matter, it might be a (non-fundamental) human right, welfare right, patient's right, or whatever.

Furthermore, if an alleged right could only ever protect the interests of a *sub-set* of children then one is put on one's guard that it might not properly be called a children's right under this theory. There is no difficulty with a right that only operates on children when they are in a particular situation, but the reasons for distinguishing that situation from other situations then come under scrutiny. For example, the foundational welfare principle which generates the normal case interest in child support provides good reason to distinguish between (a) children whose parents have separated and (b) children whose parents have not separated. It provides less good reason to distinguish between (a) children whose parents have separated *and whose custodians are on social security* and (b) children whose parents have separated but whose custodians are *not* on social security. The fact of a custodian's social security status would need positively to be shown to be relevant.

Motive is a more open-ended standard, particularly in a consequentialist theory. MacCormick advances an interest theory of children's rights and takes as his subject matter a right to be nurtured:

Consider the oddity of saying that turkeys have a right to be well fed in order to be fat for the Christmas table, or of saying that children have a right to care and nurture lest they become a charge on the taxpayer (MacCormick, 1982:159).

He regards these statements as oddities because, unpersuasively in my view, his interest theory takes the diagonal path and is rooted in a quasi-Kantian principle that 'sentient beings ought to be respected as ends in themselves' (MacCormick, 1982:161). A consequentialist theory seems actually to *invite* consideration of interests beyond those of the right-holder and is less troubled by the existence of ulterior or parallel motives. Nevertheless, the presence of these ulterior motives makes us watch closely for signs that the interest is being 'sold out', that its urgent and intense nature is being compromised and relegated to that of a goal-right. We are alerted to the possibility that, as was the case with the old child maintenance system, the interest is simply being randomly advanced where it happily coincides with other interests. Attention to motive, then, keeps the focus on the displacing or 'trumping' power which is characteristic of a right.

Benefit is a standard related closely to distinctiveness and motive. David Feldman, in a discussion of claims about the rights of animals and foetuses, examines a possible variant of the interest theory as follows: X has a right to Z as against Y if W benefits from Y behaving in accordance with X's claim. To Feldman, this is really a claim:

that W, not X has a right to Y's behaviour. Trying to impute the right to X adds nothing of substance to the claim; if anything, it tends to obscure the picture. This may be very useful in practical politics, but it does not help philosophical discourse (Feldman, 1987:107).

Feldman's example is presumably aimed at a case where W is the *exclusive* beneficiary and not where both X and W benefit from Y's behaviour. My point is different. It is that, when taken with the standards of distinctiveness and motive, the standard of benefit requires a more open-ended examination of the relative benefits that X and W receive. The more that W benefits *at the expense of X*, the less it can be said that X is truly being accorded positive rights.

Enforcement is a troubling issue in children's rights theory. The impossibility of an infant child personally enforcing (or waiving) the performance of a duty is said by will theorists to be a strong reason why young children cannot have rights at all. MacCormick (1982:157) seems to me to evade the argument by responding that it is unduly Anglo-centric to assume there cannot be a right without a remedy (although he says it in Latin). My response is that the interest theory is about ascribing rights *to* people anyway: their personal inability to enforce them is beside the point. (Indeed, the interest theory proclaims moral superiority over the will theory precisely because it embraces those who are unable to fend for themselves.) Nevertheless, the existence of an enforcement mechanism is an important *empirical* matter. Under my theory, which despite all appearances to the contrary is meant to be a practical one, an interest has not properly been promoted to right-hood if there are no adequate procedures for ensuring compliance. This is because the essential by-products of rights are unlikely to be obtained in the absence of effective enforcement procedures. The question whether an enforcement procedure is adequate to the task is, of course, also an open-ended one but here the continuing relevance of the foundation principle comes into play. Given the force behind the normal case interest one should be slow to hand over decisions about enforcement to the very adults who might have interests divergent from the child's. Were this to happen, then suspicions about distinctiveness, motive and benefit would be further aroused. We can see now how the four promotion standards fit together.

THE CHILD SUPPORT SCHEME

I mentioned in the Introduction that the main function of the Australian Child Support Scheme in this paper is to make the rights theory more concrete and enable its better evaluation. The theory is now sufficiently sketched out for it to be demonstrated in action. The questions to be asked are (i) whether the Scheme has picked out the child's interest in the correct way and (ii) whether it has protected that interest in a way which creates rights.

The normal case interest, derived from the good of non-betrayal, is the interest of a child in having the same amount of resources applied to her or him as would have been applied in a normal two-parent family on these income levels. The Scheme is only partially successful in this regard. The percentage applied to the liable parent's non-exempt income does attempt it because the formula is apparently based upon research into resource-sharing in families at different income levels. On the other hand, it applies no percentage to the *custodial* parent, partly because of a policy of trying to provide her with work incentives (which, if successful, will lead to lower social security reliance). By leaving out of account the income of the custodian (except in the rare cases where she earns above Average Weekly Earnings) the formula loses its way. The Scheme might, in some instances, actually lead to the replication of resource-sharing in a two parent family, but that will be coincidental.

Other doubts about whether the Scheme has clearly picked out the normal case interest for protection relate to opting out. The relevant provisions allow considerably more scope for adult choices where there are no social security implications. One consequence is that the custodian who is not on social security, perhaps because she has repartnered and is not within the meaning of 'single person' in the *Social Security Act*, is free to make choices that *might* disadvantage the child, whereas the same freedom is not accorded to other custodians. One needs to be careful here because this exercise must not turn into custodian-bashing. Nevertheless, children's rights are rights primarily against adults. The justification for the normal case interest is that the adverse consequences of adult choices should be avoided wherever reasonable. Opting out and the question of reasonableness are returned to shortly. Assume, for the purposes of argument, however, that the normal case interest has been correctly built into the design of the Scheme. Has it been protected in the required way?

The four related standards to be applied are those of distinctiveness, motive, benefit and enforcement. As for distinctiveness, the opting out provisions based on social security status raise doubts about whether the right-holders have been classified with sufficient distinctiveness. I mentioned above that there is no difficulty about framing rights for a subset of children: presumably all rights cater only for people when they are in a particular situation. On the other hand, the foundational welfare principle which gives rise to the normal case interest does not obviously allow that interest to be abrogated by reference to an adult's position *vis-à-vis* the state.

Dealing with motive and benefit together, the Scheme is so overladen with social security and work incentive considerations that one is left suspicious about who benefits predominantly. I said earlier that these are open-ended standards and so it becomes a matter of broad judgment. The theory does not require that there be only one motive, nor that there be an exclusive beneficiary. Detailed empirical enquiry of the kind presently being undertaken into the impact of the Scheme on different kinds of children (those in sole parent families, those in reconstituted families, those whose custodians are on social security, those whose custodians are not on social security, and so on) will be an important source of information about differential benefit.

As for enforcement, the Scheme comes out well for those children whose custodians are in receipt of, or claiming, social security. In practical terms, an application for administrative assessment must be made if eligibility is to continue. For other children, however, it leaves matters to the choices of some of the adults who failed them in the past: parents and lawyers. This might not seem a strong point but these children may be in an equally disadvantaged position. There are many reasons why people are ineligible to claim social security, or refuse to exercise their eligibility.

The Scheme is best regarded as an improved version of the old child maintenance regime. It confers upon custodial parents the right to claim money which will help them raise their children. It has changed the nature of custodians' choices whilst confining them in a different way. In the past, their choices were conditioned by the considerable expense and uncertainty involved in making a claim for child maintenance and the considerable doubt whether they could enforce any order. Now it is less expensive and more certain, and enforcement is taken out of their hands, but the choice is markedly confined where social security is in question. Within the context of an adult-centred family law this should confer greater benefits on children and is a good thing. But the point of children's rights, if they are to be instituted, may be that decisions should be approached from a different starting point.

A Scheme more obviously in line with the theory presented here would begin by assuming that the normal case interest *must* be secured where there are resources available to do so. It would require that an assessment of child support must be sought and it would guarantee that any shortfall below the normal case interest is to be made up by social security. In practical terms, this may more easily be achieved by a guaranteed state payment with a quite separate mechanism for reimbursement by the liable parent.[13]

CONCLUSION

The Convention

The general approach to children's rights taken in this paper is, in my view, capable of adoption in the interpretation and application of the Convention. Admittedly, the opening paragraph of the Preamble refers to the 'recognition of the inherent dignity and . . . equal and inalienable rights of all members of the human family' but this seems simply to be a speech-style of the United Nations rather than an insistent deontological principle.

I read the Convention as embodying liberal values about the virtues of the family as a sphere to be kept separate from, and privileged over, that of the state (see, for example, Preamble, paragraph 5 and Articles 5 and 9) and about the rights and responsibilities which parents have in priority to those of the state. Liberalism is, of course, highly elastic and the terms of the Convention are capable of diverse interpretations. Nevertheless, I guess that the major liberal societies of the world reckon that they comply with most aspects of the Convention already and that the reluctance of some to ratify it stems largely from other considerations. The theory of children's rights put forward here, with its consequentialist concerns for welfare and life chances, seems capable of adoption, however, without doing damage to a plausible reading of the relevant Articles.

Could the Theory Change Anything Fundamentally?

One reason for asking this lies in the fact that the theory is largely a formal one. My use of the Child Support Scheme was designed to illustrate some of the substantive content which could be supplied to the theory but it is clear that much depends upon the welfare values that are fed in. For example, the goal of a community in which all of its members justifiably believe that their life chances have not been impaired by the reasonably avoidable adverse consequences of past adult choices leaves many questions open. What are life chances? Which consequences are adverse? What is *reasonably* avoidable?

It is possible that conservative answers could be given to these questions. If one takes 'life chances' as synonymous with 'equality of opportunity' then one is presented with a continuum of meanings, from the most formal notion of equality to the most substantive. Much depends on where one places the starting block. The test of reasonable avoidability could even be used to justify measures that seek to inhibit parental separation.[14] If access to divorce and related relief benefits women, as manifestly it can do, then feminists would rightly be concerned about such moves. The word 'reasonable' is really the gateway for an issue that the paper has so far neglected: namely how children's rights, goal-rights and mere interests should be placed *vis-à-vis* the rights, goal-rights and mere interests of others. Any developed consequentialist theory must specify some operation for combining the theory's separate goods into a single global value so that choices between options can be made (Sumner, 1987:170). Non-consequentialist theories still face analogous problems, however. If, say, autonomy or liberty are to be used as principles from which rights are deduced or constructed than a procedure is required for dealing with the clashes of rights that inevitably soon occur.

If, however, the good of non-betrayal is capable of a conservative construction, it is also capable of a transformative one. It is commonly noted that 'equality of opportunity' has a subversive potential. If one itemizes all the obstacles to it that women face, then measures designed to promote it can slide close to those required for equality of outcome. 'Life chances' could be similarly interpreted within the good of non-betrayal. Leaving aside child support, gender patterns in child-rearing, a major obstacle to equality of outcome, could also come under critical scrutiny. The good of non-betrayal provides a mechanism by which the reasonable avoidability of various outcomes can be debated. This may be attractive to those who, like the author, are generally suspicious of rights-talk. But one merit of rights-talk has been glimpsed. If presented as a concern with outcomes, it can prise open the political dimensions of choices so that legal decisionmakers can no longer ignore them.

NOTES

[1] See, however, Parker (1991:24–57).

[2] Accountants and solicitors have been criticized in the popular media in Australia for presenting papers at conferences on methods of minimizing liability for child support. One such method is to reduce one's personal taxable income by using companies or trusts as intermediaries. More worrying, perhaps, would be any practice by solicitors or judges to reduce the custodial parent's share in the family home because of the new levels of child support. If, say, a custodial parent who might previously have received 60 per cent of the home now receives only 50 per cent then the child could, on the facts, be worse off than before.

[3] I take Lucy's elaborate thesis about the 'essential contestability' of children's rights to be saying much the same thing; see Lucy (1990:213).

[4] See for example, Sumner (1987:203–4). I leave out of account some defences of the will theory that adults can act as agents for children and exercise powers on their behalf, although the substantive issue is taken up later.

[5] I appreciate that there are also theories based somehow in nature or religion, so that rights in these theories are related back to an alleged objective existence independent of human contrivance, but I adopt Mackie's argument that a belief in objective prescriptivity cannot in the end be defended: Mackie (1977:ch 1); Waldron (1984:171). Moral entities seem to me to belong within human thinking and practice so that they are either explicitly or implicitly posited, adopted or laid down.

[6] Pettit (1990:116) puts it slightly differently: 'Deontologists say that, in some cases at least, the right option is that which honours a relevant value by exemplifying respect for it in this particular instance, whether or not honouring the value in this way promotes its realisation overall.'

[7] See for example, Smart & Williams (1973); Scheffler (1988).

[8] For a sustained contemporary defence of a modified form of rule consequentialism see Johnson (1991).

[9] As this paper was completed, a description of the consequences for girls was published but it was too late to incorporate into the text; see Maclean & Kuh (1991).

[10] See also, Wadsworth, Maclean et al (1991).

[11] See for example, Cherlin, et al (1991); McDonald (1986); Richards & Dyson (1982); Wadsworth & Maclean (1986); and Wallerstein & Kelly (1980).

[12] See further Elliott & Richards (1991), corroborating this picture of chronic disadvantage.

[13] Such a proposal is not novel. I think it was at the core of the Finer Committee's recommendations in Britain in 1974. Something similar was also proposed by the Women's Electoral Lobby in Australia. The reasons why it has not been accepted may lie in political theory, and in particular the liberal view as to the proper relationship between the state, men, women and children. This is touched on again in the Conclusion.

[14] Research into the long-term consequences of parental separation may cause dilemmas for the majority of modern family lawyers who have long supported the removal of institutional pressures on adults to stay together. The old belief that a child in an unhappy two parent family is likely to be worse off than a child who lives with one fulfilled parent may be up for reconsideration, although it is too early to say whether any different conclusions would be reached.

CHILD SUPPORT: IS THE RIGHT THE WRONG ONE? A COMMENT ON PARKER

REBECCA BAILEY-HARRIS*

The value of rights analysis and rights discourse lies in its potential to generate constructive criticism of existing institutions and thence to propose reforms (Campbell et al, 1988:1; Parker, 1991:50). Parker has advanced a theory of the child's right to financial support – formulated as the normal case interest – and explored it in the context of the current Australian Child Support Scheme. This commentary offers some further perspectives on that analysis, and raises some different issues. The generality of the right is questioned, as is the appropriateness of defining the interest in normal case terms. An alternative is formulated, and the question asked whether the current Child Support Scheme is correctly analyzed in terms of children's rights at all. Finally some implications of the United Nations Convention on the Rights of the Child for future reforms are considered.

An alleged children's right which draws sharp distinctions between various categories of children arguably lacks the degree of generality necessary for right-hood status. The Child Support Scheme operates quite differentially in relation to a number of sub-sets of children. At first glance the child's right to financial support might appear to be generalized, since the scheme now operates throughout Australia irrespective of the marital status of a child's parents – no mean achievement given the complications of the constitutional position.[1] Yet on closer examination the scheme reveals a number of significant distinctions. It divides children into two populations according to the date[2] on which the parents separated or the child was born. For the 'old' population, the scheme offers the limited benefits of an enforcement mechanism for court-obtained maintenance orders, whilst the 'new' population is afforded the full advantages of administrative assessment as well as collection (Dickey, 1990). The implications of this distinction are just now emerging. The recent Report of the Child Support Evaluation Advisory Group (Fogarty, 1990) highlights the limited effectiveness of the scheme in relation to the 'old' population; for instance, the proportion of sole parent pensioners receiving child maintenance has risen from 25.6 per cent to only 36.5 per cent, and the levels of amounts ordered

* MA, BCL; Foundation Professor of Law, The Flinders University of South Australia, GPO Box 2100, Adelaide, South Australia 5001 Australia.

have increased in real terms by only $10 or 30 per cent and on an
average of $39 per week per child are still well below the estimated
actual costs of support (Nygh, 1991).[3] By contrast the situation for the
'new' population is 'distinctly better' (Nygh, 1991:185) with 45 per cent
of sole pensioners receiving maintenance and a further 35 per cent
involved in action or negotiation. The level of assessment also reveals
how the 'new' population is advantaged over the old – by an average of
$5 per week per child more with a further guaranteed rise of $5 anticipated. Justice Nygh (Nygh, 1991) has warned that 'there is therefore a
serious risk of increasing imbalance between Stage I and Stage II.'
(Nygh, 1991:185). The Advisory Group has recommended that the eligibility distinction between the 'old' and 'new' populations be removed,
subject to certain safeguards designed primarily to protect the interests
of the non-custodial parent in the non-retrospectivity of the formula's
operation. So strongly has the latter interest been advocated that the
recommendation has not at the time of writing been implemented.
Another important distinction (aimed at saving the public purse) is that
drawn between children whose parents are in receipt of social security
benefits and those whose parents are not. The latter's parents possess a
far greater degree of freedom to opt out of the formula's operation
through unscrutinized consent agreements,[4] and to obtain substitution
orders (capital provision in place of income support)[5]than do non-
pensioner parents. Depending on the circumstances, this freedom may
operate either for or against the interests of the child concerned – who is
entitled to no separate representation in any of the proceedings involved.
This disenfranchizement of the child will be the subject of further comment later in this paper. Parker has elsewhere demonstrated yet a further distinction in the potential of the formula to operate differentially as
between successive families according to social status (Parker, 1991:45–
8). Finally, the scheme distinguishes in practice between those children
whose liable parent can afford access to the Family Court in an application for departure from formula assessment and those who cannot; the
significance of this is becoming apparent as the number of such applications increases.

It is questionable whether the child's right to financial support *should*
be defined in Parker's terms of the normal case interest. That analysis
focuses on the resources available from the child's parents, the objective
being to make available to the child the same level of support as in a two-
parent family on that income level.[6] An alternative approach would be to
identify the child's claim to a guaranteed minimum income level, under-
written by the state where parental resources are inadequate. Distributive justice requires an expansion of the financial responsibility of the
state towards the children of the poor. Despite the then Prime Minister's
pre-election rhetoric that by 1990 no Australian child would live in
poverty,[7] the Child Support Scheme was never designed nor intended as

a guaranteed minimum income scheme. In fact a primary objective was to save expenditure on social security by enforcing parental financial obligations much more effectively than before, and to prevent the use of private child support merely to 'top up' pensions where the liable parent resources are adequate (Cabinet Sub-Committee Report, 1986:8–9). The contemporaneous revision of the social security legislation was designed to provide work incentives (Graycar, 1988:80–92). A golden opportunity thus existed to channel the estimated millions of dollars to be saved on social security directly back into social security to create a guaranteed minimum income scheme, by means of substantially increased state assistance to custodial parents where the child's other parent is without resources or cannot be traced. This opportunity was not taken, and so such children remain excluded from the scheme's benefits.

Is the current Child Support Scheme really susceptible of analysis in children's rights terms? If rights analysis is employed, the Scheme may be seen as based predominantly not on children's rights but rather on the *custodian's* right to enforce the liable parent's obligation, and also on the *state's* right to enforce parental obligations. But arguably *any* rights analysis is inappropriate: the scheme is more properly viewed as being based on obligation ie the enforcement of parental *obligations* to support their children. The language employed in the Child Support (Assess-ment) Act 1989 (Cth) is of symbolic significance: it is framed entirely in terms of parental duty.[8] It is not suggested that an obligations analysis is necessarily less capable of promoting the child's interests than a rights analysis (O'Neill, 1992); nevertheless the two approaches must be recognized as conceptually distinct. If the Child Support Scheme is to be analyzed in obligation terms, the nature of the parental obligation it creates merits analysis. It arises from procreation and not from nurtur-ing; it is not necessary for a liable parent to have lived with the custodian. It is an obligation which may exist without any correlative benefit (Seymour, 1992), the legislation having set its face squarely against any necessary link between access and financial support.

What assistance can be gained from the United Nations' Convention on the Rights of the Child in suggesting reforms to the current Child Support Scheme? Article 2 (1) requires that the rights contained in the Convention (including the right to adequate financial support from parents)[9] be ensured to each child without discrimination of any kind, irrespective of, inter alia, the child or parent/guardian's birth or other status. This article could be invoked to support the removal of the sharp distinction currently drawn between the 'old' and 'new' populations of children. The unfortunate consequences of that distinction have already been canvassed, and it is a distinction based wholly on the date of the child's birth or of the parents' separation. The full formula assessment scheme could be made to operate retrospectively to cover all children.[10]

Article 12 is of great significance. It requires that the child who is capable of forming his or her own views be given the opportunity to be heard in any judicial or administrative proceedings affecting the child. In contrast to the Family Law Act 1975 (Cth) s 65, the Child Support (Assessment) Act 1988 (Cth) ss 88–95, 114–20 gives the child no right of representation in any applications made under it, for instance, for registered agreements or for departure from formula assessment. The latter are becoming increasingly common as legal practitioners become familiar with the scheme. The dangers of the emergence of a two-tier system of child support assessment, based on a parent's capacity to afford access to court proceedings, are self-evident. Finally, Article 26 can be invoked to support the establishment of a guaranteed minimum income scheme for all Australian children. It recognizes the right of every child to benefit fully from social security. Whilst both Articles 26 and 27 support the enforcement of *parental* maintenance obligations where appropriate, the provision of a proper level of *State* support precisely where those resources are *not* adequate would achieve much-needed distributive justice, and fulfil the promise that no Australian child need live in poverty.

NOTES

[1] From 1986 to 1990 all State except Western Australia referred legislative power over the maintenance of children to the Commonwealth Parliament. Western Australia passed the Child Support (Adoption of Laws) Act 1990 (WA).

[2] 1 October 1989.

[3] The cost of maintaining a teenager is currently estimated at $212 or $116 per week, depending on whether child-related costs of housing and transport, school fees and medical and dental expenses are included: Australian Institute of Family Studies (1991); CCH (1991, 3–015) (based on Lovering, 1984).

[4] Child Support (Assessment) Act 1989 (Cth) Part VI.

[5] Child Support (Assessment) Act 1989 (Cth) s 124.

[6] *Sed quaere* whether this is consistent with the ceiling on the liable parent's income upon which the formula operates: Child Support (Assessment) Act 1989 (Cth) s 42.

[7] Speech made during 1987 election campaign by R. Hawke.

[8] Child Support Assessment Act 1989 (Cth) ss 3, 4.

[9] Convention on the Rights of the Child, Article 27.

[10] Full retrospective operation would necessitate the subordination of the liable parent's interest not to have financial arrangements made under the previous law disturbed.

MEDICAL EXPERIMENTATION WITH CHILDREN

SHEILA McLEAN*

ABSTRACT

This article considers legal issues related to medical experimentation with children in the context of international humanitarian instruments, including the UN Convention on the Rights of the Child.

It is necessary at the outset to define the terms of this paper as I interpret them. Thus, a brief definition must be given both of the groups to be included and of what is meant by experimentation. The United Nations Convention on the rights of the Child says in Article 1 that a child means 'every human being below the age of 18 years unless, under the law applicable to the child, majority is attained earlier'. But it also incorporates that part of the Declaration of the Rights of the Child adopted by the UN in 1959 which states that 'the child, by reason of his physical and mental immaturity, needs special safeguards and care, including appropriate legal protection, *before as well as after birth*'. (emphasis added) If these two statements are taken together, then it would appear that a 'child' for the purposes of this Declaration might include an embryo or foetus. However, it seems that this was not the intention of this latest Convention.

In these circumstances, and for the avoidance of doubt, it should be made clear at this stage that the concern of this paper is with live born children, and not those at the embryonic or foetal stage. In particular this paper will concentrate on the problems posed by research or experimentation involving those who are entirely, or partially, unable to offer their own consent, with particular emphasis on paediatric research.

As to experimentation, this will be defined as the controlled use of innovative therapies or the controlled scrutiny of biological or developmental processes. This, therefore, excludes a doctor's individual attempt to innovate in the one to one situation where he/she might wish to exercise clinical judgement. 'Controlled' in this situation means using one group of children to match results against another group. In the interests of scientific validity, this is usually conducted on a double

* Sheila McLean, School of Law, The University, Glasgow, G12 8QQ Scotland.

blind, randomized basis. This means that children will be selected randomly for inclusion in one group or the other, and that neither the researcher nor the child (nor its parents) will know to which group the child has been allocated, thus screening out the 'placebo effect'. Quite clearly, there are ethical problems raised by the way in which these trials are carried out, but this is not the place to discuss them.

GENERAL BACKGROUND

The fundamental cornerstone of all medical intervention, experimental or not, is that it should be based on willing participation, subject only to the exception of emergency. This means that the subject of the intervention must have elected to participate, based on the provision of adequate information about risks, benefits and alternatives and by implication (at least prima facie) must have the legal capacity to provide or withhold consent. Action or inaction which did not meet these conditions would be roundly criticized as being immoral and illegal. The requirement of voluntariness is, at least in theory, reinforced by international agreements, some of which will be dealt with in a little more detail later, although a few will be referred to here.

The Council of Europe, for example, in 1990 reaffirmed that 'It is absolutely necessary to obtain the informed consent of the person undergoing medical research' (Council of Europe, 1991) and the Royal College of Physicians (UK) says that 'For consent to be valid it is self-evident that it must be offered voluntarily and based on adequate understanding' (Royal College of Physicians of London, 1990:16). There are any number of statements couched in similar terms which seem to demand the free, uncoerced and understanding participation of the research subject. Manifestly, were this the whole picture then most – if not all – children would be excluded from involvements in research. Nonetheless, reports of the involvements of children in research – with or without parental consent – continue to appear in the media. Now of course, some children – although not those on whom I wish to concentrate – may be able to express an opinion on their involvement. In certain cases, their views may be regarded as legally binding, whether or not they meet the test of 'majority', because they can be said to understand and to be involved freely.

National laws vary as to the age at which someone becomes an adult, or is deemed capable of consenting to medical treatment. But courts are not necessarily bound to follow a strict interpretation of any purported line drawn between 'child' and 'adult'. An example of courts exercising their own powers rather than bowing to legislative provisions can be found in the United Kingdom case of *Gillick* v *West Norfolk and Wisbech Area Health Authority*.[1] The facts of the case are probably widely known, but what is interesting is that the House of Lords chose to interpret statutory rules about the provision of consent for 'treatment' in the context of contraception (arguably not 'treatment') in such a way as to avoid the strict conclusion that the age at which consent to medical intervention is valid is sixteen. Although, therefore, including children under that age within the framework of those who can offer consent in their own right to (arguably) non-therapeutic intervention, the court indicated that this had to be based on a number of criteria – maturity, understanding and a 'best interests' test.

What is not clear, however, is the extent – if any – to which this judgment would cover participation in experimental procedures, although if the research was said to be 'therapeutic' then presumably it could meet Lord Fraser's requirements, as laid down in *Gillick*. What is clear is that neither the 'best interests' test nor the 'understanding' test stand alone. If intervention is 'in the best interests of the child' that child's consent (and presumably refusal) will not be legally sufficient unless they also understand the implications of their choice, and *vice versa*. If translated into the experimental setting, this dictum would seem to suggest that only those who can understand and whose interests are served by involvement could be included in research.

However, despite the apparent emphasis on voluntary participation in experimentation, it is widely known, and apparently widely accepted, that children – even very young children – are involved in research and experimentation. This need not be invasive – indeed, it may be no more than a form of observation – but it *is* something which would otherwise demand clear and unequivocal consent. One major purpose of this Declaration – not the first – on the rights of the child, is to reinforce, as did the 1971 Convention on the Rights of the Handicapped, the view that people are not less worthy of respect because of individual characteristics such as age or disability. Equally, internationally endorsed statements of this sort remind states and individuals of their obligations in respect of these groups. Before considering the reasons *why* children might be thought suitable participants, it is worth looking briefly at what guidelines were available before the recent Convention and at what, if any, provisions are made in this new statement of rights. In addition, this will be a good point to refine the definition of experimentation.

WHAT IS EXPERIMENTATION?

It is traditional to divide research into therapeutic (for the direct benefit of the patient) and non-therapeutic (having no immediate intention of benefiting the research subject). It is also customary to argue that the dividing line between these two forms is often blurred and that this description is, as often as not, a distinction without a difference. However, there is little doubt that the *aim* of an experiment may be closely linked to its consequences and that this distinction, particularly in the case of those who cannot agree to or reject involvement, might have more relevance than is generally conceded.

For example, if a clinician experiments by offering one group the established treatment and another group a new (potentially better) treatment, then – although it is arguable whether this is therapeutic or non-therapeutic – it is clearly an experiment which has a hope of success (at least for some of the participants). The group on the traditional therapy loses nothing since it is not clear that the innovative treatment *will* be better, and – at least in theory – the group receiving the new therapy can revert to the old if there are signs that the new is harmful. If it is, indeed, beneficial then they gain, and so too – in the light of that information – will all individuals suffering from the same condition. There would seem, therefore, to be no obvious losers in this scenario. In these cases, we might be said to be paying some attention to the Kantian ideal of using people not as means but rather as ends in themselves, but the difficulty remains that – even where it is hoped that benefits may accrue to some of these individuals – unless both therapies have equal success rates then there is an inherent acknowledgement that *some* are being used as a means to the end of information gathering for the benefit of future patients. It is for this reason, amongst others, that the debate continues to rage as to whether or not an experiment can ever be truly said to be therapeutic, and concern remains as to the ethical basis on which these experiments rest. Equally, where the child is not expected to benefit from the experiment, then clearly the child *is* being used as a means to the end of scientific (and ultimately, perhaps, clinical) knowledge. In situations of this sort, the philosophical underpinnings of non-voluntary involvement are blurred.

The Kantian notion, encapsulated in the prohibition on non self-willed, perhaps even non self-serving, participation might well be a consideration used in judging the ethics of experimentation, but the utilitarian calculation is generally also an inherent part of its justification. The placing at risk – actual or potential – of any individuals or groups in the interests of measuring scientific validity and perhaps obtaining clinical endorsement, even with the intention to benefit *some* of them, perhaps ultimately all of them, is nonetheless a calculation based as much on greater good as it is on respect for persons. It may encapsulate some aspects of an individualistic approach, but it also subsumes them into a wider theoretical framework.

THE INTERNATIONAL POSITION

There are a number of Codes covering human experimentation, but perhaps the most widely referred to and most widely attended to is the Declaration of Helsinki (as amended). Although not directly enforceable in national laws, its terms have formed the basis of what is generally regarded as the 'good' or 'ethical' in human experimentation. Yet, on closer scrutiny, the Declaration adopts a somewhat ambivalent attitude to the rights of those who may be involved in human experiments. On the one hand, for example, it states unequivocally that the free and informed consent of the individual is necessary before research can go ahead. On the other hand, both in therapeutic and non-therapeutic research, provision is made for the authorization of involvement by proxy.

This ambivalence may well affect a number of individuals and groups, but few so directly as children, the handicapped, the elderly and the mentally ill – groups who are already vulnerable and who might be thought to require additional protection for that reason alone. However different jurisdictions have chosen to address the problem, and whatever legal or ethical framework they have adopted, it remains the case that the provision of authority by one person on behalf of another (*incapax*) person is routinely accepted – in other words the consent of the individual subject of research is *not* uniformly sought or obtained, despite the apparent emphasis on voluntary involvement. It is worth noting in passing that recent EC guidelines, which may eventually become applicable in Member States, would seem to have gone one step further than is traditional. By insisting on a free consent in non-therapeutic research – with no apparent exceptions – the EC goes much further than its recent predecessors and seems to rule out the use of any individual in non-therapeutic research who is not legally capable of offering a free and meaningful consent. Even this statement, however, does not go as far as the 'mother' of all declarations, the Declaration of Nurnberg, which states unequivocally in Article 1: 'The voluntary consent of the human subject is absolutely essential. This means that the person involved should have legal capacity to give consent . . .'

Whatever the European Community or national laws may say, the UN Convention on the Rights of the Child was designed quite explicitly to offer support to, and further definition of, the rights which affirming states *should* give to children. So what does the Convention actually say in respect of children's status in this area? The answer is 'nothing', at least not directly. A number of Articles make specific reference to the respect to be accorded to children in general. For example, Article 16, mimicking the International Declaration of Human Rights and the European Convention on Human Rights says: 'No child shall be subjected to arbitrary or unlawful interference with his or her privacy, family, home or correspondence . . .' Article 19 commits States to taking '. . . all appropriate legislative, administrative, social and educational measures to protect the child from all forms of physical or mental violence, injury or abuse, neglect or negligent treatment, maltreatment or exploitation including sexual abuse, while in the care of parent(s), legal guardian(s) or any other person who has the care of the child'. In partial restatement of the United Nations Convention on Civil and Political Rights, the Convention in Article 37 also says 'No child shall be subjected to torture or other cruel, inhuman or degrading treatment or punishment'. Interestingly, what is omitted from this version is a crucial statement which appears in the earlier agreement, which continues 'In particular, no one shall be subjected without his free consent to medical or scientific experimentation'.

Given the obvious vulnerability of children, particularly the very young, it seems a curious omission from the Convention that the subject of involvement in experimentation was not addressed directly. I understand that the non-appearance of a direct statement on experimentation on children may have been in part due to 'lack of time'. Whatever the reason for the omission, the Australian delegation indicated that in their view it would have been preferable had there been an explicit statement on experimentation, although they felt that given the terms of other articles in the Convention, children would not be left unprotected. However, the lack of a clear statement may also reflect an ambivalence about on the one hand the perceived value of using children and on the other the clear ethical problems of the fact that their involvement would – in many cases – be non-consensual (a position which a Declaration of rights would presumably seek to avoid).

WHY USE CHILDREN?

The answer to this question need not detain us long. It is self-evident that in disease processes specific to children, or in developmental matters, the child is often the most appropriate, if not the only, person who can provide answers to the questions posed by the researcher. Thus, it would be argued, if we are to develop mechanisms for dealing with childhood diseases, or to understand better the way in which developmental stages are reached, it is essential that we use children as our subject. The *Guardian* newspaper of 9 July 1991, for example, reports that observation and minimal intrusion has provided information as to how people breathe when eating, and why it is that some children do not learn this technique. This research was non-invasive and clearly has profound and valuable consequences for children, although the bulk of the research seems to have been carried out on adults. Although this kind of research, in common with for example nutritional research, is unlikely to be particularly invasive, and therefore might not be thought of as problematic, this is only a tenable conclusion if we ignore two important things. First that even if risks *are* apparently minimal, if the person was able to offer or withhold consent we would require that decision to be made, and second, that we do not actually know that risks are minimal. A classic example of this can be found in the case of DES.

Women in the United States, with a history of miscarriage, were entered into a trial in which they were given DES which was thought likely to prevent miscarriage. There seemed to be no risk, the women were not apparently harmed and the test appeared to be successful. However, a number of years later, daughters born to women who had been given DES were found to have a higher risk of developing certain relatively rare cancers – a finding which was linked to DES. It is, therefore, seldom possible to *know* that something is minimally risky.

Children, of course, will not always be the only appropriate subject group, even in situations where they may be the major beneficiaries. However, say in developing new therapies for the treatment of certain childhood leukaemias, children *will* be the most suitable group and some of them may be very young. If this research is to be undertaken, then it will be necessary that children are used, and quite clearly the gravity of the disease may well be not unrelated to the risks associated with the existing therapy or the innovative one. Some research in which it is desirable to use children as the subject will involve considerable risk and may well demand that the very young are used. The nature of the condition for which cure is being sought may also be sufficiently grave to require highly invasive medical intervention. Yet evidently no paediatric patient is ever in a position to make a decision about involvement. Research, if carried out, must therefore amount to an acceptance that one individual (not at immediate risk) is authorized to decide for another (directly at risk) whether nor not they should be exposed to that risk. This flies in the face of the purported rationale for consent provisions.

It is one thing as a consenting adult to agree to take substantial risks – whether or not in one's best interests. It is another to endorse the taking of these risks on behalf of another. In fact, even with adult, *capax* persons, as Brahams has said: '. . . though most doctors would agree that informed consent is ideal, many clinicians consider that in the real practical world, the blanket requirements of informed consent are counter-productive and even go against the best interest of patients . . .' (Brahams 1989:331). Why this is so is not self-evident, although it almost certainly mimics Buchanan's exposition of the paternalistic approach of doctors to their patients (Buchanan 1979).

However, from whatever theoretical perspective, let us assume that there are scientific reasons for involving children in research and that it is something which is in fact happening. Neither of these would amount, of course, to a justification were one not independently available. It is necessary, therefore, to address ourselves to the crux of the question – what are the bases on which experiments are carried out and what standards are available to test the ethics or the legality of such experiments? Underlying this, of course, is the issue of the intention of the researcher, which may make a morally qualitative difference to the experiment, but is usually unknowable. I will concentrate, therefore, on the kinds of tests which have been applied by courts, legislatures and so on – tests which they themselves see (as is demonstrated in *Gillick*) as reflecting a moral rather than a strictly legal approach.

LEGAL REQUIREMENTS

UK law lays down no statutory definition of when, and what kind of, research is possible with anyone – child or not. Other jurisdictions are less reticent. In Australia, s 46.116 of the National Research Act (Public Law 93–348, 12 July 1974) says: '. . . no investigator may involve a human being as a subject in research covered by these regulations unless the investigator has obtained the legally effective informed consent of the subject or the subject's legally authorised representative'. The Californian Protection of Human Subjects in Medical Experimentation Act 1987 contains caveats about 'unauthorised' experiments, amongst others. Recent Canadian Guidelines declare that non-therapeutic research on children should be organized 'in a general federal statute on experimentation provided that all the following conditions are met:

a) the research is of major scientific importance and it is not possible to conduct it using adult subjects capable of giving consent;

b) the research is in close, direct relation to infantile diseases or pathologies;

c) the experiment does not involve any serious risks for the child;

d) the consent of a person having parental authority and of an independent third party (a judge, an ombudsman or the child's lawyer) is obtained; and

e) where possible, the consent of the child should be obtained.

Moreover, whatever the child's age, his refusal should always be respected.'

Guidelines in use in Australia following the NH & MRC Statement on Human Experimentation confirm the value of progress in the treatment of childhood diseases and indicate that 'Some programs may offer direct benefit to the individual child, while others may have a broader community purpose. In appropriate circumstances both may be ethical.' (National Health and Research Council, 1982:Supp Note 2, A (2)). The responsibilities of ethics committees in having concern for the rights and welfare of the child are reinforced, and the use of risks/benefits analysis endorsed. In therapeutic research, the statement indicates that in performing this risks/benefits analysis the committee should 'weigh the risk of the proposed research against customary therapeutic measures and the natural hazards of the disease or condition.' (1982:5(i)). In non-therapeutic research 'The risk to the child should be so minimal as to be little more than the risks run in everyday life'. (1982:5(ii)).

Each of these statements mentioned above purports to provide some guidance on when the use of children may be regarded as ethical, but arguably they are fraught with ethical and interpretational problems. Certainly, apart from the EC and Nurnberg, they all begin from the presumption that proxy consent is valid – no other conclusion can be reached, and this *ab initio* fails to address the conflict between progress and respect for persons. Moreover, they encapsulate language such as 'minimal risk', risk/benefits analysis, and so on which disguise the difficulties of making such judgements in an experimental setting. If we *knew* the risks and benefits of a therapy or a technique, it would not be experimental. It is precisely because we do not know that we wish to carry out the research. As one commentator has pointed out, the values inherent in experimentation are such that a simple risks/benefits analysis is an inadequate basis on which to make judgements. In any event, if the research carries only minimal risk – whatever that is – then it may also only produce minimal benefit, and arguably the arguments against using children at all become stronger.

Certainly there may be some circumstances where we might appear to be able to make simple assumptions, but these are not always valid. The underlying 'certainties' which form the basis of the assessment of likely risk may themselves be open to question. An example of this is the straightforward assumption that – as oxygen is essential to life – its provision is a good thing. Experiments with increased oxygenation of premature babies, however, resulted in the blinding of a number of them.

In many jurisdictions, the assessment of the validity of experiments (or at least those that come to light) is left to the ethics of the researcher, ethics committees or to the courts. Whatever the aims or motives of experimentation, it is argued here that it must be at least testable against some kind of ethical framework, and – it will be concluded – even if we do not intuitively *like* the principles we have adopted, we nonetheless should state them clearly.

The primary requirement of the law, and of international agreements, concerning experimentation using *any* human subject is that of consent. Failure to obtain a real consent – generally described as a consent which is free, uncoerced and knowledgeable – makes, it is claimed, any experiment unethical and unlawful. This, it must be said, may, however, be too sweeping a generalization since it must also be the case that the experiment is of a type to which consent can be given. Thus, purported consent to an experiment which would have death as a more than likely outcome would probably not be regarded as valid or binding. However, assuming the research to have genuine scientific and clinical goals, and the risks/benefits balance seems acceptable, we do not need to concern ourselves with this here.

It is conceded, to paraphrase the words of Mr. Justice Cardozo in *Schloendorff*,[2] that the sane, adult person has the right to make decisions

about what can and cannot be done with his or her body. Whilst this
case was about general consent, it can probably be translated into the
experimental situation also. In fact the Canadian case of *Halushka* v
University of Saskatchewan[3] would suggest that the consent criteria would
be even more strict in the case of experimental procedures.

This takes us, then to the crux of the question. Given that (apart from
parts of recent EC guidelines and the Nurnberg Code) all Declarations,
and most national laws or guidelines where they exist, presume that
research *can* involve children using the device of proxy consent – what
tests, if any, are suitable in judging whether or not this proxy consent is
satisfactory? Whatever age one sets for legal capacity to consent, it is
clear that – particularly if one looks at paediatric medicine – there will
be cases where no consent other than that given by an authorized other
will be available. The next section will, therefore, seek to identify and
evaluate the tests which are currently used in assessing the validity of
proxy consents.

These tests are, of course, not the only way in which we might try to
reach conclusions about the validity of a proxy decision. There are any
number of other considerations which might be weighed in the balance,
such as motive, likelihood of success and so on. But they *are* the tests
which address themselves to the child him or her self and not to the
project or the researcher. For this reason, they are particularly important. In dealing with those who have legal capacity the model by which
we proceed is unashamedly founded in the concept of autonomy. Whilst
it is conceded that it makes no sense to talk of the paediatric patient as
having decision-making capacities which would enhance autonomy, it
does not make no sense to argue that the values which facilitate decision-
making in the adult are valuable also in the context of the paediatric
patient. Few, if any, would argue that a temporary incapacity to make
decisions which bear on autonomy provides a justification for the uncontrolled use of children in research.

Some attempts have been made to reach a compromise position – to
enter a number of *caveats*, defences almost, but set nonetheless against a
background which presumes that children will be involved in research.
Dickens, for example, suggests:

> Minors should not be involved where adults would equally meet the scientific
> requirements of the study; minors should not be exposed to procedures which
> have not been used, if they are appropriate to be used, on adults; if only minors
> can serve a study, those at the upper ages, with a capacity for independent
> consent and effective refusal, should be approached in preference to younger
> children; if only younger children are suitable for the study, parents of healthy
> children living at home should be approached in preference to guardians of
> institutionalised children; if sick children are alone suitable, the non-
> institutionalised should be preferred over those in institutional care. (Dickens,
> 1979:44–5)

Whilst this formulation does avoid using tests such as 'best interests', and to that extent removes some of the more contentious issues from the equation, it does not and cannot solve the problem of what basis should be used by those where proxy consent will still be the authorizing consent. At this point, therefore, it seems appropriate to turn our attention to the tests which are currently in use and to assess their contribution to decision-making and their underlying principles. By and large, courts and decision-makers – such as ethical committees – appear to concentrate on two main mechanisms in reaching decisions in these questions – 'best interests' and 'substituted judgement'. Dworkin (1987:201 et seq) also proposes that a 'not against the best interests of the child' test might be applied, and this will also be considered briefly. In addition, we should not forget the 'scientific interest or validity' test, which will be considered briefly at the end of the paper.

BEST INTEREST/WELFARE

This test is very much in line with the terms of the UN Convention. Article 3 states: 'In all actions concerning children, whether undertaken by public or private social welfare institutions, courts of law, administrative authorities or legislative bodies, the best interests of the child shall be a primary consideration'. It is worth noting that this phrasing only makes best interests *a* primary consideration, not *the* primary consideration, thereby not ruling out completely the application of other tests in appropriate circumstances. It is, however, a tradition of Anglo systems of law that the 'best interest of the child' shall be a paramount consideration.

The application of 'best interests' is common in cases involving children and those who are accorded similar status, such as the mentally handicapped. Recent judgements in the United Kingdom have shown the extent to which the courts are prepared to utilize this concept, both in therapeutic situations and those which arguably are non-therapeutic. Recently, for example, UK Courts authorized the abortion of a twelve-year-old girl on the grounds that she both understood the implications of it and that it was 'in her best interests' despite parental objections. In what was described as the 'difficult balancing exercise as to what was in L's best interests' the Court had regard to 'the girl's age, her wishes and the wishes of those concerned with her, and the conflicting medical opinions and counsel's submissions'.[4] In other words, the assessment of what is in the child's best interests, even in circumstances where the *child* is clear as to what these might be, is no simple task.

In a series of cases, British Courts have also authorized the sterilization of mentally handicapped women (whether or not over the age of majority) by applying this test.[5] Interestingly, unlike their Canadian counterparts,[6] the UK courts refused to consider whether or not there was any value in differentiating between therapeutic and non-therapeutic, seeming rather to assume that the degree of overlap would be so substantial as to make this distinction unnecessary. This might – in the experimental setting – justify the imposition of presumed consent to a risk, great or small, on the basis that society has the right to enforce altruism in situations where no express contrary wish is expressed (or expressable) by the individual, and society will gain. Just as society might seem to gain by preventing the handicapped from procreating, so too it might benefit if children are the subjects of research. But, if we return to the distinction between 'therapeutic' and 'non-therapeutic' experimentation for a moment, and seek to apply the 'best interest' test, it would seem that some conclusions might be drawn.

Therapeutic Research

The application of a 'best interests' test to situations where the child is expected to benefit from the research would seem to lead to the conclusion that proxy authorization should be upheld. Certainly, courts and others would be reluctant to refuse validation to a decision to involve a child in something which could be of benefit. However, endorsing decisions based on perceived 'best interests' presupposes two fundamentals: 1) that there *is* good reason to believe the research to be in the best interests of the child (and this will generally mean medical interests) and 2) therefore, that an adequate risk/benefit analysis has been or can be carried out. Both of these are potentially tricky conclusions to reach with any degree of certainty. In particular, the risks/benefits analysis is a profoundly difficult one to make with any real confidence – the very fact that something *is* experimental makes it difficult to know, or perhaps even be reasonably sure, that the 'best interests' of a given child or group of children can readily be identified. In addition, given the definition of experimentation used here, what of those who are not given the opportunity of the new therapy or the safety of the old? Since neither group (nor those authorized to offer consent or refuse participation on their behalf) will know exactly what is happening, how can we easily define 'best interests' unless there is subsumed into it the notion of ultimate gain for those not directly participating and not exposed to the risks?

Non-Therapeutic Research

Despite the fact that, for example, the Declaration of Helsinki explicitly countenances the provision of proxy consent in non-therapeutic situations, it is difficult to see how this could be done on a 'best interests' test. We are not obliged either to act altruistically nor are we assumed inevitably to benefit, spiritually or morally, from such a course. Indeed – even if we were – quite clearly there can be no reasonable expectation of any recognizable form of benefit to the very young child resulting from participation at that time. Of course it might, for example, be argued that the child's involvement in non-therapeutic research *is* in his or her best interests because, once grown up, they might look back and decide that they would have wanted to participate. This is a tricky argument, and one which does not immediately appeal since it amounts to an intellectual or emotional sleight of hand. Equally, it bears some resemblance to the next test to be considered and shares the same flaws.

If the above fail to satisfy, then the justification for authorizing the involvement of the child must be found outside the 'best interests' test – most likely from the utilitarian one of benefit to others or to the community as a whole. Use of the 'best interests' test, therefore, would seem to rule out the involvement of children in non-therapeutic research by proxy consent, unless we can be certain that, once they reach the age of maturity they would wish that they had been involved, and that they are in some way harmed by this wish not having been fulfilled.

SUBSTITUTED JUDGEMENT

One way round the difficulties of trying to work out what is in anybody else's 'best interests' is to approach the question from an apparently different angle. The question posed here would be: What would the incompetent person want if he/she were in a position to give an answer? American and other courts have applied this sort of test in a variety of cases involving children. In medical cases, they have addressed themselves also to a further issue and that is the extent to which decisions need to be made *pro tem* in order that a free exercise of choice can be made by the individual when capacity is gained. A further variation, mentioned above, would be to say that when the child is old enough to understand he/she would have wanted to have participated. This argument is one commonly used in other areas, based on the notion that, if you have a right to do something then just because you are in some way handicapped should not preclude you from having the opportunity to do so. It is, for example, an argument in favour of sterilizing the mentally handicapped on the grounds that if other women have a right to control their fertility then they should not be denied it because they can't legally authorize the procedure which permits such control. However, I am dubious as to whether this translation can be made. The 'right' to control fertility is arguably a right of a different sort from the 'right' to involve oneself in risky procedures. The latter is a right which is based on, not separate from, capacity.

Therapeutic Research

Where an experiment has a sufficiently high probability of meeting the risks/benefits equation, then the substituted judgement test might provide one way round the problems of deciding on 'best interests' although it effectively would address similar questions. We might for example simply assume that any individual, faced with a possible benefit, would choose to accept it (if they were able to), and thereby given acceptance of the clinical proposition that benefit can be expected, agree that proxy consent is soundly based. There are, however, also problems with this. First, we do not always prefer to accept a benefit and certainly are under no obligation so to do. Our presumption in favour, therefore, whilst not objectionable, is similar in kind to the decision of the doctor in a casualty unit who saves the life of an attempted suicide. There is no way of knowing whether or not the attempt is real and therefore both law and intuition would most likely support (or at least not condemn) the decision to save life. In the experimental setting, however, there is a further problem relating to the notion of 'benefit' which might impact on this conclusion. Given that clinical expectation is not infallible and is scarcely testable by the law or by parents, there is a remaining uncertainty about whether or not a benefit *is* likely to accrue.

And, of course, in the case of children, there is a further refinement which may come into play – that is the notion that we can justify proceeding or not by reference to whether or not the proxy decision can be seen as 'facilitating future autonomy'. Although this amounts to a modification of the substituted judgement test it is not uncommonly used in tandem with it, since it provides a partial answer to the former problem. What it does is to say that until the individual is able to make his/her own choice, we may have an obligation to protect him/her so that there is a possibility of autonomy being exercised in the future. This, however, only meets the problem in situations where a failure to authorize some intervention would preclude the possibility of reaching the stage at which capacity exists, or where authorization of procedures seems likely to ensure that the autonomous stage is reached. In the experimental setting, then, this test could be applied where the experiment is one which is designed to save life (or perhaps even mental capacity), but not where its purpose is less immediate and the risks are not minimal (however we might assess this).

Any other application of this test actually makes it virtually indistinguishable from a best interests one.

Non-Therapeutic Research

In this situation it is very difficult to see how the substituted judgement test could sanction the use of children. Not only is it unusual to presume that people would want to choose to take risks for other, but the difficulty of working out what others would do in this situation is compounded by the fact that no benefit is intended for them. Here the criticism of LaForest, J in the *Eve* case[7] becomes particularly poignant. In denouncing the substituted judgement test as a vehicle for judicial or other decision-making on someone else's behalf in a non-therapeutic setting, he said:

. . . it is obviously fiction to suggest that a decision so made is that of the mental incompetent. What the incompetent would do if he or she could make the choice is simply a matter of speculation.[8]

In any event, it has long been assumed, for example by the (UK) Medical Research Council, that '. . . in the strict view of the law parents and guardians of minors cannot give consent on their behalf to any procedures which are of no particular benefit to them and which may carry some risk of harm.' (Medical Research Council, 1964). Or, as has been said, albeit in a different situation:

Parents may be free to become martyrs themselves. But it does not follow [that] they are free, in identical circumstances, to make martyrs of their children . . .[9]

This statement is very much in line with subequent US decisions concerning parental refusal of treatment in the face of serious risk to the child (Sher, 1983). Indeed, it is an attitude which has been taken even in the face of the request of (apparently) competent adults for withdrawal of treatment, inevitably resulting in harm. Again, therefore, it would appear that this test might endorse the use of children in the therapeutic experiment, but not in the non-therapeutic. Even if we were to endorse the final variation of the substituted judgement test – that is why should children be denied the opportunity to participate simply because of their age – we would still need a much clearer definition of what risks are 'minimal' and a much more sophisticated basis for the risks/benefits analysis. The latter may prove impossible to achieve, whilst the former is an enduring feature of life. It is not foreign to the kind of community in which we live for decisions to be made on behalf of others that they should not be allowed (for reasons of morality or pragmatics) to do something which others can do. For example, we are all entitled to drive, but only once tests have been gone through – tests which have a rigorous, thought-out content relevant to the permission being sought.

NOT AGAINST THE BEST INTERESTS OF THE CHILD

This particular test would ask yet another question. To what extent would the child be harmed by any proposed research? Using this approach as the basis for testing the validity of proxy decisions would also lead to different conclusions depending on whether or not the research is therapeutic.

Therapeutic Research

If the therapeutic research genuinely *is* research designed to benefit the child, and has a reasonable expectation of so doing, with an acceptable level of risk (however this is defined) it seems unlikely that proxy consent based on this analysis would be seen as invalid. In fact, the terms of the

test do not seem either to be particularly demanding or to be significantly different from the 'best interests' test – at least to the extent that
they require consideration of similar issues.

However, this test is not a panacea. Even therapeutic research which
has a known risk of causing harm *could* be excluded on this analysis since
any harm might be said to be 'against the best interests of the child' even
if *some* benefit can be anticipated (but probably never actually known).
The balancing of interests under this test is arguably more complex than
under the straightforward 'best interests' test.

Non-Therapeutic Research

As with the other tests considered, a decision to authorize involvement
in research using this analysis would manifestly preclude involvement
since there will almost certainly be a risk which the child need not
experience and it is generally likely to be assumed that exposure to
unnecessary risk is against the best interests of the child.

CONCLUSIONS

It can be seen in this brief review of the methods available and used to
test the validity of proxy decision-making that – unless we are prepared
to impose on children a level of altruism that we do not impose on those
with legal capacity – there is no test which would easily permit of the use
of children in non-therapeutic experimentation. Yet, of course, non-
therapeutic experimentation is said to be an important part of the
armoury of medical progress. Indeed, even in the therapeutic situation,
it would appear – in line with some national guidelines – that research
based on proxy consent would only be permissible where benefits are
real and risks minimal. The major difficulty is to assert tht this will be
the outcome with any real confidence.

Over the years following Nurnberg, however, our capacity for
tolerance seems to have changed and a number of tests have been
developed and utilized which are designed to authorize research on
those who lack the capacity to agree or disagree on their own behalf.
There are a number of reasons which can be promulgated for such
change. One, and perhaps an overriding one, is that medical science has
become so widely perceived as a miracle worker. What medicine can do
is viewed with awe and amazement. The repeated claims made for
experimentation as an integral, indeed an essential and preliminary,
part of modern medical miracles have a powerful hold on the imagination. So, into the ethical codes governing human experimentation crept –
unexplained – the concept of proxy consent. Even if we concede that
there are situations where we would wish to endorse proxy decision-
making, this does not answer the questions which this paper has sought
to address, namely is there a standard, explicable and explained, which

we can comfortably use, and once we find this (if we do) what are its consequences for particular types of experimentation?

A recent paper sought to show that, whatever subsequent declarations have done, the Nurnberg Code remains at the heart of guidance on human experimentation. Yet subsequent statements have deviated from its unequivocal terms substantially. Most particularly, this has been done by the gradual intrusion of the notion of proxy consent, a notion unexplained beyond the legalistic mechanics of who is entitled to provide it. No mention is made of the way in which the authorized person should approach the task they have undertaken or had thrust upon them. The Convention on the Rights of the Child is no different, failing even to address the question of experimentation head on.

What is being confronted, then, is a serious and weighty matter. The United Nations Convention on the Rights of the Child fundamentally avoids the issue of participation in research, yet we all know that it is going on all the time. Indeed, sometimes it is done without even seeking consent of a proxy. There is an inherent need for concern about this silence. Given the extent to which this Convention borrows from others, it might be accused of being even less committed to the rights of children in research than those from which it so obviously borrows. A valuable opportunity to re-evaluate the principles underlying the use of children as research subjects has been lost. This Convention might have strengthened procedures, reassessed the whole issue of proxy consent and encapsulated tests to which all jurisdictions would be expected to subject proxy decisions were they to be authorized. Instead the Convention maintains silence on these matters. The view of the Australian delegation that children were adequately protected by the invocation of other articles in the Declaration might seem somewhat naïve in the face of an exposition of the complexities which are unique to human experimentation. Experimentation may well be necessary (however it is defined) and we as communities of nations may wish to endorse it. It may be done in the name of progress or in the name of patient care. But that this Convention omits even to address itself to these questions is surprising.

To return to the question of the child who is, by any jurisdiction's standards, unable to offer a consent or refuse to participate, the *Journal of Medical Ethics* makes the following point about the Convention:

Paediatric medicine abounds with examples of issues which the Convention could not settle without further interpretation. There are, for example, the many types of case which concern the respective powers of parents and children to grant or withhold consent to medical treatment. If the relevance of the Convention to the medical profession were thought to depend upon its capacity to shed light on these hard cases, then it would be a document with only a slight claim upon the attention of doctors in liberal democracies. Perhaps, then, the strongest basis for the Convention's claim on the attention of the medical profession in general, and paediatricians in particular, is in the opportunity it provides for an appraisal of the broader implications and limitations of appeals to children's rights in medical ethics (Briefings in Medical Ethics, 1991).

But is this enough? The broad brush with which the Convention tackles at least this aspect of children's rights described by Manciaux as reflecting both 'consensus and compromise' (Manciaux, 1991:167) might well be as satisfactory as it was inevitable, were we confident that clear principles existed already which could guide us to an ethical position. However, what I have tried to show is that the formulae for decision-making which are used are inherently flawed and are seldom subject to rigorous scrutiny. In any event, – even were they not flawed – they cannot justify on a strict or a liberal interpretation at least some of the research which is carried out.

It may be that what this tells us is something basic about the way in which we view children when they are in potential conflict with the interests of others or the 'rights' of parents and guardians. It may also say that we think of children as automatically being protected by those who make decisions on their behalf. Can we really believe this in a world in which it is necessary to draw up a Convention of this sort in the first place? At the moment children are being conceived specifically in order that they may donate bone marrow, for example to save the life of an existing sibling. Anencephalics are used as organ donors even although they cannot satisfy the criteria for death. Children in hospitals are involved in research projects (invasive or not) without the consent of them or their parents. In all, it presents an uncomfortable picture. On the one hand, we are all generally convinced of the value of scientific and medical progress. On the other our courage fails when it comes to adopting identifiable standards against which to test our goals. I suspect that this is because we do not wish to own up to the fact that – despite grandiose international statements to the contrary – we *do* maintain the inequality of power between some groups and others without adequately examining either the source of this or the justification (if there is one) for continuing to do so. The UN Convention goes no further than pre-existing statements towards resolving these problems.

Nor can it be assumed that the problems are minimized or qualms stilled by, for example, the existence of ethics committees to scrutinize proposed experiments. The evidence in the United Kingdom, for example, suggests that these committees are dominated by those with scientific backgrounds, that many of them were unaware of what their task was, that the frequency and style of their meetings and the numbers of their membership varied considerably – in other words, they can scarcely be seen as truly effective. And it is here that the last test – that of scientific and clinical interest – is most important. Doctors are required to participate in research, to break new (and publishable) ground if they wish to progress in their careers. Even the professional sanctions which exist – such as not publishing anything which has not been scrutinized and approved by an ethics committee – are only as good as the committees themselves.

Of course, it may be that by improving these committees we remove many of the problems, but not all of them. We still need a test with which we can be comfortable. Improving the work of the committees, however, would also provide an additional safeguard. One possibility is to establish two levels of committee – one which considers scientific validity (and which could, therefore, be substantially drawn from those with the necessary scientific expertise) and one which considers the ethics of the proposal (dominated here by non-scientists). Review of the decisions of these committees should be available through the courts, and perhaps even a children's advocate should be available on all occasions where decisions are made, in much the same way as the Official Solicitor in England will take cases in respect of the mentally handicapped.

Doubtless much has been learned from the use of children as experimental subjects. Doubtless also many children (and others) have benefited from it, directly or indirectly. But we must ask what is the greater good. No international statement of recent years has done this, no national guidelines demand an answer. In fact, whilst Codes become more sophisticated in terms of requirements about information disclosure and compensation in the event of harm caused, the underlying need to address the competing values involved in using children is obfuscated by the mantra-like repetition of the value of research and progress and the ethical and legal soundness of proxy consent.

NOTES

[1] [1985] 3 All ER 402.
[2] *Schloendorff* v *Society of New York Hospitals*, (1914) 105 NE 92.
[3] 1966, 53 DLR (2d) 436.
[4] *Re B (A Minor)* The *Guardian*, 21 May 1991, 35.
[5] Cf *Re B (A Minor) (Wardship: Sterilisation)* [1988] AC 199; *T* v *T & Anor* [1988] 1 All ER 613; *Re F (Mental Patient: Sterilisation)* 2 AC 1.
[6] *Re Eve* (1987) 31 DLR 1.
[7] Id.
[8] Ibid.
[9] *Prince* v *Massachusetts* 328 US 158, 170.

CHILDREN'S RIGHTS: SOME FEMINIST APPROACHES TO THE UNITED NATIONS CONVENTION ON THE RIGHTS OF THE CHILD

FRANCES OLSEN*

ABSTRACT

This article views the UN Convention on the Rights of the Child in the light of four feminist perceptions of children's rights: legal reformist, law as patriarchy, feminist critical legal theory and post-modern feminism. These perspectives permit a multi-dimensional critique of the Convention.

Feminists have a complex and ambiguous relationship to legal rights. On one hand, much or most progress for women from the time of feudalism on has seemed to many to come in the form of liberal rights for women. On the other hand, the notion of liberal rights and indeed liberalism as a whole are properly subject to sharp feminist critique, and the use of legal rights as an analytical tool has not served women well.[1]

The complex and ambiguous relationship feminists have to rights is mirrored in their relationship to law. On one hand, law has served as an instrument of reform. The role and status of women has generally improved significantly when women have been allowed greater participation in the legal system. Especially in certain developing countries, law seems to be operating as a nudge to improve the societal role of women. On the other hand, law has been developed in a strikingly male-dominated atmosphere, and the values, goals and attributes associated with women have generally not been highly valued in law. Legal theorists are not without significant supporting evidence when they assert that law is 'male' or part of the 'patriarchal system'.[2] (Olsen, 1990).

Feminists also have a complex and ambiguous relationship to legal protection for children. On one hand, the neglect and abuse of children is often part and parcel of the neglect and abuse of women. As the predominant caretakers of children, women are greatly influenced by the role and status of children. Where conditions are good for children, they are generally good for women. Where society neglects and abuses chil-

* Professor Dr Frances Olsen, University of Frankfurt, Senckenberganlage 31/VI, Frankfurt am Main, D-6000 Germany. I would like to thank Philip Alston and Ludwig Salgo for comments on an earlier draft and Tom Campbell for being a constructive commentator at the presentation of this paper.

dren, it is likely also to neglect and abuse women. Women's role as primary caretakers of children gives them a particular interest in the welfare of children.[3]

On the other hand, women's role as primary caretakers of children has contributed greatly to the impoverishment and oppression of women. Women who are caring for children are likely to spend fewer years in school and likely to have less good jobs throughout their lives than men with children or than women who do not have children. Children have been used as hostages to force women to remain in completely unreasonable marriages and domestic situations. Many wives experience not marriage but the birth of a child as the point at which they lose their freedom. Legal protection of children can be and has been used as a basis for controlling women.

Finally, feminists have a complex and ambiguous relationship to international human rights law. On one hand, feminist human rights lawyers have found ways to use the norms of international human rights to identify and enforce rights for women that can improve, and perhaps already have improved the lives of women (Engle, 1991a). Even feminists who find the institutional structures formed by international law to be unreasonably male-dominated have nevertheless been able to create spaces within these structures that they can occupy for the benefit of women (Engle, 1991a).

On the other hand, human rights law has been dominated by men and the human rights system not only tolerates but in significant ways perpetuates the international subordination of women (Engle, 1991a). Some human rights lawyers reject the notion of women's rights as a distraction from human rights and may even see feminist demands for change to be a threat to human rights. Feminists have argued that the international human rights system is disingenuous in its assertion of protecting human rights insofar as it fails to protect the rights of half of humankind. An important body of feminist thought suggests that 'international human rights will require reconceptualizing and redefining before it can accommodate women's rights'.[4] (Engle, 1991b) Moreover, it is not clear whether even with such re-conceptualization and redefinition international human rights discourse and doctrine can actually help to create a better world for women. There is serious question whether human rights discourse is capable of assimilating women's issues (Engle, 1991b).

This paper discusses four feminist views of children's rights, in general and specifically as articulated and promoted in the United Nations Convention on the Rights of the Child. The first view, 'Legal Reformist',[5] focuses on a doctrinal examination of the Convention to determine how it might be interpreted to benefit women (broadly including children's interests as well as many other societal interests) and what provisions present problems or pitfalls. This approach also looks at the effect the Convention might have on expanding and enriching the use of rights; how it might set and revise agendas, encouraging the establishment of useful committees and other institutions; and whether it might promote a culture of human rights, paving the way for those countries that have ratified the Convention on the Rights of the Child but have not previously ratified human rights conventions to begin to ratify other human rights documents.[6]

The problems and pitfalls of the Convention on the Rights of the Child examined by a 'Legal Reformist' approach include provisions that could serve to control and constrain women (including in ways that actually undermine what many would see as the interests or rights of children). The 'Legal Reformist' approach also focuses on particular omissions of the document. For example, it deals with child military service, which mostly affects boy children, but not with child marriage, which most affects girl children.[7] This approach questions whether the 'gender-blind' language of the document is consistent with and reinforces its provisions against sex discrimination or rather serves to obfuscate and leave in place gender discrimination, such as the disproportionate share of child care done by women and the severe discrimination against girl children in parts of the world.[8] Not only could the language of 'legal protection, before as well as after birth'[9] be employed by anti-abortionists to interfere with women's health care,[10] but the document seems to provide no role for the gestational parent in determining when a foetus shall receive legal protection.[11]

The second feminist approach, 'Law as Patriarchy' is the paradigmatic approach of those often characterized as 'cultural feminists'. A major concern is the ways in which the Convention deals with interests frequently associated with women: an appreciation of the importance and pervasiveness of human relationships, a concern with an ethic of care (as well as or perhaps rather than an ethic of rights),[12] issues raised by connection rather than a preoccupation with issues of separation (Chodorow (1978); Dinnerstein (1977)), and a concern with complexity, context and continuity. This approach may take the form of a feminist elaboration and development of the communalist critique of the allegedly atomistic nature of rights. Alternatively, under the 'law as patriarchy' approach, the Convention could be seen as a crucially important document in a move toward a fuller, more feminist (or feminine) view of rights.

The third and fourth views are nearer one another than the other approaches. The third approach I refer to as 'Feminist Critical Legal Theory'. It has several components, including a critique of the public/private dichotomy,[13] an elaboration of the feminist critique of the liberal notion of consent and choice,[14] and a feminist version of the critique of the project of rights *analysis* as doomed by the pervasiveness of *conflicting* rights. The Convention can be seen as a broadside attack on the public/

private dichotomy,[15] but it can also be seen to reinforce and presuppose a very conventional notion of the family as the centre of affective life and a sharp split between affective and productive life. The notion of choice is enshrined in the Convention. The only recognized inhibition to the exercise of choice seems to be the age and maturity of the child; power is either simple and blatant, or nowhere to be found in the Convention (unlike in real life where innumerable subtle as well as blatant exercises of power constrain and indeed structure choices to such an extent that choice may be as meaningless for competent adults as it is for disempowered children). The Convention is indeterminate insofar as it supports flatly conflicting and contradictory rights. Children's right to care conflicts with their right to autonomy, their right to formal equality with their right to substantive equality, their and others' right to security with their and others' right to freedom of action, and their rights with the rights of others, especially mothers. A world with rights everywhere one looks can hardly be said to be less 'dismal' than a 'world without rights'. (Freeman, 1992).

The fourth approach I refer to as 'Post-Modern Feminism'. It shares much with 'Feminist Critical Legal Theory', but the emphasis is different. This fourth approach is concerned with false universalisms and the feminist critique of abstraction. White people think of themselves as universal and without a race, just as men (and often women) consider gender to be an issue for *women*. The claim of unsituatedness is made by and on behalf of those with power. To the extent the Convention deals with children as unspecified, unsituated people, it tends in fact to deal with white, male, relatively privileged children. The Convention fails to the extent it fails to challenge the categories through which we understand the world. Arguably, the Convention could be seen ironically as the final deconstruction of the notion of rights. A post-modernist might delight in the Convention as the explosion of rights, breaking apart the concept. From this fourth perspective, the value of the Convention lies in its ability (if it is able) to open spaces for children to redefine childhood. The question is whether children are empowered.

LEGAL REFORMIST APPROACHES

Legal reformist is a broad category in which I intend to include probably most feminist lawyers and liberal legal scholars. The important shared view is that the current inequality between men and women could be changed by allowing women to enjoy the privileges currently all too much reserved to men. Some legal reformists would also like to see other societal changes, but the identifying characteristic is that the primary goal is to include women in the existing structure, not wait until some more global change takes place, and not base hopes for improving the role and status of women on any other major changes in values, technology, social systems or economics. Law is valued for its ability to abstract from particularistic situations and provide a relatively neutral playing field on which reason and principle may prevail over the dead hand of tradition and over a wide variety of forms of illegitimate power.

Most of the legal reforms that have improved the role and status of women have taken place within a broad liberal legal reformist perspective. While I believe it is important to be critical of this perspective, it would be foolish not to recognize both its practical value and the widespread perception that liberal reformism is the approach that works 'in the real world'. From such a perspective, rights for children, and specifically the United Nations Convention on the Rights of the Child, can be seen to have both positive and negative potentials.

Positive

Rights for women and children are usually seen as complementary, not as a zero sum game. The patriarchal family is generally understood to have denied rights to both women and children. The problem with the ideology of liberal rights is often seen to be that it is too limited in that it too often provides only for the 'Rights of Man'. The legal and social treatment of women and of children during much of the past two or three centuries has been criticized as 'feudal'.[16] Thus, the extension of rights to children is in one sense simply a more or less logical next step after the extension of rights to women.

Moreover, insofar as the largest share of the day-to-day care of children generally falls on mothers, women as a group stand to benefit from improvements in the conditions under which children are raised. Article 23 of the United Nations Convention on the Rights of the Child, for example, provides that subject to available resources, physically or mentally disabled children should receive publicly financed special care and education to achieve the fullest possible individual development and social integration into the community. The Article specifically provides for the extension of assistance to 'those responsible for' such a child's care. Thus, subject to the available resources, this Article could not only radically improve the lives of disabled children but also significantly reduce the despair and isolation often experienced by their mothers, especially mothers in economically disadvantaged circumstances.

Similarly, Article 24, encouraging states to provide health care to children and take measures to diminish infant and child mortality, aids parents and especially mothers, who most often care for children in illness. Whether or not, as many believe, mothers as a group suffer more than fathers as a group from the death of a child, it is generally mothers who bear most of the emotional burden of helping siblings deal with the death of a child. Women have a strong interest in reducing infant and child mortality.

Article 18 makes particular reference to the 'children of working parents' and provides that governments 'shall render appropriate assistance to parents . . . in the performance of their child-rearing responsibilities and shall ensure the development of institutions, facilities and services for the care of children'. Even more directly serving the interest of mothers, Article 24(2)(d) provides for 'appropriate pre-natal and post-natal health care for mothers'.

The provisions in Article 17 suggesting that states should 'encourage the production and dissemination of children's books' and 'encourage the mass media to have particular regard to the linguistic needs of the child who belongs to a minority group or is indigenous' are likely to help children's primary caretakers. So too might the provisions in Article 31 recognizing the 'right of the child . . . to engage in play and recreational activities appropriate to the age of the child and to participate freely in cultural life and the arts' and specifying that states 'shall encourage the provision of appropriate and equal opportunities' for such activities.

A particularly positive aspect of the Convention from a feminist legal reformist perspective is its prohibition of sex discrimination. Article 2 (1) requires enforcement of children's rights 'without discrimination of any kind, irrespective of the child's or his or her parent's or legal guardian's . . . sex . . . or birth . . .'. This section prohibits discrimination specifically on the basis of the child's sex and also on the basis of the marital status of the mother when the child is born. The old notion of 'illegitimacy' harmed children and penalized women who did not marry before having a child.[17] Article 2 (2) provides that 'States Parties shall take all appropriate measures to ensure that the child is protected against all forms of discrimination', based on 'the status, activities, expressed opinions or beliefs of the child's parents, legal guardians, or family members'. This section requires that governments not only themselves refrain from discriminating on the forbidden bases, but also that they take 'all appropriate measures' to prevent any discrimination on these bases. One would hope that the language of Section 2 (1) that governments 'shall respect and ensure the rights set forth in the present convention' without discrimination will also be understood broadly to require governments to undertake to prevent all forms of so-called 'private' discrimination against children on the basis of race, sex, and the other forbidden grounds. For example, in many societies more resources are devoted to educating boys than girls. This form of discrimination should be ended, and girls should receive as good education as boys throughout the world.

Similarly positive from a feminist reform perspective is the Convention's prohibition against sexual abuse by parents or others, Article 19, its forbidding of traffic in children, Article 35, and its prohibition against the 'exploitative use' of children in prostitution and in pornography, Article 34. Article 34 also prohibits the 'inducement or coercion of a child to engage in any unlawful sexual activity'.[18] Each of these Articles require States Parties to undertake to protect children through national laws or through international co-operation or both.

Another positive but more complex aspect of the Convention from a feminist liberal reformist perspective is its relentlessly gender neutral language. The child is always referred to as 'he or she' and the parent, not the father or the mother, is referred to throughout the document. The only exception is in Article 24(2)(d) which refers to pre- and post-natal care for 'mothers'.[19] Although the issue of the value of 'gender neutral' language is a nuanced and controversial one, one body of opinion would commend the Convention for always using 'he or she' and 'his or hers' when referring to children and for never assuming in its language that women are the only caretakers of children,[20] thus refusing to provide the ideological support to the status quo that language too often provides.

The strong emphasis on 'positive' rather than just 'negative' rights will be seen by many feminists to be beneficial. The Convention expands the notion of rights in ways quite amenable to women as a group. While 'negative' rights may limit the power of the government to enact policies to change the status quo, 'positive' rights are likely to require a change in the status quo, often a change that improves the situation of the relatively powerless.

One does not have to believe naïvely that the specification of positive rights will lead directly to their fulfilment to be supportive of the concept. The Convention on the Rights of the Child and its listing of positive rights can have a significant and beneficial effect on the way that agendas are set. It can, and indeed has, led to the establishment of committees, agencies and other instituitons that are likely to improve the lives of children, and of their primary caretakers. We can expect, for example, that most parties will seek to comply with Article 44's requirement to submit a report on 'the measures they have adopted which give effect to the rights recognized herein and on the progress they have made on the enjoyment of those rights' within two years of the Convention coming into force in a country and every five years thereafter. In a number of countries, the process of making such a report will provide access to government agencies and ministers to groups and individuals formerly denied such access. In this and other ways it may increase the power and legitimacy of those concerned with the interests of children.

Negative

Yet there are also less positive evaluations of the Convention on the Rights of the Child to be made from a feminist liberal reform perspective. One of the most significant of these concerns is whether the Convention may be used to control and confine women. Children, and the expressed interest in their welfare (expressed often by people who show no other interest in children) have often been used to control women.

Efforts to bar women from the professions and from other forms of paid employment have often been explained as being for the benefit of children. Increasingly the movement to forbid abortion focuses on an asserted concern with the welfare of foetuses rather than with religious obligations or with sexual morality.

As well as supporting a child's caretaker, the provisions of the Convention may also impose heavy burdens upon the caretaker. Even Article 31's language that the State 'shall encourage the provision of appropriate and equal opportunities for cultural, artistic, recreational and leisure activity' could be understood to justify the State's imposition upon caretakers of the obligation individually to provide their children with these opportunities. Article 27 places 'the primary responsibility' for financial support of the child on '[t]he parent(s) or others responsible for the child'. Article 18 makes a clear statement that '[p]arents or, as the case may be, legal guardians, have the primary responsibility for the upbringing and development of the child'. Having primary responsibility for the upbringing and development of a child has often resulted in mothers being isolated with their children. A fear might be that these provisions could in actual practice tend to cancel out other provisions that provide for more communally shared responsibility. Regarding parents' care for children, the Convention specifies that '[t]he best interests of the child will be their basic concern'. These provisions could arguably be interpreted as providing a basis for justifying intrusive surveillance of parents in general, and the more specific the provision, the more directly it could impact upon the primary caretakers of children.

Although the provisions making *both* parents responsible for children would seem to be generally beneficial to women, who otherwise too often wind up solely responsible for children, the provisions may also work against the interests of women as a group. It may well be that the obligations placed 'equally' upon fathers will turn out to be unenforceable as a practical matter,[21] but that the provisions can be used by 'father's rights' groups, composed often of recently-divorced, angry and misogynistic men, to harass the women who are taking care of 'their' children. In Germany, for instance, some 'father's rights' advocates are claiming that the Convention would require courts ordinarily to award joint custody of a child upon divorce (Steindorff, 1991). The Convention provides in Article 9, that 'a child shall not be separated from his or her parents against their will, except when competent authorities subject to judicial review determine . . . that such separation is necessary for the best interests of the child'. It also provides that '[s]uch determination may be necessary . . . where the parents are living separately and a decision must be made as to the child's place of residence'. Although German legal scholars strongly refute the assertion that Article 9 would limit the courts' ability to decide custody upon divorce, 'father's rights' groups could gain political momentum in their claim for joint custody, despite the growing evidence from the United States that court-ordered joint custody may be detrimental to mothers and children.[22]

Although many national laws already provide for visitation in the case of divorce, the Convention on the Rights of the Child offers further support for visitation, perhaps even in cases where it is clearly against the interest of the custodial parent (usually the mother) and of questionable value or against the interests of the child. Article 9 (3) protects 'the right of the child who is separated from one or both parents to maintain personal relations and direct contact with both parents on a regular basis, except if it is contrary to the child's best interest'. In the recent highly publicized case in which Dr. Elizabeth Morgan spent more than two years in a Washington, D.C. jail for contempt of court when she refused to subject her child to unsupervised visitation with the girl's father in the face of evidence that he had raped the girl, the Convention could justify the father's visitation. Although one would expect any court to conclude that visitation with a molesting father would be against the child's interests, and Article 19 specifically requires states to protect children from abuse by their own parents, courts may be quite reluctant to conclude that apparently 'normal' men are child abusers. The trial judge in the Morgan case ordered visitation when he believed that the child might or might not have been molested by her father.[23] Moreover, the provisions of Article 11 combating the 'illicit' transfer of children abroad could be used to force the return of the child from New Zealand, where she was living with her maternal grandparents under an assumed name while her mother was in jail.

The issue of 'illicit transfer' of children is a complex one. Certainly it would generally seem best that children not be taken from one jurisdiction to another in custody fights, and certainly women may suffer disproportionally insofar as fathers are more likely to have the financial resources to kidnap a child. Yet, the willingness of desperate women to relocate with their children has served as an important final resort for women deprived of their children by unfair, patriarchal laws. One example is the case in nineteenth-century England which led finally to the enactment of Lord Talfourd's Act, allowing mothers as well as fathers to have custody. The father in that case was alleged to have carried out a threat that if the wife continued her ecclesistical action against him for adultery, he would deprive her of their children, whom he had abandoned. The mother fled from England to keep her children, and Lord Talfourd, the attorney for the father, was so appalled by his 'victory' that he introduced a bill into Parliament that he hoped would prevent similar injustices in the future.[24]

Provisions of the Convention on the Rights of the Child could also be read to justify intrusive questioning of a woman regarding her sexual behaviour in order to find the father of a child in cases in which the mother does not wish for the father to be involved. Or, suppose that a woman were to become pregnant as a result of being gang-raped. If she chose to continue the pregnancy or were barred from having an abortion, would the Convention on the Rights of the Child require the mother to co-operate with blood tests to determine which of the rapists was the father of the child she bore? Article 7 guarantees a child the right to know and be cared for by parents 'as far as possible'. So if this man chose, could he assert a father's right to contact with the child? Surely such a father would be an 'interested part[y]' with a right 'to participate in the proceedings and make [his] views known'. And, 'except if it is contrary to the child's best interests' the father would seem entitled to 'direct contact . . . on a regular basis' with the child.

It is uncertain what effect the Convention would have on the practice of artificial insemination by anonymous donor. Would the consenting husband be considered for all purposes the father, as under certain national laws? Or would the child have a right to discover his or her 'real' father? And if the former, what effect would the Convention have on the struggles of unmarried women, including women in stable domestic partnership with another woman, to have access to artificial insemination by anonymous donor? It is difficult to believe that children will benefit if society forces women to have sexual intercourse with a man if they wish to become pregnant.

Article 21 permits adoptions that are in 'the best interests of the child', but, combined with Article 7's provision that a child has 'as far as possible, the right to know and be cared for by his or her parents' the Convention may limit the practice of 'closed' adoptions, in which the identity of the natural parent is concealed. Although it may usually be good for all involved for adoptions to be open and for children to be able to know their natural parents, as long as many societies in the world seriously penalize unmarried women who give birth to a child, there is some question whether a woman should not be entitled to maintain her anonymity when she gives a child up for adoption. It might well be that children will be better off if young, relatively powerless women are not denied the option of anonymous adoption. Society should remove the stigma of unwed pregnancy before it eliminates possibilities for avoiding that stigma, both for the mothers and for their children.

The provision in the preamble that children need protection before birth may be used to harass women. The provision was inserted at the last minute upon the urging of representatives who had not previously been actively involved in the drafting of the document, and there seems to be a general consensus that the provision will not bar abortion. Indeed, anti-abortionists may be concerned that the provisions regarding a child's right to medical care and provisions regarding family planning (Article 24) will undermine their efforts to chip away at abortion where it is legally available. Nevertheless, arguments will be made and some courts may issue orders harassing pregnant women on the basis of the preamble. Moreover, it may be used in a variety of countries to justify some of the various forms of intrusion to which women in the United States have been subjected, including criminal prosecution of drug-addicted women who have been barred from drug-treatment programmes because of their pregnancy, forced Caesarian sections in cases in which some doctor considers it advisable, and un-consented pre-natal operations upon foetuses. Such actions are particularly likely to harm children in a society such as the United States where poor women have long been denied adequate pre-natal care and may be intimidated against seeking care otherwise available. Inadequate pre-natal care is a leading cause of the extraordinarily high infant mortality rate in the United States. In the case of babies born to drug-addicted mothers, adequate pre-natal care is particularly important and can make the difference between a relatively mild medical problem and long-term or permanent damage to the child (Roberts, 1991).

Although the issue of medical treatment of severely disabled newborns is complex, the better opinion seems to be that parents may be in the best position to make decisions about consenting to medical care that would prolong a short life of pain for newborn babies. For those societies that can afford such care, it seems civilized to make it available even though the child may suffer pain for very little benefit. Yet, when parents conclude that in a hopeless case it would be better to let the child die, for the State to force medical care seems brutal and inappropriate (Minow, 1985). The provisions of Article 23 protecting disabled children and Article 6, protecting the right to life, will surely be interpreted by some to eliminate the possibility of parents choosing against medical care that would prolong the life of a newborn, no matter how hopeless the situation was.

LAW AS PATRIARCHY

The 'Law as Patriarchy' approach is less familiar to most people than the legal reformist approach and seems to some to make less positive contribution. Nevertheless, it is important to understand this approach and particularly to understand the critique it presents of liberal feminist legal reform. Moderate versions of the 'Law as Patriarchy' approach may play a particularly important role in dealing with children's rights issues. Just as a legal reformist approach is associated with and resonates with liberal feminism, the 'Law as Patriarchy' approach is associated with and resonates with the feminist movement referred to (especially by those who do not consider themselves part of the movement) as 'cultural feminism'.

Cultural feminists criticize legal reformist demands for women's equality with men as settling for too little. Men do not represent an adequate aspiration. The greatest problem with society is not just the suppression of women, but the suppression of the values associated with women. Indeed, the effort to achieve legal and social equality could even contribute to the devaluation and suppression of those values. The American women's movement has been criticized, though probably unjustly, for devaluing the work of housewives and mothers and glorifying work in the marketplace and the liberal values identified with men – independence, self-assertion, self-aggrandizement. Cultural feminism tries instead to revalue the traits, morals, and aspirations associated with women. Although many cultural feminists ground their claims about women upon biology (and thus are charged with essentialism) the claims do not require such essentialist grounding.

Cultural feminism is progressive, in my view, insofar as it challenges the devaluation of certain aspects of life, in particular values associated with women. A major weakness of liberal legal reform feminism is its tendency to accept the dominant values of society and to devalue, often inadvertently, those areas of life traditionally associated with women. Cultural feminism is conservative of the status quo, however, insofar as it supports an exaggerated notion of the differences between men and women. While trying to revalue the traits traditionally associated with women, cultural feminists may concede to men, even if inadvertently, positively-connoted traits that a great many men simply do not possess and that many women do in fact possess.

Cultural feminism has gained considerable momentum and prestige through the work of Carol Gilligan. In her enormously popular book *In a Different Voice*, Gilligan presented a politically respectable theoretical basis for reasserting the differences between men and women. She showed how the psychological theory of Kohlberg and others is male-biased in that it described the moral development of *boys* (girl subjects actually being excluded from most of the studies) while it purported to discuss the moral development of *children*. She challenged the ways boys are said to develop moral maturity and the moral maturity claimed by men as partial and incomplete. Writing within the feminist tradition of women scholars filling in the gaps left by male scholarship and often in the process re-conceptualizing an entire field, Gilligan examined the moral development of girls in American society.

Gilligan's study is particularly useful for considering issues of children's rights. She characterized the moral ethic American society teaches girls as an 'ethic of care' and contrasted it with the 'ethic of rights' that our society particularly develops in boys. These two ethics fit very neatly into discussions of children's rights, or parents' obligations to care for children. The Convention could be seen to import the (male) ethic of rights into a field long dominated by women and an ethic of care. This interpretation of the Convention says little about whether importing an ethic of rights is good or bad. On one hand, Gilligan talks about

the need for balance and completion. To the extent an ethic of rights
dominates, a situation can be improved by the insertion of an ethic of
care, and vice versa. She concludes that growth for men might well lie in
their adoption of an ethic of care (which she says some men do in their
later life) while growth for women may lie in their greater adoption of an
ethic of rights. Thus, to the extent the care of children has been dominated by an ethic of care, perhaps the importation of an ethic of rights
could be a very good thing. Some liberal feminist supporters of children's rights might well endorse this view.[25]

On the other hand, cultural feminists might well condemn the importation of an ethic of rights into the field of child care or parent–child
relations. The Convention on the Rights of the Child could represent yet
another field being taken away from women and the values associated
with women being supplanted once again. The most interesting and
sophisticated statement I have found that broadly critiques the notion of
adopting an ethic of rights with respect to children is a 1988 essay by
Onora O'Neill (O'Neill, 1992).

An alternative view of the Convention, from a perspective generally
critical of individual rights, would see the Convention as a potentially
important expansion and re-conceptualization of the basic notion of
rights. This positive vision of rights for children is well illustrated in a
1986 article by Martha Minow that discusses such potentials for children's rights, though it does not address the Convention in particular. It
is not pure happenstance that my two main examples are from people
who do not fit neatly into the 'Law as Patriarchy' camp and would
probably be rather startled to find themselves considered cultural feminists. Moderate instances of the 'Law as Patriarchy' approach tend to
seem useful to law in a way that the more pure expressions of the
position do not.

Negative

In her provocative essay, Onora O'Neill argues that a focus on the
obligations of adults rather than on the rights of children provides a
clearer and more complete view of ethical aspects of children's lives.
O'Neill's opposition to rights is limited. She believes that positive or
legal rights may be useful and that it is only 'when it aspires to become
the sole or fundamental ethical category' that 'the legitimacy of the
discourse of rights becomes problematic'. (O'Neill, 1992:36). O'Neill
introduces three categories of obligations and two categories of rights.
'Universal obligations' owed to all children and 'special obligations'
owed to particular, specified children, can be expressed, without great
loss, in terms of the universal rights of children or the special rights of
the specified children. The third category of obligation, however, cannot
be alternatively expressed in terms of a right. 'Imperfect obligations'
refer to obligations adults owe to children, but not to all children and,

until the obligations are institutionalized, to children who cannot be *specified*. The imperfect obligation owed by adults to unspecified children cannot be expressed as a right, since there is no specified child who can be said to have a corresponding right.

O'Neill considers imperfect obligations to be very important, especially in the lives of children. For this reason, she opposes the open-ended 'right to liberty' supported by libertarians and by many 'deontological liberals', which would deny the existence of any obligation that lacked a corresponding right. O'Neill argues that '[i]f rights are taken as the starting point of ethical debate, imperfect obligations will drop out of the picture because they lack corresponding rights' (O'Neill, 1992:28). Such a 'narrowing of ethical vision' (O'Neill, 1992:28) is particularly harmful for children, whose lives would be diminished if they are to receive no more than their enforceable claims against others. '[A] shift to the idiom of rights in discussions of children risks excluding and neglecting things that matter for children' (O'Neill, 1992:35–6).

A shift to the idiom of rights may, according to O'Neill, be harmful not only to children, but also to any 'lives that are dependent and vulnerable', (O'Neill, 1992:34) which includes all human beings. 'Human beings are . . . vulnerable and needy . . . in the sense that their rationality and their mutual independence – the very basis for their agency – is incomplete, mutually vulnerable and socially produced' (O'Neill, 1992:34). O'Neill points out that '[i]mperfect obligations are traditionally thought to comprise matters such as help, care or consideration'. These are concerns that an ethic of care can address, but that are likely to be overlooked in an ethic of rights. O'Neill does not oppose positive or legal rights for children, but she dismisses the United Nations Declaration of the Rights of the Child as promulgating mere 'manifesto' rights (O'Neill, 1992:37). The Convention on the Rights of the Child would seem to avoid this criticism only to the extent that it can institutionalize the rights and secure enforceable claims.

Of particular interest to us is O'Neill's assertion that rights for children are politically questionable. The popularity of rights discourse she attributes to history. In the eighteenth century, rights were a powerful statement that the recipient was 'no mere loyal subject who petitions for some boon or favour but, rather, a claimant who demands what is owed and is wronged if a rightful claim is denied'. 'The rhetoric of rights', according to O'Neill, 'disputes established powers and their categories and seeks to empower the powerless; it is the rhetoric of those who lack power but do not accept the status quo' (O'Neill, 1992:36). Such a perspective she finds not useful to children. Children's dependence on others is not like the dependence of oppressed social groups for whom rights rhetoric has been empowering. Women, minorities and colonial peoples all had 'capacities for rational and independent life' that were 'demonstrably there but thwarted' by the denial of rights. The dependence of children is very different. If children are old enough to respond to the appeal to rights, 'they will probably find themselves well on the way to majority and to the ending of the forms of disability and dependence that are peculiar to children'. Although children are powerless, 'their main remedy is to grow up' (O'Neill, 1992:39). With respect to oppressed groups, it was important to repudiate the paternalistic model. Not so with children, according to O'Neill. '[P]aternalism may be much of what is ethically required when dealing with children' (O'Neill, 1992:40).

Although O'Neill's essay is interesting and appealing, it is also mistaken in important ways. She has in mind children who are being raised relatively well, she is not thinking of children at risk. Her recognition of abuse stops at 'cold, distant or fanatical parents and teachers' who may deny children 'the genial play of life' (O'Neill, 1992:28). She wants children to be raised to 'learn to share or to show "the unbought grace of life"' (O'Neill, 1992:29). This is all very nice, but it has nothing to do with the lives of millions of the world's children. She is correct, of course, that the situation of children is not exactly like that of women or minorities. The more relevant comparison, however, might be between abused children and oppressed groups. In this sense, the rights of the child are like the Rights of Man. Lots of men did not 'need' any rights. So too lots of children do not 'need' rights because they are cared for well in a supportive environment. O'Neill is correct that children are dependent in many ways that adults are not dependent, but this difference is not itself a problem for children. The problem children have is not dependency, but the abuse or violation of dependency. Again, O'Neill's focus is on relatively emotionally privileged children. Unless we recognize her limited perspective, O'Neill's suggestion that children just need to grow up would seem callous. For abused or neglected children, it is no remedy 'to grow up' (O'Neill, 1992:39). Their problem is how they can manage to grow up, to raise themselves without the help they need.

I am generally sympathetic with O'Neill's support for paternalism toward children. Although the Roman origins of the word, combined with the role of the *pater* in Roman law (and perhaps life) (Dixon, 1988) give one pause, paternalism often gets unduly maligned.[26] What is properly and positively referred to as paternalism is based on connection and intersubjecivity, which are good, not evil. It seems to me, however, that there is some slipperiness in O'Neill's use of the term 'paternalism'. The primary evil of 'paternalistic' behaviour toward adults is really not that it treats an adult with the kind of care and concern that would be proper toward a child. As O'Neill recognizes, the claim of fatherly concern by those exercising illegitimate power over women, minorities, colonial peoples, or other oppressed groups is generally not made in good faith but is 'highly political rhetoric' (O'Neill, 1992:38). The same kind of negative, bad faith 'paternalism' that oppresses adults is just as oppressive to children[27]. Once again, O'Neill's analysis is limited by her focus on emotionally privileged children who are being raised relatively well.

Positive

One can recognize the cogency of many critiques of rights and still have a more optimistic view of children's rights. For example, in a 1986 article, Martha Minow discussed many problems and pitfalls of rights, but argued that the development of children's rights could lead to a productive re-conceptualization of the whole notion of rights (Minow, 1986). Her analysis was informed, as she characterized it, 'by three feminist concerns: appreciation of relationships, a commitment to a vision of the self forged in connection with – not just through separation from – others, and a preference for glimpses of complexity, contextual detail, and continuing conversation' (Minow, 1986:15). The dominant conception of rights presupposes an autonomous individual who has a direct relationship with the state. This conception is problematic with respect to children, who are not autonomous but dependent (both 'in their lives as lived' (Minow, 1986:18) and as a result of legal rules denying them independence) and whose relationship to the State is generally not direct but mediated by their parents. Like O'Neill, Minow recognizes that the liberal conception of an autonomous individual is also problematic with respect to adults. Unlike O'Neill, Minow finds in children's rights possibilities for expanding and enriching rights, for adults as well as for children.

Minow traces the history of the legal treatment of children in America and finds a 'contest between two competing principles: the principle of individual rights, and the principle that the care and custody of children by adults serves the interests of both' (Minow, 1986:13). The shared interests perspective 'suggests that individual rights are not just unnecessary, but may actually damage the relationship between [adult] and child, because children need authority, not rights' (Minow, 1986:13). Minow's response to this argument is to 'challenge simplistic conceptions of rights' and 'offer an avenue for developing richer notions of rights'. (Minow, 1986:15).

Minow looks to 'earlier and persistent uses of law to facilitate interpersonal relationships' (Minow, 1986:16) and finds a conception of rights at odds with the claim that rights protect personal autonomy rather than human relationship or connection. She invites us to reject the view that rights run only between an individual and the State and that rights only mark and preserve the distance between people. Although children's rights are often designed to constrain abuses of power by the State or by parents, there exists also another concept of children's rights, in some tension with this first understanding – rights that promote the ability of children 'to form relationships of trust, meaning, and affection with people in their daily lives and their broader communities'. (Minow, 1986:24). This tension between rights to autonomy and to connect is obvious with children, but it exists with adults also. 'Rights could be part of legal arrangements that permit, not to mention promote, relationships for adults – while also combating hierarchy and fixed assignments of status.' (Minow, 1986:17–18). An important goal is to devise 'rights for children that can promote relationships while protecting autonomy'. (Minow, 1986:18).

Minow suggests that the notion of 'duty' can enrich the discussion. Duty 'introduce[s] a bilateral dimension to rights that gives them content'. (Minow, 1986:23). The task of formulating duties 'would direct people's attention to aspects of rights committed to facilitating interpersonal connection'. (Minow, 1986:23). In this way, it expresses a social commitment to 'individual freedom to form relationships with others'. (Minow, 1986:23). 'The critical need for . . . institutions addressing children's rights . . . is to focus on the preconditions for relationships'. (Minow, 1986:23). The goal of autonomy should not be abandoned, but it must be joined with the goal of affiliation. From this perspective, many of the most valuable provisions of the United Nations Convention on the Rights of the Child may be those O'Neill might consider mere 'manifesto' rights, in that they may be those rights least able to be institutionalized or to secure enforceable claims.

FEMINIST CRITICAL LEGAL THEORY

One important distinguishing feature of Critical Legal Studies is that it tries to challenge simultaneously the assertion that law is rational, abstract and principled – characteristics valued as manly – and at the same time challenge the valuation of these characteristics. Law is neither the enemy of women nor the privileged arena for feminist struggles. Not all work considered to fall within the realm of Critical Legal Studies makes such a challenge. The concern of this paper is with the work that does, not with Critical Legal Studies in general.

Many different positions have been put forward by scholars associated with the Critical Legal Studies movement. The ones that are most important for the purposes of a feminist critical legal theory perspective on the Convention on the Rights of the Child include the challenge to the public/private distinction (questioning both the state/society and the family/market dichotomies), a critical examination of the notion of 'choice' central to liberal political theory, and a critique of rights analysis as indeterminate.

State/Society

The public/private distinction has two important dimensions. First, the distinction refers to the dichotomy between state action and non-state, or private action. Drawing on the insights of the American Legal Realists (1920s–30s), scholars working in the Critical Legal Studies tradition have shown the manipulability and ultimately the incoherence of the distinction between state action and non-state action. My own work has developed this critique specifically in the context of the question of state 'intervention' in the family. In my relatively early article, 'The Family and the Market: A Study of Ideology and Legal Reform' (Olsen, 1983) and again more explicitly in 'The Myth of State Intervention in the Family' (Olsen, 1985) I show how 'the family' and roles within the family are constructed by law, and that state intervention in the family is not an analytical concept but rather an ideological one. Family law is an arena for ideological struggle over what it means to be a mother, daughter, wife, and so forth, as well as an arena for overt political struggle over power within the family and upon the breakup of a marriage (Olsen, 1984b; Olsen, 1986b). One of the most important questions about the Convention on the Rights of the Child is how it affects these political and ideological struggles.

Family/Market

A second dimension of the public/private distinction is the dichotomy between the 'private' family or domestic world, and the 'public' commercial world. A critical examination of this distinction allows us to 'denaturalize' the family, and to recognize the contingent character of family life. The Convention on the Rights of the Child is striking in its ability to bridge over different family forms found throughout the world. Someone whose only knowledge of life on earth came from a careful reading of the Convention would be puzzled by the occasional references to 'traditional practices' and 'those responsible for children' other than parents. Throughout most of the document, one would assume that all children were born into two-parent families that look a lot like the family of my first grade reader – Dick, Jane and Baby Sally, Mom baking cookies at home, Daddy coming home from the office in a nice suit and playing with the children. Although cookie baking is clearly *productive* work, this family displays a sharp split between productive work in the market and affective life at home with the family. The family is the private haven to which Dick and Jane return from the public world of school and Daddy from the public world of work. Baby Sally and Mom stay at home, non-productive. If Sally helps bake the cookies, we all know that this is not child labour.

In the family worlds of many societies, life is not so easy and pleasant. It is not always clear when a child is being allowed to participate in the life of the community, and when the child is being exploited.[28] The radical separation of home from work place is taken for granted, and the separation is assumed to be a good thing. The alternative possibility of making work places healthy and educational environments for children seems never to have been considered.[29]

'Choice'

The third issue of particular importance to a critical feminist analysis of the Convention on the Rights of the Child is the question of choice. Feminists have shown how the concept of 'choice' is problematic. The anti-rape work of feminists such as Andrea Dworkin and Catharine MacKinnon shows the problems with the liberal concept of choice as it applies to the consent standard in sexual crimes. To the extent that rape law ignores power differentials and treats women's consent to intercourse as an un-coerced norm, it has difficulty dealing with the myriad of ways that women are pressured, coerced and forced into unwanted sexual contact. The failure of rape law to enforce women's choice not to have sex in many situations has the effect of enforcing women's 'consent' to unwanted sexual contact.

Feminists have shown the difficulty with choice in other contexts as well. In a recent article, Vicki Schultz studied sex discrimination cases that raised the issue of whether women were under-represented in certain jobs because of employers' discrimination or because of women's choice. She examined a variety of ways in which the work place constructs jobs and the people who fill those jobs. Specifically, the desire or lack of desire of women to work at 'non-traditional' jobs cannot intelligently be considered to be given in sex discrimination law. The experience of women on the job and the images and ideas about the work that are promulgated by the employer radically influence – indeed construct – the desire of women to work or not to work at particular jobs. The image of a woman worker that is put forth will affect how many women apply for (well-paying) jobs and how many get hired, as well as how difficult a time a woman who is not hired will have trying to prove that the reason she did not get the job was that she was a woman (Schultz, 1990).

Given the difficulty with 'choice' as applied to adults, it should be no surprise that there are problems with applying the notion to children. The United Nations Convention on the Rights of the Child tries to finesse the issue. The major provision dealing with the child's choices is Article 12, which states that a 'child who is capable of forming his or her own views' must be given the 'right to express those views freely in all matters affecting the child' and that these views must be 'given due weight in accordance with the age and maturity of the child'. In particular, the child must 'be provided the opportunity to be heard in any judicial and administrative proceedings affecting the child either directly, or through a representative or an appropriate body'.

As well as 'age and maturity', the Convention speaks of children's 'evolving capacities'. Article 5 refers to parents providing 'direction and guidance' to the child to exercise the rights recognized in the Convention 'in a manner consistent with the evolving capacities of the child'. Article

14 protects the child's 'freedom of thought, conscience and religion' and mentions the 'duties' of parents and guardians again 'to provide direction to the child in the exercise of his or her right in a manner consistent with the evolving capacities of the child'. Choice, coercion and consent of children involve questions of power and present more problems than just 'evolving capacities' of the 'age and maturity' of the child. In ignoring questions of power and treating choice as a matter of age and maturity, the convention may miss dealing with some of the harder questions.

One context in which the question of a child's choice arises in a crucially important way is in child abuse. The provisions in the convention for children's input are probably not specific enough for ratification of the convention to help abused children in the United States, for example, where child abuse is widespread and government policies on child abuse often do as much harm to children as good for them. Although child abuse is dealt with on a state-by-state basis, common problems arise from the failure to listen to children and the endemic overriding of the child's stated wishes. The flip side of ignoring the power that restricts choice is to ignore the choices that children nevertheless make in the face of power.

On one hand, children's reports of abuse are not believed. American cities are filled with homeless adolescents whose wishes to leave abusing parents were not recognized or respected by government authorities. The protestations of young children of divorced parents are often discounted as being merely the result of the negative influence of one parent on the child, as in Dr. Elizabeth Morgan's case, and the children are forced to visit their other parent unless and until abuse can be proven to the satisfaction of an often sceptical court. Too often children seeking help are ignored or silenced. In the rare cases in which a child is driven to strike back at an abusing parent, the history of abuse is usually treated as no defence and long jail terms are not uncommon. On occasion judges may even acknowledge that they are giving a harsh sentence to deter other children from 'taking the law into their own hands'. Even if the judges are not consciously trying to contribute to a broader message that children had better remain passive and not try to do anything about abuse, that is all too much the message children consistently receive.

On the other hand, when governmental authorities conclude that child abuse has taken place, children's wishes are often overridden, or their wishes never even become known because the authorities still do not listen to the children. Pleas of the child to remain with his or her parents are often discounted and ignored. Article 9 requires States Parties to 'ensure that a child shall not be separated from his or her parents against *their* will' [emphasis added] except if State authorities properly determine such separation 'is necessary for the best interests of the child'. Although section (2) of the Article would seem certainly to include the child as one of the 'interested parties' who 'shall be given an opportunity to participate' and 'make their views known' in such a determination, children would benefit from a provision that a child may not be separated from his or her parents against *the child's* will. Virtually all choices are coerced in a sense, and few if any choices are so coerced that they should be ignored.

However well intentioned government workers may be, the actual effect of their refusal to respect the wishes of children is to make the government into an accessory to child abuse. Most child abuse – especially sexual abuse – depends upon secrecy. In the United States most child neglect also depends upon secrecy. An abuser maintains this secrecy most often through threats of the dire consequences that would ensue were the secret to be made public. Even in cases in which the government worker is acting in complete good faith and is generally competent, the reaction by the authorities to child abuse is likely to reinforce the abuser's message: 'Don't tell or there'll be real trouble.'

From the point of view of the authorities evaluating the child's choice, it is easy to say that the child is too immature to exercise a proper choice. The crucial factor that such an analysis leaves out, however, is that kids do make choices. Often they choose to go along with the secrecy deman- ded by the abusing parent. However much we may disparage the 'choice' and point out the child's lack of freedom to choose, we must accept our responsibility for further constraining the choices children feel are open to them. If society is really interested in stopping child abuse, every effort should be made to encourage the exposure of abuse and to help children protect themselves. To avoid silencing children, a primary rock-solid principle must be that a child *never* be worse off for telling about abuse. All too often, the child is worse off. The child is often worse off by almost anyone's criterion; certainly the child is often worse off by his or her own criterion. No abused or neglected child should have the added burden of being afraid that social workers may discover the child's plight and act against the child's wishes.

If the child says she or he wishes to stay in the family, this wish should be respected. Children need this security if they are to be able to break silence and to protect themselves effectively. The furthest any govern- ment worker should ever be allowed to go is to ensure the child has the opportunity to state her or his preferences in some environment free from immediate coercion by any member of the family *and* free of coercion by anyone else, including the government worker. If the child continues to express a desire to remain home, even in a risky environ- ment, the State should be required to limit itself to alternative methods of protection. Certainly electronic alarms that can be activated by the child are a possibility in western industrialized countries such as the United States. Even adding a social worker to the household of the abused child would be possible. In the long run, such a policy would be no more expensive than the ineffective alternatives currently in use.

In treating choice as too simple an issue, subject to a child's evolving capacities and limited by a child's age and maturity, the Convention avoids dealing with many of the factors that actually limit children's choices. It neglects the subtle as well as blatant exercises of power that constrain and indeed structure the choices of adults and of children. Nevertheless, the provisions requiring children to be heard are to be commended. It may be that the Convention will encourage adults to develop habits of listening to children. Such habits could significantly improve children's lives and encourage children who are trying, however ambiguously, to expose neglect or abuse, to do so and to be heard.

Rights Analysis: Gaps, Conflicts and Ambiguities

The United Nations Convention on the Rights of the Child illustrates the broader problems with any project of trying to improve the life situation of a group by conferring rights. But laws conferring rights will have gaps, conflicts and ambiguities. In the case of children's rights, these gaps, conflicts and ambiguities are if anything more pronounced. There is an often noted conflict between children's rights against their parents (protected by empowering the State) and their rights against the State (usually protected by empowering their parents). The classic conflict between substantive equality and formal equality takes the form of a conflict between children's rights to be protected (and have their youth recognized) and their rights to receive the same treatment as anyone else (which usually means being treated as an adult). If we add in Martha Minow's rights that promote children's ability 'to form relationships of trust, meaning, and affection with people in their daily lives and their broader communities', we have even more conflicts, or at least 'tensions'.

To give some specific examples from the Convention, children have a right to be protected from pornography, but the child's right to freedom of expression includes the right to 'receive and impart information and ideas of all kinds', Article 13. Pornography may be the most effective means of imparting the idea that women are inferior to men and that violence against women and the degradation of women are sexy. While the Convention certainly takes a different view of women and their roles, no one would limit the freedom to receive and impart ideas to those ideas the Convention promotes. Primary education is compulsory, Article 28 and shall 'be directed to' the 'preparation of the child for responsible life in a free society, in the spirit of understanding, peace, tolerance, equality of sexes, and friendship among all peoples'. To one who does not support these ideals, this direction is likely to sound more like propaganda than education.[30] This education toward tolerance, equality between the sexes, and friendship conflicts with various religions, which the Convention guarantees to children the right to practice. A child has the right to practice his or her religion, yet the State must protect the child from denial of medical care (required by some religions)[31] and 'illicit use of narcotic drugs and psychotropic substances' (central to some religions).

Articles 38 and 13 provide an interesting example of conflicting rights. Certainly, the Convention's specification that children under the age of fifteen should not be soldiers is an appropriate humanitarian gesture (and indeed it should be embarrassing to Americans that it was United States representatives who prevented the adoption of a stronger provision) (Hammarberg, 1990:101). Yet the philosophy behind this provision can come into conflict with the provision in Article 13 that children have a right to have and express political views. Especially children in irregular or guerilla armies may be expressing their political views, perhaps in the only way that they would consider effective. Children participating in Civil Rights demonstrations in the United States in the 1960s and 1970s were subjected to some of the same kinds of danger and stresses that children soldiers are. Were the children at Wounded Knee, South Dakota, during the uprising of 1973 adequately protected from the evils of soldiering as long as they were not allowed to carry a gun? Many of the people at Wounded Knee considered themselves to be using guns purely for self-defence; and many of the children would say that even if they had been allowed to carry a gun, they would still have been exercising their freedom of expression, not acting as soldiers. Insofar as all the people at Wounded Knee were in the line of fire of the US Marshals and the FBI troops, who seemed at times to be viewing them all as hostile soldiers, it could be argued that the philosophy behind the Convention's limitation on children soldiers should bar children from participating in such potentially dangerous social protest actions.[32] Any such interpretation, however, would begin to limit children's rights to express their political views to those expressions of views that are relatively uncontroversial or unopposed. Rights analysis does not resolve any of these conflicts, but at most re-expresses them.

POST-MODERN FEMINISM

As I mentioned in the introduction, the distinction between Critical Feminism and Post-Modern Feminism is not a sharp or clear division, but rather more a matter of emphasis. Each challenges both the gendering of life and law, and the claimed differences between men and women. The different emphasis relates to the fact that what I refer to as postmodern feminism focuses on the rejection of dichotomization as such and is more concerned with the positive views of difference. Like cultural feminism, post-modernism has a conservative aspect. The conservative aspect of post-modernism lies not in its acceptance of the difference asserted between men and women but rather in its tendency to dissolve the category of women altogether, rendering problematic feminist politics. Post-modernism throws into question the bases underlying judgements about what is progressive.

The concerns of post-modern feminism that bear most closely on the Convention on the Rights of the Child include the whole notion of a universal document to deal with all children, throughout the world; the concern that such an effort will almost inevitably result in a western-oriented document that merely purports to be universal; and, more positively, the question of the category 'child' and the status of that category.

Universalism and Grand Approaches

Some writers admire the Convention for its universalism. For example, Michael Jupp reports happily on the drafting of the Convention that it was 'an exemplary exercise in international consensus-building and demonstrates that the values associated with the family are, indeed, universal' (Jupp, 1990:134). Given the variety of family forms and the variety of 'values' that might be found to be 'associated with' any of these family forms, Jupp's statement could be considered either self-evident or astounding. I am not sure which way I am more inclined to view it. 'Family values' has been used in the United States as a tag line or code for conservative, anti-feminist views, just as 'states' rights' in the 1960s and 1970s was a tag line or code for supporting racism. Even more than 'states' rights', however, it seems important not to abandon 'family values' to its limited, coded use. And many of the values that Michael Jupp probably has in mind when he refers to 'the values associated with the family' are values of particular importance to women as a group. Universal standards have a strong appeal. Especially for people who are often omitted from various benefits or in other ways feel left out of society, something *universal* has appeal in part because of its promised inclusion.

Universal standards have serious problems, however. One such problem is that they seem to overlook particular social meanings. The social meaning of a law forbidding abortion for sex selection, for example, is very different in India than in the United States. In the United States where there is no history of gender-specific abortion nor a realistic danger of the practice, such a law serves the purpose of chipping away at the woman's right to abortion by entitling the State to harass a woman with questions regarding why she is choosing to have an abortion. At some point, it may serve to drive women to overseas or back-alley abortions. In India, the meaning is different. There amniocentesis has been used specifically to determine the sex of a foetus and if the sex is female, the pregnancy is in most instances terminated. Moreover, in India the abortion decision is all too often forced upon women by their families. The anti-sex-selection laws recently enacted in the Indian states of Maharashtra and Goa are part of the state Governments' attempt to protect girl children from systematic exploitation and relative neglect (Lingam, 1991; Mendonca, 1990).[33]

Another important criticism of universal standards is that their promise of inclusion is so often broken. Universalism can be a camouflage hiding some of the worst forms of cultural chauvinism.

Cultural Chauvinism

During the debates over the draft convention, writers such as Russell Barsh raised the issue of cultural chauvinism. He pointed out that only four Articles referred to parties beyond 'parents' and 'legal guardians' (Barsh, 1989). During the earlier years of the drafting process, the Convention had a considerably stronger 'Western industrialized bias', which was moderated only by the 'more active participation of countries outside the Western group' later in the process and the advocacy of Non-Governmental Organizations ('NGO's') and UN special agencies (Miljeteig-Olssen, 1990:151).

The final version of the Convention can be seen as either cultural pluralist or cultural chauvinist, depending upon one's expectations and upon one's understanding of how the document will be interpreted. There are a number of references to respecting different cultural practices, and the failure to define 'parent' raises possible pluralist interpretations. For example, there is really nothing in the Convention to prevent two women in a stable domestic partnership, as in the example presented in Part 1 above, from being both considered 'parents' of a child born of one of them through artificial insemination by anonymous donor. Other such pluralist interpretations could enable the recognition of a multiplicity of family forms. The right of the child to protect his or her identity could mean biological identity, but it could also refer to cultural identity.

The Category 'Child'

An examination of the provision in Article 8 that State Parties must 'respect the right of the child to preserve his or her identity' may suggest a more complex process than that envisioned by the Argentine representatives who sought support in the Convention to prevent the kinds of abuses that occurred under the military dictatorship. The provision was designed to mean that children must not be abducted or 'disappear' and that the children of the victims of political terror cannot be stolen by adoptive parents. These are important issues. This kind of problem has appeared before, as for instance in Nazi Germany; and it unfortunately may arise again, in nearly any country. It is important for the Convention and the international community to offer as much support as possible to those fighting to prevent such tragedies.

It should not interfere with this primary use of Article 8, however, to consider additional possible uses to be made of the Article. As one author has suggested, 'the future interpretation of the Convention could be made more comprehensive by the addition . . . of aspects of identity not envisaged by the authors of the text themselves' (Cerda, 1990:116). In a complex way, our identities are not established by our birth or by our parents but are made or created by ourselves in the process of our interactions in society. And they are constantly in the process of being remade. A right to an identity could imply anything from respect for chosen (or not consciously chosen) sexual orientation to respect for all the child's efforts to remake his or her identity. Indeed, the basic concept of childhood could be thrown open for redefinition.

CONCLUSIONS

I have examined four different approaches feminists might take in evaluating the Convention on the Rights of the Child. Each of the approaches I have studied has something to recommend it, though none is without its difficulty. None of the approaches fully explains my own view of the Convention, which is generally positive. Like the proposed Equal Rights Amendment (ERA) to the United States Constitution, the Convention on the Rights of the Child is not a document I would have drafted and chosen to focus energies upon. Nevertheless, just as the failure thus far to ratify the ERA is a travesty, so too is the failure of the United States thus far to ratify the Convention on the Rights of the Child a travesty (Olsen, 1991). Whatever criticisms I may have of the Convention, I believe it is better for it to be ratified and enforced than for it not to be. There will undoubtedly be some aspects of the enforcement of the Convention that I will find wrong-headed and destructive, but overall it may stand to improve the status and lives of children. This is an enormously worthwhile project.

NOTES

[1] *See generally* Olsen (1984a).

[2] A related view is reflected in the subtitle of a set of conference papers recently published in Germany: *Menschenrechte haben (k)ein Geschlecht* ('Human Rights have [a/no] Sex'), Gerhard (1990).

[3] Some argue that women's role as *bearers* of children gives them a greater interest than men in the welfare of children. Perhaps or perhaps not. The cultural meaning of pregnancy and childbirth, not the simple biological fact, is the crucial issue. In any event, women's role as primary caretakers alone is certainly sufficient to explain the greater stake women seem to have in children.

[4] See also Charlesworth, Chenkin and Wright (1991). A book by these authors on the same topic is scheduled to be published in 1993 by Manchester University Press, with a working title of 'The Rules of the Game'.

[5] This terminology derives from Olsen (1990a). See also Olsen (1990b); Olsen (1990c); Olsen (1987).

[6] A more complicated question is whether the Convention on the Rights of the Child may promote human rights in general. It has been signed and ratified with unprecedented speed. Countries that have not agreed to other human rights provisions have accepted it. It may be that

these countries will now be less reluctant to sign other human rights agreements. On the other hand, having signed one may relieve the pressure they could otherwise feel to join other human rights initiatives. In addition, to whatever extent the Convention may be less enforceable than other human rights documents, it may undermine actual compliance with other human rights norms, setting a precedent, as it were, for noncompliance.

[7] It should be noted, however, that other documents deal with child marriage and that many consider the Convention's treatment of children in the military to be a step backward from the humanitarian law in other documents. See eg, Hammarberg (1990:101).

Other significant omissions are less clearly gender-related. For example, except for the reference in Article 24(2)(c) to 'the risks of environmental pollution', the Convention is silent on environmental questions, although children are more dramatically affected than adults by the degradation of the environment, both at the present time and in terms of the future. Children's bodies absorb more pollutants because children are growing faster than adults. Some pollutants particularly affect children in utero, or even while they are still eggs and sperm.

[8] See generally *Special Issue on the Girl Child* (1991) (detailing severe discrimination against girl children in India).

[9] Preamble, para 9, quoting from the Declaration of the Rights of the Child, Resolution 1386 (XIV), third preambular paragraph.

[10] But see Alston (1990) (showing inconsistency between an anti-abortion interpretation of Convention and the intent of its drafters). See discussion *infra*.

[11] For my argument that society should recognize the gestational parent's central role in determining if and when before birth her creation should be valued, and that society would take such a role for granted, except for the fact that this gestational parent is always female, combined with the tradition of devaluing women, women's moral status, and the work that women do, see Olsen (1989); see also Olsen (1991). On the pervasive devaluation of women's work, see Olsen (1988).

[12] See Gilligan (1983), discussed *infra*.

[13] This critique is stated more fully in Olsen (1983).

[14] This critique has been well developed in respect to sexual offences against women, see, eg, MacKinnon (1983), and more recently with respect to women's employment in non-traditional jobs. See Schultz (1990) criticizing the dichotomization of women being excluded from traditionally male jobs because of unlawful discrimination or because they *choose* not to seek such employment.

[15] Bettina Cass, comments made on 16 July 1991, at the conference on 'Children, Rights and the Law', in Canberra, Australia, sponsored by the Centre for International and Public Law, Australian National University, 15–18 July 1991.

[16] See sources cited in Olsen (1983).

[17] Traditionally, in Anglo-American law, as in other systems also, the marital status of the father was irrelevant. As long as the mother was married, the child would be 'presumed' to be legitimate (Teichman, 1982; Laslett, Oosterveen & Smith, 1980).

[18] One would hope that 'exploitative use' is designed for emphasis and not that the drafters envision many *non-exploitative* uses for children in pornography and prostitution. Similarly, one might wonder about the qualifier *'unlawful* sexual activity' and hope that no one intends for children to be coerced into forms of sexual activity that happen not yet to have been outlawed. I wonder whether the use of terms like 'exploitative' and 'unlawful' are more likely to be added to provisions dealing with sexuality than to provisions involving topics thought to be less personal.

[19] Article 24(2)(e) refers to education on the benefits of breast-feeding. Insofar as only women lactate (to any significant extent), some might argue that this provision is gender specific in effect. Virtually the whole document, however, is gender specific in effect. That one could imagine a world in which most provisions would cease to be in effect gender specific but in which the provision on breast-feeding would continue to be gender-specific in effect is perhaps interesting but of uncertain relevancy.

[20] Further, Article 18 directs states to encourage 'recognition of the principle that both parents have common responsibilities for the upbringing and development of the child'.

[21] For a useful recent discussion of the difficulty in the United States of enforcing parental obligations of divorced fathers, see Furstenberg & Cherlin (1991).

[22] See eg Furstenberg & Cherlin (1991).

[23] The trial judge referred to the evidence that the father did molest his daughter and the

evidence that he did not molest his daughter as being in 'equipose'. Much may depend upon the trial judge. In a previous case involving the same father and a daughter by an earlier marriage, a different judge, faced with similar evidence of molestation of that daughter, refused to order visitation. We must remember also that child abuse is found throughout society, and it is probable that a certain percentage of cases will be decided by judges who have molested their own sons or daughters. In a case something like the *Morgan* case in Germany, the divorced father accused of molesting his daughter is a judge.

[24] Cited and discussed in Olsen (1982).

[25] Although cultural feminists have found her work useful, Gilligan is distinguishable from cultural feminists in that she considers the differences between men and women culturally created rather than natural or inevitable and she would support a reduction in the differences between men and women. She does not share the conservatism of cultural feminism.

Her work is however, capable of a conservative interpretation. She provided support for the general assertion that women's moral development is *different* from men's. Although she does not intend to be supporting the false assertion of women's essential difference from men, people have used her work for just such a purpose, and indeed its ability to be so used has contributed to its enormous popularity.

[26] For my qualified defence of paternalism, see Olsen (1986:1531–4).

[27] A particular problem of 'paternalism' toward women is that the person exhibiting the 'paternalistic' behaviour claims a relationship of intimacy or intersubjective sharing with the woman that she often has rejected or would like to reject. Thus 'paternalism' is also involved with the problem of men as a group feeling all too justified in forcing intimacy upon the women with whom they choose to relate. See Olsen (1984a:393–4).

For another interesting view on the paternalism issue, consider the traditional uses in German of the familiar pronoun 'du' and formal 'Sie'. Adults use the 'Sie' form to each other unless and until they achieve a certain intimacy and interdependency. Adults on 'du' terms have traditionally been expected to recognize significant obligations of care and protection toward one another. Adults call all children 'du', while children call adults outside their intimate circle 'Sie'. One understanding of this practice is that adult–child obligations are not mutual: although the child has no corresponding obligation to protect or defend an adult stranger, adults are supposed to protect all children with the kind of care and concern they would show to their 'du' friends. To claim a 'du' relationship and then not carry through on it properly is one understanding of the problem of paternalism. (A very different understanding of the adult–child relationship emerges from a comparison to hierarchical relationships in which the adult inferior uses the respectful 'Sie' to his superior but is in turn referred to by the familiar 'du' form.)

[28] The domestic labour of daughters in many Indian households is quite exploitative (Nayar, 1991).

[29] It should be clear that I in no way intend to diminish or downplay the evil of the abuses involved with child labour. Under present conditions, child labour is an important concern of children's rights and human rights activists. See Alston (1989). My point is simply that we should not take for granted that the only solution for this evil is the exclusion of children from productive work and the continued split between our affective lives, in families, and our productive lives, in a marketplace unfit for children.

[30] The American folk singer Pete Seeger made a related point nicely when he pointed out that to a child a lullaby is a form of propaganda.

[31] Although the religion called 'Christian Science' is the best known opponent of medical care, Jehovah's Witnesses are also often required by their faith to forgo medical care. Catholics have been forbidden to use birth control or have abortions, even in cases in which pregnancy will kill a woman. See Pius XI (1930:paras 53–8) (proclaiming every form of birth control to be 'shameful and intrinsically vicious', a 'horrible crime', and 'a grave sin'); see Pius XI (1930:para 64) (proclaiming that 'however much we may pity the mother whose health and even life is gravely imperiled', doctors who perform therapeutic abortions act from 'misguided pity' and 'show themselves most unworthy of the noble medical profession').

[32] Although the United States does not draft children this young into its own army, the United States Government has often supported the exploitation of very young boys as soldiers, for example in Korea, in Vietnam and in the 'Contra' army against Nicaragua.

[33] See Lingham (1991); Ingrid Mendonca (1990).
It should be noted that the laws in Maharashtra and Goa do not try to restrict abortion, which

could simply put more pressure on pregnant women. The Maharashtra Regulation of Use of Prenatal Diagnostic Techniques Act of 1988, for example, bans the practice of using the tests to determine sex and 'declares illegal any advertisements regarding the availability of facilities for prenatal prediction of sex at clinics[,] laboratories [, and] centres'. (Lingam, 1991).

THE IMPORTANCE OF THINKING THAT CHILDREN HAVE RIGHTS

JOHN EEKELAAR*

ABSTRACT

In declaring that children have rights, the United Nations may have been unaware that philosophers and jurists have differed among themselves over the basis for conceiving that children may have rights. It is suggested in this paper that the problem is compounded by the practice of framing policy towards children in the form of general duties to promote their welfare. It is argued that legal relationships of this kind exclude the essential features of rights-based relationships. The paper offers a theoretical basis on which assertions that children have rights may be grounded and an explanation of the social significance of making such assertions. It closes by placing the United Nations Convention on the Rights of the Child within this framework.

PART ONE

Suppose that all adults were held to be under a duty (legal or moral) to promote the welfare of all children. The analytic proposition that duties entail rights[1] would compel the conclusion that the children would have a right that the adults should promote their welfare. It will be argued that this formalistic perception of rights conceals the centrally significant feature about thinking that people have rights and, furthermore, that that feature is absent in the circumstances hypothesized in the opening sentence. I will then examine the implications of this argument for difficult issues in child law and, finally, for the United Nations Convention on the Rights of the Child.

A A Socialist Vision of Rights

In *The Left and the Rights* (1983) Tom Campbell wished to rebut the 'revolutionary' socialist argument that legal rights and socialism were incompatible. His strategy was first to identify those elements in 'bourgeois' concepts of rights to which the revolutionary objects: these are that the idea of rights is *necessarily* associated with (1) a society governed by rules; (2) a system of social coercion; (3) the recognition of

* Fellow of Pembroke College, Oxford, OXI 1DW, United Kingdom; Reader in Law at the University of Oxford. I am grateful to the other contributors to this volume for their criticisms and observations of an earlier draft of this paper.

selfish individual interests and (4) an acceptance of moral values outwith the social structure. His next step was to *assume* the possibility of a 'truly' socialist society in which: (1) as in a paradigm of the family, the motivation for action is not rule-based, but springs from spontaneous care for others; (2) coercion is therefore irrelevant; (3) individuals are not concerned with advancing their selfish interests and (4) moral claims outside social behaviour are not acknowledged.

Campbell then argued that, even within such a society, there will be a place for a system of rights. Rights will be possible, or even necessary, as organizational measures to ensure the distribution of social resources. But they will not be identified by reference to the 'selfish' interests of individuals but by reference to *those things in which the individual 'is interested' (in the sense of 'concerned')*. These need not necessarily be things which are in his selfish interest, and in socialist society, would not be.

... while the 'selfish' interpretations of 'interests', in which it is assumed that a person's interests are self-regarding (that is, directed towards benefiting himself) are characteristic of a society in which 'individualism' implies the propriety of each seeking his own benefit except in so far as he is constrained by custom or law from harming others in the process, *it would not be so in a society such as the socialist envisages.* (Campbell, 1983:95). (emphasis supplied)

Furthermore, since individuals will be acting altruistically and not out of self-interest, the obligation to respect these rights will be non-coercive (Campbell, 1983:187). But, and this was Campbell's thesis, these will nevertheless be rights and obligations, conceptually related to present juristic analyses, though operating within a socialist society. Campbell advances the idea that rights can be conceptualized in terms of objects which people may be 'interested in' because he wished to salvage the idea of rights within a society in which people are not motivated by selfishness. But if I am interested, in this disinterested way, in your welfare, who has the right? Campbell seemed to say that it is my right.

It is not being argued, however, that just any interest in a person or event will be an adequate ground for the acquisition of a right, but only that such interests are candidates for having the protection of right-conferring rules. And in those cases where the interests in question do not relate to a condition which involves the right-holder it still remains the case that the right is his because its justification relates to the fact that it is his interest in the person or event that is the grounds (sic) for establishing and maintaining the right. (Campbell, 1983:101).

Campbell observed that this right may be compatible with a right held by the person in whom I am interested, but added:

It is not hard to give examples of existing rights which are based on the individual's concern for others, such as the rights which parents may have for support in the care of their children.

In socialist society, this will be the 'standard' type of right. He went on:

The fact that it may seem strange to regard the standard right as arising from a non-self-centred interest may derive more from the fact that in the societies with which we are most familiar self-directed interests are those which are most prized and protected. But there is no logical reason why this should be so.

Such a right, Campbell concluded 'accords well with the socialist ideal of man as an active, project-pursuing and creative being'.

I wish to stress the primacy afforded in this analysis to the 'right' of A to enhance B's welfare. It is true that it somewhat mitigated when, later in his book, Campbell offered arguments according to which socialists could commend specific rights (Campbell, 1983:ch 7). An important one was that needs should be met. The needy clearly have rights (these must be self-regarding) but, since in socialist society no one is privileged, they have the right to provide also for others. Campbell assumed, however, that A wants to give B what A thinks B needs and that B wants exactly what A thinks he needs, no more, no less. This assumption of perfect congruence between all members of this utopian society, however, prevented Campbell from exploring the possibility that B might conceive his or her needs differently from the way A conceived them. This leads to the central issue of this paper: if someone has the right to determine my welfare, do I have rights in any meaningful sense?

B A Counter-Vision

I shall begin my attempt at answering this question from an oblique and, apparently, distant point. In an important article published in 1981 Dworkin began with a critique of the Report of the Committee on Obscenity and Film Censorship (1979), chaired by the eminent philosopher, Bernard Williams, which reported in 1979 (and remains unimplemented). The Committee proposed that a distinction should be drawn between certain kinds of pornography which should be totally prohibited, and other kinds, which should be permitted but subjected to various restrictions (especially regarding publicity). The basis on which the Committee grounded this distinction was that the law should seek to promote the welfare of society and that this was best done by encouraging a society 'that is most conducive to human beings making intelligent decisions about what the best lives to them to lead are, and then flourishing in those lives' (Dworkin, 1981:180).[2] The Committee accepted J. S. Mill's insistence that, because knowledge is uncertain, human flourishing is best promoted by the free flow of ideas. Although this did not in itself justify pornography, the difficulties in framing restrictive laws warranted a very powerful presumption against censorship. This could be overcome only if the acts or publications in question very clearly impeded human flourishing.

Dworkin's critique proceeded simultaneously from opposite directions. He tried to demonstrate that the Committee's reasoning could justify either total freedom or total prohibition. It could be maintained that *any restrictions* (for example, those which allow private consumption of pornography but prohibit public displays) reflect evaluations of current moral judgements (here, of the proper boundaries between the public and the private) which is just the kind of issue which, according to the Committee's basic premises, should be subject to scepticism and free-flowing experimentation. But equally it could be argued that *total prohibition* of pornographic experience, even in private, would be justified because, if the advocates of this form of society are to be given a fair opportunity to 'test' their perception of the best context for human flourishing, this option should not be closed to them. In the result, the Committee's strategy collapses into incoherence. Because the basic criterion for intervention is a perception of what is best for the flourishing of society, and this is treated as being inherently uncertain, the justification for any laws against pornography can only be a society's particular view of human flourishing at a specific point in time.

As an alternative strategy, Dworkin argued that individuals have a *right* to 'moral independence', which must (unless there are strong justifications) be respected *even if the community would be better off if they did not exercise it* (and, although Dworkin did not develop this point, presumably even if the community believes the individual is worse off by exercising it). The 'right' to consume pornography, at least in private, can be seen as an aspect of this moral independence. The right to moral independence is defended because it is only in this way that individual preferences can be given equal respect to those of each other person in the community. It is not my intention to trace the defence Dworkin makes of his position against a more straightforward utilitarian political theory. My purpose in referring to Dworkin's piece is to set the idea of rights found there against the concept of rights elaborated by Campbell. For Dworkin, the whole *point* of introducing the concept of rights into theoretical discourse is to make provision for, first, recognizing that individuals may wish to engage in activities and organize their lives inconsistently with societal preferences and, second, securing social arrangements whereby those individuals may live their life as they choose. For Campbell, the position is reversed. The predominant idea of 'right' lies in the social recognition of the desires of the community to enhance its members' well-being.

Further analysis indicates that Dworkin's position may be more 'goal-based' than his argument suggests (Allan, 1983).[3] He did not, of course, suggest that commitment to recognition of everyone's moral independence demands social toleration of *anything* any individual may want to do. You have to weigh the degree to which an individual's actions might inhibit the development others wish for themselves. This could allow restrictions 'provided the damage done to those who are affected adversely is not serious damage, even in their own eyes' (Allan, 1983:206). But this balancing will inevitably reveal a vision of what is believed to be a desirable form of social ordering. It is noticeable that, when he discussed the 'right' to moral independence, Dworkin slid away from using indulgence in pornography as examples and focused upon homosexuality. But how do we react to the claim a child pornographer might make to moral independence? Apart from the risks of lapses from fantasy into practice, the very availability of pornographic materials implies exploitation of children. There may be some forms of 'moral independence' whose very existence threaten important rights of others and a community's self-image.[4]

The whole question whether to endow individuals with rights to 'moral independence', and which individual wants are to count as such rights,[5] seems to turn on what vision is held of the appropriate balance between conflicting claims and of what is a desirable social ordering. If this is so, does a rights-based approach ultimately collapse into a welfarist one: that people have, or are to be thought of having, only such rights which are consistent with the community's vision of its own welfare? Does the fact that the ascription of rights is controlled by a concept of community well-being lead to the conclusion that everyone is ultimately obliged to further the community's best interests as communally perceived and that rights, if they exist at all, do so only as subordinate facets of the general duty?

C Rights as Claims

It is this scenario which Feinberg (1980) sketched for Nowheresville. There everyone acted benevolently towards each other. They were under a duty to do so but this duty was owed, not to one another, but to an external source. Feinberg wished to demonstrate how such a society might seem deficient. He thought that its deficiency lay in the absence of any sense that its individual members made *claims*. He refers here not to claims that X is the case (these are *assertions*) but to claims *to* X. Unless people do this, Feinberg says, they have no sense of their own moral worth. To make such a claim 'enables us to "stand up like men", to "look others in the eyes"'. For the rest of the community, 'to respect a person, and to think of him as possessed of human dignity, simply *is* to think of him as a potential maker of claims' (Feinberg, 1980:151).

A perception of this kind must form part of an undisclosed background to Dworkin's argument for 'moral independence'. There must indeed be a profound distinction between a social order which acts under the normative directive that the community must enhance the welfare of its members (in accordance with the perception held by some members of a community of what constitutes that community's welfare) and one which regards each of its members as potential makers of claims. This latter orientation does not, of course, commit the community to the realization of everyone's claim (in Feinberg's terms: to treat all claims as 'valid'). For one thing, they may conflict one with another. But it does allow the perception of the community's welfare to be *constructed around* the corpus of such claims. To the extent that a claim is recognized, it can be said to have fructified into a right. Of course it is also true that the differential accordance of the status of rights to various claims in any particular community reflects a particular social vision: perhaps even a vision of the community's welfare. But, unlike the welfarist vision, this normative order results from the admixture of claims recognized at any particular moment. A normative order constructed in this way may or may not be attractive. That issue is not my present concern. I wish only to emphasize the centrality of the ideas of rights to this process. Either the process generates an idea of rights, or ideas of rights impel a society towards this process.

Why should the idea of rights be associated with giving effect to people's claims and not with what are believed to be their interests, which could be ascertained by empirical observation or *a priori* conceptions of human nature? It has been recently argued that the idea of rights could be conceived in either sense and that there is no conclusive argument in favour of either (Lucy, 1990). But the presence or possibility of the exercise of choice will standardly be found to determine the appropriateness of thinking whether or not people have rights. For if it were sufficient for my having a right only that another had a duty to advance my interests, and it turned out that the other mistakenly assessed my interests, I would have had a right that my interests should be prejudiced. This seems strange, and would seem stranger still had I disputed the assessment of my interests. If, under the guise of advancing my interests, the other had, consciously or otherwise, promoted interests other than mine, I would have had the right to have been the agent for the advancement of others at my expense. We cannot avoid these conclusions by stipulating that I have had a right only if the action turns out to have been in my interests. For at what point do we assess whether the action was in my interests? And we do not normally wait until we know how things turn out before deciding whether we have rights. We more characteristically think of people having rights when they choose an action irrespective of whether that choice eventually promotes their interests or not.

Is the idea that some rights are inalienable inconsistent with this position? We comfortably think that some rights (to life, to marry, to vote) may be held by, or conferred on, a population even if it is unaware it has them. But in so thinking, we surely assume that, when fully informed, the people would choose to have these rights. It would be meaningless to describe as rights options which we know *no one* would wish to exercise. Moreover, if individuals were compelled to live, marry, vote etc against their will, these would not be rights but duties. But they are rights because they may be chosen. Choice implies the possibility of rejection. Individuals may, exceptionally, reject choice itself (by deciding according to lot, or delegation to another) but to do so in significant life events would substantially diminish the person as a human agent. Conversely, to grant people choice in such matters is central to recognition of their human worth. Hence, if I cannot formulate for myself what my interests are, but leave them to others to determine, have I not abdicated my humanity?

It is necessary to keep clear that the reasons for believing oneself to be obligated towards others may be quite independent from the claims/choices those others may make.[6] I have elsewhere (Eekelaar, 1991a) tried to outline a moral basis underlying parental duties towards their children. Such duties may coincide with the informed wishes of mature children, and could therefore be said to respect their rights. But they need not do so. If your (moral or legal) duty towards me conflicts with my claim, it may still bind you (morally or legally), but not consequential to any right of mine. So if you believe yourself morally obliged to refuse to assist someone's suicide bid, your obligation holds, but cannot be presented as supporting the other's 'right'. Similarly, I may perceive my actions towards non-human life in terms of moral obligation without conceding that such life has rights, except perhaps metaphorically.

It is also necessary to note the obvious point that, just as moral duties may exist independently of the recognition of claims, the fact that claims are made does not compel their recognition. 'Righthood' is achieved only when sufficient duties or powers are conferred on others that the claim can realistically be realized. So, while owing duties to others does not necessarily imply that the others have rights (except in a formalistic sense), no one can have rights unless the claims which they embody are protected by duties on others (Eekelaar, 1986). The process of transition from social recognition of claims to their legal protection treads the borderline between legal and social reality which is rich in theoretical debate. I have elsewhere (Eekelaar, 1989) suggested that the key might lie in the current perception of where the public interest lies. I mean the expression in a very broad sense. It will comprise a perspective of the 'proper' ordering of relationships and, crucially for present purposes, the extent to which children's claims should be secured against the countervailing claims of adults. Rights have also a fundamental, residual, quality in that they determine the ultimate entitlements of actors 'at the end of the day'. The social fabric consists of more than the mere assertion of claim and counter-claim. A woman may have the 'right' to divorce her husband, but morality, sensitivity and humanity may dictate that all avenues should be explored before its exercise.

PART TWO

Summary Thus Far

My arguments so far have sought to show: first, that a fundamental distinction can be drawn between actions motivated solely by the purpose of promoting the welfare of another (which I call 'welfarism') and actions consequential to recognizing claims made by another; second, that the idea of rights is in some way related to the perception that people make claims and, third, that a claim simply that people should act to further my welfare as they define it is in reality to make no claim at all. Running behind these explicit propositions lies the suggestion that to treat someone fully as an individual of moral worth implies recognizing that that person makes claims and exercises choices: that is, is a potential right-holder. But rights do not constitute the sole source of justifications for holding that people owe duties to one another (or to non-humans) and many considerations are relevant to the translation of claims into rights.

D Children's Rights

It is now necessary to consider how far the general theoretical discussion can be applied to the idea of children's rights. The structural relationship will be immediately obvious. A general legal injunction to an actor to act towards a child in accordance with the actor's perception of the child's welfare may be seen to correspond to the welfarist model discussed above. The primary right lies in the disinterested provider of welfare; there is assumed to be no conflict between this and the 'interests' of the child. The discussion has, however, suggested not only that this assumption cannot be made, but also that it fails to give proper respect to the human worth of the child.

The starting-off point, then, of any rights-based approach to social policy is to have regard to claims which people make and to provide opportunities for claims to be made. What these claims actually are is an empirical matter. This is not simply a theoretical point. It involves the process, so easy for politicians, welfare professionals and even academics to forget: *listening to people*. No social organization can hope to be built on the rights of its members unless there are mechanisms whereby those members may express themselves and wherein those expressions are taken seriously. *Hearing what children say* must therefore lie at the root of any elaboration of children's rights. No society will have begun to perceive its children as rightholders until adults' attitudes and social structures are seriously adjusted towards making it possible for children to express views, and towards addressing them with respect.

We now confront the problem faced by all children's rights theorists: children may be too young to say anything. Even if they are not, their opinions may be coloured by ignorance or parental influence. Yet they surely have rights. We may be tempted, then, to abandon the claim theory entirely.[7] But we should remember the example given above where rights are conferred on or held by an ignorant population. They take their force as rights only to the extent that it can reasonably be assumed that, when fully informed, the people will wish to exercise them. If this is implausible (for example, a 'right' granted to a rebellious populace to serve in the army) we cannot sensibly think that a right has been conferred at all. So adults' duties towards young children cannot be convincingly perceived as reflecting rights held by the children unless it can be plausibly assumed that, if fully informed of the relevant factors and of mature judgement, the children would want such duties to be exercised towards them.

This hypothetical judgement is necessary in order to maintain theoretical coherence with the central character of rights asserted here. As a construct, it is partly an artefact constrained by the assumptions of full information and maturity. This precludes contemplating the conditioning of children so as to ensure that when they reach adulthood they will always approve of whatever was done to them during their childhood. The assumptions of information and maturity incorporate into rights-based decision-making regarding young children the requirement that such decisions promote the goal of maturity, which is taken to be the ability to confront the truth and exercise self-determination. Maturity opens up options; it does not close them down.

Despite these external constraints, the hypothetical judgement does not abstract the child from his or her context. On the contrary, it stipulates a *process* which requires serious attention to be given to what *the child in question*, of his or her gender, ethnicity and other personal and social characteristics, is likely to have wanted if fully informed and mature. This has important consequences. General theories of what comprises children's best interests will not in themselves suffice as grounds for decision-making. Also, since children mature gradually, it will always be necessary to observe the child closely for indications of what is important *for that child*, and why. This is in direct opposition to the devastating neglect of children's own opinions which has characterized much of the welfarist approach hitherto. Finally, the process looks forward to the future adult. It is easy (though not inevitable) that the welfarist approach should emphasize short-term effects over potential long-term consequences. A child's immediate contentment is of course important to the development of an integrated adult personality. But the hypothetical viewpoint demands serious attention to be paid also to the social and cultural environment into which the child is likely to grow. What is important about this is not so much the particular answer given in a particular case, but in the territory which this process opens up. Decisions which are taken about children will need to be justified by articulating how they may plausibly relate to the child's hypothesized viewpoint. This carries with it the discipline of precise specification. It could never be enough to assert simply that an action will be in the child's welfare.[8] We now need to think how the action could be one which the child might plausibly want. We need to consider closely the child's individual circumstances, to separate the child's claims from competing claims and relate the proposed action to both.

Since the reference to the hypothetical viewpoint is a process and not an end-result (as in the welfarist model) it will not always reveal a clear-cut conclusion. On such occasions we can assume only that the child would expect adults to make their best assessment of his or her welfare according to their own lights. But the process could lead to a re-evaluation of some current assumptions of welfarist thinking. For example, the concealment from a child of information about its birth by artificial insemination is usually justified on the ground that this is in the child's best interests. But the rights perspective poses the question: would that child, as an adult, be likely to choose to live his or her life on the basis of a deliberate deception about his or her origins? It would also ask: would a child born as a result of embryo donation choose to be brought up into the family of its gestational or its genetic parents? Similar re-framing could have significant consequences in the context of inter-racial adoption or fostering placements. It could be important also in decisions about secular and religious education and the exposure of children to literature and ideas.

As the creation of children can now be engineered by technological means as a deliberate act of social policy, it is important to protect the human rights of people so created. It is therefore inadequate to require, as s 13 (5) of the United Kingdom Human Fertilisation and Embryology Act does, merely that regard should be paid to other people's perception of the welfare of any child who may be so born. It could be claimed that it must almost always be better to be born than not.[9] The only way such rights can be addressed is by asking whether a perseon would *choose* to be born into a context and in the circumstances contemplated. This compels some regulation of these procedures.

It is intrinsic to rights-based thinking that the question: 'what claims may children make?' is essentially an empirical one. Evidence can be acquired, and must be continually revised, about what people want when they are young and how they later feel adults should have behaved towards them when they were young. I have advanced a framework of the kinds of claims which it seems children may plausibly make or wish to make if they could (Eekelaar, 1986). There is no originality in this; the list is very similar to Freeman's (1983:56). Indeed, if these representations of what children actually claim or may plausibly be thought to want to claim have any accuracy, one would expect this, although it is important to remember that such a list must always be open to discussion and revision in the light of empirical evidence. Under my ordering, the claims revolve around children's 'basic' interests (to physical, emotional and intellectual care); their 'developmental' interests (that their potential should be developed so that they enter adulthood as far as possible without disadvantage) and their 'autonomy' interests (the freedom to choose a life-style of their own). The first of these has pre-eminent status. The other two can reasonably be compromised. For example, surely no one would have wanted, when very young, to have been left uncontrolled in dangerous situations. But the plausibility of the claim that children would wish to be provided with equal life-chances has the potential for considerable social impact.

E The UN Convention and Children's Rights

I now turn to the UN Convention on the Rights of the Child and evaluate how far it reflects a concept of children's rights consistent with the viewpoint adopted in this paper. The Convention imposes a series of duties on contracting states which are owed sometimes to children and sometimes to adults. Article 3 states:

1. In all actions concerning children, whether undertaken by public or private social welfare institutions, courts of law, administrative authorities or legislative bodies, the best interests of the child shall be a primary consideration.
2. States Parties undertake to ensure the child such protection and care as is necessary for his or her well-being, taking into account the rights and duties of his or her parents, legal guardians, or other individuals legally responsible for him or her, and, to this end, shall take all appropriate legislative and administrative measures.

Interpreted in the light of the paragraph in the Preamble which runs:

Taking due account of the importance of the traditions and cultural values of each people for the protection and harmonious development of the child

the way seems open for almost unrestricted welfarism by the injection of adult values into a conception of what constitutes the 'best interests' of the child. But Article 3 requires only that the children's interests shall be 'a' primary consideration, not 'the' primary consideration. What is the significance of this?

The obvious answer (supported by the history of the preparation of the Convention) (McGoldrick, 1991) is that the child's 'welfare' may in some cases need to be compromised in the light of 'cultural values and traditions'. But it must also be read in the context of the series of explicit rights which the Convention protects. These are: 'the inherent right to life' (Art 6); 'the right from birth to a name, the right to acquire a nationality and, as far as possible, the right to know and be cared for by his or her parents' (Art 7); 'the right of the child to preserve his or her identity, including nationality' (Art 8); 'the right of the child who is separated from one or both parents to maintain personal relations and direct contact with both parents on a regular basis, except if it is contrary to the child's best interests' (Art 9(3): cf also Art 10(2)); 'the right (of a child who is capable of forming his or her own views) to express those views freely in all matters affecting the child, the views of the child being given due weight in accordance with the age and maturity of the child' (Art 12); 'the right to freedom of expression' (Art 13); 'the right of the child to freedom of thought, conscience and religion' (Art 14(1); subject to Art 14(2)); 'the rights of the child to freedom of association and to freedom of peaceful assembly' (Art 15); 'the right to the protection of the law against (arbitrary or unlawful interference with his or her privacy, family, home or correspondence and unlawful attacks on his or her honour and reputation)' (Art 16); 'the right of the child to the enjoyment of the highest attainable standard of health and to facilities for the treatment of illness and rehabilitation of health' (Art 24); 'the right of a child who has been placed by the competent authorities for the purposes of care, protection or treatment of his or her physical or mental health, to a periodic review of the treatment provided to the child asnd all other circumstances relevant to his or her placement' (Art 25); 'the right to benefit from social security' (Art 26); 'the right of every child to a standard of living adequate for the child's physical, mental, spiritual, moral and social development' (Art 27); 'the right of the child to education' (Art 28); 'the right, in community with other members of his or her group, to enjoy his or her own culture, to profess and practice his or her own religion, or to use his or her own language' (Art 30); 'the right of the child to rest and leisure, to engage in play and recreational activities appropriate to the age of the child and to participate freely in cultural life and the arts' (Art 31); 'the right of the child to be protected from economic exploitation and from performing any work that is likely to be hazardous or to interfere with the child's education' (Art 32); 'the right of every child alleged as, accused of, or recognized as having infringed the penal law to be treated in a manner consistent with the promotion of the child's sense of dignity and worth' (Art 40).[10]

The whole edifice can be seen as elaborations of the trilogy of claims I suggested children may plausibly be taken to make or wish to make. They are not only of a 'protective' nature. The right to 'know' his or her parents (Art 7(1)) and the right to 'preserve his or her identity' can be characterized as human rights which transcend the immediate welfare of a young child. The constituents of 'freedom of expression' as defined in Article 13 (which include the 'right to seek, receive and impart information and ideas of all kinds'), and the right in Article 14 to 'freedom of thought, conscience and religion' also look forward to the adult human being.

The rights in the Convention are all subject to Article 5:

States Parties shall respect the responsibilities, rights and duties of parents or, where applicable, the members of the extended family or community as provided for by local custom, legal guardians or other persons legally responsible for the child, to provide, in a manner consistent with the evolving capacities of the child, appropriate direction and guidance in the exercise by the child of the rights recognized in the present Convention.

This article recognizes that the Convention is not simply an exercise in abstraction. These interests are part of real life. They are not self-enforcing, or even immediately self-evident to children. The article therefore *assumes* that certain adults are entrusted with the role of ensuring that these interests are promoted and requires that states must 'respect' the exercise of this role by those adults. No doubt all communities constitute categories of such adults for most of their children (usually, of course, the parents); the implication of the rest of the Convention is that, if there are classes of children with respect to whom no adults have been so assigned, this should be done. But the greater difficulty lies in the assumption that these adults will promote these rights. The article allows the adults 'direction and guidance': but this must be *in the exercise* of the rights, not in derogation of the rights. Similarly, in regard to the 'right of the child to freedom of thought, conscience and religion', Article 14(2) requires states to respect the 'rights and duties of parents and, when applicable, legal guardians to provide direction *in the exercise of his or her right* in a manner consistent with the evolving capacities of the child'. The directions cannot therefore be inconsistent with the rights. Parents are not given a free hand.

It seems, therefore, that neither the 'responsible' adults, nor the State itself in pursuance of its duty under Article 3, nor an invocation of the 'welfare principle' of Article 3(1), which is not overriding, can cut down on the substance of the specific rights inasfar as such rights are delineated in the Convention. Yet is this enough to ensure that the Convention itself is soundly based on a defensible concept of children's rights? Has the adult world merely met together and given children a package which adults think is good for them? How are we to know if children want the 'rights' which the Convention gives them? They may want more, or different, rights. Very importantly, they may believe that their protection is imperfect: that the 'direction' given by adults in their exercise of these rights is no longer guidance but obstruction.

The only provision in the Convention which has a bearing on these issues is Article 12.

1. States Parties shall assure to the child who is capable of forming his or her own views the right to express those views freely, in all matters affecting the child, the views of the child being given due weight in accordance with the age and maturity of the child.
2. For this purpose, the child shall in particular be provided the opportunity to be heard in any judicial and administrative proceedings affecting the child, either directly, or through a representative or an appropriate body, in a manner consistent with the procedural rules of national law.

It is very important that the generality of the first paragraph of this article should not be overshadowed by the particularity of the second. The second paragraph is, indeed, very important. It provides a counter-weight to the broad provisions of Article 3 that, in all 'actions' concerning children (including administrative and legal actions), 'the best interests of the child shall be a primary consideration', for it allows the children a voice in such actions. But the first paragraph goes further. Children who are capable of forming their views must be 'assured' the 'right' to express them *on all matters affecting* children, and these views must be given 'due weight'. It seems unlikely that the framers of the Convention followed their own precepts and consulted with children. But the implications of the Article could, and should, be far-reaching. It may be that the prospect of the formation of children's pressure groups (that is, pressure groups *run by children*) and representative committees looks unattractive and even unrealistic. But lines of communication with children are being opened up. Specialist newspapers aimed at youthful readership are seriously canvassing their readers' opinions. Organizations such as (in England) 'Childline' (a confidential telephone service for children) and the Children's Legal Centre have been able to bring to public attention children's feelings and wishes.[11]

F CONCLUSION

It would be logically possible to have framed the Convention on the Rights of the Child as a list of duties owed by adults to children. But that would have revealed a negative, suspicious, view of human nature; it would have seen people as servile, responding best to restraint and control. The strength of the rights formulation is its recognition of humans as individuals worthy of development and fulfilment. This is not an appeal to narrow self-interest. On the contrary, it recognizes the insight that people can contribute positively to others only when they are respected and fulfilled. And to recognize people as having rights from the moment of their birth continuously into adulthood could turn out, politically, to be the most radical step of all. If all *young people* are secured all the physical, social and economic rights proclaimed in the Convention, the lives of millions of adults of the next generation would be transformed. It would be a grievous mistake to see the Convention as applying to childhood alone. Childhood is not an end in itself, but part of the process of forming the adults of the next generation. The Convention is for all *people*. It could influence their entire lives. If its aims can be realized, the Convention can truly be said to be laying the foundations for a better world.

NOTES

[1] The perception of such a logical relationship derives from Hohfeld (1919).

[2] I adopt Dworkin's statement of the Committee's strategy because this is the starting point of his theoretical discussion.

[3] Allan questions Dworkin's analysis from the opposite direction when he suggests that the position of the Williams Committee may be not so far removed from that of Dworkin.

[4] A similar argument, that pornography harms society by degrading women, can also, of course, be made.

[5] Dworkin has argued that a distinction should be drawn between holding a moral position and mere prejudice or emotion (Dworkin, 1977: ch 10). In his essay on pornography, he does not explain whether a claim to 'moral independence' requires holding a 'moral position' and whether an individual who wishes to indulge in pornography can be said to hold such a position.

[6] See O'Neill (1992), arguing that rights analysis fails to account for 'imperfect obligations' towards children and Raz (1984b), who argues against a rights-based foundation of moral obligation. I agree, but argue that thinking that children have rights can significantly influence the content of the obligations held to be owed towards children.

[8] This argument has serious implications for the way in which courts make many decisions about children. On the view taken here, it is insufficient to base a decision on broad welfarist grounds. For a fuller discussion, see Eekelaar (1991b:136–8; 1991c:386–9).

[9] But see Morgan (1990) who proposes that abortion may sometimes be justified on the ground that this is in the best interests of the child in question on analogy with withholding life-sustaining measures from living children. The idea that people might be entitled to cause the death of others because *they think* that is in those others' best interests is perhaps the most dangerous form of welfarism. In *re J* [1990] 3 All ER 930 the Court of Appeal authorized the withholding of life-sustaining measures from a severely brain-damaged child on the basis of the 'assumed point of view of the patient', rather than of the decision-makers.

[10] There may be no significance in the decision to express those interests in the language of rights, whereas other interests, such as that of protection against sexual exploitation and abuse, are found within the imposition of various protective duties upon States (Art 34). The creation of such specific duties might also, then, be thought of as expressing rights.

[11] In 1991 a call was made that a Children's Rights Commissioner should be established in the United Kingdom, Rosenbaum and Newell (1991).

MASTER REFERENCE LIST

Abrams, N. (1979), 'Problems in Defining Child Abuse and Neglect' in O'Neill & Ruddick, (eds) (1979), *Having Children: Philosophical and Legal Reflections On Parenthood*, New York, Oxford University Press.

Allan, T. (1983), 'A Right to Pornography?', *Oxford Journal of Legal Studies*, 3, 376–81.

Alston, P. (1989), 'Implementing Children's Rights: The Case of Child Labour', *Nordic Journal of International Law*, 58, 35.

Alston, P. (1990), 'The Unborn Child and Abortion Under the Draft Convention on the Rights of the Child', *Human Rights Quarterly*, 12, 156.

Anderson, R. *et al* (1975), *Voices From Wounded Knee*, 1973.

Andrews, R. & Cohn, A. (1974), 'Ungovernability: The Unjustifiable Jurisdiction', *Yale Law Journal* 83, 1383.

Aries, P. (1962), *Centuries of Childhood*, London, Jonathon Cape.

Aristotle, *Nicomachean Ethics* Book II ch 4.

Australian Institute of Family Studies (1991), *Family Matters*.

Australian Law Reform Commission (1987), *Child Welfare*, Canberra, Australian Government Publishing Service.

Bailey-Harris, R. & Naffine, N. (1988), 'Gender, Justice and Welfare in South Australia: A Study of the Female Status Offender', *International Journal of Law and the Family* 2, 214–33.

Balkin, R. P. & Davis, J. L. R. (1991), *Law of Torts*, Sydney, Butterworths.

Bankowski, Z. & Mungham, G. (1976), *Images of Law*, London, Routledge & Kegan Paul.

Barber, S. (1990), 'Heading Off Trouble', *Community Care*, 840, 23.

Barsh, R. (1989), 'The Draft Convention on the Rights of the Child: A Case of Eurocentricism in Standard-Setting', *Nordic Journal of International Law*, 58, 24.

Bayer, R. (1981), 'Crime, Punishment and the Decline of Liberal Optimism', *Crime and Delinquency*, 27 (1), 169.

Bedau, H. (1984), 'Why do We Have the Rights We Do?', *Social Philosophy and Policy*, 1, 56.

Benn, S. (1988), *A Theory of Freedom*, Cambridge, Cambridge University Press.

Berlin, I. (1969), *Four Essays on Liberty*, Oxford, Oxford University Press.

Bitensky, S. (1990), 'Educating The Child for a Productive Life' in Cohen, C. & Davidson, H. (eds) *Children's Rights in America*, Washington, American Bar Association.

Bittner, R. (1975), 'Maximen', *Akten des 4. Internationalen KantKongresses*, Berlin, G. Funke, Teil II, 2, 485–9.

Blackmore, R. (1990), 'Response to Hogan: Children's Courts: To Be or What to Be?' for National Workshop on Juvenile Justice, Australian National University, Canberra.

Blackstone (1791), *Commentaries on the Laws of England*, Vol I (11th ed).

Blumberg, A. (1976), *Criminal Justice*, Chicago, Quadrangle.

Blustein, J. (1982), *Parents And Children: The Ethics Of The Family*, New York, Oxford University Press.

Borowski, A. & Murray, J. (eds) (1985), *Juvenile Delinquency in Australia*, Melbourne, Methuen.

Bortner, M. (1982), *Inside a Juvenile Court: The Tarnished Ideal of Individualized Justice*, New York, New York University Press.

Bradshaw, J. (1990), *Child Poverty and Deprivation in the U.K.*, London, National Children's Bureau.

Brahams, D. (1989), 'Informed Consent and Randomized Controlled Trials', *Law Society Gazette*, 331.

Brandt, R. (1979), *A Theory of The Good and The Right*, Oxford, Oxford University Press.

'Briefings in Medical Ethics No 9: The UN Convention on the Rights of the Child' (1991) *Journal of Medical Ethics*, 17, 4.

Buchanan, A. (1979), 'Medical Paternalism', *Philosophy and Public Affairs*, 7, 49.

Cabinet Sub-Committee (1986), *Child Support: A Discussion Paper on Maintenance*, Canberra, AGPS.

Cain, M. (1976), 'Necessarily out of Touch: Thoughts on the Social Organization of the Bar' in Carlen, P. (ed) *The Sociology of Law*, Keele University, Sociological Review Monograph.

Campbell, T. (1983), *The Left and Rights: A Conceptual Analysis of the Idea of Socialist Rights*, Routledge & Kegan Paul.

Campbell, T. (1985), 'Philosophy, Ideology and Rights', *Legal Studies*, 5, 10–20.

Campbell, T. (1985), 'The Rights Approach to Mental Health' in A. Phillips Griffiths (ed) *Philosophy and Practice*, Cambridge University Press.

Campbell, T. (1992), 'The Rights of the Minor: As Person, As Child, As Future Adult', in this volume.

Campbell, T. & Heginbotham, C. (1991), *Mental Illness: Prejudice, Discrimination and the Law*, Dartmouth.

Campbell, T. & McKay, A. (1978), 'Antenatal Injury and the Rights of the Foetus', *Philosophical Quarterly*, 28, 17–30.

Campbell, T., Goldberg, D., McLean, S. & Mullen, T. (1988), *Human Rights: From Rhetoric to Reality*, Oxford, Blackwell.

Carlen, P. (1976), *Magistrates' Justice*, Oxford, Martin Robertson.

Carney, T. (1985), 'The Interface between Juvenile Corrections and Child Welfare: philosophy pragmatism or professionalisation?', in Borowski, A. & Murray, J. (eds) *Juvenile Delinquency in Australia*, Melbourne, Methuen, 202–20.

Carney, T. (1991), *Law at the Margins: Towards social participation?*, Melbourne, Oxford University Press.

CCH (1991), Australian Family Law Court Handbook.

Cerda, J. (1990), 'The Draft Convention on the Rights of the Child: New Rights', *Human Rights Quarterly*, 12, 115.

Charlesworth, H., Chenkin, C. & Wright, S. (1991), 'Feminist Approaches to International Law', *American Journal of International Law*, 85, 613.

Cherlin, A. *et al* (1991), 'Longitudinal Studies of Effects of Divorce on Children in Great Britain and the United States', *Science*, 252, 1386.

Chisholm, R. (1985), *Black Children: White Welfare? Aboriginal Child Welfare Law and Policy in New South Wales*, SWRC Reports and Proceedings, No 52, University of New South Wales.

Chodorow, N. (1978), *The Social Reproduction of Mothering*, Berkeley, University of California Press.

Clarke, J. (1985), 'Whose Justice? The Politics of Juvenile Control', *International Journal of the Sociology of Law*, 13, 407.

Coady, C. (1986), 'The Idea of Violence', *Journal of Applied Philosophy*, 3, 3–20.

Coady, M. & Coady, C. (1992), 'There Ought to be a Law Against It: Reflections On Child Abuse, Morality And Law', in this volume.

Cohen, C. & Davidson, H. (1990), *Children's Rights in America*, Washington, American Bar Association.

Cohen, H. (1980), *Equal Rights for Children*, Totowa, N.J., Littlefield, Adams.

Cotterrell, R. (1986), *The Sociology of Law*, London, Butterworths.

Council of Europe, Committee of Ministers (1990), 'Concerning Medical Research on Human Beings', Recommendation No. R(90)3.

Craig, G. & Glendinning, D. (1990), *The Impact of Social Security Changes: The Views of Families Using Barnardo's Pre-School Services*, Barkingside, Barnardo's Research and Development Section.

CYPF Act (1989), Children, Young Persons and their Families Act 1989 (NZ).

Dalley, G. (1988), *Ideologies of Caring*, London, MacMillan.

Debele, G. (1987), 'The Due Process Revolution and the Juvenile Court: The Matter of Race in the Historical Evolution of a Doctrine', *Law and Inequality*, 5, 512.

Declaration of the Rights of the Child, General Assembly res 1386 (XIV) of 20 November 1959.

Dickens, B. (1979), 'Human Rights in Medical Experimentation', *Israeli Yearbook on Human Rights*, 9, 23.

Dickens, C. (1846), *Dombey and Son*, London, Oxford University Press (1953 Reprint).

Dickey, A. (1990), *Family Law in Australia*, Sydney, Law Book Company.

Dingwall, R. & Eekelaar, J. (1984), 'Rethinking Child Protection' in Freeman, M. (ed) *The State, The Law and the Family: Critical Perspectives*, London, Tavistock Publications, 93–114.

Dinnerstein, D. (1977), *The Mermaid and the Minotaur*, New York, Harper & Row.

Dixon, S. (1988), *The Roman Mother*, Norman and London, University of Oklahoma Press.

Duane, M. (1972), 'Freedom and The State System of Education', in Adams, P. *et al.*, *Children's Rights*, London, Panther Books.

Dworkin, G. (1972), 'Paternalism', in Wasserstrom, R. (ed) *Morality and The Law*, California, Wadsworth.

Dworkin, G. (1987), 'Law and Medical Experimentation: Of Embryos, Children and Others with Limited Legal Capacity', *Monash University Law Review*, 13, 189.

Dworkin, G. (1988), *The Theory and Practice of Autonomy*, Cambridge, Cambridge University Press.

Dworkin, R. (1977), 'Taking Rights Seriously' in R. Dworkin (1977), *Taking Rights Seriously*, Duckworth, 184–205.

Dworkin, R. (1977, 1978), *Taking Rights Seriously*, London, Duckworth.

Dworking, R. (1978a), 'Liberalism', in Hampshire, S. (ed) *Public and Private Morality*, Cambridge, Cambridge University Press, 113–43.

Dworkin, R. (1981), 'Is there a Right to Pornography?', *Oxford Journal of Legal Studies*, 1, 177–212.

Edelman, M. (1977), *Political Language; Words That Succeed and Policies That Fail*, New York, Academic Press.

Edwards Report (1982), *The Treatment of Juvenile Offenders, A Study of the Treatment of Juvenile Offenders in Western Australia as part of an Overall Review of the Child Welfare Act*, Western Australian Government.

Eekelaar, J. (1986), 'The Emergence of Children's Rights', *Oxford Journal of Legal Studies*, 6, 161.

Eekelaar, J. (1989), 'What is "Critical" Family Law?', *Law Quarterly Review*, 105, 244–61.

Eekelaar, J. (1991a), Are Parents Morally Obliged to Care for their Children?, *Oxford Journal of Legal Studies*, 11, 340–53.

Eekelaar, J. (1991b), *Regulating Divorce*, Oxford, Clarendon Press.

Eekelaar, J. (1991c), *Law Quarterly Review*, 107, 386–9.

Eekelaar, J. (1992), 'The Importance of Thinking that Children Have Rights', in this volume.

Eekelaar, J. & Maclean, M. (1986), *Maintenance After Divorce*, Clarendon Press.

Eekelaar, J. & Pearl, D. (eds) (1989), *An Aging World – Dilemmas and Challenges for Law and Social Policy*, Oxford, Clarendon Press.

Elliott, B. J. & Richards, M. P. M. (1991), 'Children and Divorce: Educational Performance and Behaviour before and after Parental Separation', 5 *International Journal of Law and the Family*, 258–76.

Engle, K. (1991a), 'Female Subjects of International Human Rights Discourse', paper presented at Harvard Law School, March 1991.

Engle, K. (1991b), 'Clitoridectomy', paper presented in Damwoude, the Netherlands, 24 June 1991.

Farson, R. (1978), *Birthrights*, Harmondsworth, Penguin Books.

Feeley, M. (1979), *The Process is the Punishment*, New York, Russell Sage.

Feinberg, J. (1966), 'Duties, Rights and Claims', *American Philosophical Quarterly*, 3, 137.

Feinberg, J. (1980), 'The Nature and Value of Rights' in Feinberg, J., *Rights, Justice and the Bounds of Liberty: Essays in Social Philosophy*, Princeton, Princeton University Press, 143–55.

Feinberg, J. (1986), *Harm to Self, The Moral Limits of The Criminal Law*, 3, New York, Oxford University Press.

Feinberg, J. (ed) (1980), *Rights, Justice and the Bounds of Liberty: Essays in Social Philosophy*, Princeton, Princeton University Press.

Feldman, D. (1987), 'Rights, Capacity and Social Responsibility', *Anglo-American Law Review*, 16, 97.

Flekkoy, M. (1991), *A Voice For Children*, London, Jessica Kingsley.

Fogarty (1990), *Report of the Child Support Evaluation Advisory Group*, Canberra, AGPS.

Foucault, M. (1967), *Madness and Civilisation*, London, Tavistock.

Frankena, W. (1962), 'The Concept of Social Justice', in Brandt, R. (ed) *Social Justice*, Englewood Cliffs, N.J., Prentice Hall.

Frankfurt, H. (1981), 'Freedom of the Will and the Concept of a Person', *Journal of Philosophy*, 68, 829.

Freeman, M. (1983), *The Rights and Wrongs of Children*, London, Frances Pinter.

Freeman, M. (1985), 'Doing His Best To Sustain The Sanctity of Marriage' in Johnson, N. (ed) *Marital Violence*, London, Routledge & Kegan Paul.

Freeman, M. (1988a), 'Sterilising the Mentally Handicapped' in Freeman, M. (ed) *Medicine, Ethics and the Law*, London, Stevens.

Freeman, M. (1988b), 'Time to Stop Hitting Our Children', *Childright*, 51, 5.

Freeman, M. (1989), 'Cleveland, Butler-Sloss and Beyond', *Current Legal Problems*, 42, 85.

Freiberg, A., Fox, R. & Hogan, M. (1988), *Sentencing Young Offenders*, Canberra, AGPS.

Furstenberg, F. & Cherlin, A. (1991), *Divided Families*, Harvard University Press.

Gallie, W. (1964), *Philosophy and Historical Understanding*, London, Chatto & Windus.

Gamble, H. (1985), 'The Status Offender', in Borowski, A. & Murray, J. (eds) *Juvenile Delinquency in Australia*, Melbourne, Methuen, 95–111.

Gamble, H. (1986), *Law for Parents and Children*, 2nd ed, Sydney, Law Book Company.

Garbarino, J. & Gilliam, G. (1980), *Understanding Abusive Families*, Lexington Books.

Gardner, R. (1987), *Who Says? Choice and Control in Care*, London, National Children's Bureau.

Gerhard, U. *et al* (1990), 'Differenz und Gleichheit, Menschenrechte haben (k)ein Geschlecht', Frankfurt.

Gewirth, A. (1977), *Reason and Morality*, University of Chicago Press.

Gewirth, A. (1982), *Human Rights: Essays on Justification and Applications*, Chicago, Chicago University Press.

Gilligan, C. (1982), *In a Different Voice*, Cambridge, Mass, Harvard University Press.

Glendon, M. (1991), *Rights Talk*, New York, Free Press.

Goddard, C. (1988), 'A Child Sexual Abuse Police Tracking Project', *Sexual Offences Against Children: Research Reports*, Melbourne, Law Reform Commission of Victoria.

Goldstein, J., Freud, A., Solnit, A. (1979), *Before the Best Interests of the Child*, New York, Free Press.

Goodin, R. (1991), 'Utility and the Good', in Singer, P. (ed) *A Companion to Ethics*, Oxford, Blackwell.

Goodin, R. & Le Grande, J. (1987), *Not Only the Poor*, London, Allen & Unwin.

Gosling, J. & Diarists (1989), *One Day I'll Have a Place of My Own*, London, Central London Social Security Advisors' Forum and Shelter.

Gosse, E. (1984), *Father and Son*, Harmondsworth, Penguin.

Graycar, R. (1988), 'Family Law and Social Security in Australia: The Child Support Connection', *Australian Journal of Family Law*, 70–92.

Graycar, R. & Morgan, J. (1990), *The Hidden Gender of Law*, Sydney, Federation Press.

Graycar, R. (ed) (1990), *Dissenting Opinions. Feminist Exploration in Law and Society*, Sydney, Allen & Unwin.

Griffin, J. (1985), 'Towards a Substantive Theory of Rights' in Frey, R. (ed) *Utility and Rights*, Oxford, Blackwell.

Groner, J. (1991), *Hilary's Trial*, New York, Simon & Schuster.

Grylls, D. (1978), *Guardians and Angels: Parents and Children in Nineteenth-Century Literature*, London, Faber & Faber.

Guest, S. (1991), *Ronald Dworkin*, Edinburgh, Edinburgh University Press.

Gutmann, A. (1987), *Democratic Education*, Princeton, Princeton University Press.

Hacking, I. (1988), 'The Sociology of Knowledge About Child Abuse', *Nous*, 22.

Hafen, B. (1976), 'Children's Liberation and the New Egalitarianism: Some Reservations about Abandoning Children to their "Rights"', *Brigham Young ULR*, 605–58.

Hafen, B. (1977), 'Puberty, Privacy and Protection: the Risks of Children's Rights', *American Bar Association Journal*, 63, 1383.

Hammarberg, T. (1990), 'The UN Convention on the Rights of the Child – and How to Make it Work', *Human Rights Quarterly*, 12, 99.

Hampton, J. (1984), 'The Moral Education Theory of Punishment', *Philosophy and Public Affairs*, 13 (3), 208–38.

Hare, R. (1962), *Freedom and Reason*, Clarendon Press.

Harris, D. (1987), *Justifying State Welfare: The new right versus the old left*, Oxford, Basil Blackwell.

Harris, R. (1985), 'Towards Just Welfare: A Consideration of Current Controversy in the Theory of Juvenile Justice', *British Journal of Criminology*, 25 (1), 31.

Hart, H. (1955), 'Are There Any Natural Rights?', *Philosophical Review*, 63, 175–91.

Hart, H. (1982), 'Legal Rights' in *Essays on Bentham – Studies in Jurisprudence and Political Theory*, Oxford, Clarendon Press, 162–93.

Hart, H. (1982), *Essays on Bentham – Studies in Jurisprudence and Political Theory*, Oxford, Clarendon Press.

Hassall, I. & Maxwell, G. (1991), 'The Family Group Conference; a new statutory way of resolving care, protection and justice matters affecting children', in Office of the Commissioner for Children, *An Appraisal of the first Year of the Children, Young Persons and Their Families Act 1989*, Wellington, 1–13.

Haworth, L. (1986), *Autonomy*, New Haven, Yale University Press.

Heath, I. (1985), *Incest: A Crime Against Children*, Melbourne, Director of Public Prosecutions.

Hobbes, T. (1651), *Leviathan*.

Höffe, O. (1977), 'Kants kategorisher Imperativ als Kriterium des Sittlichen', *Zeitschrift fur philosophische Forschung 31*, 354–84.

Hogan, M. (1990), 'Children's Courts: To Be or What to Be?' for National Workshop on Juvenile Justice, Australian National University, Canberra.

Hohfeld, W. (1919), *Fundamental Legal Conceptions as Applied in Judicial Reasoning*, New Haven, Yale UP.

Hohfeld, W. (1923), *Fundamental Legal Conceptions as Applied in Judicial Reasoning and Other Legal Essays*, 23–64, New Haven, Yale UP.

Holmes, O. (1897), 'The Path of the Law', *Harvard Law Review*, 10, 457.

Holt, J. (1975), *Escape From Childhood*, Harmondsworth, Penguin Books.

Houlgate, L. (1988), *Family and State: The Philosophy of Family Law*, Totowa, N.J., Rowman & Littlefield.

Hoyles, M. (ed) (1979), *Changing Childhood*, London, Writers & Readers Publishing Co-operative.

Hughes, R. (1988), *The Fatal Shore: A History of the Transportation of Convicts to Australia 1787–1868*, London, Pan Books.

Illich, I. (1973), *Celebration of Awareness*, Harmondsworth, Penguin Books.

James, A. & Prout, A. (1990), *Constructing and Reconstructing Childhood*, Basingstoke, Falmer Press.

Johnson, C. (1991), *Moral Legislation: A Legal–Political Model for Indirect Consequentialist Reasoning*, Cambridge University Press.

Jupp, M. (1990), The UN Convention on the Rights of the Child: An Opportunity for Advocates', *Human Rights Quarterly*, 12, 130.

Kant, I. (1785), in H. Paton, *The Moral Law* (1948), London, Hutchinson.

Kaplan, A. (1964), *The Conduct of Inquiry*, San Francisco, Chandler Publishing.

Kaufman, T. (1988), 'Reporting Sexual Offences Against Children', *Sexual Offences Against Children Research Reports*, Melbourne, Law Reform Commission of Victoria.

Keane, M. (1982), *Good Behaviour*, London, Sphere Books.

Kellmer-Pringle, M. (1980), *The Needs of Children*, London, Hutchinson.

Kelly, L. (1988), *Surviving Sexual Violence*, Cambridge, Polity Press.

Kleinig, J. (1976), 'Mill, Children and Rights', *Educational Philosophy and Theory*, 8, 14.

Kleinig, J. (1982), *Philosophical Issues in Education*, London, Croom Helm.

Kleinig, J. (1989), 'Persons, Lines and Shadows', *Ethics*, 100, 108.

La Fontaine, J. (1990), *Child Sexual Abuse*, Oxford, Polity Press.

Land, H. (1979), 'The Boundaries between the State and the Family' in Harris, C. (ed) *The Sociology of the Family*, University of Keele, Sociological Review Monograph.

Laslett, P., Oosterveen, K., & Smith, R. M. (1980), *Bastardy and its Comparative History*, Cambridge, Harvard University Press.

Levy, A. & Kahan, B. (1991), *The Pindown Experience and the Protection of Children*, Stafford, Staffs C.C.

Lindley, R. (1986), *Autonomy*, London, Macmillan.

Lingam (1991), 'Sex-Detection Tests and the Female Foeticide – Discrimination Before Birth', *Indian Journal of Social Work*, 52, 13.

Lomasky, L. (1987), *Persons, Rights and the Moral Community*, New York, Oxford University Press.

Lovering, K. (1984), *Cost of Children in Australia*, AIFS Working Paper, Melbourne, Australian Institute of Family Studies.

Lowy, C. (1988), 'The Doctrine Of Substituted Judgment In Medical Decision Making', *Bioethics*, 15–21.

Lucy, W. (1990), 'Controversy about Children's Rights', in Freestone, D. (ed) *Children and the Law: Essays in Honour of Professor H. K. Bevan*, Hull, Hull University Press.

Luke, G. (1990), 'Back to Justice: An Evaluation' for National Workshop on Juvenile Justice, Australian National University, Canberra.

Mabbott, J. (1967), *The State and the Citizen*, London, Hutchinson.

MacCormick, D. (1976), 'Children's Rights: A Test-Case for Theories of Right', *Archiv fur Recht-und Sozialphilosophie* (1976) LXII, 305–16, reprinted in MacCormick, D. (1982), *Legal Right and Social Democracy*, Oxford, Clarendon Press, ch 8.

MacCormick, D. (1983), 'Dworkin as Pre-Benthamite' in Cohen, M. (ed), *Ronald Dworkin and Contemporary Jurisprudence*.

MacCormick, N. (1982) *Legal Right and Social Democracy: Essays in Legal and Political Philosophy*, Oxford, Clarendon Press.

MacDonald, P. (ed) (1986), *Settling Up: Property and Income Distribution on Divorce in Australia*, Prentice-Hall.

Mackie, J. (1977), *Ethics, Inventing Right and Wrong*, Harmondsworth, Penguin.

Mackie, J. (1984), 'Can There Be a Right-Based Moral Theory?' in Waldron, J. (ed) *Theories of Rights*, Oxford, Oxford University Press.

MacKinnon, C. (1983), 'Feminism, Marxism, Method and the State: Toward Feminist Jurisprudence', *Signs*, 8, 635.

Maclean, M. & Kuh, D. (1991) 'The long term effects for girls of parental divorce', in Maclean, M. & Groves, D., *Women's Issues in Social Policy*, Routledge & Kegan Paul.

Maclean, M. & Wadsworth, M. (1988), 'The Interests of Children After Parental Divorce: A Long-term Perspective', *International Journal of Law and the Family*, 2, 155.

Manciaux, M. (1991), 'The United Nations Convention on the Rights of the Child', *International Dif. Health Legislation*, 42, 165.

Margolin, C. (1978), 'Salvation Versus Liberation: The Movement for Children's Rights In a Historical Context', *Social Problems*, 22, 441.

Marshall, T. (1973), *Sociology at the Crossroads and other Essays*, London, Heinemann.

Martin, R. & Nickel, J. (1980), 'Recent Work on the Concept of Rights', *American Philosophical Quarterly*, 17, 165.

Mason, A. (1987), 'Future Directions in Australian Law' *Australian Bar Review*, 4, 93.

Max, L. (1990), *Children: An Endangered Species?*, Auckland, Penguin Books.

Mayor, R. (1973), *The Rector's Daughter*, Harmondsworth, Penguin.

McBarnet, D. (1981), *Conviction: Law, the State and the Construction of Justice*, London, Macmillan.

McBarnet, D. (1981a), 'Magistrates' Courts and the Ideology of Justice', *British Journal of Law and Society*, 8 (2), 197.

McCloskey, H. (1973), *Our Freedom and its Responsibilities*, Melbourne, LaTrobe.

McGoldrick, D. (1991), 'The United Nations Convention on the Rights of the Child', *International Journal of Law and the Family*, 5, 132–69.

Medical Research Council (UK) (1964), 'Responsibilities in Investigations on Human Subjects', in the *Report of the Medical Research Council for the Year 1962–63*, London, HM Stationery Office.

Melton, G. (1987), *Reforming The Law*, New York, Guilford Press.

Mendonca, I. (1990), 'The Girl in India: A Deprived Child', Centre for Women's Studies, Department of Sociology, University of Poona, Pune, India.

Miljeteig-Olssen (1990), 'Advocacy of Children's Rights – The Convention as More than a Legal Document', *Human Rights Quarterly*, 22, 149.

Mill, J. S. (1859), *On Liberty*.

Mill, J. S. (1957), *Utilitarianism, Liberty and Representative Government*, London, Everyman's Library, J. Dent & Sons.

Miller, A. (1984), *Thou Shalt Not Be Aware*, New York, Farrar, Straus & Giroux.

Miller, A. (1987), *The Drama of Being A Child*, London, Virago Press.

Minow, M. (1985), 'Beyond State Intervention in the Family: For Baby Jane Doe', *University of Michigan Journal of Law Reform*, 18, 933.

Minow, M. (1986), 'Rights for the Next Generation: A Feminist Approach to Children's Rights', *Harvard Women's Law Journal*, 9, 1.

Mnookin, R. (1978), 'Children's Rights: Legal and Ethical Dilemmas', *The Transcript*, 11, 5.

Mohr Report (1977), *Report of the Royal Commission into the Administration of the Juvenile Courts Act and Other Associated Matters Part 2*, South Australian Government.

Montgomery, J. (1988), 'Children as Property?', *Modern Law Review*, 51, 323–42.

Morgan, D. (1990), 'Abortion: The Unexamined Ground', *Criminal Law Review*, 687.

Morgan, J. (1988), 'Feminist Theory as Legal Theory', *Melbourne University Law Review*, 16, 743–59.

Morris, A. & Giller, H. (1987), *Understanding Juvenile Justice*, London, Croom Helm.

Morris, A. *et al* (1980), *Justice for Children*, London, Macmillan.

Mulholland, L. (1990), *Kant's System of Rights*, New York, Columbia University Press.

Naffine, N. (1990a), *Law and the Sexes: Explorations in Feminist Jurisprudence*, Sydney, Allen & Unwin.

Naffine, N. (1990b), 'Trends in Juvenile Justice', Paper prepared for the planned publication of the proceedings of the National Workshop on Juvenile Justice.

Naffine, N. & Wundersitz, J. (1991a), 'Charge Negotiations in the Children's Court', *Criminology Australia* 2 (4), 21.

Naffine, N. & Wundersitz, J. (1991b), 'Lawyers in the Children's Court', *Crime and Delinquency*, 37 (3), 374.

Naffine, N., Wundersitz, J., & Gale, F. (1990), 'Back to Justice for Juveniles: The Rhetoric and Reality of Law Reform', *Australian and New Zealand Journal of Criminology*, 23, 192.

Narveson, J. (1985), 'Contractarian Rights' in Frey R. (ed) *Utility and Rights*, Oxford, Blackwell.

National Children's Home (1989), *Children in Danger*, NCH Factfile About Children Today.

National Health and Research Council (Australia) (1982), *First Report by the National Health and Research Council Working Party on Ethics in Medical Research: Research on Humans*.

National Workshop (1990), Unpublished Proceedings of the National Workshop on Juvenile Justice, Australian National University, Canberra.

Nayar (1991), 'Labour of the Indian Girl Child: Multi-Curse, Multi-Abuse, and Multi-Neglect', *Indian Journal of Social Work*, 52, 37.

Nelson, S. (1987), *Incest: Fact and Myth*, Edinburgh, Stramullion.

Newell, P. (1989), *Children Are People Too*, London, Bedford Square Press.

Newell, P. (1991), *The UN Convention and Children's Rights in the UK*, London, National Children's Bureau.

Nichols, H. (1981), 'Courts and Panels for Young Female Offenders in South Australia', 51st ANZAAS Conference, Brisbane.

Nozick, R. (1974), *Anarchy, State and Utopia*, Oxford, Blackwell.

Nygh, P. (1991), 'Evaluation of the Child Support Scheme', *Australian Journal of Family Law*, 5, 183.

O'Hagan, T. (1984), *The End of Law?*, Oxford, Blackwell.

O'Neill, O. (1979–80), 'The Most Extensive Liberty', *Proceedings of the Aristotelian Society*, 80, 45–59.

O'Neill, O. (1985a), 'Between Consenting Adults', *Philosophy and Public Affairs*, 44, 252–77.

O'Neill, O. (1985b), 'Rights, Obligations and Needs', *Logos*, 6, 29–47.

O'Neill, O. (1986), *Faces of Hunger: An Essay on Poverty, Development and Justice*, London, George Allen & Unwin.

O'Neill, O. (1988), 'Ethical Reasoning and Ideological Pluralism', *Ethics*, 98, 705–22.

O'Neill, O. (1992), 'Children's Rights and Children's Lives', in this volume.

O'Neill, O. & Ruddick, W. (eds) (1979), *Having Children: Philosophical and Legal Reflections On Parenthood*, New York, Oxford University Press.

Okin, S. (1989), *Justice, Gender and the Family*, New York, Basic Books.

Olsen, F. (1983), The Family and the Market: A Study of Ideology and Legal Reform', *Harvard Law Review*, 96, 1497.

Olsen, F. (1984a), 'Statutory Rape: A Feminist Critique of Rights Analysis', *Texas Law Review*, 64, 387.

Olsen, F. (1984b), 'The Politics of Family Law', *Law & Inequality*, 2, 1.

Olsen, F. (1984c), 'Socrates on Legal Obligation: Legitimation Theory and Civil Disobedience', *Georgia Law Review*, 18, 929.

Olsen, F. (1985), 'The Myth of State Intervention in the Family', *University of Michigan Journal of Law Reform*, 18, 835.

Olsen, F. (1986), 'From False Paternalism to False Equality: Judicial Assaults on Feminist Community, Illinois 1869–1895', *Michigan Law Review*, 84, 1518.

Olsen, F. (1986b), 'De politieke dimensies van het familiercht', *Nemesis*, 2, 144–54.

Olsen, F. (1987), 'Feminism, Post-Modernism, and Critical Legal Studies', Working Paper 29, University College, London.

Olsen, F. (1988), 'Foraeldremyndighed og reproduktionsteknologi', *Retfaerd*, 11, 61–72.

Olsen, F. (1989), 'Unravelling Compromise', *Harvard Law Review*, 103, 105.

Olsen, F. (1990a), 'The Sex of Law', in Kairys, D. (ed) *The Politics of Law* (1990) (2nd ed).

Olsen, F. (1990b), 'Feminism and Critical Legal Theory: An American Perspective', *International Journal of the Sociology of Law*, 18, 199–215.

Olsen, F. (1990c), 'Das Geschlecht des Rechts', *Kritische Justiz*, 3, 303–17.

Olsen, F. (1991), 'A Finger to the Devil: Abortion, Privacy and Equality', *Dissent*.

OPCS, Occupational Mortality 1979–80 & 1982–83' in Social Services Committee (1988), *Perinatal, Neonatal and Infant Mortality*, First Report, Session 1988–89, H.C.54, London, HMSS.

Packer, H. (1964), 'Two Models of Criminal Justice', *University of Pennsylvania Law Review*, 113, 1.

Parfit, D. (1984), *Reasons and Persons*, Oxford, Oxford University Press.

Parker, S. (1991), 'Child Support in Australia: Children's Rights or Public Interest?', *International Journal of Law and the Family*, 5, 24–57.

Parsloe, P. (1978), *Juvenile Justice in Britain and the United States: The Balance of Needs and Rights*, London, Routledge & Kegan Paul.

Parton, N. (1985), *The Politics of Child Abuse*, London, Macmillan.

Pateman, C. (1989), *The Disorder of Women*, Cambridge, Polity.

Paton, G. (1972), *A Text Book of Jurisprudence*, Oxford, Oxford University Press.

Paulsen, M. (1974), 'The Law and Abused Children' in Helfer, R. & Kempe, C. (eds) *The Battered Child*, Chicago, University of Chicago Press.

Pearce, D., Campbell, E. & Harding, D. (1987), *Australian Law Schools: A Discipline Assessment for the Commonwealth Tertiary Education Commission*, Canberra, AGPS.

Peller, G. (1985), 'The Metaphysics of American Law, *California Law Review*, 73, 1151.

Pettit, P. (1986), 'Can the Welfare State Take Rights Seriously?' in Sampford, C. & Galligan, D. J. (eds) (1986), *Law, Rights and the Welfare State*, London, Croom Helm.

Pettit, P. (1990), 'The Consequentialist Can Recognise Rights', *The Philosophical Quarterly*, 38, 42.

Pfuhl, S. (1980), *The Deviance Process*, New York, D.0. 31 Van Nostrand.

Pius XI (1930), 'Casti connubi', in Ihm, C. (1981), *The Papal Encyclicals 1903–1939*, McGrath.

Pollock, L. (1983), *Forgotten Children*, Cambridge, Cambridge University Press.

Pratt, J. (1989), 'Corporatism: The Third Model of Juvenile Justice', *British Journal of Criminology*, 29 (3), 236.

Rawls, J. (1971), *A Theory of Justice*, Cambridge, Mass., Harvard University Press.

Rawls, J. (1972), *A Theory of Justice*, Oxford, Oxford University Press.

Rawls, J. (1980), 'Kantian Constrictivism and Moral Theory', *Journal of Philosophy*, 77, 515–72.

Rawls, J. (1982), 'Social Unity and Primary Goods' in Sen, A. & Williams, B. (eds) *Utilitarianism and Beyond*, Cambridge, Cambridge University Press.

Rawls, J. (1987), 'On the Idea of an Overlapping Consensus', *Oxford Journal of Legal Studies*, 7, 1.

Raz, J. (1984a), 'Legal Rights', *Oxford Journal of Legal Studies*, 4, 1–21.

Raz, J. (1984b), 'Right-based Moralities', *Theories of Rights*, ed Waldron, J., Oxford, Oxford University Press, 182–200.

Richards, D. (1981), 'Rights and Autonomy', *Ethics*, 92, 3.

Richards, M. & Dyson, M. (1982), *Separation, Divorce and the Development of Children: A Review*, Cambridge Child Care and Development Group.

Roberts, D. E. (1991), 'Punishing Drug Addicts Who Have Babies: Women of Color, Equality, and the Right to Privacy', *Harvard Law Review*, 104, 1419.

Rogers, C. & Wrightsman, L. (1978), 'Attitudes Toward Children's Rights: Nurturance or Self-Determination', *Journal of Social Issues*, 34 (2), 59.

Rosenbaum, M. & Newell, P. (1991), *Taking Children Seriously*, Calouste Gulbenkian Foundation.

Royal College of Physicians of London (1990), *Research Involving Patients*.

Ryan, W. (1976), *Blaming the Victim*, New York, Vintage Books.

Sallmann, P. (1985), *Report on Criminal Trials*, Canberra, Australian Institute of Judicial Administration.

Sampford, C. (1986), 'The Dimensions of Liberty and their Judicial Protection', *Law in Context*, 4, 29–51.

Scheffler, S. (ed) (1988), *Consequentialism and its Critics*, Oxford University Press.

Schoeman, F. (1980), 'Rights of Children, Rights of Parents, and the Moral Basis of the Family', *Ethics*, 91, 6–19.

Schultz, V. (1990), 'Telling Stories About Women and Work', *Harvard Law Review*, 103, 1750.

Scutt, J. (1983), *Even in the Best of Homes: Violence in the Family*, Ringwood, Penguin.

Seidler, V. (1986), *Kant, Respect and Injustice*, London, RKP.

Seymour, J. (1988), *Dealing with Young Offenders*, Sydney, Law Book Co.

Seymour, J. (1990), 'Comments on J Pratt, "The Philosophy of Juvenile Justice", for National Workshop on Juvenile Justice, Australian National University, Canberra.

Sher, E. (1983), 'Choosing for Children: Adjudicating Medical Disputes between Parents and the State', *New York University Law Review*, 58, 157.

Shrag, F. (1980), 'Children: their Rights and Needs', *Whose Child? Children's Rights, Parental Authority and State Power*, Aiken, W. & La Folette, H. (ed), Totowa, N.J., Rowman and Littlefield, 237–53.

Shue, H. (1980), *Basic Rights: Subsistence, Affluence and U.S. Foreign Policy*, Princeton, N.J., Princeton University Press.

Simmonds, N. (1985), 'Rights, Socialism and Liberalism'; *Legal Studies*, 5, 1–9.

Simmonds, N. (1986), *Central Issues In Jurisprudence*, London, Sweet & Maxwell.

Skinner, Q. (1984), 'The Idea of Negative Liberty: *Philosophy in History*, Rorty, R., Schneewind, J., & Skinner, Q. (eds) Cambridge, Cambridge University Press.

Skolnick, J. (1966), *Justice Without Trial*, Chichester, Wiley.

Smart, J. & Williams, B. (1973), *Utilitarianism: For and Against*, Cambridge, Cambridge University Press.

Special Issue on the Girl Child (1991), *Indian Journal of Social Work*, 52.

Spitzer, S. (1975), 'Toward a Marxian Theory of Deviance', *Social Problems*, 22, 638.

Steindorff (1991), 'Die UN-Kinderrechtskonvention als Legitimationsgrundlage fur Elternrechte?', *Familie und Recht*, 4, 214.

Steiner, H. (1974), 'Individual Liberty', *Proceedings of the Aristotelian Society*, 75, 33–50.

Sugarman, D. (1986), 'Legal Theory, the Common Law Mind and the Making of the Textbook Tradition', in Twining, W. (ed) *Legal Theory and Common Law*, Oxford, Basil Blackwell.

Summers, A. (1975), *Damned Whores and God's Police: the Colonization of Women in Australia*, London, Penguin.

Sumner, L. (1987), *The Moral Foundation of Rights*, Oxford, Clarendon Press.
Taylor, C. (1985), 'What's Wrong with Negative Liberty?' reprinted in *Philosophy and the Human Sciences*, Cambridge, Cambridge University Press, vol 2, 211–29.
Teichman, J. (1982), *Illegitimacy: A Philosophical Examination*, Oxford, Blackwell.
Thompson, J. (1986), *Rights, Restitution, and Risk*, Cambridge, Mass., Harvard University Press.
Tuck, R. (1979), *Natural Rights Theories*, Cambridge, Cambridge University Press.
UNICEF (1991), *The State of the World's Children 1991*, Oxford, Oxford University Press.
Victorian Law Reform Commission (1988), *Sexual Offences Against Children*, Report No 18.
Wadsworth, M. & Maclean, M. (1986), 'Parents' Divorce and Children's Life Chances', *Children's and Youth Services Review*, 8, 144.
Wadsworth, M. *et al* (1991), 'Children of Divorce and Separated Parents', *Sauvegard de l'Enfance*, 152.
Wald, M. (1976), 'State Intervention on Behalf of "Neglected" Children: A Search for Realistic Standards', in Rosenheim, M. (ed) *Pursuing Justice for the Child*, Chicago, University of Chicago Press, 246–78.
Wald, M. (1982), 'State Intervention on Behalf of Endangered Children – A Proposed Legal Response', *Child Abuse and Neglect*, 6, 3–45.
Waldron, J. (ed) (1984), *Theories of Rights*, Oxford, Oxford University Press.
Waldron, J. (1987), *Nonsense Upon Stilts*, London, Methuen.
Wallerstein, J. & Kelly, J. (1980), *Surviving the Breakup*, London, Grant Macintyre.
Wasserstrom, R. (1964), 'Rights, Human Rights and Racial Discrimination', *Journal of Philosophy*, 61, 628.
Wellman, C. (1982), *Welfare Rights*, Totowa N.J., Rowman and Allenheld.
Wellman, C. (1984), 'The Growth of Children's Rights', *Archives for Philosophy of Law and Social Philosophy*, 70, 441–53.
Westen, P. (1990), *Speaking of Equality*, Princeton, Princeton University Press.
Wiggins, D. (1985), 'Claims of Need', in Honderich, T. (ed) *Morality and Objectivity*, London, Routledge & Kegan Paul, 149–202.
Wikler, D. (1979), 'Paternalism and the Mildly Retarded', *Philosophy and Public Affairs*, 8, 377.
Wilkinson, M. (1986), 'Good Mothers – Bad Mothers: State Substitute Care of Children in the 1960's' in Marchant, H. & Waring, B. (eds) *Gender Reclaimed*, Sydney, Hale & Iremonger.
Williams Report (1979), *Report of the Committee on Obscenity and Film Censorship*, Cmnd 7772, HM Stationery Office.
Woodhead, M. (1990), 'Psychology and The Cultural Construction of Children's Needs' in James, A. & Prout, A. (eds), *Constructing and Reconstructing Childhood*, Basingstoke, Falmer Press.
Woolf, H. (1991), *Prison Disturbances April 1990*, London, HMSO.
Worsfold, V. (1974), 'A Philosophical Justification for Children's Rights', *Harvard Educational Review*, 44, 142.
Wundersitz, J., Naffine, N., & Gale, F. (1991), 'The Production of Guilt in the Juvenile Justice System', *Howard Journal of Criminal Justice* (in press).
Young, R. (1986), *Personal Autonomy: Beyond Negative and Positive Liberty*, London, Croom Helm.
Zahn-Waxler, C., Radke-Yarrow, M., & King, R. (1979), 'Child Rearing and Children's Prosocial Initiations Towards Victims of Distress', *Child Development*, 50.
Zaretsky, E. (1976), *Capitalism, the Family and Personal Life*, London, Pluto Press.
Zines, L. (1986), *The High Court and the Constitution* 2nd ed North Ryde, Sydney, Butterworths.

UNITED NATIONS CONVENTION ON THE RIGHTS OF THE CHILD

PREAMBLE

The States Parties to the present Convention,

Considering that, in accordance with the principles proclaimed in the Charter of the United Nations, recognition of the inherent dignity and of the equal and inalienable rights of all members of the human family is the foundation of freedom, justice and peace in the world,

Bearing in mind that the peoples of the United Nations have, in the Charter, reaffirmed their faith in fundamental human rights and in the dignity and worth of the human person, and have determined to promote social progress and better standards of life in larger freedom,

Recognizing that the United Nations has, in the Universal Declaration of Human Rights and in the International Covenants on Human Rights, proclaimed and agreed that everyone is entitled to all the rights and freedoms set forth therein, without distinction of any kind, such as race, colour, sex, language, religion, political or other opinion, national or social origin, property, birth or other status,

Recalling that, in the Universal Declaration of Human Rights, the United Nations has proclaimed that childhood is entitled to special care and assistance,

Convinced that the family, as the fundamental group of society and the natural environment for the growth and well-being of all its members and particularly children, should be afforded the necessary protection and assistance so that it can fully assume its responsibilities within the community,

Recognizing that the child, for the full and harmonious development of his or her personality, should grow up in a family environment, in an atmosphere of happiness, love and understanding,

Considering that the child should be fully prepared to live an individual life in society, and brought up in the spirit of the ideals proclaimed in the Charter of the United Nations, and in particular in the spirit of peace, dignity, tolerance, freedom, equality and solidarity,

Bearing in mind that the need to extend particular care to the child has been stated in the Geneva Declaration of the Rights of the Child of 1924 and in the Declaration of the Rights of the Child adopted by the General Assembly on 20 November 1959 and recognized in the Universal Declaration of Human Rights, in the International Covenant on Civil and Political Rights (in particular in articles 23 and 24), in the International Covenant on Economic, Social and Cultural Rights (in particular in article 10) and in the statutes and relevant instruments of specialized agencies and international organizations concerned with the welfare of children,

Bearing in mind that, as indicated in the Declaration of the Rights of the Child, 'the child, by reason of his physical and mental immaturity, needs special safeguards and care, including appropriate legal protection, before as well as after birth',

Recalling the provisions of the Declaration on Social and Legal Principles relating to the Protection and Welfare of Children, with Special Reference to Foster Placement and Adoption Nationally and Internationally; the United Nations Standard Minimum Rules for the Administration of Juvenile Justice (The Beijing Rules); and the Declaration on the Protection of Women and Children in Emergency and Armed Conflict,

Recognizing that, in all countries in the world, there are children living in exceptionally difficult conditions, and that such children need special consideration,

Taking due account of the importance of the traditions and cultural values of each people for the protection and harmonious development of the child,

Recognizing the importance of international co-operation for improving the living conditions of children in every country, in particular in the developing countries,

Have agreed as follows:

PART I

Article 1

For the purposes of the present Convention, a child means every human being below the age of eighteen years unless, under the law applicable to the child, majority is attained earlier.

Article 2

1. States Parties shall respect and ensure the rights set forth in the present Convention to each child within their jurisdiction without discrimination of any kind, irrespective of the child's or his or her parent's or legal guardian's race, colour, sex, language, religion, political or other opinion, national, ethnic or social origin, property, disability, birth or other status.

2. States Parties shall take all appropriate measures to ensure that the child is protected against all forms of discrimination or punishment on the basis of the status, activities, expressed opinions, or beliefs of the child's parents, legal guardians, or family members.

Article 3

1. In all actions concerning children, whether undertaken by public or private social welfare institutions, courts of law, administrative authorities or legislative bodies, the best interests of the child shall be a primary consideration.

2. States Parties undertake to ensure the child such protection and care as is necessary for his or her well-being, taking into account the rights and duties of his or her parents, legal guardians, or other individuals legally responsible for him or her, and, to this end, shall take all appropriate legislative and administrative measures.

3. States Parties shall ensure that the institutions, services and facilities responsible for the care or protection of children shall conform with the standards established by competent authorities, particularly in the areas of safety, health, in the number and suitability of their staff, as well as competent supervision.

Article 4

States Parties shall undertake all appropriate legislative, administrative, and other measures for the implementation of the rights recognized in the present Convention. With regard to economic, social and cultural rights, States Parties shall undertake such measures to the maximum extent of their available resources and, where needed, within the framework of international co-operation.

Article 5

States Parties shall respect the responsibilities, rights and duties of parents or, where applicable, the members of the extended family or community as provided for by local custom, legal guardians or other persons legally responsible for the child, to provide, in a manner consistent with the evolving capacities of the child, appropriate direction and guidance in the exercise by the child of the rights recognized in the present Convention.

Article 6

1. States Parties recognize that every child has the inherent right to life.

2. States Parties shall ensure to the maximum extent possible the survival and development of the child.

Article 7

1. The child shall be registered immediately after birth and shall have the right from birth to a name, the right to acquire a nationality and, as far as possible, the right to know and to be cared for by his or her parents.

2. States Parties shall ensure the implementation of these rights in

accordance with their national law and their obligations under the relevant international instruments in this field, in particular where the child would otherwise be stateless.

Article 8

1. States Parties undertake to respect the right of the child to preserve his or her identity, including nationality, name and family relations as recognized by law without unlawful interference.

2. Where a child is illegally deprived of some or all of the elements of his or her identity, States Parties shall provide appropriate assistance and protection, with a view to speedily re-establishing his or her identity.

Article 9

1. States Parties shall ensure that a child shall not be separated from his or her parents against their will, except when competent authorities subject to judicial review determine, in accordance with applicable law and procedures, that such separation is necessary for the best interests of the child. Such determination may be necessary in a particular case such as one involving abuse or neglect of the child by the parents, or one where the parents are living separately and a decision must be made as to the child's place of residence.

2. In any proceedings pursuant to paragraph 1 of the present article, all interested parties shall be given an opportunity to participate in the proceedings and make their views known.

3. States Parties shall respect the right of the child who is separated from one or both parents to maintain personal relations and direct contact with both parents on a regular basis, except if it is contrary to the child's best interests.

4. Where such separation results from any action initiated by a State Party, such as the detention, imprisonment, exile, deportation or death (including death arising from any cause while the person is in the custody of the State) of one or both parents or of the child, that State Party shall, upon request, provide the parents, the child or, if appropriate, another member of the family with the essential information concerning the whereabouts of the absent member(s) of the family unless the provision of the information would be detrimental to the well-being of the child. States Parties shall further ensure that the submission of such a request shall of itself entail no adverse consequences for the person(s) concerned.

Article 10

1. In accordance with the obligation of States Parties under article 9, paragraph 1, applications by a child or his or her parents to enter or

leave a State Party for the purpose of family reunification shall be dealt with by States Parties in a positive, humane and expeditious manner. States Parties shall further ensure that the submission of such a request shall entail no adverse consequences for the applicants and for the members of their family.

2. A child whose parents reside in different States shall have the right to maintain on a regular basis, save in exceptional circumstances, personal relations and direct contacts with both parents. Towards that end and in accordance with the obligation of States Parties under article 9, paragraph 1, States Parties shall respect the right of the child and his or her parents to leave any country, including their own, and to enter their own country. The right to leave any country shall be subject only to such restrictions as are prescribed by law and which are necessary to protect the national security, public order (*ordre public*), public health or morals or the rights and freedoms of others and are consistent with the other rights recognized in the present Convention.

Article 11

1. States Parties shall take measures to combat the illicit transfer and non-return of children abroad.

2. To this end, States Parties shall promote the conclusion of bilateral or multilateral agreements or accession to existing agreements.

Article 12

1. States Parties shall assure to the child who is capable of forming his or her own views the right to express those views freely in all matters affecting the child, the views of the child being given due weight in accordance with the age and maturity of the child.

2. For this purpose, the child shall in particular be provided the opportunity to be heard in any judicial and administrative proceedings affecting the child, either directly or through a representative or an appropriate body, in a manner consistent with the procedural rules of national law.

Article 13

1. The child shall have the right to freedom of expression; this right shall include freedom to seek, receive and impart information and ideas of all kinds, regardless of frontiers, either orally, in writing or in print, in the form of art, or through any other media of the child's choice.

2. The exercise of this right may be subject to certain restrictions, but these shall only be such as are provided by law and are necessary:

(a) For respect of the rights or reputations of others; or

(b) For the protection of national security or of public order (*ordre public*), or of public health or morals.

Article 14

1. States Parties shall respect the right of the child to freedom of thought, conscience and religion.

2. States Parties shall respect the rights and duties of the parents and, when applicable, legal guardians, to provide direction to the child in the exercise of his or her right in a manner consistent with the evolving capacities of the child.

3. Freedom to manifest one's religon or beliefs may be subject only to such limitations as are prescribed by law and are necessary to protect public safety, order, health or morals, or the fundamental rights and freedoms of others.

Article 15

1. States Parties recognize the rights of the child to freedom of association and to freedom of peaceful assembly.

2. No restrictions may be placed on the exercise of these rights other than those imposed in conformity with the law and which are necessary in a democratic society in the interests of national security or public safety, public order (*ordre public*), the protection of public health or morals or the protection of the rights and freedoms of others.

Article 16

1. No child shall be subjected to arbitrary or unlawful interference with his or her privacy, family, home or correspondence, nor to unlawful attacks on his or her honour and reputation.

2. The child has the right to the protection of the law against such interference or attacks.

Article 17

States Parties recognize the important function performed by the mass media and shall ensure that the child has access to information and material from a diversity of national and international sources, especially those aimed at the promotion of his or her social, spiritual and moral well-being and physical and mental health. To this end, States Parties shall:

(a) Encourage the mass media to disseminate information and material of social and cultural benefit to the child and in accordance with the spirit of article 29;

(b) Encourage international co-operation in the production, exchange and dissemination of such information and material from a diversity of cultural, national and international sources;

(c) Encourage the production and dissemination of children's books;

(d) Encourage the mass media to have particular regard to the linguistic needs of the child who belongs to a minority group or who is indigenous;

(e) Encourage the development of appropriate guidelines for the protection of the child from information and material injurious to his or her well-being, bearing in mind the provisions of article 13 and 18.

Article 18

1. States Parties shall use their best efforts to ensure recognition of the principle that both parents have common responsibilities for the upbringing and development of the child. Parents or, as the case may be, legal guardians, have the primary responsibility for the upbringing and development of the child. The best interests of the child will be their basic concern.

2. For the purpose of guaranteeing and promoting the rights set forth in the present Convention, States Parties shall render appropriate assistance to parents and legal guardians in the performance of their child-rearing responsibilities and shall ensure the development of institutions, facilities and services for the care of children.

3. States Parties shall take all appropriate measures to ensure that children of working parents have the right to benefit from child-care services and facilities for which they are eligible.

Article 19

1. States Parties shall take all appropriate legislative, administrative, social and educational measures to protect the child from all forms of physical or mental violence, injury or abuse, neglect or negligent treatment, maltreatment or exploitation, including sexual abuse, while in the care of parent(s), legal guardian(s) or any other person who has the care of the child.

2. Such protective measures should, as appropriate, include effective procedures for the establishment of social programmes to provide necessary support for the child and for those who have the care of the child, as well as for other forms of prevention and for identification, reporting, referral, investigation, treatment and follow-up of instances of child maltreatment described heretofore, and, as appropriate, for judicial involvement.

Article 20

1. A child temporarily or permanently deprived of his or her family environment, or in whose own best interests cannot be allowed to remain in that environment, shall be entitled to special protection and assistance provided by the State.

2. States Parties shall in accordance with their national laws ensure alternative care for such a child.

3. Such care could include, *inter alia*, foster placement, *kafalah* of

Islamic law, adoption or if necessary placement in suitable institutions for the care of children. When considering solutions, due regard shall be paid to the desirability of continuity in a child's upbringing and to the child's ethnic, religious, cultural and linguistic background.

Article 21

States Parties that recognize and/or permit the system of adoption shall ensure that the best interests of the child shall be the paramount consideration and they shall:

(a) Ensure that the adoption of a child is authorized only by competent authorities who determine, in accordance with applicable law and procedures and on the basis of all pertinent and reliable information, that the adoption is permissible in view of the child's status concerning parents, relatives and legal guardians and that, if required, the persons concerned have given their informed consent to the adoption on the basis of such counselling as may be necessary;

(b) Recognize that inter-country adoption may be considered as an alternative means of child's care, if the child cannot be placed in a foster or an adoptive family or cannot in any suitable manner be cared for in the child's country of origin;

(c) Ensure that the child concerned by inter-country adoption enjoys safeguards and standards equivalent to those existing in the case of national adoption;

(d) Take all appropriate measures to ensure that, in inter-country adoption, the placement does not result in improper financial gain for those involved in it;

(e) Promote, where appropriate, the objectives of the present article by concluding bilateral or multilateral arrangements or agreements, and endeavour, within this framework, to ensure that the placement of the child in another country is carried out by competent authorities or organs.

Article 22

1. States Parties shall take appropriate measures to ensure that a child who is seeking refugee status or who is considered a refugee in accordance with applicable international or domestic law and procedures shall, whether unaccompanied or accompanied by his or her parents or by any other person, receive appropriate protection and humanitarian assistance in the enjoyment of applicable rights set forth in the present Convention and in other international human rights or humanitarian instruments to which the said States are Parties.

2. For this purpose, States Parties shall provide, as they consider appropriate, co-operation in any efforts by the United Nations and other competent inter-governmental organizations or non-governmental organizations co-operating with the United Nations to protect and assist

such a child and to trace the parents or other members of the family of any refugee child in order to obtain information necessary for reunification with his or her family. In cases where no parents or other members of the family can be found, the child shall be accorded the same protection as any other child permanently or temporarily deprived of his or her family environment for any reason, as set forth in the present Convention.

Article 23

1. States Parties recognize that a mentally or physically disabled child should enjoy a full and decent life, in conditions which ensure dignity, promote self-reliance and facilitate the child's active participation in the community.

2. States Parties recognize the right of the disabled child to special care and shall encourage and ensure the extension, subject to available resources, to the eligible child and those responsible for his or her care, of assistance for which application is made and which is appropriate to the child's condition and to the circumstances of the parents or others caring for the child.

3. Recognizing the special needs of a disabled child, assistance extended in accordance with paragraph 2 of the present article shall be provided free of charge, whenever possible, taking into account the financial resources of the parents or others caring for the child, and shall be designed to ensure that the disabled child has effective access to and receives education, training, health care services, rehabilitation services, preparation for employment and recreation opportunities in a manner conducive to the child's achieving the fullest possible social integration and individual development, including his or her cultural and spiritual development.

4. States Parties shall promote, in the spirit of international co-operation, the exchange of appropriate information in the field of preventive health care and of medical, psychological and functional treatment of disabled children, including dissemination of and access to information concerning methods of rehabilitation, education and vocational services, with the aim of enabling States Parties to improve their capabilities and skills and to widen their experience in these areas. In this regard, particular account shall be taken of the needs of developing countries.

Article 24

1. States Parties recognize the right of the child to the enjoyment of the highest attainable standard of health and to facilities for the treatment of illness and rehabilitation of health. States Parties shall strive to ensure that no child is deprived of his or her right of access to such health care services.

2. States Parties shall pursue full implementation of this right and, in particular, shall take appropriate measures:

(a) To diminish infant and child mortality;

(b) To ensure the provision of necessary medical assistance and health care to all children with emphasis on the development of primary health care;

(c) To combat disease and malnutrition, including within the framework of primary health care, through, *inter alia*, the application of readily available technology and through the provision of adequate nutritious foods and clean drinking-water, taking into consideration the dangers and risks of environmental pollution;

(d) To ensure appropriate pre-natal and post-natal health care for mothers;

(e) To ensure that all segments of society, in particular parents and children, are informed, have access to education and are supported in the use of basic knowledge of child health and nutrition, the advantages of breast-feeding, hygiene and environmental sanitation and the prevention of accidents;

(f) To develop preventive health care, guidance for parents and family planning education and services.

3. States Parties shall take all effective and appropriate measures with a view to abolishing traditional practices prejudicial to the health of children.

4. States Parties undertake to promote and encourage international co-operation with a view to achieving progressively the full realization of the right recognized in the present article. In this regard, particular account shall be taken of the needs of developing countries.

Article 25

States Parties recognize the right of a child who has been placed by the competent authorities for the purposes of care, protection or treatment of his or her physical or mental health, to a periodic review of the treatment provided to the child and all other circumstances relevant to his or her placement.

Article 26

1. States Parties shall recognize for every child the right to benefit from social security, including social insurance, and shall take the necessary measures to achieve the full realization of this right in accordance with their national law.

2. The benefits should, where appropriate, be granted, taking into account the resources and the circumstances of the child and persons having responsibility for the maintenance of the child, as well as any other consideration relevant to an application for benefits made by or on behalf of the child.

Article 27

1. States Parties recognize the right of every child to a standard of living adequate for the child's physical, mental, spiritual, moral and social development.

2. The parent(s) or others responsible for the child have the primary responsibility to secure, within their abilities and financial capacities, the conditions of living necessary for the child's development.

3. States Parties, in accordance with national conditions and within their means, shall take appropriate measures to assist parents and others responsible for the child to implement this right and shall in case of need provide material assistance and support programmes, particularly with regard to nutrition, clothing and housing.

4. States Parties shall take all appropriate measures to secure the recovery of maintenance for the child from the parents or other persons having responsibility for the child, both within the State Party and from abroad. In particular, where the person having financial responsibility for the child lives in a State different from that of the child, States Parties shall promote the accession to international agreements or the conclusion of such agreements, as well as the making of other appropriate arrangements.

Article 28

1. States Parties recognize the right of the child to education, and with a view to achieving this right progressively and on the basis of equal opportunity, they shall, in particular:

(a) Make primary education compulsory and available free to all;

(b) Encourage the development of different forms of secondary education, including general and vocational education, make them available and accessible to every child, and take appropriate measures such as the introduction of free education and offering financial assistance in case of need;

(c) Make higher education accessible to all on the basis of capacity by every appropriate means;

(d) Make educational and vocational information and guidance available and accessible to all children;

(e) Take measures to encourage regular attendance at schools and the reduction of drop-out rates.

2. States Parties shall take all appropriate measures to ensure that school discipline is administered in a manner consistent with the child's human dignity and in conformity with the present Convention.

3. States Parties shall promote and encourage international co-operation in matters relating to education, in particular with a view to contributing to the elimination of ignorance and illiteracy throughout the world and facilitating access to scientific and technical knowledge

and modern teaching methods. In this regard, particular account shall be taken of the needs of developing countries.

Article 29

1. States Parties agree that the education of the child shall be directed to:

(a) The development of the child's personality, talents and mental and physical abilities to their fullest potential;

(b) The development of respect for human rights and fundamental freedoms, and for the principles enshrined in the Charter of the United Nations;

(c) The development of respect for the child's parents, his or her own cultural identity, language and values, for the national values of the country in which the child is living, the country from which he or she may originate and for civilizations different from his or her own;

(d) The preparation of the child for responsible life in a free society, in the spirit of understanding, peace, tolerance, equality of sexes, and friendship among all peoples, ethnic, national and religious groups and persons of indigenous origin;

(e) The development of respect for the natural environment.

2. No part of the present article or article 28 shall be construed so as to interfere with the liberty of individuals and bodies to establish and direct educational institutions, subject always to the observance of the principles set forth in paragraph 1 of the present article and to the requirements that the education given in such institutions shall conform to such minimum standards as may be laid down by the State.

Article 30

In those States in which ethnic, religious or linguistic minorities or persons of indigenous origin exist, a child belonging to such a minority or who is indigenous shall not be denied the right, in community with other members of his or her group, to enjoy his or her own culture, to profess and practise his or her own religion, or to use his or her own language.

Article 31

1. States Parties recognize the right of the child to rest and leisure, to engage in play and recreational activities appropriate to the age of the child and to participate freely in cultural life and the arts.

2. States Parties shall respect and promote the right of the child to participate fully in cultural and artistic life and shall encourage the provision of appropriate and equal opportunities for cultural, artistic, recreational and leisure activity.

Article 32

1. States Parties recognize the right of the child to be protected from economic exploitation and from performing any work that is likely to be hazardous or to interfere with the child's education, or to be harmful to the child's health or physical, mental, spiritual, moral or social development.

2. States Parties shall take legislative, administrative, social and educational measures to ensure the implementation of the present article. To this end, and having regard to the relevant provisions of other international instruments, States Parties shall in particular:

(a) Provide for a minimum age or minimum ages for admission to employment;

(b) Provide for appropriate regulation of the hours and conditions of employment;

(c) Provide for appropriate penalties or other sanctions to ensure the effective enforcement of the present article.

Article 33

States Parties shall take all appropriate measures, including legislative, administrative, social and educational measures, to protect children from the illicit use of narcotic drugs and psychotropic substances as defined in the relevant international treaties, and to prevent the use of children in the illicit production and trafficking of such substances.

Article 34

States Parties undertake to protect the child from all forms of sexual exploitation and sexual abuse. For these purposes, States Parties shall in particular take all appropriate national, bilateral and multilateral measures to prevent:

(a) The inducement or coercion of a child to engage in any unlawful sexual activity;

(b) The exploitative use of children in prostitution or other unlawful sexual practices;

(c) The exploitative use of children in pornographic performances and materials.

Article 35

States Parties shall take all appropriate national, bilateral and multilateral measures to prevent the abduction of, the sale of or traffic in children for any purpose or in any form.

Article 36

States Parties shall protect the child against all other forms of exploitation prejudicial to any aspects of the child's welfare.

Article 37

1. States Parties shall ensure that:

(a) No child shall be subjected to torture or other cruel, inhuman or degrading treatment or punishment. Neither capital punishment nor life imprisonment without possibility of release shall be imposed for offences committed by persons below eighteen years of age;

(b) No child shall be deprived of his or her liberty unlawfully or arbitrarily. The arrest, detention or imprisonment of a child shall be in conformity with the law and shall be used only as a measure of last resort and for the shortest appropriate period of time;

(c) Every child deprived of liberty shall be treated with humanity and respect for the inherent dignity of the human person, and in a manner which takes into account the needs of persons of his or her age. In particular, every child deprived of liberty shall be separated from adults unless it is considered in the child's best interest not to do so and shall have the right to maintain contact with his or her family through correspondence and visits, save in exceptional circumstances;

(d) Every child deprived of his or her liberty shall have the right to prompt access to legal and other appropriate assistance, as well as the right to challenge the legality of the deprivation of his or her liberty before a court or other competent, independent and impartial authority, and to a prompt decision on any such action.

Article 38

1. States Parties undertake to respect and to ensure respect for rules of international humanitarian law applicable to them in armed conflicts which are relevant to the child.

2. States Parties shall take all feasible measures to ensure that persons who have not attained the age of fifteen years do not take a direct part in hostilities.

3. States Parties shall refrain from recruiting any person who has not attained the age of fifteen years into their armed forces. In recruiting among those persons who have attained the age of fifteen years but who have not attained the age of eighteen years, States Parties shall endeavour to give priority to those who are oldest.

4. In accordance with their obligations under international humanitarian law to protect the civilian population in armed conflicts, States Parties shall take all feasible measures to ensure protection and care of children who are affected by an armed conflict.

Article 39

States Parties shall take all appropriate measures to promote physical and psychological recovery and social reintegration of a child victim of: any form of neglect, exploitation or abuse, torture or any other form of cruel, inhuman or degrading treatment or punishment, or armed conflicts. Such recovery and reintegration shall take place in an environment which fosters the health, self-respect and dignity of the child.

Article 40

1. States Parties recognize the right of every child alleged as, accused of, or recognized as having infringed the penal law to be treated in a manner consistent with the promotion of the child's sense of dignity and worth, which reinforces the child's respect for the human rights and fundamental freedoms of others and which takes into account the child's age and the desirability of promoting the child's reintegration and the child's assuming a constructive role in society.

2. To this end, and having regard to the relevant provisions of international instruments, States Parties shall, in particular, ensure that:

(a) No child shall be alleged as, be accused of, or recognized as having infringed the penal law by reason of acts or omissions that were not prohibited by national or international law at the time they were committed;

(b) Every child alleged as or accused of having infringed the penal law has at least the following guarantees;

(i) To be presumed innocent until proven guilty according to law;

(i) To be informed promptly and directly of the charges against him or her, and, if appropriate, through his or her parents or legal guardians, and to have legal or other appropriate assistance in the preparation and presentation of his or her defence;

(iii) To have the matter determined without delay by a competent, independent and impartial authority or judicial body in a fair hearing according to law, in the presence of legal or other appropriate assistance and, unless it is considered not to be in the best interest of the child, in particular, taking into account his or her age or situation, his or her parents or legal guardians;

(iv) Not to be compelled to give testimony or to confess guilt; to examine or have examined adverse witnesses and to obtain the participation and examination of witnesses on his or her behalf under conditions of equality;

(v) If considered to have infringed the penal law, to have this decision and any measures imposed in consequence thereof reviewed by a higher competent, independent and impartial authority or judicial body according to law;

(vi) To have the free assistance of an interpreter if the child cannot understand or speak the language used;

(vii) To have his or her privacy fully respected at all stages of the proceedings.

3. States Parties shall seek to promote the establishment of laws, procedures, authorities and institutions specifically applicable to chil-

dren alleged as, accused of, or recognized as having infringed the penal law, and, in particular:

(a) The establishment of a minimum age below which children shall be presumed not to have the capacity to infringe the penal law;

(b) Whenever appropriate and desirable, measures for dealing with such children without resorting to judicial proceedings, providing that human rights and legal safeguards are fully respected.

4. A variety of dispositions, such as care, guidance and supervision orders; counselling; probation; foster care; education and vocational training programmes and other alternatives to institutional care shall be available to ensure that children are dealt with in a manner appropriate to their well-being and proportionate both to their circumstances and the offence.

Article 41

Nothing in the present Convention shall affect any provisions which are more conducive to the realization of the rights of the child and which may be contained in:

(a) The law of a State Party; or

(b) International law in force for that State.

PART II

Article 42

States Parties undertake to make the principles and provisions of the Convention widely known, by appropriate and active means, to adults and children alike.

Article 43

1. For the purpose of examining the progress made by States Parties in achieving the realization of the obligations undertaken in the present Convention there shall be established a Committee on the Rights of the Child, which shall carry out the functions hereinafter provided.

2. The Committee shall consist of ten experts of high moral standing and recognized competence in the field covered by this Convention. The members of the Committee shall be elected by States Parties from among their nationals and shall serve in their personal capacity, consideration being given to equitable geographical distribution, as well as to the principal legal systems.

3. The members of the Committee shall be elected by secret ballot from a list of persons nominated by States Parties. Each State Party may nominate one person from among its own nationals.

4. The initial election to the Committee shall be held no later than six months after the date of the entry into force of the present Convention and thereafter every second year. At least four months before the date of

each election, the Secretary-General of the United Nations shall address a letter to States Parties inviting them to submit their nominations within two months. The Secretary-General shall subsequently prepare a list in alphabetical order of all persons thus nominated, indicating States Parties which have nominated them, and shall submit it to the States Parties to the present Convention.

5. The elections shall be held at meetings of States Parties convened by the Secretary-General at United Nations Headquarters. At those meetings, for which two thirds of States Parties shall constitute a quorum, the persons elected to the Committee shall be those who obtain the largest number of votes and an absolute majority of the votes of the representatives of States Parties present and voting.

6. The members of the Committee shall be elected for a term of four years. They shall be eligible for re-election if renominated. The term of five of the members elected at the first election shall expire at the end of two years; immediately after the first election, the names of these five members shall be chosen by lot by the Chairman of the meeting.

7. If a member of the Committee dies or resigns or declares that for any other cause he or she can no longer perform the duties of the Committee, the State Party which nominated the member shall appoint another expert from among its nationals to serve for the remainder of the term, subject to the approval of the Committee.

8. The Committee shall establish its own rules of procedure.

9. The Committee shall elect its officers for a period of two years.

10. The meetings of the Committee shall normally be held at United Nations Headquarters or at any other convenient place as determined by the Committee. The Committee shall normally meet annually. The duration of the meetings of the Committee shall be determined, and reviewed, if necessary, by a meeting of the States Parties to the present Convention, subject to the approval of the General Assembly.

11. The Secretary-General of the United Nations shall provide the necessary staff and facilities for the effective performance of the functions of the Committee under the present Convention.

12. With the approval of the General Assembly, the members of the Committee established under the present Convention shall receive emoluments from United Nations resources on such terms and conditions as the Assembly may decide.

Article 44

1. States Parties undertake to submit to the Committee, through the Secretary-General of the United Nations, reports on the measures they have adopted which give effect to the rights recognized herein and on the progress made on the enjoyment of those rights:

(a) Within two years of the entry into force of the Convention for the State Party concerned;

(b) Thereafter every five years.

2. Reports made under the present article shall indicate factors and difficulties, if any, affecting the degree of fulfilment of the obligations under the present Convention. Reports shall also contain sufficient information to provide the Committee with a comprehensive understanding of the implementation of the Convention in the country concerned.

3. A State Party which has submitted a comprehensive initial report to the Committee need not, in its subsequent reports submitted in accordance with paragraph 1 (b) of the present article, repeat basic information previously provided.

4. The Committee may request from States Parties further information relevant to the implementation of the Convention.

5. The Committee shall submit to the General Assembly, through the Economic and Social Council, every two years, reports on its activities.

6. States Parties shall make their reports widely available to the public in their own countries.

Article 45

In order to foster the effective implementation of the Convention and to encourage international co-operation in the field covered by the Convention:

(a) The specialized agencies, the United Nations Children's Fund, and other United Nations organs shall be entitled to be represented at the consideration of the implementation of such provisions of the present Convention as fall within the scope of their mandate. The Committee may invite the specialized agencies, the United Nations Children's Fund and other competent bodies as it may consider appropriate to provide expert advice on the implementation of the Convention in areas falling within the scope of their respective mandates. The Committee may invite the specialized agencies, the United Nations Children's Fund, and other United Nations organs to submit reports on the implementation of the Convention in areas falling within the scope of their activities;

(b) The Committee shall transmit, as it may consider appropriate, to the specialized agencies, the United Nations Children's Fund and other competent bodies, any reports from States Parties that contain a request, or indicate a need, for technical advice or assistance, along with the Committee's observations and suggestions, if any, on these requests or indications;

(c) The Committee may recommend to the General Assembly to request the Secretary-General to undertake on its behalf studies on specific issues relating to the rights of the child;

(d) The Committee may make suggestions and general recommendations based on information received pursuant to articles 44 and 45 of the present Convention. Such suggestions and general recommendations shall be transmitted to any State Party concerned and reported to the General Assembly, together with comments, if any, from States Parties.

PART III

Article 46

The present Convention shall be open for signature by all States.

Article 47

The present Convention is subject to ratification. Instruments of ratification shall be deposited with the Secretary-General of the United Nations.

Article 48

The present Convention shall remain open for accession by any State. The instruments of accession shall be deposited with the Secretary-General of the United Nations.

Article 49

1. The present Convention shall enter into force on the thirtieth day following the date of deposit with the Secretary-General of the United Nations of the twentieth instrument of ratification or accession.

2. For each State ratifying or acceding to the Convention after the deposit of the twentieth instrument of ratification or accession, the Convention shall enter into force on the thirtieth day after the deposit by such State of its instrument of ratification or accession.

Article 50

1. Any State Party may propose an amendment and file it with the Secretary-General of the United Nations. The Secretary-General shall thereupon communicate the proposed amendment to States Parties, with a request that they indicate whether they favour a conference of States Parties for the purpose of considering and voting upon the proposals. In the event that, within four months from the date of such communication, at least one third of the States Parties favour such a conference, the Secretary-General shall convene the conference under the auspices of the United Nations. Any amendment adopted by a majority of States Parties present and voting at the conference shall be submitted to the General Assembly for approval.

2. An amendment adopted in accordance with paragraph 1 of the present article shall enter into force when it has been approved by the General Assembly of the United Nations and accepted by a two-thirds majority of States Parties.

3. When an amendment enters into force, it shall be binding on those States Parties which have accepted it, other States Parties still being

bound by the provisions of the present Convention and any earlier amendments which they have accepted.

Article 51

1. The Secretary-General of the United Nations shall receive and circulate to all States the text of reservations made by States at the time of ratification or accession.

2. A reservation incompatible with the object and purpose of the present Convention shall not be permitted.

3. Reservations may be withdrawn at any time by notification to that effect addressed to the Secretary-General of the United Nations, who shall then inform all States. Such notification shall take effect on the date on which it is received by the Secretary-General.

Article 52

A State Party may denounce the present Convention by written notification to the Secretary-General of the United Nations. Denunciation becomes effective one year after the date of receipt of the notification by the Secretary-General.

Article 53

The Secretary-General of the United Nations is designated as the depositary of the present Convention.

Article 54

The original of the present Convention, of which the Arabic, Chinese, English, French, Russian and Spanish texts are equally authentic, shall be deposited with the Secretary-General of the United Nations.

In witness thereof the undersigned plenipotentiaries, being duly authorized thereto by their respective Governments, have signed the present Convention.

INDEX